SECOND EDITION

TECHNICAL DRAWING 101

A Multidisciplinary Curriculum
for the First Semester

D1607156

SECOND EDITION

TECHNICAL DRAWING 101

A Multidisciplinary Curriculum for the First Semester

DOUGLAS SMITH

Austin Community College

ANTONIO RAMIREZ

Austin Community College

Prentice Hall

Boston   Columbus   Indianapolis   New York   San Francisco   Upper Saddle River
Amsterdam   Cape Town   Dubai   London   Madrid   Milan   Munich   Paris   Montréal   Toronto
Delhi   Mexico City   São Paulo   Sydney   Hong Kong   Seoul   Singapore   Taipei   Tokyo

Editorial Director: Vernon R. Anthony
Acquisitions Editor: Sara Eilert
Editorial Assistant: Doug Greive
Director of Marketing: David Gesell
Marketing Manager: Kara Clark
Senior Marketing Coordinator: Alicia Wozniak
Marketing Assistant: Les Roberts
Senior Managing Editor: JoEllen Gohr
Associate Managing Editor: Alexandrina
  Benedicto Wolf
Project Manager: Louise Sette
AV Project Manager: Janet Portisch

Senior Operations Supervisor: Patricia
  Tonneman
Operations Specialist: Deidra Skahill
Senior Art Director: Diane Ernsberger
Cover Designer: Jason Moore
Cover Art: © Olivier Cirendini
Full-Service Project Management: Lisa
  Garboski, bookworks
Composition: S4Carlisle Publishing Services
Printer/Binder: Courier Kendallville, Inc.
Cover Printer: Lehigh-Phoenix Color/Hagerstown
Text Font: Times New Roman

Disclaimer

The publication is designed to provide tutorial information about AutoCAD® and/or other Autodesk computer programs. Every effort has been made to make this publication complete and as accurate as possible. The reader is expressly cautioned to use any and all precautions necessary, and to take appropriate steps to avoid hazards, when engaging in the activities described herein.

Neither the author nor the publisher makes any representations or warranties of any kind, with respect to the materials set forth in this publication, express or implied, including without limitation any warranties of fitness for a particular purpose or merchantability. Nor shall the author or the publisher be liable for any special, consequential or exemplary damages resulting, in whole or in part, directly or indirectly, from the reader's use of, or reliance upon, this material or subsequent revisions of this material.

Credits and acknowledgments borrowed from other sources and reproduced, with permission, in this textbook appear on appropriate page within text.

Library of Congress Control Number: 2010925301

10 9 8 7 6 5 4 3 2 1

Prentice Hall
is an imprint of

www.pearsonhighered.com

ISBN 10: 0-13-254495-4
ISBN 13: 978-0-13-254495-5

— USING THIS BOOK

The following features were designed to provide easy navigation and quick reference for students and professionals who look to Smith/Ramirez as a helpfully organized teaching text and a lasting reference for technical drawing information.

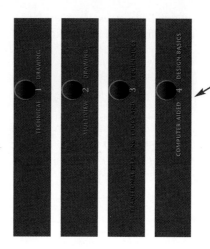

Chapters are keyed in alternating colors to help you locate frequently referenced content by memory.

CHAPTER OPENER SECTIONS

A bold vertical color band and oversized number on the first page of each chapter help you flip to find topics quickly.

Topics that you can expect to learn about in this chapter are listed here.

A large illustration and an interesting overview give you a real-world context for what this chapter is about.

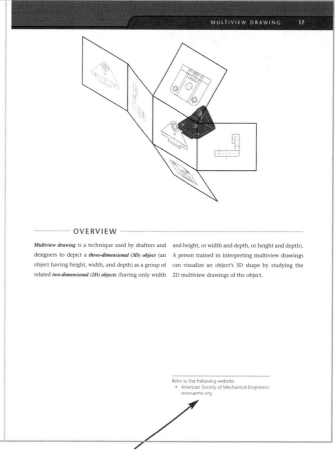

CHAPTER TWO

MULTIVIEW DRAWING

— OBJECTIVES —

After studying the material in this chapter, you should be able to:

1. Explain what multiview drawings are and their importance to the field of technical drawing.
2. Explain how views are chosen and aligned in a multiview drawing.
3. Visualize and interpret the multiviews of an object.
4. Describe the linetypes and lineweights used in technical drawings as defined by the *ASME Y14.2* standard.
5. Explain the difference between drawings created with first-angle and third-angle projection techniques.
6. Use a miter line to project information between top and side views.
7. Create multiview sketches of objects including the correct placement and depiction of visible, hidden, and centerlines.

Refer to the following standard(s):
* ASME Y14.2-2008 Line Conventions and Lettering
* ASME Y14.1-2005 Decimal Inch Drawing Sheet Size and Format
* ASME Y14.3-2003 Multiview and Sectional View Drawings
* ASME Y14.1M-2005 Metric Drawing Sheet Size and Format

— OVERVIEW —

Multiview drawing is a technique used by drafters and designers to depict a *three-dimensional (3D) object* (an object having height, width, and depth) as a group of related *two-dimensional (2D) objects* (having only width and height, or width and depth, or height and depth). A person trained in interpreting multiview drawings can visualize an object's 3D shape by studying the 2D multiview drawings of the object.

Refer to the following website:
* American Society of Mechanical Engineers: www.asme.org

Standards that apply to this chapter are shown here.

Handy Websites that apply to this chapter are shown here.

"STEP-BY-STEP" ACTIVITIES

Throughout the book, complicated processes are shown as step by step activities with each illustration right next to the text that explains it.

"Step by Step" tab identifies these activities.

CHAPTER REVIEW PAGE

You will find Key Words, Chapter Summary, and Review Questions sections at the end of each chapter.

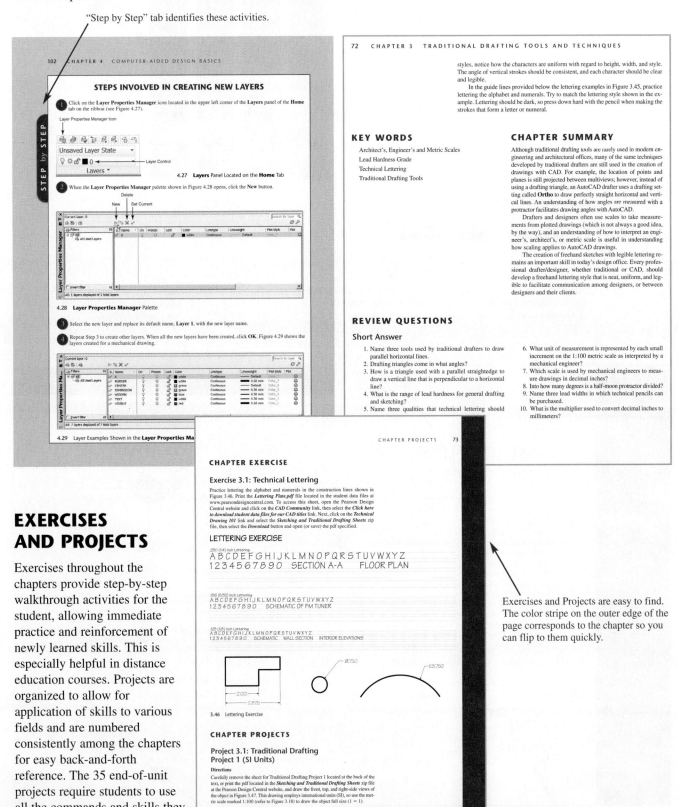

STEPS INVOLVED IN CREATING NEW LAYERS

1. Click on the **Layer Properties Manager** icon located in the upper left corner of the **Layers** panel of the **Home** tab on the ribbon (see Figure 4.27).

Layer Properties Manager Icon

Unsaved Layer State ▼

— Layer Control

Layers ▼

4.27   Layers Panel Located on the **Home** Tab

2. When the **Layer Properties Manager** palette shown in Figure 4.28 opens, click the **New** button.

Delete

New   Set Current

4.28   Layer Properties Manager Palette

3. Select the new layer and replace its default name, **Layer 1**, with the new layer name.

4. Repeat Step 3 to create other layers. When all the new layers have been created, click **OK**. Figure 4.29 shows the layers created for a mechanical drawing.

4.29   Layer Examples Shown in the Layer Properties Ma...

---

styles, notice how the characters are uniform with regard to height, width, and style. The angle of vertical strokes should be consistent, and each character should be clear and legible.

In the guide lines provided below the lettering examples in Figure 3.45, practice lettering the alphabet and numerals. Try to match the lettering style shown in the example. Lettering should be dark, so press down hard with the pencil when making the strokes that form a letter or numeral.

KEY WORDS

Architect's, Engineer's and Metric Scales
Lead Hardness Grade
Technical Lettering
Traditional Drafting Tools

CHAPTER SUMMARY

Although traditional drafting tools are rarely used in modern engineering and architectural offices, many of the same techniques developed by traditional drafters are still used in the creation of drawings with CAD. For example, the location of points and planes is still projected between multiviews; however, instead of using a drafting triangle, an AutoCAD drafter uses a drafting setting called **Ortho** to draw perfectly straight horizontal and vertical lines. An understanding of how angles are measured with a protractor facilitates drawing angles with AutoCAD.

Drafters and designers often use scales to take measurements from plotted drawings (which is not always a good idea, by the way), and an understanding of how to interpret an engineer's, architect's, or metric scale is useful in understanding how scaling applies to AutoCAD drawings.

The creation of freehand sketches with legible lettering remains an important skill in today's design office. Every professional drafter/designer, whether traditional or CAD, should develop a freehand lettering style that is neat, uniform, and legible to facilitate communication among designers, or between designers and their clients.

REVIEW QUESTIONS

Short Answer

1. Name three tools used by traditional drafters to draw parallel horizontal lines.
2. Drafting triangles come in what angles?
3. How is a triangle used with a parallel straightedge to draw a vertical line that is perpendicular to a horizontal line?
4. What is the range of lead hardness for general drafting and sketching?
5. Name three qualities that technical lettering should

6. What unit of measurement is represented by each small increment on the 1:100 metric scale as interpreted by a mechanical engineer?
7. Which scale is used by mechanical engineers to measure drawings in decimal inches?
8. Into how many degrees is a half-moon protractor divided?
9. Name three lead widths in which technical pencils can be purchased.
10. What is the multiplier used to convert decimal inches to millimeters?

CHAPTER EXERCISE

Exercise 3.1: Technical Lettering

Practice lettering the alphabet and numerals in the construction lines shown in Figure 3.46. Print the **Lettering Plate.pdf** file located in the student data files at www.pearsondesigncentral.com. To access this sheet, open the Pearson Design Central website and click on the **CAD Community** link, then select the **Click here to download student data files for our CAD titles** link. Next, click on the **Technical Drawing 101** link and select the **Sketching and Traditional Drafting Sheets** zip file, then select the **Download** button and open (or save) the pdf specified.

LETTERING EXERCISE

.250 (1/4) Inch Lettering
ABCDEFGHIJKLMNOPQRSTUVWXYZ
1234567890   SECTION A-A   FLOOR PLAN

.156 (5/32) Inch Lettering
ABCDEFGHIJKLMNOPQRSTUVWXYZ
1234567890   SCHEMATIC OF FM TUNER

.125 (1/8) Inch Lettering
ABCDEFGHIJKLMNOPQRSTUVWXYZ
1234567890   SCHEMATIC   WALL SECTION   INTERIOR ELEVATIONS

Ø.750

R3.750

2.00
2.875

3.46   Lettering Exercise

CHAPTER PROJECTS

Project 3.1: Traditional Drafting Project 1 (SI Units)

Directions
Carefully remove the sheet for Traditional Drafting Project 1 located at the back of the text, or print the pdf located in the **Sketching and Traditional Drafting Sheets** zip file at the Pearson Design Central website, and draw the front, top, and right-side views of the object in Figure 3.47. This drawing employs international units (SI), so use the metric scale marked 1:100 (refer to Figure 3.18) to draw the object full size (1 = 1).

EXERCISES AND PROJECTS

Exercises throughout the chapters provide step-by-step walkthrough activities for the student, allowing immediate practice and reinforcement of newly learned skills. This is especially helpful in distance education courses. Projects are organized to allow for application of skills to various fields and are numbered consistently among the chapters for easy back-and-forth reference. The 35 end-of-unit projects require students to use all the commands and skills they have learned cumulatively.

Exercises and Projects are easy to find. The color stripe on the outer edge of the page corresponds to the chapter so you can flip to them quickly.

PREFACE

ABOUT THIS BOOK

In the Architectural and Engineering Computer-Aided Design program at Austin Community College, we take our Introduction to Technical Drawing class very seriously. In fact, although we offer 26 CAD-related courses, we believe Introduction to Technical Drawing is *the* most important class. Our reasoning is simple: Many years of experience tell us that students will decide whether to major in our department based on their success and satisfaction with their first technical drawing course. So, if we don't do a great job teaching this course, students don't enroll for the other 25. You may have found this to be true in your department as well.

Each semester, when a new crop of students enroll in our Introduction to Technical Drawing classes, our department has a unique opportunity to recruit and retain these students, and we feel that the best way to accomplish this is to offer them a course that is challenging, interesting, and supportive. With this philosophy in mind, the authors began in the spring of 2000 to create a curriculum system (text and supporting materials) that would assist both students and faculty through the process of successfully learning and teaching the basics of technical drawing, including AutoCAD fundamentals, in a one-semester course (about 80 class hours). We have worked to improve this system every semester since. To date more than 1200 students have successfully completed this curriculum in our CAD labs at Austin Community College. The best proof we can offer of the efficacy of this system with regard to student retention is that in the 2009/2010 academic year our department had more than 1100 enrollments.

THE CURRICULUM

Technical Drawing 101 covers topics ranging from the most basic, such as making freehand, multiview sketches of machine parts, to the advanced—creating an AutoCAD dimension style containing the style settings defined by the *ASME Y14.5-2009 Dimensioning and Tolerancing* standard. But unlike the massive technical drawing reference texts on the market, *Technical Drawing 101* aims to present just the right mix of information and projects that can be reasonably covered by faculty, and assimilated by students, in one semester.

The CAD portion of the text incorporates drafting theory whenever possible and covers the basics of drawing setup (units, limits, and layers), the tools of the **Draw, Modify,** and **Dimension** toolbars, and the fundamentals of 3D modeling. By focusing on the fundamental building blocks of CAD, *Technical Drawing 101* provides a solid foundation for students going on to learn advanced CAD concepts and techniques (paper space, viewports, xrefs, annotative scaling, etc.) in intermediate CAD courses.

In recognition of the diverse career interests of our students, *Technical Drawing 101* includes projects in which students create working drawings for a mechanical assembly as well as for an architectural project. We include architectural drawing because our experience has shown that many (if not most) first-semester drafting students are interested in careers in the architectural design field, and that a traditional technical drawing text, which focuses solely on mechanical drawing projects, holds little interest for these students. The multidisciplinary approach of this text and its supporting materials is intended to broaden the appeal of the curriculum and increase student interest and, it is hoped, future enrollments. To be sure, this is not intended to be an architectural drafting text, but the steps involved in drawing the elevation views of a building dovetail nicely with the concepts and techniques of multiview drawing. Most CAD tools and techniques are basically the same whether applied to a mechanical or an architectural project.

HIGH SCHOOL AND TECH PREP PROGRAMS

Our program at Austin Community College has Tech-Prep agreements with many Austin area high schools, and each year our department provides faculty development training to the CAD faculty from these schools. By requiring that our high school partners adopt the *Technical Drawing 101* curriculum, both programs can be confident that our curricula are aligned and equivalent in scope and quality, thus facilitating the awarding of college credit to students for the work completed at the high school level. By building relationships with high school faculty in our area, we are maintaining an important pipeline for recruiting well-prepared students into our program at Austin Community College.

FEATURES NEW TO THE SECOND EDITION

The second edition of *Technical Drawing 101* has a new design layout intended to highlight the step-by-step instruction of drafting and CAD techniques.

AutoCAD's ribbon interface is the primary workspace of the second edition, rather than the classic interface presented in the first edition (the steps involved in setting the workspace to *AutoCAD Classic* are still included in Chapter 4). However, even with the tools of the ribbon displayed, students are encouraged to open the **Draw, Modify, Osnap,** and **Dimension** toolbars and dock them on the side of the drawing window, as this will help beginners become acquainted with these icons more quickly. The steps for opening these toolbars while operating in the ribbon workspace are presented in Chapter 4.

To help users who are migrating from the classic workspace to the ribbon environment, a tutorial featuring the tabs and panels of the AutoCAD 2011 ribbon, including accessing advanced help features, and controlling the size of the ribbon, is included in Appendix E.

The second edition has been updated to reflect the latest ASME (and other) standards applying to the creation of engineering drawings including the *ASME Y14.5-2009 Dimensioning and Tolerancing* standard.

SUPPLEMENTS AND ONLINE RESOURCES FOR INSTRUCTORS AND STUDENTS

Technical Drawing 101 is intended to be a complete turnkey curriculum that provides supporting materials for both full-time and adjunct faculty, thus improving the consistency and quality of instruction across the curriculum.

INSTRUCTOR RESOURCES

To access supplementary materials online, instructors need to request an instructor access code. Go to **www.pearson highered.com/irc,** where you can register for an instructor access code. Within 48 hours after registering, you will receive a confirming e-mail, including an instructor access code. Once you have received your code, go to the site and log on for full instructions on downloading the materials you wish to use.

Supplements available to instructors include:

- A comprehensive Instructor's Manual that explains how to present the material in each chapter, and the resources available to both teachers and students

- Lecture materials for each chapter in PowerPoint format
- Check prints consisting of AutoCAD dwg files with solutions to all drawing problems
- Prototype drawings for each CAD assignment in AutoCAD dwg file format
- Syllabus, tests, quizzes, answer keys, and sketching and traditional drafting files in doc and pdf format

STUDENT RESOURCES

Students can access supplementary materials in the student data files located at **www.pearsondesigncentral.com.** To access these tutorials, go to **www.pearsonhighered.com/irc** and click on the *CAD Community link*, then select the *Click here to download student data files for our CAD titles* link. Next, click on the *Technical Drawing 101* link and select the *AutoCAD Tutorial Videos* zip file, then select the *Download* button and open (or save) the desired supplements.

Supplements available to students include:

- Video tutorials for the commands on AutoCAD's **Draw, Modify, Dimension** and **Object Snap** toolbars, including Osnap's temporary track point feature to project through a miter line when creating multiview drawings (students can refer to these videos as needed for help outside of class)
- AutoCAD prototype drawings for each CAD assignment
- Lettering practice sheets and multiview sketching grid sheets in pdf format

A FINAL WORD

In the spring of 2010, our department offered nine sections of Introduction to Technical Drawing, each with a limit of 14 students. At the end of the registration period, every section was full, for a total of 126 beginning students. To frame it another way—126 opportunities to present CAD-related career fields *and* our department in the best possible light to students who are making important decisions about their educational and career paths. We feel that the curriculum presented in this book, along with the supplementary materials, positions our department to deliver the best training possible to these students. They deserve nothing less, and the future of our department depends on it.

ACKNOWLEDGMENTS

Tony Ramirez would like to thank his wife, Janice, and Doug Smith would like to thank his wife, Robin, and son, Carson, for their encouragement, understanding, and support during the development of the second edition.

The authors would like express our sincere thanks to our students and colleagues whose suggestions, expertise, and encouragement help us constantly improve this curriculum, especially Sam Gideon, Kim Duren, Alicia Norman, Mischon Olger, Trang Ong, Matt Wilson, Jana Schmidt, Ashleigh Fuller, Jeffrey Muhammad, and Quinn Stewart.

The authors would also like to thank the many reviewers who offered valuable comments and insight:

Tarek Abdel-Salam, East Carolina University; Theodore J. Branoff, North Carolina State University; Fred Brasfield, Tarrant County College; Charles Richard Cole, Southern Polytechnic State University; Steven L. Dulmes, College of Lake County; James Freygang, Ivy Tech Community College; Luis Gast, Robert Morris University; Ramarathnam Narasimhan, University of Miami; Frank H. Ortiz, Houston Community College; Karen Riethmiller, Butler County Community College; and Vivek Tandon, The University of Texas at El Paso.

Tony Ramirez and Douglas Smith,
Austin Community College, Austin, Texas

CONTENTS

CHAPTER FOUR
COMPUTER-AIDED DESIGN BASICS 78

CHAPTER FIVE
DIMENSIONING MECHANICAL DRAWINGS 204

CHAPTER SIX
DIMENSIONING ARCHITECTURAL DRAWINGS   260

SECOND EDITION

TECHNICAL DRAWING 101

A Multidisciplinary Curriculum
for the First Semester

CHAPTER ONE

TECHNICAL DRAWING

OBJECTIVES

After studying the material in this chapter, you should be able to:

1. Explain what technical drawings are.

2. Explain the terminology used to describe the process of creating technical drawings.

3. Explain how technical drawings are produced.

4. Explain the training needed to become an engineer, architect, designer, or drafter.

5. Describe the process of obtaining employment in the technical drawing field and the qualities that employers seek.

6. Describe what career prospects and opportunities, including salary ranges, are available in the field of technical drawing.

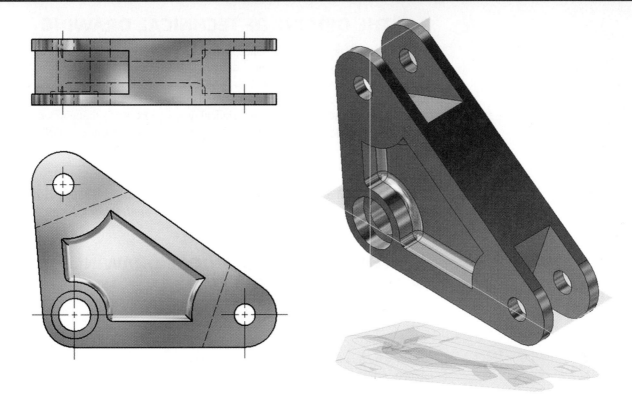

OVERVIEW

Technical drawings are the graphics and documentation (including notes and specifications) used by manufacturers to fabricate electronic and mechanical products and by construction professionals to produce houses, commercial buildings, roads, bridges, and water and wastewater systems. In fact, technical graphics are produced before almost all products are manufactured—from the integrated circuits inside your computer to the buttons on your shirt.

Refer to the following websites:
- American Design Drafting Association: www.adda.org
- American Institute of Architects: www.aia.org
- American Society for Engineering Education: www.asee.org
- National Society of Professional Engineers: www.nspe.org
- U.S. Department of Labor: www.bls.gov

1.1 THE ORIGINS OF TECHNICAL DRAWING

Technical drawing is not a new concept; archeological evidence suggests that humans first began creating crude technical drawings several thousand years ago. Through the ages, architects and designers, including Leonardo Da Vinci, created technical drawings. However, a French mathematician, Gaspard Monge, is considered by many to be the founder of modern technical drawing. Monge's thoughts on the subject, *Géométrie Descriptive* (Descriptive Geometry), published around 1799, became the basis for the first university courses. In 1821, the first English-language text on technical drawing, *Treatise on Descriptive Geometry*, was published by Claudius Crozet, a professor at the U.S. Military Academy.

Other terms often used to describe the creation of technical drawings are ***drafting***, ***engineering graphics***, ***engineering drawings***, and ***computer-aided design*** (**CAD**).

1.2 THE ROLE OF TECHNICAL DRAWING IN THE DESIGN PROCESS

To appreciate technical drawing's role in the design process, you must first understand some basics about design process itself.

For most projects, the first phase of a design project is to define clearly the design criteria that the finished design must meet to be considered a success. Many designers refer to this phase in the design process as *problem identification*. For example, before designing a house, an architectural designer needs to know the size and style of home the client wants, the number of bedrooms and baths, and the approximate budget for the project. The designer also needs information about the site where the house will be built. Is it hilly or flat? Are there trees, and if so, where are they located? What is the orientation of the site relative to the rising and setting of the sun? These concerns represent just a few of many design parameters that the designer needs to define before beginning the design process.

Once the design problem is clearly defined, the designer begins preparing preliminary designs that can meet the parameters defined during the problem identification phase. During this step, multiple solutions to the design problem may be generated in the form of freehand sketches, formal CAD drawings, or even rendered three-dimensional (3D) models. Designers refer to this process of generating many possible solutions to the design problem as the *ideation*, or *brainstorming*, phase of the process.

The preliminary designs are shown to the client to determine whether the design is in line with the client's expectations. This step allows the designer to clarify the client's needs and expectations. It also is an opportunity for a designer to educate the client about other, possibly better, solutions to the design problem.

After the client decides on a preliminary design that meets the criteria established in the first problem identification phase, the designer begins preparing design inputs that more clearly define the details of the design project. Design inputs may include freehand sketches with dimensional information, detailed notes, or even CAD models. Figure 1.1 shows an example of an architectural designer's sketch of a foundation detail for a house.

When the design inputs are finished, they are given to the drafter(s) responsible for preparing the technical drawings for the project. ***Drafters*** are individuals who have received specialized training in the creation of technical drawings. One of the most important skills that drafters must acquire during their training is the ability to interpret design inputs and transform them into technical drawings. Drafters usually work closely with other members of the design team, which may include designers, checkers, engineers, architects, and other drafters during the creation of technical drawings.

Most drafters use CAD software to prepare the drawings. CAD allows drafters to produce drawings much more quickly than traditional drafting techniques. Popular CAD programs include AutoCAD®, Revit®, Autodesk® Inventor®, SolidWorks®, and Pro/ENGINEER®. CAD software can range in price from several hundred to thousands of dollars per station depending on the software. Figure 1.2 shows an AutoCAD drawing prepared from the designer's sketch shown in Figure 1.1.

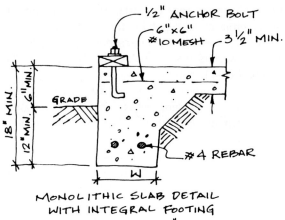

1.1 Architectural Designer's Sketch of a Foundation Detail

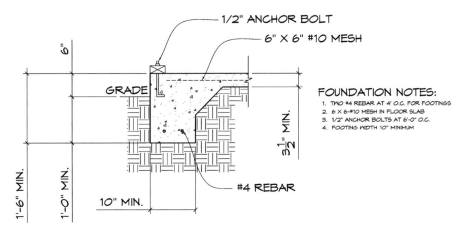

1.2 Detail Prepared from Architectural Designer's Sketch in Figure 1.1

JOB SKILLS

Although modern drafters use CAD tools to create drawings, traditional drafting skills such as sketching and blueprint reading are still very important for facilitating communication between drafters and designers.

When the drafter is finished preparing the technical drawings, the designer, or in some cases a *checker*, reviews the drawings carefully for mistakes. If mistakes are found, or if the design has been revised, the drafter will make the necessary corrections or revisions to the drawings. This process is repeated until the construction drawings are considered to be complete. When the entire set of construction drawings is finalized, the drafter and designer(s) put their initials in an area of the drawing called the *title block*.

The finished construction drawings represent the master plan for the project. Everything required to complete the project, from applying for a building permit to securing financing for the project, revolves around the construction drawings. Building contractors use the construction documents to prepare bids for the project, and the winning bidders will use them to construct the building.

Engineering designers follow a similar process when designing products. Most engineering projects begin with a definition of initial design criteria and progress through the phases of preliminary design, design refinement, preparation of technical drawings, manufacturing, and inspection.

The trend in modern design, whether architectural or engineering, is to use CAD tools to create a dynamic, often three-dimensional, database that can be shared by all members of the design team. Increasingly, others in the organization, such as those involved in marketing, finance, or service and repair, will access information from the CAD database to accomplish their jobs.

JOB SKILLS

Catching problems and mistakes during the design and drafting stages of the project can result in huge savings versus correcting mistakes on the job site or after the project has been built or manufactured. An example is the enormous cost incurred by an automobile manufacturer who has to recall thousands of cars to correct a design problem versus the cost of catching the problem on the technical drawing before the cars are manufactured.

1.3 TRAINING FOR CAREERS IN TECHNICAL DRAWING

Most drafters acquire their training by attending community college or technical school programs that lead to a certificate or associate's degree in drafting and design or CAD. These programs usually take from one to two years to complete and focus on the skills necessary to work as a drafter in industry, such as drafting techniques, knowledge of drafting standards, and the use of CAD programs to create drawings. Although most employers do not require that drafters be certified, the American Design Drafting Association (ADDA) has established a certification program for drafters. Individuals seeking certification must pass a test, which is administered periodically at ADDA-authorized sites. Some publishers of CAD software also offer certification on their products through authorized training sites.

TIP

You can learn more about the American Design Drafting Association by visiting its website at www.adda.org.

Most drafters are full-time employees of architectural and engineering firms. Usually, drafters qualify for overtime pay when they work in excess of 40 hours per week. However, some drafters prefer to work as nonemployee contractors. Contractors are usually very experienced drafters who often earn higher salaries than direct employees but have less job stability. Some organizations allow drafters to telecommute and transfer drawing files to the office via the Internet.

Designers are often former drafters who have proven their ability to take on more responsibility and decision-making duties. Designers usually earn higher salaries than drafters because they are charged with more responsibility for the design, and even the successful completion, of the project.

To become an engineer or architect, an individual must first earn a bachelor's degree in engineering or architecture from a university program. Bachelor's degree programs generally take four to five years to complete and usually require a mastery of higher level courses in mathematics and physics.

After earning a degree, an engineer may become a ***professional engineer*** **(P.E.)**, and an architect may become *licensed*, through a process involving both work experience and rigorous professional exams. The accrediting body for architects is the ***American Institute of Architects (AIA)***. The accrediting agency for engineers is the ***National Society of Professional Engineers***.

> ─── **TIP** ──────────────────────────────
>
> You can learn more about the American Institute of Architects and the National Society of Professional Engineers by visiting their websites at www.aia.org and www.nspe.org, respectively.

Career Paths in Technical Drawing

Architectural drafters work with architects and designers to prepare the drawings used in construction projects. These drawings may include floor plans, elevations, and construction details. Study of construction techniques and materials, as well as building codes, is important to the education of an architectural drafter. Some architectural drafters specialize in residential architecture (houses), whereas others may specialize in commercial architecture (buildings and apartments) or structural drafting (steel buildings or concrete structures). Figures 1.3 and 1.4 show details from a set of architectural drawings prepared by an architectural design drafter using Autodesk® Revit® CAD software.

Mechanical drafters work with mechanical engineers and designers to prepare detail and assembly drawings of machinery and mechanical devices. Mechanical drafters are usually trained in basic engineering theory as well as drafting standards and manufacturing techniques. They may be responsible for specifying items on a drawing such as the types of fasteners (nuts, bolts, and screws) needed to assemble a mechanical device or the fit between mating parts. Figure 1.5 shows a 3D model of a bellcrank created with Autodesk® Inventor® CAD software.

Aeronautical or ***aerospace drafters*** prepare technical drawings used in the manufacture of spacecraft and aircraft. These drafters often split their duties between mechanical drafting and electrical/electronics drafting and are sometimes referred to as ***electro/mechanical drafters***.

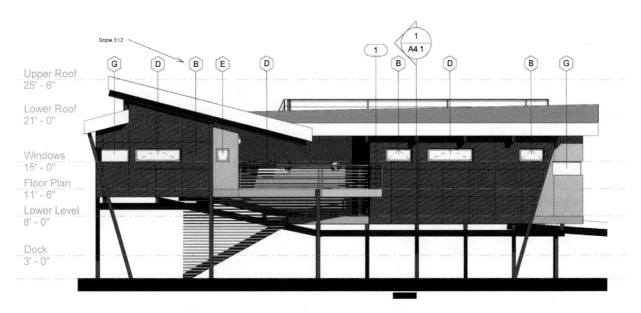

1.3   Elevation View of a Custom Home Created with 3D Modeling Software. *Image courtesy David Naumann.*

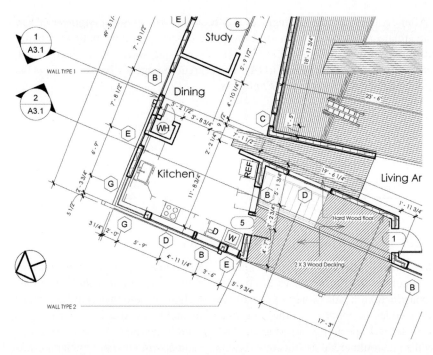

1.4 Detail from the Floor Plan of the Home Shown in Figure 1.3. *Image courtesy David Naumann.*

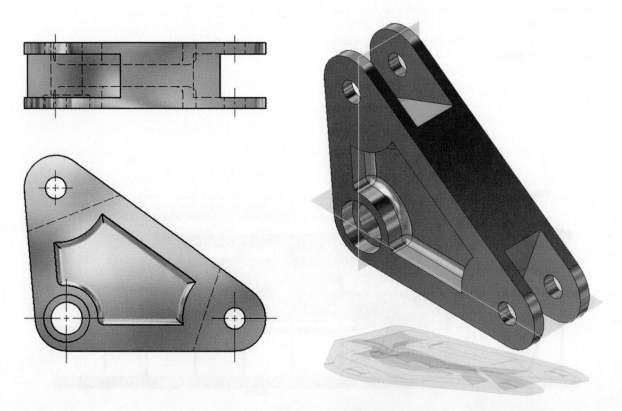

1.5 Model of a Machine Part Created with 3D Modeling Software

Civil drafters and *design technicians* prepare construction drawings and topographical maps used in civil engineering projects. Civil projects may include roads, bridges, and water and wastewater systems. Civil drafters may also work for *surveying* companies to create site plans and plats for new subdivisions. Figure 1.6 shows an image of a subdivision plat created with AutoCAD Civil 3D® CAD software.

Electrical drafters prepare diagrams used in the installation and repair of electrical equipment and building wiring. Electrical drafters create documentation for systems ranging from low-voltage fire and security systems to high-voltage electrical distribution networks.

Electronics drafters create schematic diagrams, printed circuit board (PCB) artwork, integrated circuit layouts, and other graphics used in the design and maintenance of electronic (semiconductor) devices. Figure 1.7 shows a detail from an electronics schematic drawing.

Figure 1.8 shows a detail of a PCB prepared from the schematic shown in Figure 1.7.

Pipeline drafters and *process piping drafters* prepare drawings used in the construction and maintenance of oil refineries, oil production and exploration industries,

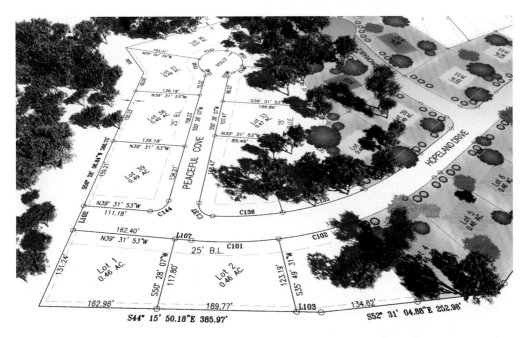

1.6   Civil Engineering Image Created for a Subdivision Plat. *Image courtesy Jeffrey B. Muhammad.*

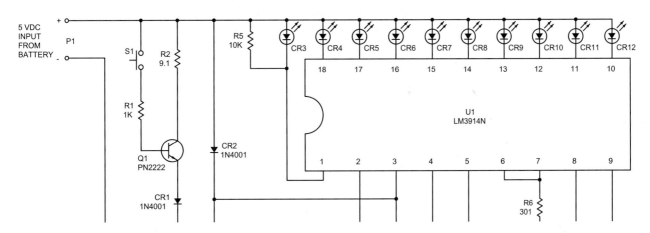

1.7   Detail from an Electronics Schematic

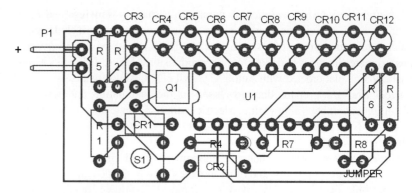

1.8   Detail of a Printed Circuit Board Prepared from the Schematic Shown in Figure 1.7

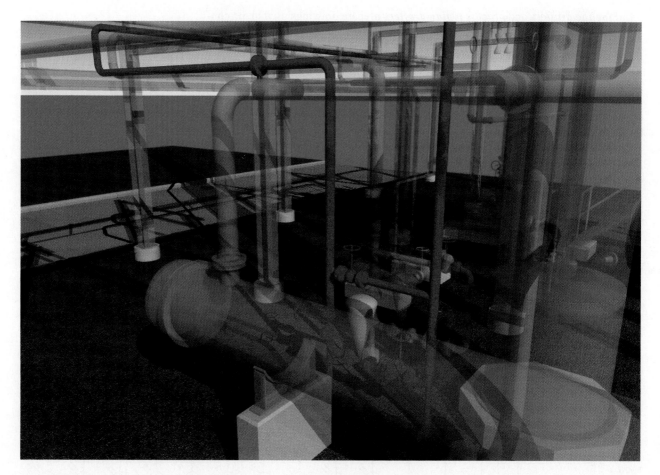

1.9   3D CAD Model of a Process Piping Design. *Image courtesy Mustang Engineering L.P.*

chemical plants, and process piping systems such as those used in the manufacture of semiconductor devices. Figure 1.9 shows a 3D CAD model of a process piping system created using CADWorx® Plant software.

Qualities That Employers Look for in Drafters

Most employers are very careful in making hiring decisions. Interviews are usually very thorough; in extreme cases, the interview process may take several hours. Candidates may be called back for more than one interview.

When interviewing for a job, the candidate may interview with one person or with the entire design team. In the modern engineering or architectural office, the candidate's attitude regarding work and his or her ability to learn quickly and contribute to the team immediately is factored into the hiring decision. Often, tests are administered during the interview to measure proficiency with CAD or the candidate's understanding of necessary concepts that should have been mastered while in college or during other training.

Typical Interview Questions

- Are you a quick learner (will you contribute to the organization quickly)?
- Are you intelligent, competent, and energetic?
- Will you fit into the team? Do you get along with others?
- Did you make good grades in your major? Will your instructors give you a good recommendation?
- Do you meet deadlines?
- Are you able to work successfully both in groups and individually?
- Did your training prepare you for this job?
- Do you communicate well with others (both verbally and in writing)?
- Do you have good work habits? Are you dependable?
- Will the employer profit from your work?

JOB SKILLS

If you are interested in working in the technical drawing field, develop good work habits while you are in school. Set high standards for your work, strive to create outstanding drawings for your portfolio, and be able to explain how the drawings in your portfolio were created and why. Come to class prepared and on time, meet your deadlines, and try to impress your instructors with your work habits and attitude. Very often the recommendation of a current or former instructor will determine whether you get a job.

Salary Information for Drafters, Architects, and Engineers

Earnings for drafters vary depending on the specialty (architecture, mechanical, electrical/electronics, etc.), level of responsibility, and geographic area. According to U.S. Department of Labor statistics (May 2008), median annual earnings for architectural and civil drafters were $44,490 ($21.39 per hour). Median annual earnings for architects were $70,325. Median annual earnings for civil engineers were $74,610.

Median annual earnings for mechanical drafters were $46,640 ($22.42 per hour). Median annual earnings for mechanical engineers were $74,922.

Median annual earnings for electrical and electronics drafters were $51,320 ($24.67 per hour). Median annual earnings for electrical engineers were $82,160.

NOTE

Salary data taken from the Bureau of Labor Statistics, U.S. Department of Labor, *Occupational Outlook Handbook,* 2010-11 Edition, Drafters, on the Internet at http://www.bls.gov/oes/2008/may/oes_nat.htm#b17-0000.

Job Prospects for Drafters

According to the U.S. Department of Labor, approximately 251,900 people were employed as drafters nationwide in 2008. Overall employment for drafters is expected to grow by 4% between 2008 and 2018; however, growth in architectural and civil drafting is expected to increase by 9% during that period. Growth will vary by geographic region.

> ── NOTE ──
> The median is the middle of a distribution; that is, half the earnings are above the median, and half are below the median.

The Department of Labor's Bureau of Labor Statistics predicts that "opportunities should be best for individuals with at least 2 years of postsecondary training in a drafting program that provides strong technical skills, as well as considerable experience with CADD (computer aided design and drafting) systems. CADD has increased the complexity of drafting applications while enhancing the productivity of drafters. It also has enhanced the nature of drafting by creating more possibilities for design and drafting. As technology continues to advance, employers will look for drafters with a strong background in fundamental drafting principles, a high level of technical sophistication, and the ability to apply their knowledge to a broader range of responsibilities."

> ── TIP ──
> You can find out more about careers in drafting by visiting the U.S. Department of Labor website at www.bls.gov/oco/ocos111.htm.

1.4 THREE TECHNICAL DRAWING SUCCESS STORIES

Jeffrey Muhammad first began taking drafting courses at Temple College in Temple, Texas, and later transferred to Austin Community College (ACC) in Austin, Texas. In 1996, before he completed the requirements for his associate's degree at ACC, Jeffrey was hired by Wenzel Engineering in Austin. While at Wenzel, Jeffrey used AutoCAD to prepare site-plan development drawings and on-site wastewater management systems. Jeffrey continued to take classes at night and in 2003 received his Associate of Applied Science degree in Architectural and Engineering Computer Aided Design at ACC. Jeffrey's next position was with Loomis Austin, a civil engineering firm, where he was involved in subdivision platting, street design, utility design, site-plan development, and land planning. While employed by Loomis, Jeffrey used AutoCAD® Land Desktop and AutoCAD® Civil 3D® software to perform his job functions.

At present, Jeffrey is employed as a full-time instructor in the CAD program at Austin Community College, where he is the coordinator of the Civil CAD program.

Elain Dalton already had a bachelor's degree from the University of Oregon when she decided to take a drafting course at the University of Houston "just for fun." Using the skills she developed in that class, Elain was able to find a job with Johnson Controls' "Star Wars" defense base in the Marshall Islands (a U.S. territory in the South Pacific) doing facilities operations and master planning. The job required that Elain split her time between two CAD programs: AutoCAD® and Microstation. There was only one small snag—Elain would have to teach herself to use both programs, which she did. When Elain returned to the continental United States, she took a job with Carrier Corporation and enrolled in the drafting program at San Jacinto Community College in Pasadena, Texas, earning an Associate of Applied Science degree in 1996. Her work with Carrier Corporation involved mechanical, electrical, and pipe drafting for clients such as Dow Chemical, Vulcan Chemicals, DuPont, and other corporations using commercial heating and cooling systems. She was also responsible for ensuring that the drawings complied with *American Society of Mechanical Engineers* standards.

Elain is currently employed as a drafter/designer with Lubrizol Chemical Corporation, where she uses AutoCAD to create mechanical, civil, site-mapping, and piping drawings.

Bryan Lym began his path to a career in architecture in an unusual way—he dropped out of high school. After working at a variety of jobs, he was encouraged by a friend to take the GED® test at El Centro College, a community college in Dallas, Texas. Bryan passed his test and went on to enroll in the architectural drafting program at El Centro. In these drafting classes, Bryan discovered that both his aptitudes and interests lay in the field of architecture. Near the end of his second year at El Centro, he was accepted into the School of Architecture at the University of Texas. On his graduation day in 1997, Bryan received two degrees: a Bachelor of Architecture *and* a Bachelor of Science in Architectural Engineering. Following graduation, Bryan held positions with RNL Design, Beck Construction, and Carter and Burgess. While employed at Carter and Burgess, Bryan began taking the licensure exams of the American Institute of Architects, and in 2003 he became a licensed architect. That same year, he began his own firm, Lym Architecture. Today his practice focuses primarily on designs for commercial remodels. His office uses a variety of software including AutoCAD, 3D Studio Max®, Sketch Up, Adobe® Photoshop® and Illustrator®, Word®, Excel®, and Adobe Acrobat®.

Because he had dropped out of high school, Bryan believes that if he had not been offered the second chance at El Centro College, he would never have been accepted into the architecture program at the University of Texas.

KEY WORDS

Aeronautical or Aerospace Drafters
American Institute of Architects
American Society of Mechanical Engineers
Architectural Drafters
Civil Drafters
Computer-Aided Design (CAD)
Designers
Design Technicians
Drafters
Drafting
Electrical Drafters
Electro/mechanical Drafters
Electronics Drafters
Engineering Drawings
Engineering Graphics
Mechanical Drafters
National Society of Professional Engineers
Pipeline Drafters
Process Piping Drafters
Professional Engineer
Technical Drawings

CHAPTER SUMMARY

The curriculum of this course is designed to introduce students to the field of technical drawing. This course is a good way to explore whether you possess the interests and aptitudes to pursue a career in which technical drawings are created or interpreted. If you wish to pursue more training, most community colleges and many universities offer specialized courses in engineering or architectural drawing. Your instructor may also be able to advise you on training opportunities and possible career paths.

REVIEW QUESTIONS

Short Answer

1. Name three terms that are used to describe the creation of technical drawings.
2. In which field must a drafter be familiar with floor plans, elevations, and construction details?
3. How can an employer find out about a student's CAD skills, work habits, and dependability?
4. A drafter who divides his or her duties between mechanical drafting and electrical/electronics drafting is known as what kind of drafter?
5. Name the job titles of people who might constitute a design team.

Multiple Choice

1. The acronym AIA stands for what?
   a. Architectural Institute of America
   b. American and International Architects
   c. American Institute of Architects
   d. Association of International Architects

2. According to the U.S. Department of Labor Statistics (2008), which field of drafting has the highest median salary?
   a. Architectural
   b. Mechanical
   c. Electronics
   d. Radiological

3. In which field must a drafter be familiar with roads, bridges, water and wastewater systems, and surveying techniques?
   a. Architectural
   b. Civil
   c. Electronics
   d. Mechanical

4. Which of the following attributes do most employers value?
   a. Ability to fit into a team
   b. Ability to work independently
   c. Ability to communicate clearly
   d. All the above

5. Designers have a higher salary than drafters because:
   a. They usually have advanced technical degrees.
   b. They are licensed.
   c. They work longer hours than drafters.
   d. They have a higher degree of responsibility for the success of the project.

Matching

Column A

a. Mechanical
b. Process piping
c. Bachelor's
d. Electronics
e. Associate's

Column B

1. Type of college degree held by most engineers and architects
2. Drafting field concerned with chemical plants and oil refineries
3. Type of college degree held by many drafters
4. Drafting field concerned with screw threads and fasteners
5. Drafting field concerned with design of semiconductor devices

CHAPTER EXERCISES

Exercise 1.1: Locate Bachelors Degree Programs in Architecture or Engineering

Search the Internet for university programs in your geographic area offering a bachelor's degree in architecture and/or engineering. Try to locate an online degree plan for each major, and compare the courses required for each degree.

Exercise 1.2: Locate Associates Degree Programs in CAD

Search the Internet for community college or technical school programs in your geographic area offering an associate's degree in CAD or a related field. Try to locate an online degree plan for the program. Compare the courses required for the associate degree with the courses required in the bachelor's degree program.

MULTIVIEW DRAWING

---- OBJECTIVES ----

After studying the material in this chapter, you should be able to:

1. Explain what multiview drawings are and their importance to the field of technical drawing.

2. Explain how views are chosen and aligned in a multiview drawing.

3. Visualize and interpret the multiviews of an object.

4. Describe the linetypes and lineweights used in technical drawings as defined by the *ASME Y14.2* standard.

5. Explain the difference between drawings created with first-angle and third-angle projection techniques.

6. Use a miter line to project information between top and side views.

7. Create multiview sketches of objects including the correct placement and depiction of visible, hidden, and centerlines.

Refer to the following standard(s):
- ASME Y14.2-2008 Line Conventions and Lettering
- ASME Y14.1-2005 Decimal Inch Drawing Sheet Size and Format
- ASME Y14.3-2003 Multiview and Sectional View Drawings
- ASME Y14.1M-2005 Metric Drawing Sheet Size and Format

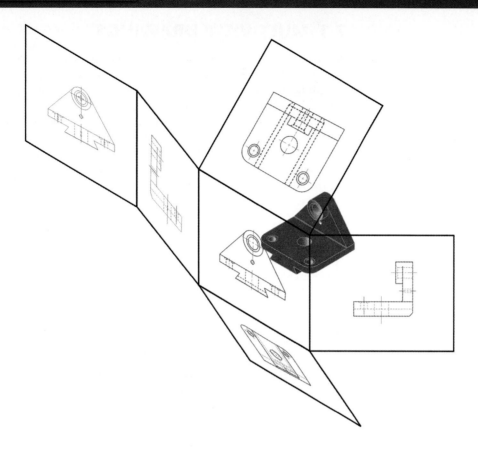

OVERVIEW

Multiview drawing is a technique used by drafters and designers to depict a *three-dimensional (3D) object* (an object having height, width, and depth) as a group of related *two-dimensional (2D) objects* (having only width and height, or width and depth, or height and depth). A person trained in interpreting multiview drawings can visualize an object's 3D shape by studying the 2D multiview drawings of the object.

Refer to the following website:
• American Society of Mechanical Engineers: www.asme.org

2.1 MULTIVIEW DRAWINGS

Figure 2.1 represents a 3D image of a school bus. The 3D image of the bus is very helpful in visualizing its shape, because the viewer can quickly get an idea of the overall height, width, and depth of the bus. However, the 3D view cannot show the viewer all the sides of the bus, or its true length, width, or height. On the other hand, a multiview drawing (Figure 2.2) can provide the viewer with all the sides of a bus, represented in its true proportions: width, height, and depth. The six views representing the bus in Figure 2.2—the front, top, right side, left side, back, and bottom—are referred to in technical drawing terminology as the six *regular views*.

TIP

Although a total of six views are possible using the multiview drawing technique, drafters draw only the views necessary to show clearly all the features of the object. Dimensional information for the features is added to these views. If no dimensions are placed on a view, the view is probably unnecessary.

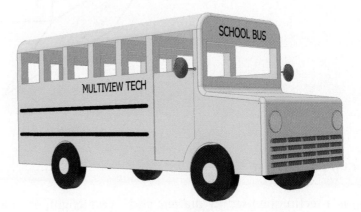

2.1   A Three-Dimensional Image of a School Bus

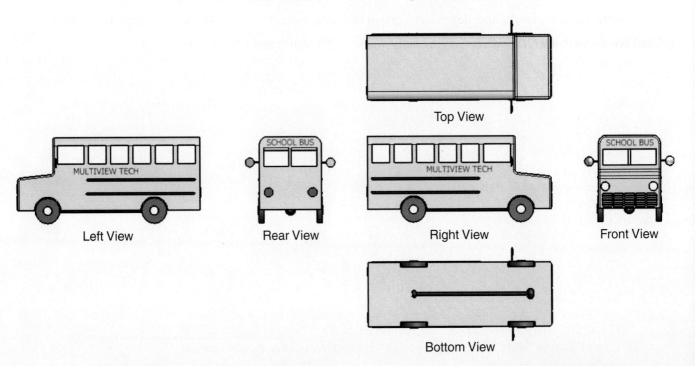

Top View

Left View   Rear View   Right View   Front View

Bottom View

2.2   The Multiviews of the Bus Depicting the Six Regular Views—Front, Top, Bottom, Right, Left, and Rear

When the multiview drawing of the bus is created, the front, or principal, view is drawn first. The top, bottom, right-, and left-side views are drawn by rotating the bus at 90° intervals relative to the front view. For example, the top view is created by rotating the front view 90° toward the top; the right-side view is created by rotating the front view 90° to the right.

TIP

When choosing the front, or principal, view of an object, select the view you would choose if you could show the viewer only one view to describe the object.

2.2 VIEW SELECTION AND ALIGNMENT OF MULTIVIEW DRAWINGS

In Figure 2.2, the *side* view of the bus was chosen to be the front, or principal, view because it provides the viewer with the most information about the shape of the bus. The actual *front* of the bus is drawn as the right-side view. The top view is a bird's-eye view from directly above the front view. The left-side view shows the back of the bus, and the rear view of the bus is projected from this view. The bottom view is drawn directly below the front view. Features of the bus, such as the headlights, tires, and windows, are aligned in all views.

Because the front view is the principal view of the bus, it is drawn first. The other views are created by *projecting* from the geometry of the front view. For example, after the width of the front view has been measured and drawn it can be projected to the top and bottom views, so the drafter doesn't need to remeasure the width in those views. Likewise, the height of the front view can be projected to the right- and left-side views. Because drafters can avoid remeasuring features by projecting between views, multiview drawing is an efficient way to create technical drawings.

2.3 USING PROJECTION PLANES TO VISUALIZE MULTIVIEWS

If a house were placed inside a glass box as in Figure 2.3, the glass sides of the box would create **projection planes** (also referred to as *viewing planes*). If the 3D geometry of the front, side, and top of the house were projected onto the corresponding 2D projection plane, the resulting 2D image would represent a front, top, or side view as shown in Figures 2.4, 2.5, and 2.6, respectively.

In Figure 2.7, the front, top, left-, and right-side views of the house are shown as they would be arranged in a multiview drawing. In the creation of this drawing, the front view was drawn first. Then, the top view was drawn directly above the front view. Next, the right and left views were drawn directly to the right and left of the front view, respectively. Architects refer to multiview drawings of the exterior of a house as **elevation drawings**.

Notice that a feature in the front view, such as the peak of the roof, is exactly in line with the top of the roof in both the left and right views. Also note how the features of the chimney are aligned in each of the views.

The planes representing the roof in the right, left, and top views appear as rectangles in the multiviews, but by studying them in relation to the front view, you will see that they actually represent the sloping or **inclined planes** of the roof. Because the planes of the roof, as projected to the top and side viewing planes, are sloping, they are not drawn actual, or true, size. In technical drawing, this phenomenon is referred to as **foreshortening**.

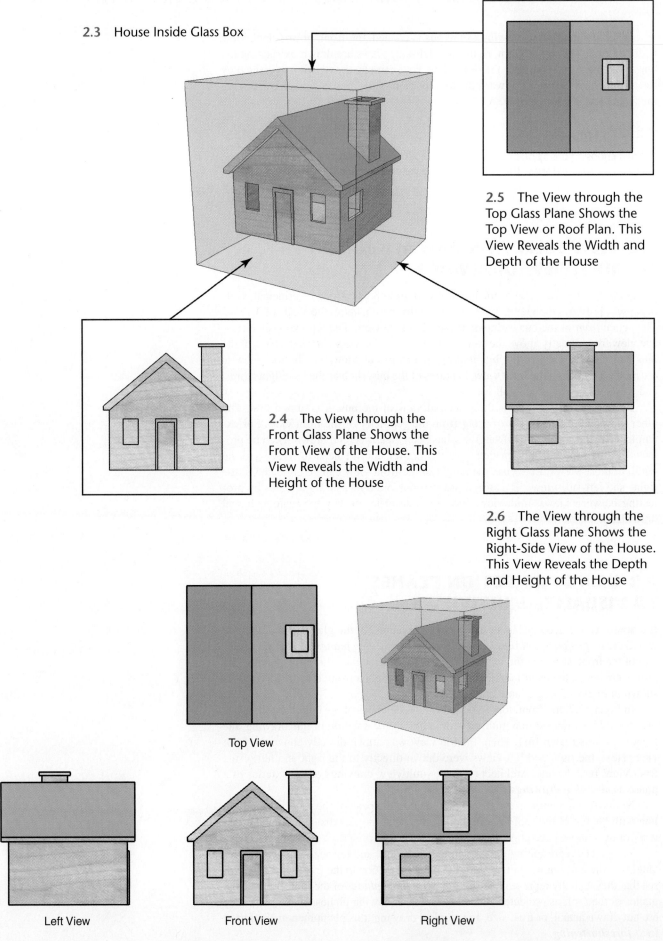

2.3 House Inside Glass Box

2.5 The View through the Top Glass Plane Shows the Top View or Roof Plan. This View Reveals the Width and Depth of the House

2.4 The View through the Front Glass Plane Shows the Front View of the House. This View Reveals the Width and Height of the House

2.6 The View through the Right Glass Plane Shows the Right-Side View of the House. This View Reveals the Depth and Height of the House

Top View

Left View

Front View

Right View

2.7 The Elevations of a House as They Would Be Arranged in a Multiview Drawing

USING THE GLASS BOX TECHNIQUE OF VISUALIZING MULTIVIEWS

Figure 2.3 introduced the concept of placing an object inside a glass box to create viewing planes. This method of visualizing multiviews is known as the *glass box technique*. This technique is often helpful for beginners who are learning the process of visualizing an object's multiviews. The following steps detail the process of using the glass box technique to visualize the multiviews of the object in Figure 2.8.

1 Imagine the object shown in Figure 2.8 is centered inside a glass box and its six regular views are projected out to the glass planes surrounding the object (see Figure 2.9). The plane on which the front view is projected is called the *frontal plane*.

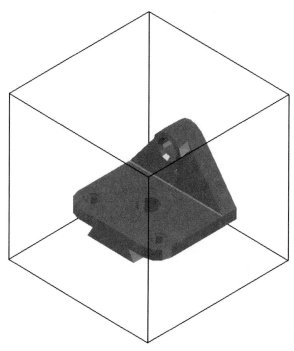

2.8 Object Centered Inside Glass Box

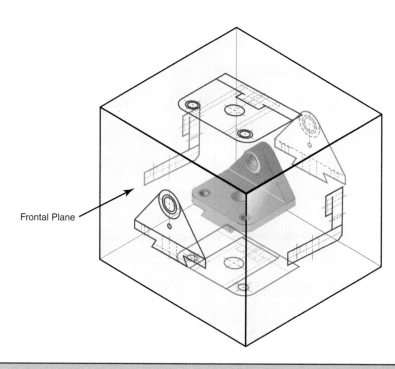

Frontal Plane

2.9 Multiviews of Object Projected onto Glass Planes

STEP by STEP

2 Unfold the glass box as if the four sides of the frontal plane were hinged, as shown in Figures 2.10 and 2.11.

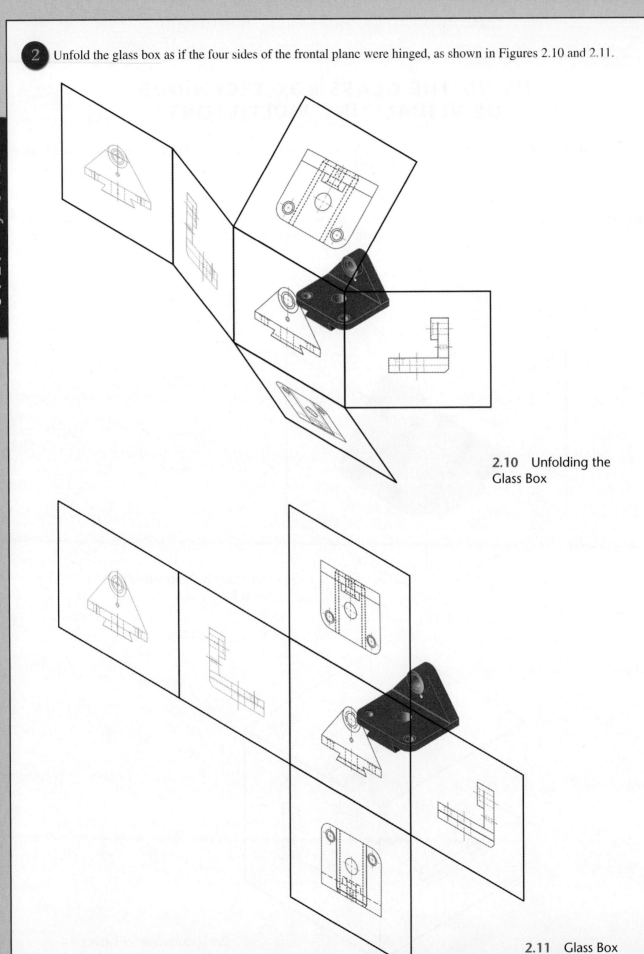

2.10 Unfolding the Glass Box

2.11 Glass Box Unfolded

3 After the sides of the glass box are unfolded, the six regular views of the object (front, top, bottom, right, left, and rear) are displayed in their "projected" positions, as shown in Figure 2.12. Note that the front, right, left and rear views are aligned horizontally, and the front, top, and bottom views are in vertical alignment.

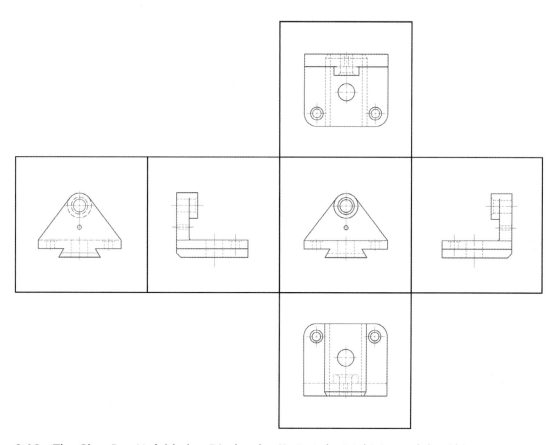

2.12 The Glass Box Unfolded to Display the Six Regular Multiviews of the Object

2.4 LINETYPES AND LINEWEIGHTS IN MULTIVIEW DRAWINGS

The features of an object are shown with differing ***linetypes*** and ***lineweights***. Commonly used linetypes include *visible lines,* which show the visible edges and features of an object; *hidden lines,* which represent features that would not be visible; and *centerlines,* which locate the centers of features such as holes and arcs. The terminology used for the various linetypes is shown in Figure 2.13.

Lineweight refers to the width of the lines in a technical drawing. Standard linetypes and lineweights have been established by the American Society of Mechanical Engineers (ASME). The ASME standard for line conventions and lettering is *ASME Y14.2-2008.* The lineweights for lines specified by this standard for use on technical drawings are shown in Table 2.1.

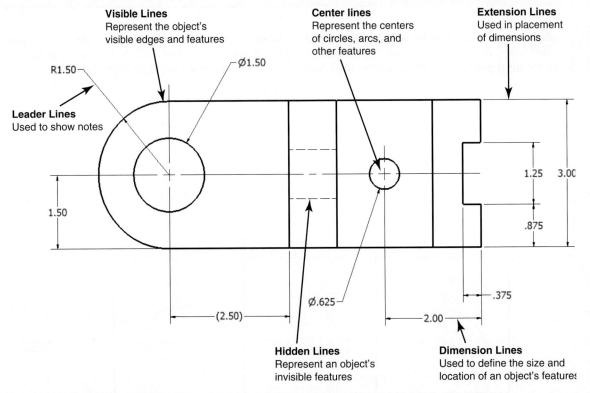

Visible Lines
Represent the object's
visible edges and features

Center lines
Represent the centers
of circles, arcs, and
other features

Extension Lines
Used in placement
of dimensions

R1.50

Ø1.50

Leader Lines
Used to show notes

1.50

1.25   3.00

.875

.375

(2.50)

Ø.625

2.00

Hidden Lines
Represent an object's
invisible features

Dimension Lines
Used to define the size and
location of an object's features

2.13   Linetype Terminology

NOTE
ASME describes these line
thicknesses as the *approximate*
widths.

Table 2.1 ASME Y14.2 Line Thickness
Standard

Visible line = .6mm thick
Hidden line = .3mm thick
Centerline = .3mm thick
Dimension line = .3mm thick
Extension line = .3mm thick
Cutting plane line = .6mm thick
Section line = .3mm thick

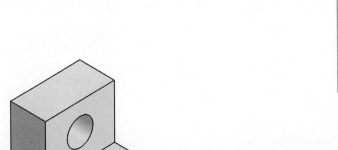

**2.14   Object to Be
Visualized with
Multiviews**

2.5 HIDDEN FEATURES AND CENTERLINES IN MULTIVIEW DRAWINGS

Figure 2.15 shows the six regular views of the object shown in Figure 2.14. Study
these examples and note how features that would otherwise be invisible in a view,
such as the edges of the hole and slot in the side views, are depicted with hidden lines.
Also, note the different ways that the centerlines representing the center of the hole
are drawn in each view.

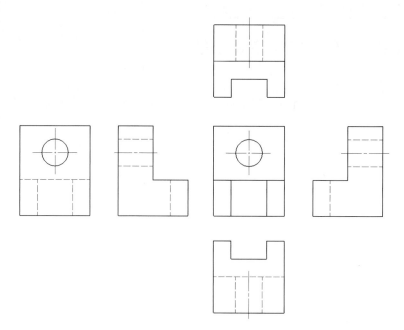

2.15 The Six Regular Views of the Object in Figure 2.14 with Visible, Hidden, and Centerlines Displayed

2.6 USE YOUR IMAGINATION!

As a drafter-in-training, you should develop the ability to use your imagination to visualize the multiviews of an object. Engineering and architecture are fields in which a powerful imagination is an important tool for success because most of the objects being designed exist first only in the imagination of the designer(s). The challenge for the design team is to take the design from the imagination stage and turn it into a set of drawings that can be used to make the design a reality.

The following steps document the process of creating a multiview drawing for the object shown in the designer's sketch in Figure 2.16.

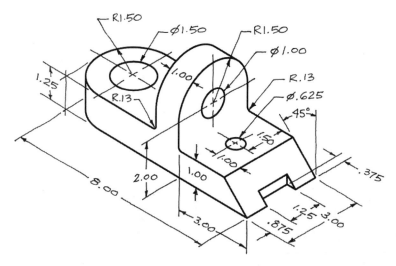

MATERIAL-ALUMINUM 6061

2.16 The Designer's Two-Dimensional Sketch of the Object to Be Visualized

CREATING A MULTIVIEW DRAWING

1 The drafter studies the designer's sketch of the object in Figure 2.16 and imagines how it might look after it has been manufactured (Figure 2.17). Next, the drafter determines the front, or principal, view of the imagined 3D object and how it may be positioned (Figure 2.18).

Then, the drafter rotates the object in his or her mind toward the top (Figure 2.19) until the top, or bird's-eye, view of the principal view is visible as shown in Figure 2.20.

Next, the drafter imagines the front view of the object rotated toward the right (Figure 2.21) until the right-side view is visible (Figure 2.22).

This process could be likened to creating a 3D movie of the object in your imagination to facilitate the visualization of the desired views.

Note that the top and right views (Figures 2.20 and 2.22) are drawn at right angles (90°), or perpendicular, to the front view (Figure 2.18).

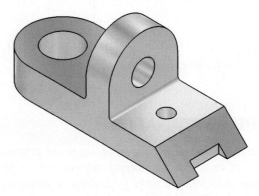

2.17   The Object Visualized as a Three-Dimensional Part

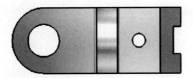

2.20   The Top View of the Object

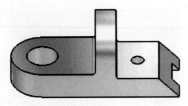

2.19   Rotating the Object toward the Top

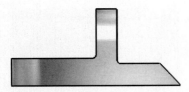

2.18   The Front of the Object

2.21   Rotating the Object toward the Right

2.22   The Right View of the Object

2 The drafter continues the process begun in Step 1, rotating the object until the six regular views of the object have been visualized (Figure 2.23).

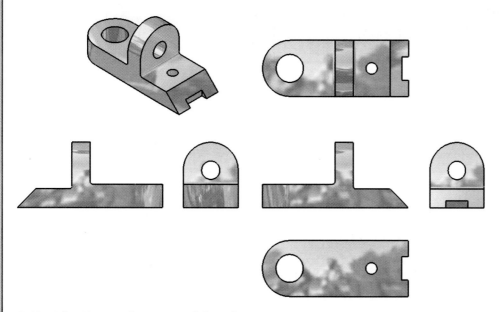

2.23 The Six Regular Views of the Object

3 The drafter visualizes the visible lines of the object (Figure 2.24).

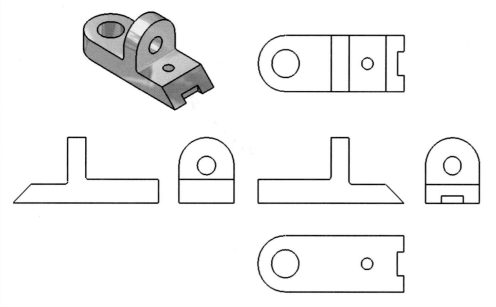

2.24 The Six Regular Views Showing the Object's Visible Lines

STEP by STEP

STEP by STEP

4 Next, the drafter visualizes the location of the object's hidden and centerlines (Figure 2.25).

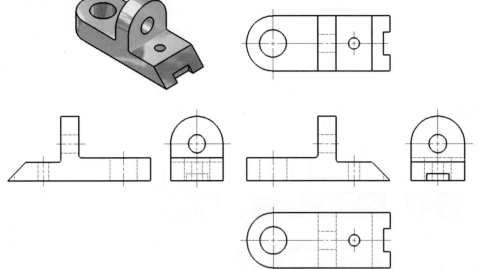

2.25 The Six Regular Views of the Object Including Hidden and Centerlines

5 In the last step, the drafter determines which of the six views will be necessary to describe the object and places dimensions on the part (Figure 2.26).

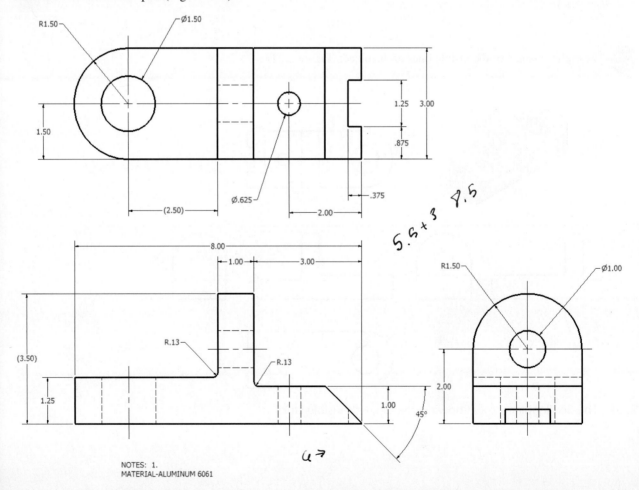

NOTES: 1.
MATERIAL-ALUMINUM 6061

2.26 The Views Necessary to Describe the Object Including Dimensions

2.7 VISUALIZING THE MULTIVIEWS OF BASIC GEOMETRIC SHAPES

The multiview representations of some basic geometric shapes are shown in Figures 2.27 through 2.40. Shapes such as boxes, cylinders, cones, spheres, wedges, and prisms are often referred to as **graphic primitives**, because by combining, or *unioning,* these shapes, or in some cases *subtracting* the geometry of one shape from another one, more complicated shapes can be formed. Graphic primitives can be considered as building blocks used to construct more complex objects. Students who learn to visualize the multiviews of graphic primitives will find it easier to visualize the multiviews of the more complicated shapes formed when they are combined.

Study Figures 2.27 through 2.40 and familiarize yourself with how the front, top, and side views of the graphic primitives and their combinations are drawn, including how hidden and centerlines are placed.

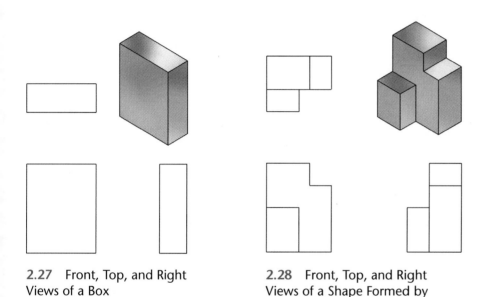

2.27 Front, Top, and Right Views of a Box

2.28 Front, Top, and Right Views of a Shape Formed by Unioning and Subtracting Boxes

2.29 Front, Top, and Right Views of a Cylinder

2.30 Front, Top, and Right Views of a Shape Formed by Subtracting a Cylinder from a Box

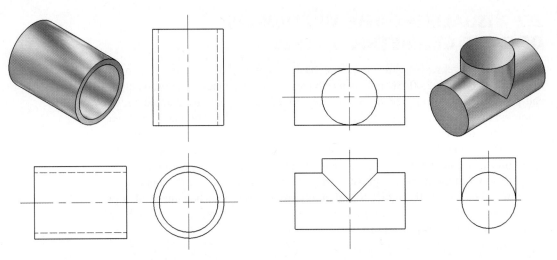

2.31　Front, Top, and Left Views of a Cylinder with a Smaller Cylinder Subtracted from Its Center

2.32　Front, Top, and Right Views of a Shape Formed by the Intersection of Two Cylinders of Equal Diameter

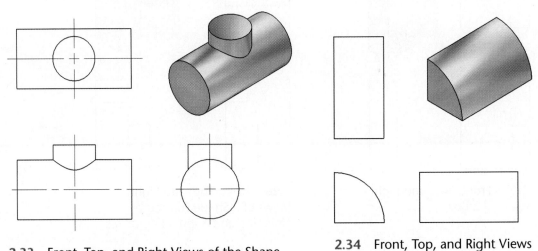

2.33　Front, Top, and Right Views of the Shape Resulting from the Intersection of Two Cylinders with Unequal Diameters

2.34　Front, Top, and Right Views of a Quarter-Round Shape

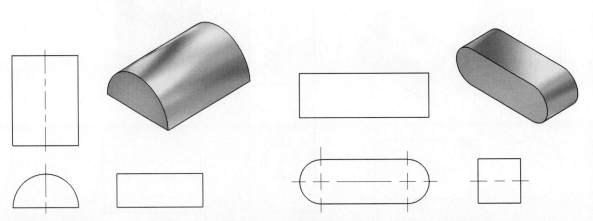

2.35　Front, Top, and Right Views of a Half-Round Shape

2.36　Front, Top, and Right Views of a Shape Resulting from the Union of a Box and Two Half-Rounds

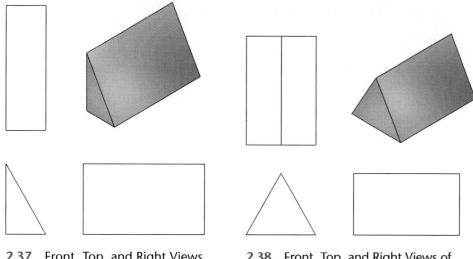

2.37 Front, Top, and Right Views
of a Wedge

2.38 Front, Top, and Right Views of
a Prism

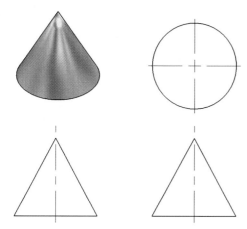

2.39 Front, Top, and Left Views of
a Cone

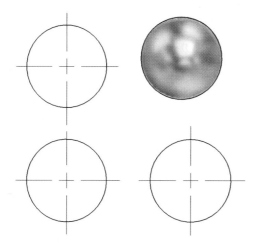

2.40 Front, Top, and Right Views of
a Sphere

2.8 ORTHOGRAPHIC PROJECTION

Orthographic projection is the technique employed in the creation of multiview drawings to project the size and location of geometric features (points, lines, planes, or other features) from one view to another. Light construction lines are usually drawn between views to facilitate the transfer of this information. Projecting information in this manner is a more efficient way to construct technical drawings than by remeasuring the features in each view.

The orthographic projection technique also utilizes a *miter line* drawn at 45°, which allows geometric information to be projected between the top and side views.

Figure 2.41 shows an example of this technique. Dotted lines illustrate how the size and location of the object's features can be projected from view to view. Note how the 45° miter line is used to facilitate the transfer of information between the top and side views.

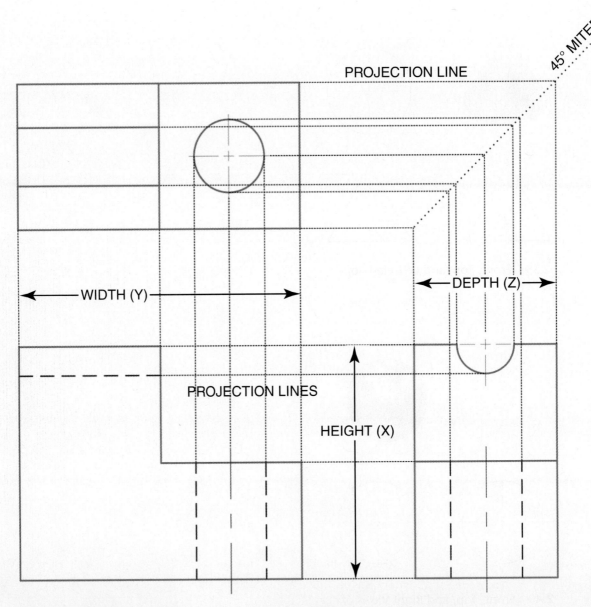

2.41   Multiview Drawing of an Object Using Orthographic Projection Techniques

UTILIZING ORTHOGRAPHIC PROJECTION TECHNIQUES TO CREATE MULTIVIEW SKETCHES

1 Study the sketch of the part shown in Figure 2.42 and try to imagine it as a 3D object. With this 3D image in mind, visualize the front, top, and right-side views.

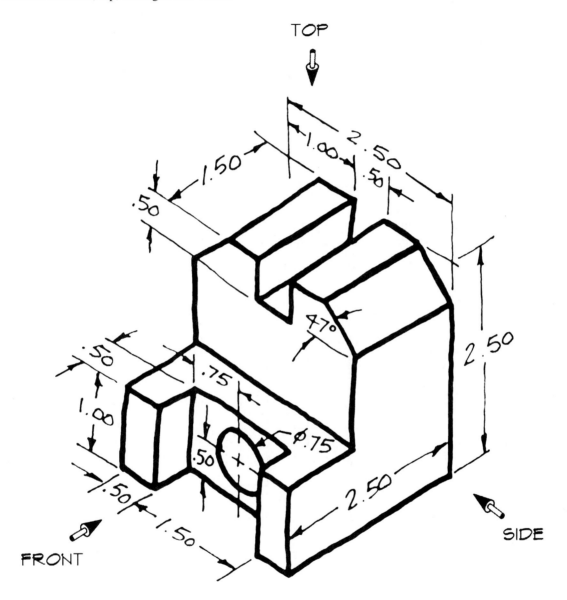

2.42 Sketch of Object to Be Drawn as a Multiview Drawing

NOTE

The American Society of Mechanical Engineers Standard for creating multiview drawings is *ASME Y14.3-2003*.

STEP by STEP

2 Sketch the front view of the object. Try to sketch the part proportionally to the dimensions specified on the sketch. Extend light construction lines out from the features of the front view to the top and right sides and place a 45° miter line as shown in Figure 2.43.

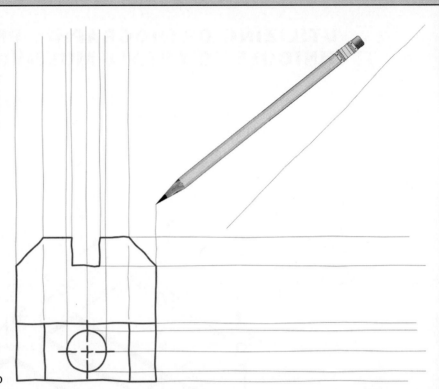

2.43 Extending Construction Lines from the Features of the Front View to the Side and Top

3 Sketch the top and right-side views of the object as shown in Figure 2.44. Use the construction lines projected from the front view, and construction lines projected through the miter line, to locate the features of each view. Darken the visible, hidden, and centerlines as needed. Erase construction lines that appear too dark.

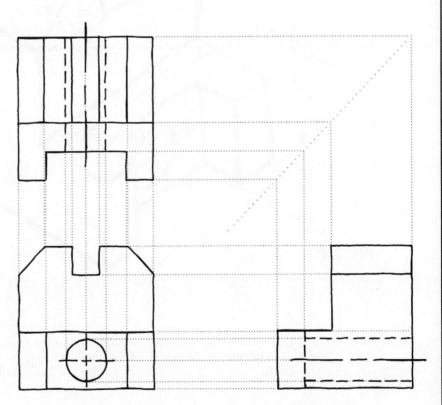

2.44 Sketching the Top and Right-Side Views

2.9 DRAWING OBJECTS TO SCALE

In technical drawings, objects are often drawn *to scale*. This term refers to the relationship between the size of the object in the drawing and the actual size of the object after it is manufactured. Following are four of the scales most commonly used in the creation of mechanical drawings:

- **Full Scale**   This means that the size of the object in the drawing will be the same size as the object after it is manufactured. This is usually only feasible on smaller objects such as machine parts (to draw an average-size house at full scale, you might need a sheet of paper that is 136′ long by 88′ wide). When noting on a drawing that the object is drawn full scale, the drafter may write 1 = 1, 1/1, or 1:1.
- **Half Scale**   This means that the size of the object in the drawing is half the size of the object after it is manufactured. The drafter will still place the full-size dimensions on the views of the object so that even though the drawing is half size, the part will be manufactured full size. When noting on a drawing that the object is drawn half scale, the drafter may write 1 = 2, 1/2, .5X, or 1:2.
- **Quarter Scale**   This means that the size of the object in the drawing is one fourth the size of the object after it is manufactured. The drafter will still place the full-size dimensions on the views of the object so that even though the drawing is one-fourth size, the part will be manufactured full size. When noting on a drawing that the object is drawn quarter scale, the drafter may write 1 = 4, 1/4, .25X, or 1:4.
- **Double Scale**   This means that the size of the object in the drawing is twice the size of the object after it is manufactured. The drafter will still place the full-size dimensions on the views of the object so that even though the drawing is twice the size, the part will be manufactured full size. This scale is used for smaller objects that would be difficult to dimension if drawn at actual size. When noting on a drawing that the object is drawn double scale, the drafter may write 2 = 1, 2/1, 2:1, or 2X.

2.10 DRAWING ARCHITECTURAL PLANS TO SCALE

Following are two of the scales most commonly used in the creation of architectural drawings:

- **Quarter Inch Equals One Foot**   This means that every 1/4″ on the plotted drawing represents a measurement of 1′ on the actual construction project. For example, a wall that is to be built 16′ in length will measure 4″ on the drawing. This allows a drafter to fit a house that is 100′ long and 50′ wide on a sheet of paper measuring only 36″ by 24″. The 100′ distance will measure only 25″ on the drawing sheet (100 × 1/4″ = 25″), and 50′ will measure 12.5″ on the sheet (50 × 1/4″ = 12.5″). The dimensions on the drawing will be labeled at the actual distance (in feet and inches) required to construct the building full size. When noting on a drawing that the object is drawn to this scale, the drafter would write 1/4″ = 1′ -0″.
- **Eighth Inch Equals One Foot**   This means that every 1/8″ on the plotted drawing will represent a measurement of 1′ on the actual construction project. For example, a wall that is to be built 16′ in length will measure 2″ on the drawing. This allows a drafter to fit a house that is 200′ long and 100′ wide on a sheet of paper measuring only 36″ by 24″. The distance of 200′ will measure only 25″ on the drawing sheet (200 × 1/8″ = 25″), and 100′ will measure 12.5″ on the sheet (100 × 1/8″ = 12.5″). The dimensions on the drawing will be labeled at the actual distance (in feet and inches) required to construct the building full size. When noting on a drawing that the object is drawn to this scale, the drafter would write 1/8″ = 1′-0″.

2.11 DRAWING SHEET SIZES

ASME and other standards organizations have defined standardized *sheet sizes* for the preparation of technical drawings. These sheet sizes vary depending on the type of drawing and/or the unit of measurement used to create the drawing.

The ASME standard for decimal sheet sizes is *ASME Y14.1-2005*. The sheet sizes defined in this standard begin with an A sheet, which is 11″ × 8.5″. A B sheet's dimensions are 17″ × 11″, which is the equivalent of two A sheets laid side by side. A C sheet is 22″ × 17″, which is the equivalent of two B sheets laid side by side. A D sheet is 34″ × 22″, which is the equivalent of two C sheets laid side by side. Figure 2.45 illustrates the sheet sizes used in mechanical drawings.

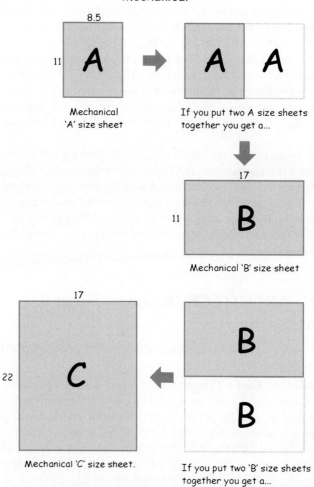

2.45 Sheet Sizes for a Mechanical Drawing

The ASME standard for metric sheet sizes is *ASME Y14.1M-2005*. In this standard, an A4 sheet measures 297 × 210 millimeters (mm), an A3 sheet measures 420 mm × 297 mm, an A2 sheet measures 594 mm × 420 mm, an A1 sheet measures 841 mm × 594 mm, and an A0 sheet measures 1189 mm × 841 mm.

For architectural drawings in which inches are used as the unit of measurement, an A sheet measures 12″ × 9″, a B sheet is 18″ × 12″, a C sheet is 24″ × 18″, and a D sheet is 36″ × 24″.

A high-quality paper known as *vellum*, or tracing paper, is used to plot drawings that are made to be reproduced by blueprinting. Vellum is a strong, thin paper that allows light to pass through it relatively easily. Vellum can be purchased in rolls 24″ to 36″ in width or in standard sheet sizes. Vellum can also be purchased with preprinted title blocks.

2.12 THIRD-ANGLE PROJECTION VERSUS FIRST-ANGLE PROJECTION

The method of arranging multiviews shown in Figure 2.46, with the top view drawn above the front view and the right-side view drawn to the right of the front view, is called ***third-angle projection***. This method is widely used in technical drawings created in the United States. In a third-angle projection, the image is projected onto a viewing plane that is located between the object and the viewer.

In many parts of the world, multiviews are arranged using ***first-angle projection*** instead of third-angle projection. A first-angle projection is drawn as though the object is between the observer and the projection plane. For this reason, when a drawing is created with first-angle projection, the right-side view appears to the *left* of the front view, and the top view appears *below* the front view, as shown in Figure 2.47.

> ## NOTE
> The American Society of Mechanical Engineers standard for creating and interpreting multiview drawings using first- and third-angle projection techniques is *ASME Y14.3-2003*.

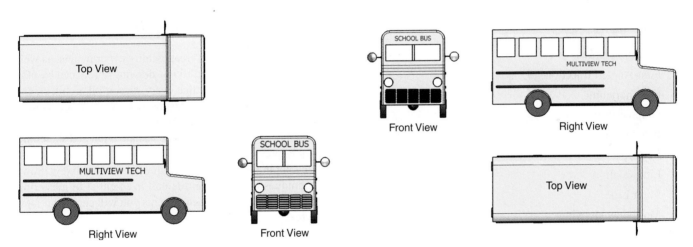

2.46   Third-Angle Projection Example

2.47   Arrangement of Views in First-Angle Projection

To avoid confusion, it may be necessary to note on the drawing whether first- or third-angle projection was used to create the drawing. For this reason, symbols have been developed to distinguish between the two types of projection techniques.

Third-angle projection can be noted on drawings by placing the symbol shown in Figure 2.48 in, or near, the title block.

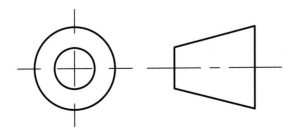

2.48   Third-Angle Projection Symbol

> **NOTE**
>
> The American Society of Mechanical Engineers standard governing the symbols used for first- and third-angle projection is *ASME Y14.1-2005.*

The first-angle projection technique can be noted on drawings with the symbol shown in Figure 2.49. The letters *SI* (International System of Units) indicate that the drawing was prepared using metric units. The unit of measurement commonly used in the creation of mechanical engineering drawings is the millimeter.

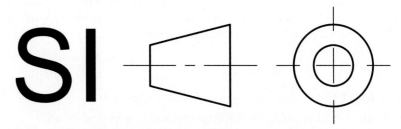

2.49 First-Angle Projection Symbol. SI Signifies That the Drawing Was Created in Metric Units

KEY WORDS

Elevation Drawings

First-Angle Projection

Foreshortening

Graphic Primitives

Inclined Plane

Linetype

Lineweight

Miter Line

Multiview Drawing

Orthographic Projection

Projection Planes

Regular Views

Sheet Sizes

Third-Angle Projection

Three-Dimensional (3D) Object

Two-Dimensional (2D) Object

CHAPTER SUMMARY

The ability to visualize and create multiview drawings, as well as the ability to interpret multiview drawings produced by others, is an essential job skill that every successful architect, engineer, designer, and drafter must possess. Some students may find that to develop this skill they will need to devote a significant amount of time practicing the visualization and sketching techniques presented in this unit.

Developing a solid understanding of the multiview drawing techniques presented in this unit is essential to mastering the concepts and drawing assignments you will encounter later in this text.

REVIEW QUESTIONS

Short Answer

1. Name the six regular views of an object.
2. How does a drafter determine which view will be the front view?
3. How many views of an object should a drafter draw?
4. What does *quarter scale* mean?
5. Name the standard that controls line thickness in an ASME drawing.

Multiple Choice

1. What is the sheet size for an architectural D sheet?
   a. 12 × 9
   b. 297 × 210
   c. 36 × 24
   d. 18 × 12

2. What is the sheet size for a mechanical B size sheet?
   a. 17 × 11
   b. 18 × 12
   c. 841 × 594
   d. 36 × 24

3. Which ratio indicates that a drawing is full size?
   a. 1 = 1
   b. 1/1
   c. 1:1
   d. All the above

4. A C sheet is equal in size to two of these sheets laid side by side:
   a. A
   b. B
   c. D
   d. None of the above

5. What does 1/4″ = 1′-0″ represent on an architectural drawing of a house?
   a. The scale of the drawing is 1 = 4.
   b. One foot on the construction site equals 1/4 inch on the drawing.
   c. The house should be built one-quarter scale.
   d. A distance of 100 feet will measure 12.5 inches on the drawing.

Matching

Column A

a. 2 = 1

b. .3mm

c. .3mm

d. 1 = 2

e. .6mm

Column B

1. Ratio indicating a drawing is half scale

2. ASME line thickness for a visible line

3. Ratio indicating a drawing is double scale

4. ASME line thickness for a centerline

5. ASME line thickness for a hidden line

CHAPTER EXERCISES

— NOTE —
Remove the grid sheets by carefully tearing along the perforation. If you need extra grid sheets, print the **Multiview Grid Sheet.pdf** file located in the Sketching and Traditional Drafting Sheets folder located in the student data files at **www .pearsondesigncentral .com.** To access this sheet, open the *Pearson Design Central* website and click on the **CAD Community** link, then select the **Click here to download student data files for our CAD titles** link. Next, click on the **Technical Drawing 101** link and select the **Sketching and Traditional Drafting Sheets** zip file, then select the **Download** button and open (or save) the pdf specified above.

The following sketching exercises are designed to help you develop multiview sketching and visualization skills.

Directions

1. On the grid sheets located at the back of the text, sketch the front, top, and side views of the objects in Exercises 2.1 through 2.6. The black arrows on each sketching exercise identify the view of the object to sketch as the front view.
2. Begin each sketch by counting the number of grids that define the features of the front view and transfer these distances to the grid sheet. Start the front view in the darkened corner located in the lower left corner of each numbered grid box (see the example shown on the Exercise 2.1 grid sheet). Begin the top and right views in the darkened corners above, or to the right, of the front view
3. Take advantage of the miter line drawn in each grid box to transfer information between the top and right views whenever possible.

If you have trouble with a sketching problem, you may find referring to Figures 2.27 through 2.40 helpful. Also, do not hesitate to ask your instructor for assistance. This activity may seem difficult at first, but keep working at it, because through practice it is possible for you to develop this important drafting skill.

Exercise 2.1

On the grid sheet located at the back of the text, sketch the front, top, and right-side views of the objects shown on page 41. Begin views in the dark corners shown in the grid.

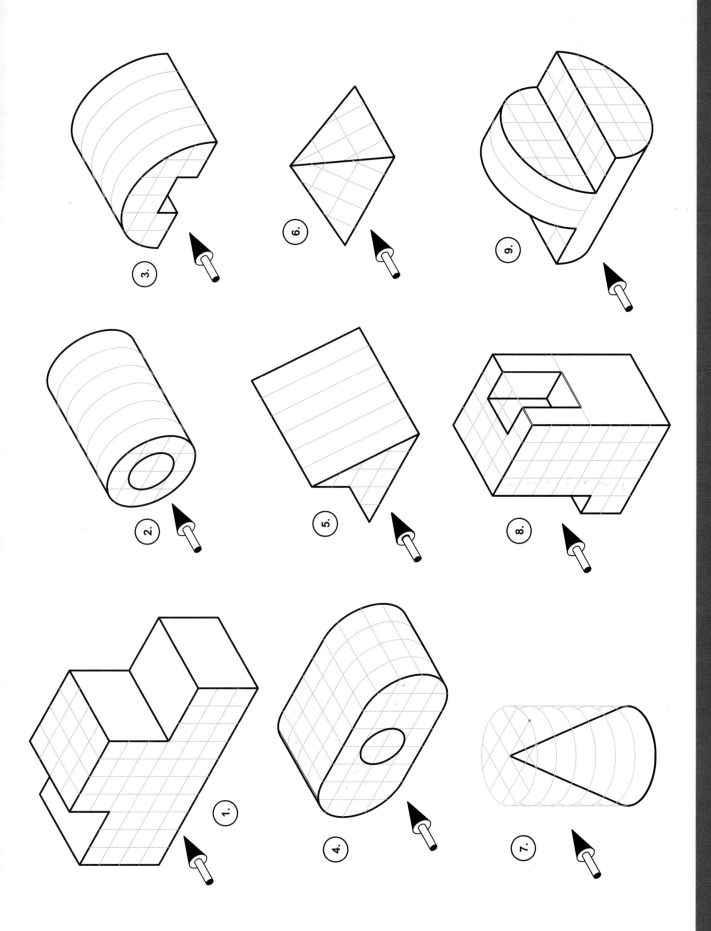

Exercise 2.2

On the grid sheet located at the back of the text, sketch the front, top, and right-side views of the objects shown on page 43. Begin views in the corners shown in the grid.

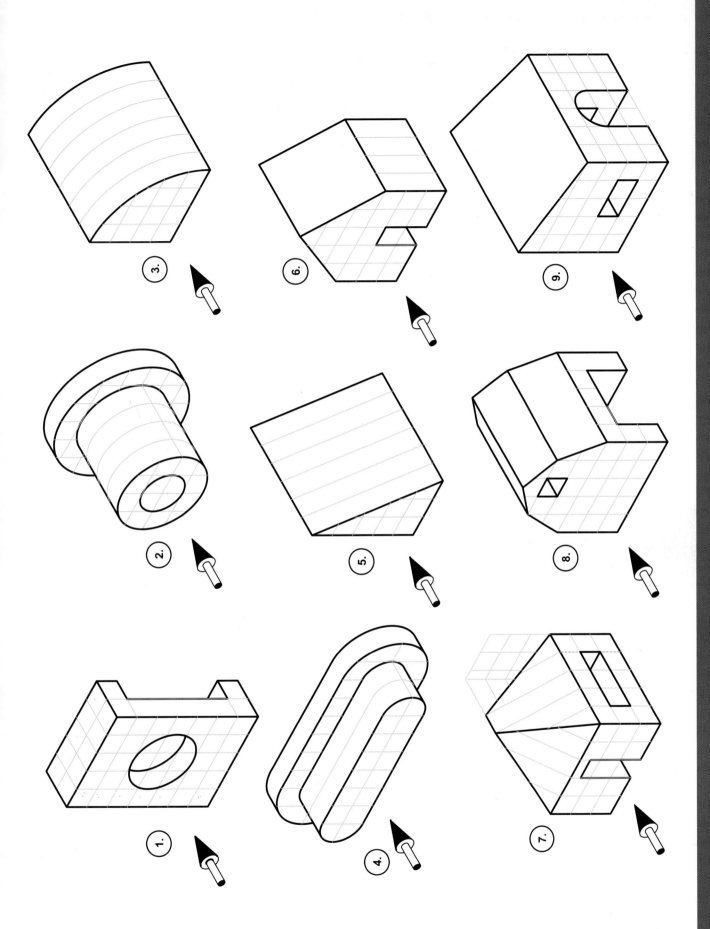

Exercise 2.3

On the grid sheet located at the back of the text, sketch the front, top, and right-side views of the objects shown on page 45. Begin views in the corners shown in the grid.

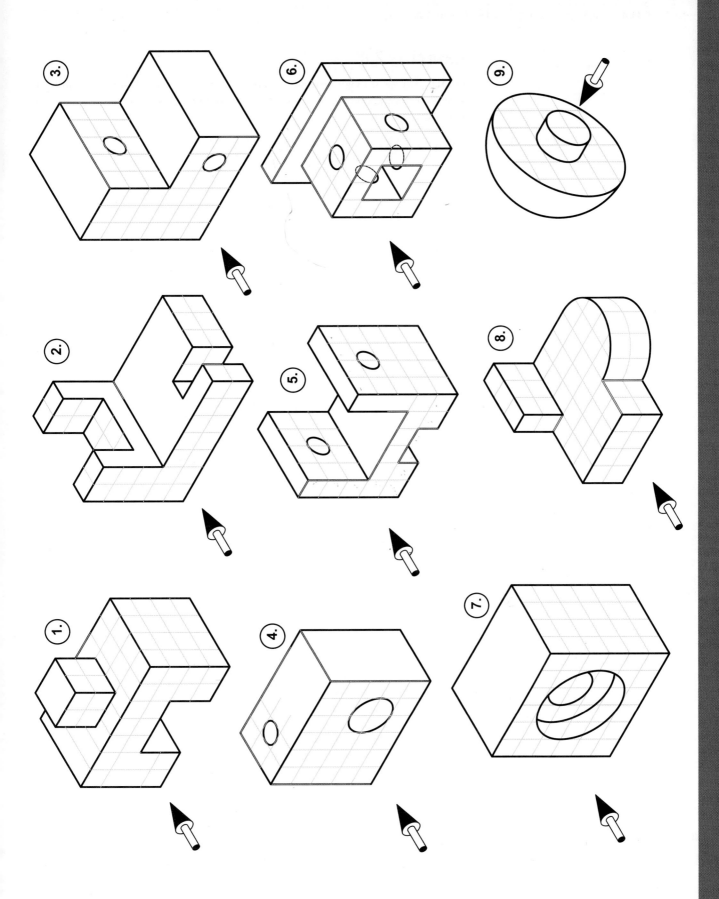

45

Exercise 2.4

On the grid sheet located at the back of the text, sketch the front, top, and right-side views of the objects shown on page 47. Begin views in the corners shown in the grid.

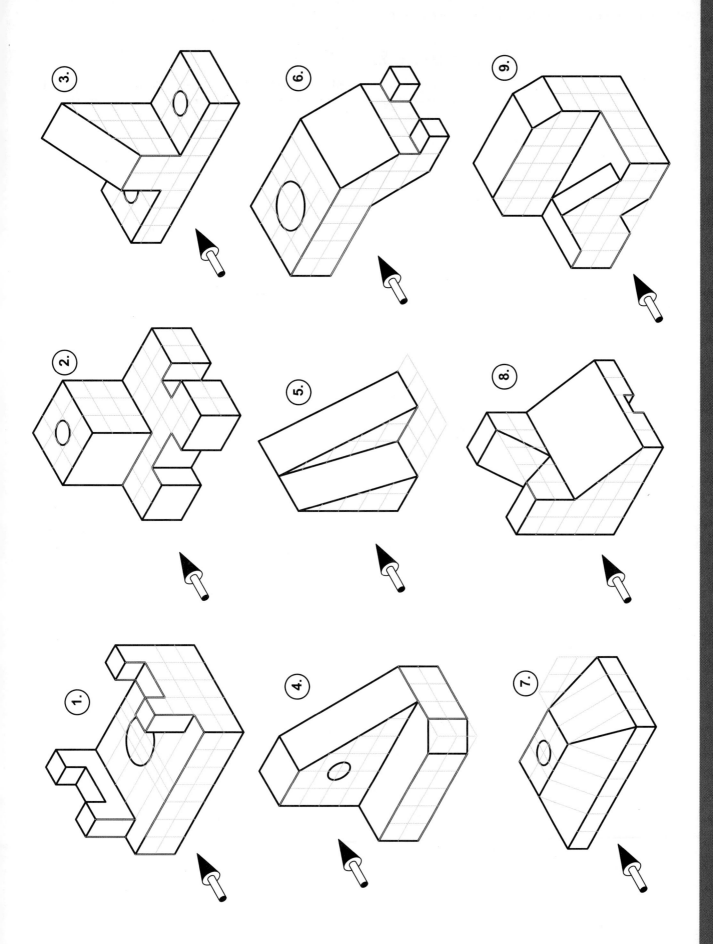

Exercise 2.5

On the grid sheet located at the back of the text, sketch the front, top, and right-side views of the objects shown on page 49. Begin views in the corners shown in the grid.

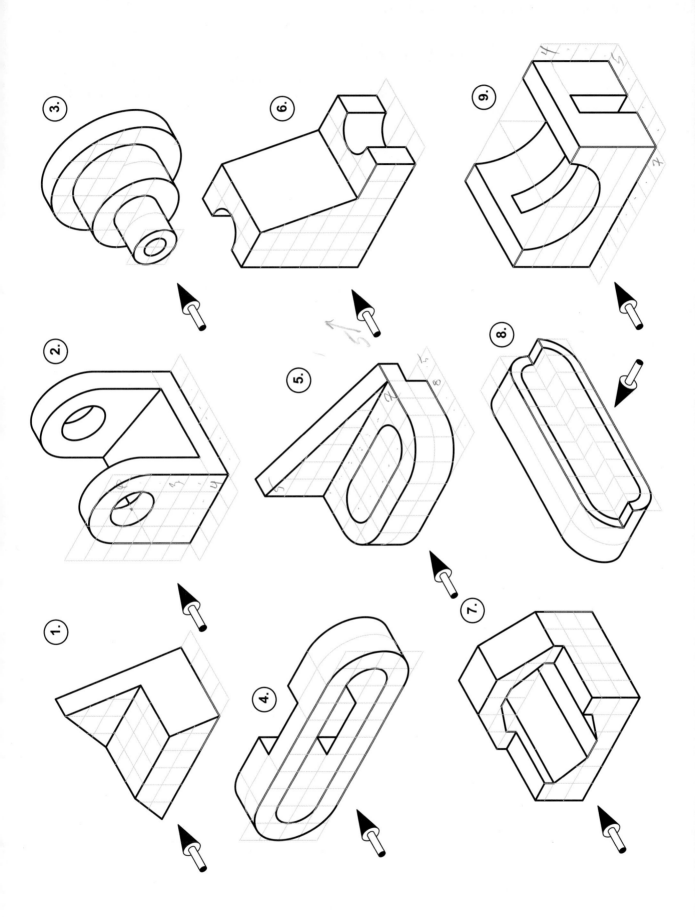

Exercise 2.6

On the grid sheet located at the back of the text, sketch the front, top, and right-side views of the objects shown on page 51. Begin views in the corners shown in the grid.

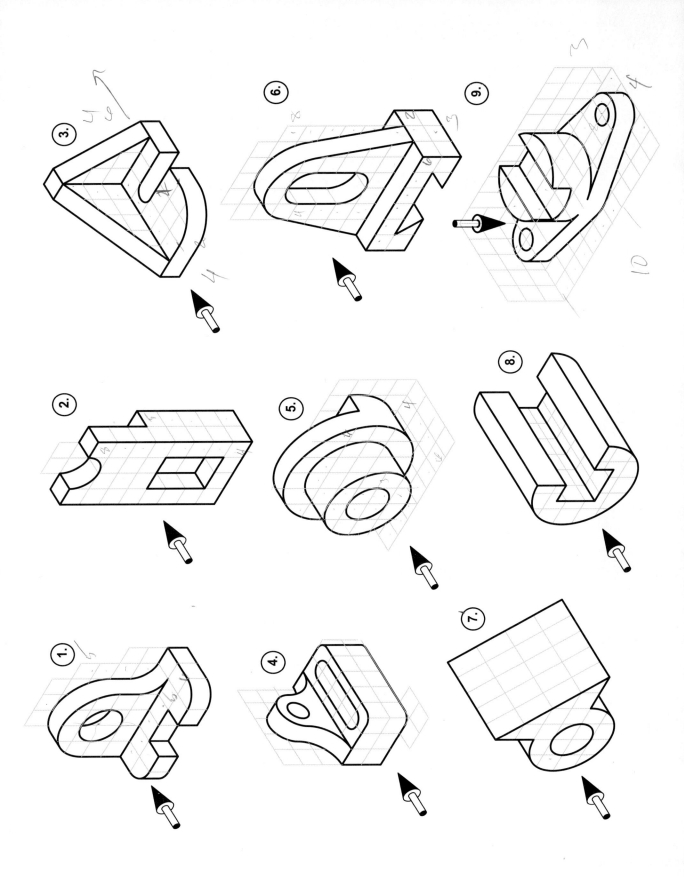

CHAPTER THREE

TRADITIONAL DRAFTING TOOLS AND TECHNIQUES

OBJECTIVES

After studying the material in this chapter, you should be able to:

1. Describe the tools and techniques used in traditional drafting.

2. Use technical pencils, straightedges, triangles, scales, protractors, and templates to construct the geometry of technical drawings.

3. Read a conversion table to convert between decimal, fractional, and metric units.

4. Use traditional drafting tools to create multiview drawings of objects including correctly placed and depicted visible, hidden, and centerlines.

5. Hand-letter notes and dimensions on technical drawings that are clear and legible.

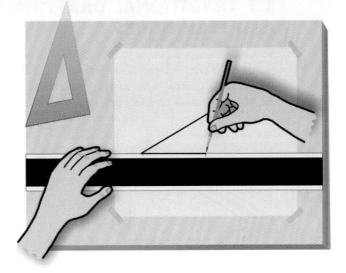

OVERVIEW

Before CAD revolutionized the way technical drawings are produced, drafters and designers sat at drawing tables and used *traditional drafting tools* like technical pens, straightedges, triangles, scales, protractors, and templates to draw on sheets of vellum or Mylar (a thin sheet of plastic with a matte surface).

In today's engineering or architectural office, it would be rare for a drafter to create a drawing in the traditional way, but many of the techniques developed by traditional drafters, such as orthographic projection, are still used to create 2D CAD drawings. The traditional tools discussed in this chapter can be purchased through drafting supply outlets.

Refer to the following websites:
- Pentel: www.pentel.com
- Staedtler: www.staedtler.com

3.1 TRADITIONAL DRAFTING TOOLS AND TECHNIQUES

Shown in Figures 3.1 through 3.3 are examples of traditional drafting equipment. A drafting machine, or a parallel straightedge, attached to the top of a drawing table allows a drafter to draw horizontal lines that are parallel to each other. Another tool that can be used to draw parallel horizontal lines is a T-square.

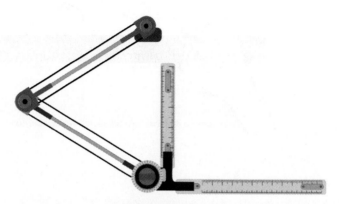

3.1 Drafting Machines Can Easily Be Adjusted for Drawing Variable Angles. Drafting Machines Were Once Common in Engineering Offices

3.2 Drawing Table with Drafting Machine

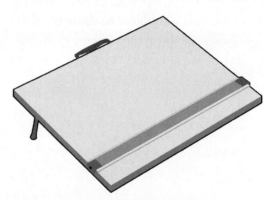

3.3 Parallel Straightedge Attached to the Top of a Portable Drawing Table

3.2 TECHNICAL PENCILS AND PENS

Professional-grade technical pens and pencils are often used by design professionals to create technical drawings and sketches (see Figure 3.4).

Leads are inserted after removing both the top cap and the eraser

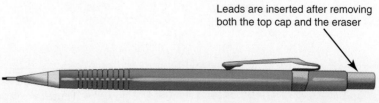

3.4 Technical Pencil

Technical pens and pencils come in differing line widths (.3mm, .5mm, .7mm, or .9mm). Leads for technical pencils are available in a variety of hardness grades, defined by the *lead hardness grade*, depending on the type of work to be performed. Table 3.1 shows the lead (graphite) hardness grades and the appropriate application for the leads in each hardness range.

Table 3.1 Lead Hardness Grades

Hard leads (4H–9H) are useful for laying out construction lines on a technical drawing.
Medium leads (3H, 2H, H, F, HB, and B) are often used for general drafting and sketching (2H is a popular medium lead).
Soft leads (2B–7B) are often used for shading and rendering drawings.

3.3 BEGINNING A TRADITIONAL DRAFTING PROJECT

Figure 3.5 illustrates the proper technique for attaching a sheet of vellum to the top of a drawing table. Align the bottom edge of the sheet with the top edge of the drafting machine arm, parallel straightedge, or T-square, and tape all four corners to the table top.

Horizontal lines are drawn along the top edge of the straightedge as shown in Figure 3.6. Right-handed drafters would hold the straightedge in place with their left hand when drawing a horizontal line.

3.4 DRAFTING TRIANGLES

Triangles, such as the ones shown in Figures 3.7 and 3.8, provide drafters with angles commonly used in technical drawings: 30°, 45°, 60°, and 90°. Triangles are usually made of acrylic plastic and are available in a variety of sizes.

3.5 Aligning the Bottom Edge of a Sheet of Vellum with the Top Edge of a Parallel Straightedge

3.6   Drawing a Horizontal Line

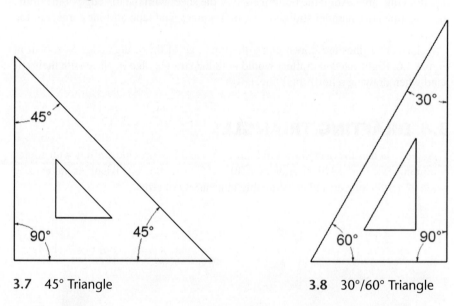

3.7   45° Triangle   **3.8**   30°/60° Triangle

TIP

Some triangles are designed for drawing with graphite, and others for drawing with pen and ink. Inking triangles have a beveled, or stepped, edge to prevent the ink from running under the edge of the triangle and smearing.

3.5 DRAWING LINES WITH TRIANGLES AND PARALLEL STRAIGHTEDGES

To draw horizontal and vertical lines that are mutually perpendicular (90°), drafters use a triangle in conjunction with a parallel straightedge.

To draw vertical lines, place the triangle on top of the straightedge, as in Figure 3.9. Hold both the straightedge and triangle with your left hand while drawing the vertical line. In this way you are assured that a vertical line will be drawn at a 90° angle relative to lines drawn along the top of the parallel straightedge. You can use either the 30°/60° triangle (as shown) or the 45° triangle.

Beginning students often erroneously believe that holding a triangle as vertical as their eyes can position it (known as "eyeballing") and drawing a line will give them

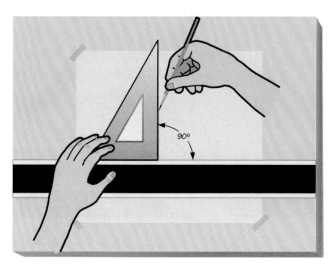

3.9 Drawing a Vertical Line

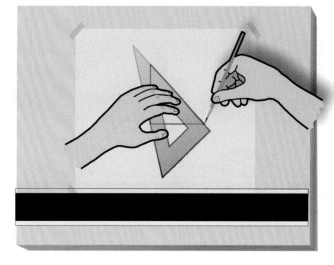

3.10 Drawing a Line between the Endpoints of Two Lines

a perpendicular vertical line, when in fact the only way to draw an accurate vertical line is to make sure the triangle rests on the straightedge as shown in Figure 3.9. However, there are occasions when the triangle is not positioned on the straightedge, for example, when connecting, two points or the ends of two lines, when the angle of the resulting line is not equal to 30°, 45°, 60°, or 90°.

Figure 3.10 illustrates how you can draw a line connecting the endpoints of vertical and horizontal lines. The desired angle does not match one of the triangle's normal angles (30°, 45°, 60°, or 90°). In this case, the triangle is floated and aligned with the ends of the vertical and horizontal lines. The line is drawn between the points along the edge of the triangle.

Placing the 30°/60° triangle on the top of the straightedge as in Figure 3.11 allows you to draw lines 30° from horizontal. You can draw these lines sloping either to the right (as shown) or to the left by flipping the triangle over.

Figure 3.12 shows lines being drawn at a 60° angle from horizontal. Flipping the triangle over allows you to draw lines sloping to the left or right as needed.

The 45° triangle can be used to draw 45° lines sloping to either the left or right, as in Figure 3.13.

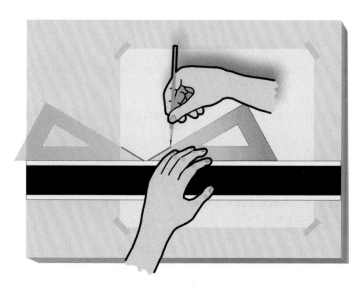

3.11 Drawing a 30° Line

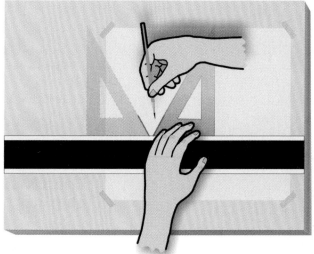

3.12 Drawing a 60° Line

3.13 Drawing a 45° Line

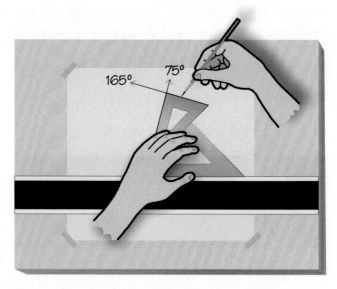

3.14 Combining Triangles to Produce 75° and 165° Lines

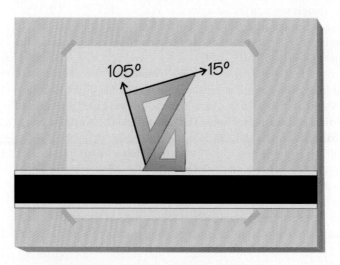

3.15 Combining Triangles to Produce 15° and 105° Lines

Using two triangles in combination allows you to draw lines at 15° increments. In Figure 3.14, the 45° and 30°/60° triangles are combined to draw lines at 75° and 165°.

In Figure 3.15, the 45° and 30°/60° triangles are combined to draw lines at 105° and 15°.

3.6 MAKING MEASUREMENTS WITH THE ENGINEER'S, ARCHITECT'S, AND METRIC SCALES

In engineering and architectural offices, designers and drafters use scales in two ways. The first is to take measurements from existing drawings or plots; the second is to lay out distances when constructing a drawing using traditional drafting techniques.

Depending on the type of drawing being created, a designer may choose the *engineer's, architect's,* or *metric scale* to measure distances (a *combination* scale is also available that has a mix of the most commonly used scales).

Reading the Engineer's Scale

The engineer's scale is used by both mechanical and civil engineers. The marks on the scale may be interpreted differently depending on the discipline. In Figure 3.16, the engineer's 10 scale is used to measure decimal inches. In Figure 3.17, the engineer's 10 scale is used to measure distances in feet.

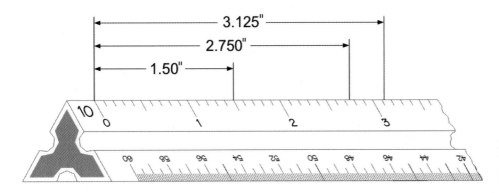

3.16 The Engineer's 10 Scale Showing Decimal Inches

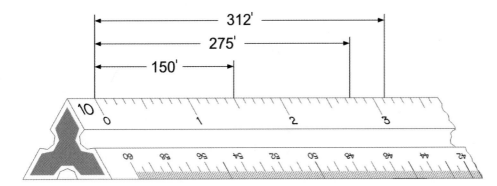

3.17 The Engineer's 10 Scale Showing Feet. This Scale Would Be Interpreted as 1" = 100'

Reading the Metric Scale

Mechanical engineers can use the metric scale shown in Figure 3.18 to measure distances in millimeters. In Figure 3.18, each small mark on the scale equals 1 millimeter.

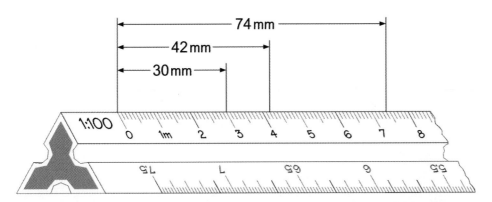

3.18 The Metric Scale Used to Measure Millimeters

Reading the Architect's Scale

The architect's scale is used to measure feet and inches on a floor plan. The architect's 1/4 scale shown in Figure 3.19 would be interpreted as 1/4" = 1'-0". This means that 1/4 inch measured on the drawing would equal 1 foot at the construction site.

Figures 3.20, 3.21, and 3.22 show examples of other commonly used architectural scales.

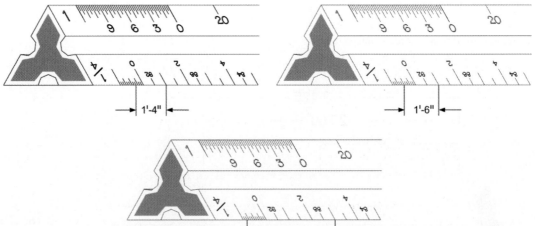

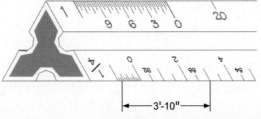

3.19 The Architect's 1/4 Scale Illustrating Several Different Measurements of Feet and Inches

The secret to using these scales is to align the numbers with the zero. Once you have done this, it becomes relatively easy to determine the required ticks for measuring.

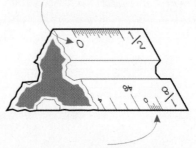

3.20 Interpreting Inch Marks on the Architect's 1/2 and 1/8 Scales

Each mark on the 1/8th scale is worth two inches (2", 4", 6", 8", etc.)

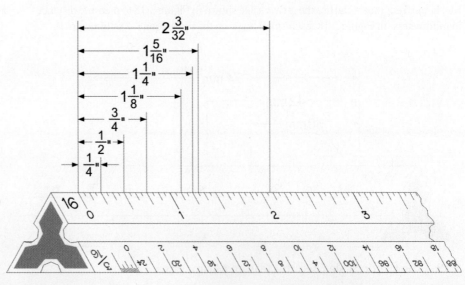

3.21 The Architect's 16 Scale Can Be Used to Measure Fractional Inches

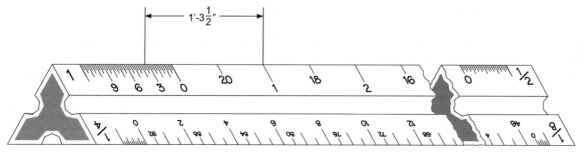

The scale along this edge - if read from the right - would be 1/8"=1'-0"

3.22   The Architect's 1 Scale Can Be Used to Measure Feet and Inches on a Floor Plan. The Scale Along the Top Edge, if Read from the Left, Would Be Interpreted as 1" = 1'-0"

> **TIP**
>
> To avoid having to search for a desired scale on a triangular scale, use a binder clip to mark your scale. For example, if using the 10 scale on an engineer's scale, attach the binder clip to the 50 scale. When you pick up your scale, the binder clip will orient you to the 10 scale.

3.7 CONVERTING UNITS OF MEASUREMENT

Drafters must sometimes convert from one unit of measurement to another. Some commonly used conversion factors are as follows:

- Fractional inches can be converted to decimal inches by dividing the numerator (the top number) by the denominator (the bottom number).
- Decimal inches can be converted to millimeters by multiplying them by 25.4.
- Millimeters can be converted to decimal inches by dividing them by 25.4.

Table 3.2 is useful for quickly finding the equivalent value among the various units listed.

3.8 READING THE PROTRACTOR

A protractor is a tool used to lay out angles on a drawing. Full-circle protractors are divided into 360°, and half-moon protractors (see Figure 3.23) are divided into 180°. Both are divided in 10° increments. Note that the protractor in Figure 3.23 is divided from 0° to 180° in both the clockwise and counterclockwise directions.

Figures 3.24 through 3.27 illustrate some of the ways the protractor can be used to measure angles.

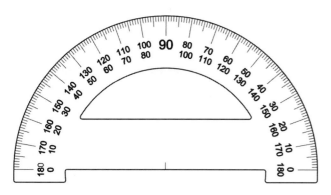

3.23   A Half-Moon, or 180°, Protractor

Table 3.2 Conversions among Fractional Inches, Decimal Inches, and Millimeters for Values Up to One Inch

Fractional Inch	Decimal Inch	Metric (mm)	Fractional Inch	Decimal Inch	Metric (mm)
1/64	.015625	0.3969	33/64	.515625	13.0969
1/32	.03125	0.7938	17/32	.53125	13.4938
3/64	.046875	1.1906	35/64	.546875	13.8906
1/16	.0625	1.5875	9/16	.5625	14.2875
5/64	.078125	1.9844	37/64	.578125	14.6844
3/32	.09375	2.3813	19/32	.59375	15.0813
7/64	.109375	2.7781	39/64	.609375	15.4781
1/8	.1250	3.1750	5/8	.6250	15.8750
9/64	.140625	3.5719	41/64	.640625	16.2719
5/32	.15625	3.9688	21/32	.65625	16.6688
11/64	.171875	4.3656	43/64	.671875	17.0656
3/16	.1875	4.7625	11/16	.6875	17.4625
13/64	.203125	5.1594	45/64	.703125	17.8594
7/32	.21875	5.5563	23/32	.71875	18.2563
15/64	.234375	5.9531	47/64	.734375	18.6531
1/4	.250	6.3500	3/4	.750	19.0500
17/64	.265625	6.7469	49/64	.765625	19.4469
9/32	.28125	7.1438	25/32	.78125	19.8438
19/64	.296875	7.5406	51/64	.796875	20.2406
5/16	.3125	7.9375	13/16	.8125	20.6375
21/64	.328125	8.3344	53/64	.828125	21.0344
11/32	.34375	8.7313	27/32	.84375	21.4313
23/64	.359375	9.1281	55/64	.859375	21.8281
3/8	.3750	9.5250	7/8	.8750	22.2250
25/64	.390625	9.9219	57/64	.890625	22.6219
13/32	.40625	10.3188	29/32	.90625	23.0188
27/64	.421875	10.7156	59/64	.921875	23.4156
7/16	.4375	11.1125	15/16	.9375	23.8125
29/64	.453125	11.5094	61/64	.953125	24.2094
15/32	.46875	11.9063	31/32	.96875	24.6063
31/64	.484375	12.3031	63/64	.984375	25.0031
1/2	.500	12.700	1	1.000	25.400

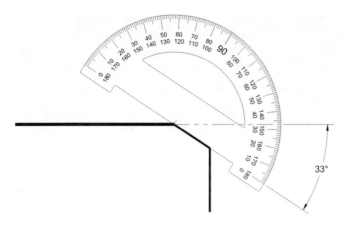

3.24 A 33° Angle Using the Inner Dial

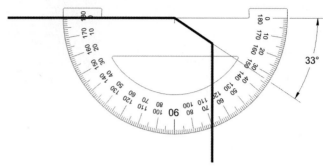

3.25 A 33° Angle Using the Outer Dial

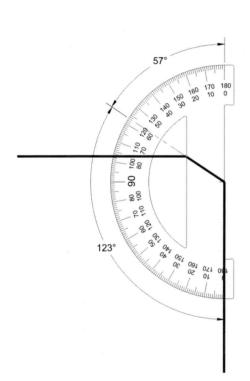

3.26 A 57° Angle Measured from Vertical

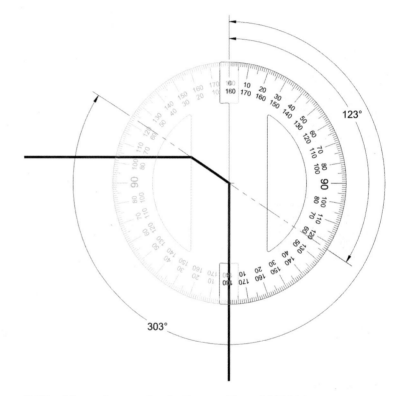

3.27 Measuring an Angle Greater Than 180° Using a Half-Moon Protractor

3.9 CIRCLE TEMPLATE

Circle templates come in a wide range of units (decimal inches, fractional inches, and millimeters) and diameters (see Figure 3.28). Figure 3.29 illustrates the steps in drawing a circle with the circle template.

3.10 ISOMETRIC ELLIPSE TEMPLATE

On isometric drawings, circles are represented as ellipses. Isometric ellipse templates allow drafters to place ellipses on isometric drawings quickly. Figure 3.30 illustrates the steps in drawing an ellipse with this template.

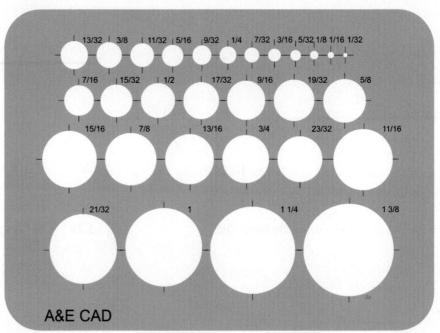

3.28 A Circle Template

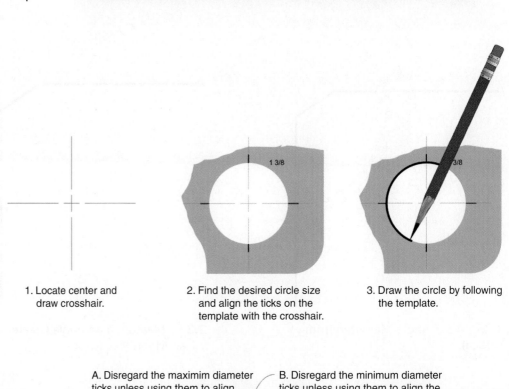

3.29 Using the Circle Template

1. Locate center and draw crosshair.

2. Find the desired circle size and align the ticks on the template with the crosshair.

3. Draw the circle by following the template.

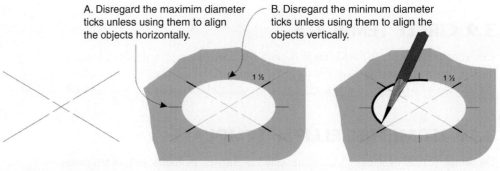

A. Disregard the maximim diameter ticks unless using them to align the objects horizontally.

B. Disregard the minimum diameter ticks unless using them to align the objects vertically.

3.30 Using the Isometric Ellipse Template

1. Locate center and draw crosshair at 30° angles.

2. Find the desired ellipse size and align the ticks on the template with the crosshair.

3. Draw the isometric ellipse by following the template.

STEPS IN CONSTRUCTING A SIMPLE DRAWING

Steps 1 through 8 illustrate how a drafter may use the triangle, scale, and parallel straightedge to construct a simple technical drawing. At the end of this chapter are drafting projects in which you will have an opportunity to apply the techniques shown in these steps.

1 Draw a light 30° construction line (Figure 3.31).

3.31 Drawing a 30° Construction Line

2 Align the scale along the construction line and place light tick marks to denote the desired measurement (Figure 3.32).

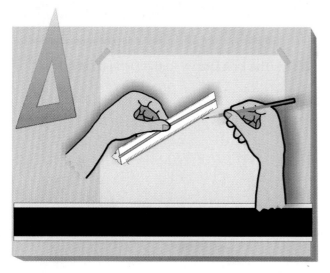

3.32 Making a Measurement along the 30° Construction Line

3 Align the edge of the 30°/60° triangle with the construction line and draw a dark line along the top edge of the triangle between the tick marks located in Step 2 (Figure 3.33).

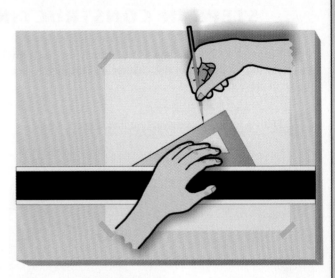

3.33　Darkening the Line

4 Draw the darkened visible line the desired distance (Figure 3.34).

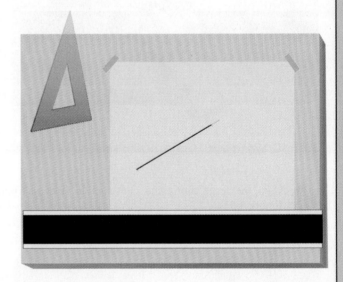

3.34　The Line Drawn to the Desired Length

5 Slide the horizontal bar until it is aligned with the lower tick mark and lightly draw a horizontal construction line (Figure 3.35).

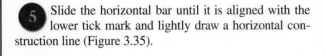

3.35　Drawing a Horizontal Construction Line

6 Measure along the horizontal construction line and mark off the required distance with a small tick mark (Figure 3.36).

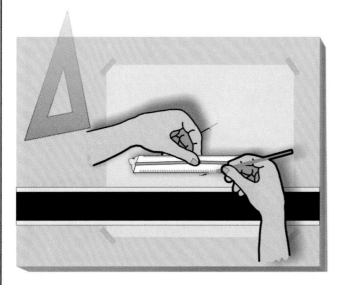

3.36 Making a Measurement along the Horizontal Construction Line

7 Draw a dark visible line between the tick marks (Figure 3.37).

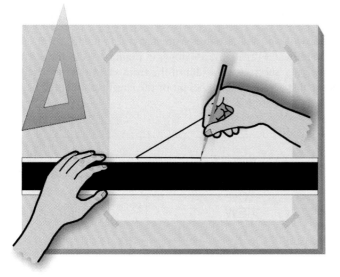

3.37 Darkening the Horizontal Line

8 Because the angle between the ends of the lines does not match an angle on either the 45° or 30°/60° triangle, move the triangle until it is aligned with the endpoints of each line and draw a dark line connecting them (Figure 3.38). The completed drawing is shown in Figure 3.39.

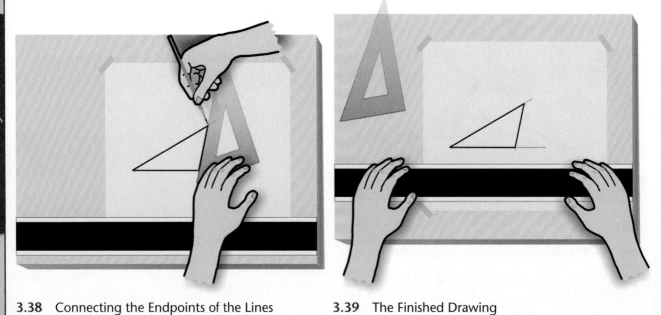

3.38 Connecting the Endpoints of the Lines

3.39 The Finished Drawing

STEPS IN CONSTRUCTING A MULTIVIEW DRAWING

The steps involved in constructing a multiview drawing with traditional tools are illustrated in Figures 3.40 through 3.44.

1 Study the width, depth, and height of the object to be drawn and use these dimensions to determine the location of the views. Views are usually equally spaced both horizontally and vertically, as shown in Figure 3.40. A formula for determining the horizontal spacing is to take the width of the sheet, subtract the width of the front view and the depth of the side view, and divide the remainder by 3. To find the vertical spacing, take the height of the sheet, subtract the height of the front view and the depth of the top view, and divide the remainder by 3.

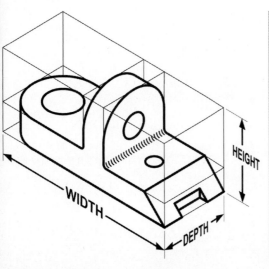

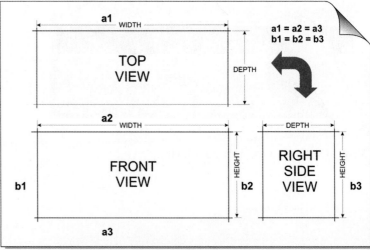

3.40 Determining View Spacing

2 Lay out the width, height, and depth of the views with light construction lines (Figure 3.41).

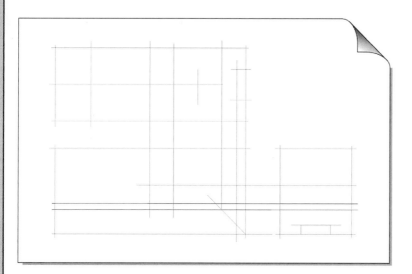

3.41 Rough Layout of Views

3 Add a miter line so that orthographic projection techniques can be used to project between the top and side views. Draw in circles lightly with a circle template or compass. Project information between views with light construction lines (Figure 3.42).

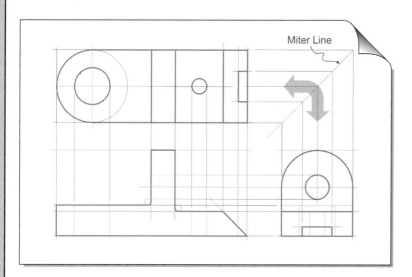

3.42 Adding Miter Line and Circles

4 Add hidden and centerlines (Figure 3.43).

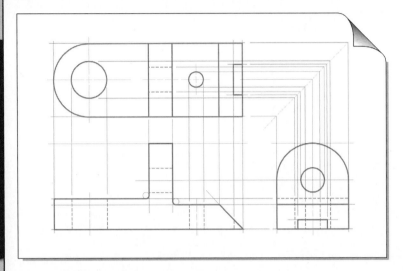

3.43   Adding Hidden and Centerlines

5 Erase the construction lines, and darken the visible, hidden, and centerlines to complete the drawing (Figure 3.44).

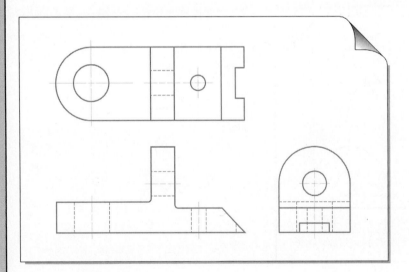

3.44   Finished Drawing

JOB SKILLS

It is best to draw all the views using construction lines. If you make a mistake, it is easier to erase a construction line than a darkened visible, hidden, or centerline. After you have drawn the views with construction lines, darken the top view first, then the front view, and the side view last. Darkening your lines in this order allows you to work away from your completed views and minimizes smudging.

3.11 TECHNICAL LETTERING

Every technical drawing text is required by law to expound on the importance of good *technical lettering* skills. Well, not really, but technical drawing teachers, as sworn defenders of an ancient art form, feel an obligation to convey the importance of this skill to their students.

During the design process, drafters and designers often make sketches that contain handwritten notes and dimensions. It is very important that any hand-lettered text on a drawing be neat, uniform, and legible. In fact, lettering that does not have these qualities would be considered unprofessional in most engineering or architectural offices. This is because poor lettering on a design sketch could cause dimensions or notes to be incorrectly depicted on a technical drawing, which could lead to a costly mistake on a construction site or manufacturing floor. It might also cost a designer his or her job.

It is hoped that last sentence caught your attention so you realize that developing good lettering skills is very important to your success as a drafter/designer. Good lettering is a skill that is mastered only through practice. Over time, most drafters and designers develop their own unique lettering style. Some drafters, especially in the architectural field, develop a lettering style that could be considered an art form. Although you may never develop a style that qualifies as "art," with practice you can develop a style that is neat, legible, and uniform.

Developing a Technical Lettering Style

Study the examples of the letters and numerals shown in Figure 3.45. The example at the top of the figure is lettered in an artistic, *architectural* style, and the example midway down the figure is lettered in a more gothic, *engineering* style. In each of the

3.45 Examples of Good Technical Lettering Styles (Top: Architectural Style; Bottom: Engineering Style)

styles, notice how the characters are uniform with regard to height, width, and style. The angle of vertical strokes should be consistent, and each character should be clear and legible.

In the guide lines provided below the lettering examples in Figure 3.45, practice lettering the alphabet and numerals. Try to match the lettering style shown in the example. Lettering should be dark, so press down hard with the pencil when making the strokes that form a letter or numeral.

KEY WORDS

Architect's, Engineer's and Metric Scales

Lead Hardness Grade

Technical Lettering

Traditional Drafting Tools

CHAPTER SUMMARY

Although traditional drafting tools are rarely used in modern engineering and architectural offices, many of the same techniques developed by traditional drafters are still used in the creation of drawings with CAD. For example, the location of points and planes is still projected between multiviews; however, instead of using a drafting triangle, an AutoCAD drafter uses a drafting setting called **Ortho** to draw perfectly straight horizontal and vertical lines. An understanding of how angles are measured with a protractor facilitates drawing angles with AutoCAD.

Drafters and designers often use scales to take measurements from plotted drawings (which is not always a good idea, by the way), and an understanding of how to interpret an engineer's, architect's, or metric scale is useful in understanding how scaling applies to AutoCAD drawings.

The creation of freehand sketches with legible lettering remains an important skill in today's design office. Every professional drafter/designer, whether traditional or CAD, should develop a freehand lettering style that is neat, uniform, and legible to facilitate communication among designers, or between designers and their clients.

REVIEW QUESTIONS

Short Answer

1. Name three tools used by traditional drafters to draw parallel horizontal lines.
2. Drafting triangles come in what angles?
3. How is a triangle used with a parallel straightedge to draw a vertical line that is perpendicular to a horizontal line?
4. What is the range of lead hardness for general drafting and sketching?
5. Name three qualities that technical lettering should possess.
6. What unit of measurement is represented by each small increment on the 1:100 metric scale as interpreted by a mechanical engineer?
7. Which scale is used by mechanical engineers to measure drawings in decimal inches?
8. Into how many degrees is a half-moon protractor divided?
9. Name three lead widths in which technical pencils can be purchased.
10. What is the multiplier used to convert decimal inches to millimeters?

CHAPTER EXERCISE

Exercise 3.1: Technical Lettering

Practice lettering the alphabet and numerals in the construction lines shown in Figure 3.46. Print the *Lettering Plate.pdf* file located in the student data files at www.pearsondesigncentral.com. To access this sheet, open the Pearson Design Central website and click on the *CAD Community* link, then select the *Click here to download student data files for our CAD titles* link. Next, click on the *Technical Drawing 101* link and select the *Sketching and Traditional Drafting Sheets* zip file, then select the *Download* button and open (or save) the pdf specified.

LETTERING EXERCISE

.250 (1/4) Inch Lettering

A B C D E F G H I J K L M N O P Q R S T U V W X Y Z
1 2 3 4 5 6 7 8 9 0   SECTION A-A   FLOOR PLAN

.156 (5/32) Inch Lettering

A B C D E F G H I J K L M N O P Q R S T U V W X Y Z
1 2 3 4 5 6 7 8 9 0   SCHEMATIC OF FM TUNER

.125 (1/8) Inch Lettering

A B C D E F G H I J K L M N O P Q R S T U V W X Y Z
1 2 3 4 5 6 7 8 9 0   SCHEMATIC   WALL SECTION   INTERIOR ELEVATIONS

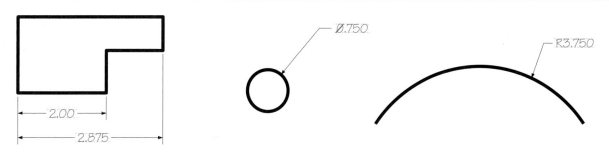

3.46 Lettering Exercise

CHAPTER PROJECTS

Project 3.1: Traditional Drafting Project 1 (SI Units)

Directions

Carefully remove the sheet for Traditional Drafting Project 1 located at the back of the text, or print the pdf located in the *Sketching and Traditional Drafting Sheets* zip file at the Pearson Design Central website, and draw the front, top, and right-side views of the object in Figure 3.47. This drawing employs international units (SI), so use the metric scale marked 1:100 (refer to Figure 3.18) to draw the object full size (1 = 1).

Add dimensions to the views as instructed by your teacher. Letter your name, the material of the part, and the scale in the guide lines provided (refer to Figure 3.48).

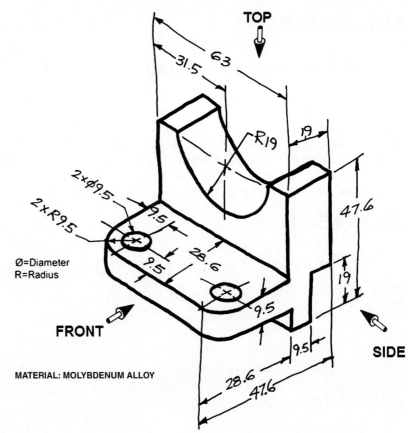

Ø=Diameter
R=Radius

MATERIAL: MOLYBDENUM ALLOY

3.47 Traditional Drafting Project 1

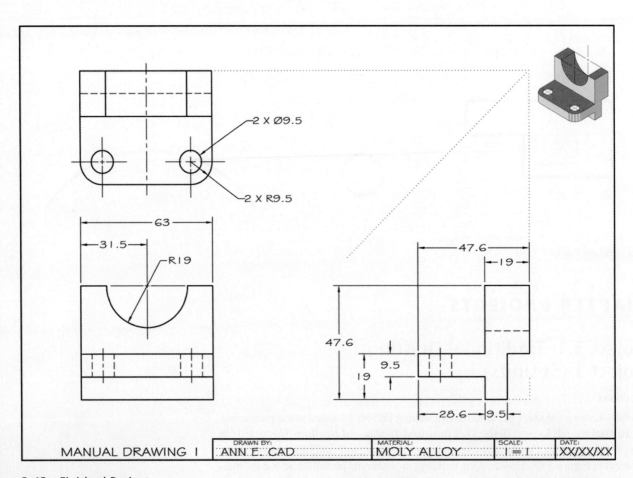

3.48 Finished Project

Project 3.2: Traditional Drafting Project 2

Directions

Carefully remove the sheet for Traditional Drafting Project 2 located at the back of the text, or print the pdf located in the ***Sketching and Traditional Drafting Sheets*** zip file at the Pearson Design Central website, and draw the front, top, and right view of the object in Figure 3.49. Using the engineer's 10 scale (refer to Figure 3.16), draw the object 3/4 size (*Note:* To convert the dimensions in Figure 3.49 to 3/4 size, multiply them by .75).

Add dimensions to the views as instructed by your teacher. Letter your name, the material of the part, and the scale in the guide lines provided (refer to Figure 3.50).

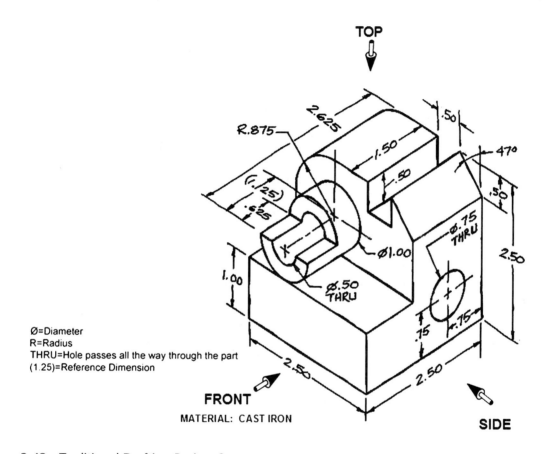

Ø=Diameter
R=Radius
THRU=Hole passes all the way through the part
(1.25)=Reference Dimension

MATERIAL: CAST IRON

3.49   Traditional Drafting Project 2

Optional Traditional Drafting Projects

The drafting projects on the following pages are designed to give you additional practice applying the tools and techniques of traditional drafting.

Directions

Follow your instructor's directions to print copies of the ***Traditional Drafting Sheet.pdf*** file located in the student data files at www.pearsondesigncentral.com. To access this sheet, open the Pearson Design Central website and click on the ***CAD Community*** link, then select the ***Click here to download student data files for our CAD titles*** link. Next, click on the ***Technical Drawing 101*** link and select the ***Sketching and Traditional Drafting Sheets*** zip file, then select the ***Download*** button and open (or save) the pdf specified. Then, draw the front, top, and right views of the objects in Figures 3.51 through 3.53. Use the appropriate scale for the units provided in the designer's sketch.

Add dimensions to the views as instructed by your teacher. Letter your name, the material of the part, and the scale in the guide lines provided.

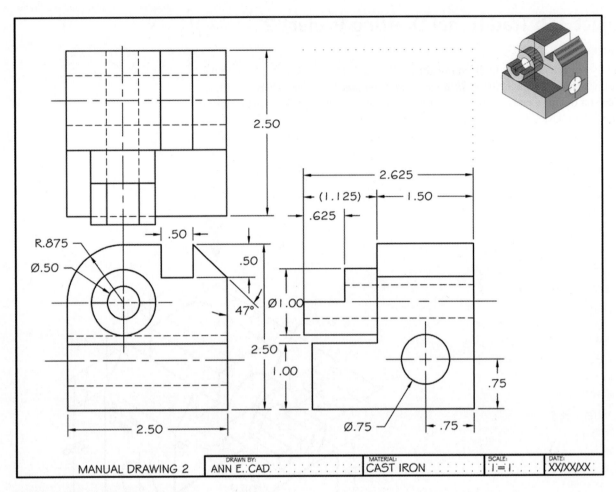

3.50 Finished Project

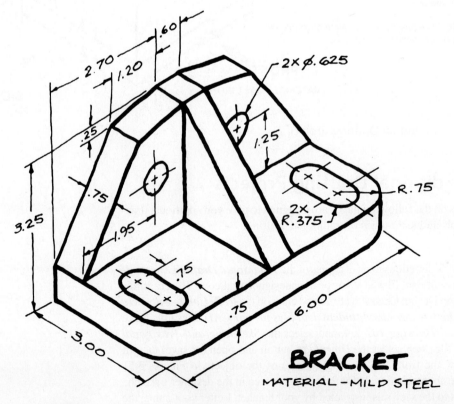

3.51 Traditional Drafting Project 3

SHAFT GUIDE

NOTES: MATERIAL – CAST IRON

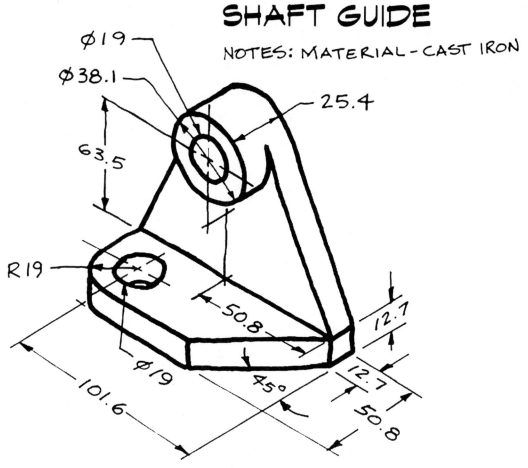

3.52 Traditional Drafting Project 4

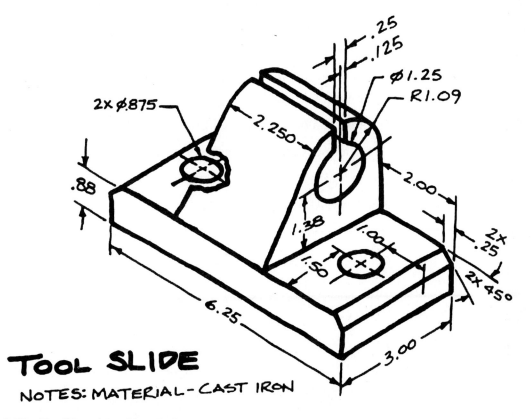

TOOL SLIDE

NOTES: MATERIAL – CAST IRON

3.53 Traditional Drafting Project 5

CHAPTER FOUR

COMPUTER-AIDED DESIGN BASICS

OBJECTIVES

After studying the material in this chapter, you should be able to:

1. Describe the AutoCAD screen layout.

2. Perform an AutoCAD drawing setup, including setting units, limits, layers, linetypes, and lineweights.

3. Explain the coordinate systems used to create AutoCAD drawings (absolute, relative, and polar coordinates).

4. Create and edit AutoCAD drawings using the commands found on the **Draw, Modify,** and **Inquiry** toolbars.

5. Employ object snaps to facilitate construction of AutoCAD drawings.

6. Use the **Properties** tool to inquire about or to change the properties of an entity.

7. Add text to a drawing and edit the text including text style.

8. Create a floor plan for a small cottage.

9. Create multiview drawings of machine parts.

10. Plot AutoCAD drawings.

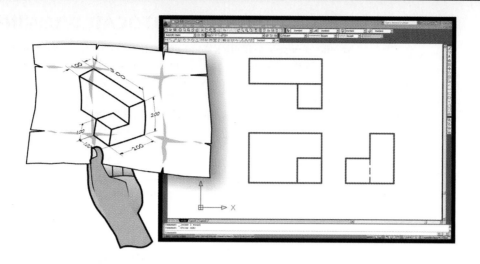

OVERVIEW

In most engineering and architectural offices, drafters and designers produce technical drawings using CAD systems. A CAD system consists of a personal computer (PC) or workstation coupled with a CAD software program. One of the most widely used CAD software programs is called *AutoCAD*. When AutoCAD was introduced in 1982, it was one of the first CAD programs that could operate on a PC. Autodesk, the parent company that publishes Auto-CAD software, reports that there are now millions of AutoCAD users worldwide. The price for a single station of AutoCAD for a professional user is about $4000, but professional users have the option of purchasing an annual software license for much less. Autodesk offers students a free trial download of AutoCAD through its website, but student versions of AutoCAD are available at discounted prices through education-related software outlets.

There are many other CAD programs on the market as well. Some CAD programs are designed to perform work in a specialized area. In mechanical design, Inventor, ProE, and Solidworks are three of the principal CAD programs; in electronics design, Cadence and Mentor are widely used. In the civil and architectural fields, Land Desktop, Civil 3D, Micro-station, and Revit are popular CAD programs.

- Autodesk (AutoCAD, Revit, Inventor): www.autodesk.com
- Bentley (Microstation): www.bentley.com
- Cadalyst: www.cadalyst.com
- Cadence: www.cadence.com
- Mentor Graphics: www.mentor.com
- PTC (ProE): www.ptc.com
- Solidworks: www.solidworks.com

4.1 BEGINNING AN AUTOCAD DRAWING

Use the mouse's left-click button to double-click on the AutoCAD 2011 icon located on the desktop of your computer. This will launch the AutoCAD program.

When the program opens, the AutoCAD user interface will appear similar to the one shown in Figure 4.1. Study the AutoCAD interface shown in Figure 4.1 and acquaint yourself with the terminology used to describe its features. Your instructor may call your attention to these features as you proceed with your CAD training. This textbook refers to these features as well.

Find the *command line* noted in Figure 4.1; it is very important for beginners to refer frequently to the command line because it offers important prompts and cues necessary to successfully complete AutoCAD commands.

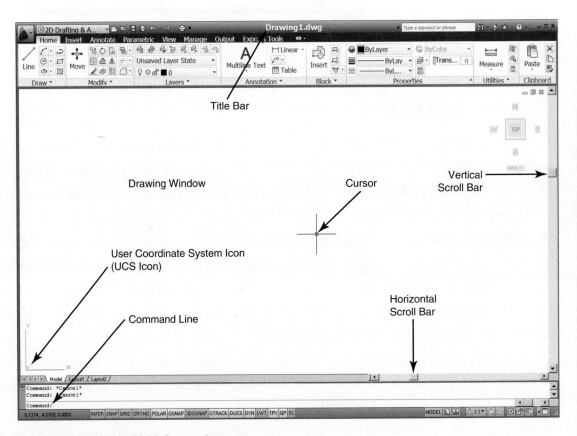

4.1   The AutoCAD 2011 Screen Layout

4.2 AUTOCAD'S RIBBON INTERFACE

NOTE

Appendix E provides a tutorial that covers the ribbon's tabs and panels in greater depth.

Since the release of AutoCAD 2009 users have had the option of displaying the AutoCAD user interface in either the ribbon or the **AutoCAD Classic** workspace mode. Figure 4.2 shows the AutoCAD 2011 interface as it appears in the ribbon mode. In the ribbon mode, many of AutoCAD's tools and settings are divided into *tabs* and *panels*.

In Figure 4.2 the **Home** tab of the ribbon is selected, which makes the **Draw, Modify, Layers, Annotation, Block, Properties, Utilities,** and **Clipboard** panels visible. Each panel contains a set of commands that are related to the function of the panel; for example, the **Draw** panel contains draw commands such as **LINE** and **CIRCLE**, and the **Modify** panel contains the **ERASE, MOVE,** and **COPY** commands. The techniques involved in using these commands will be presented later in this chapter.

Ribbon

Home Tab

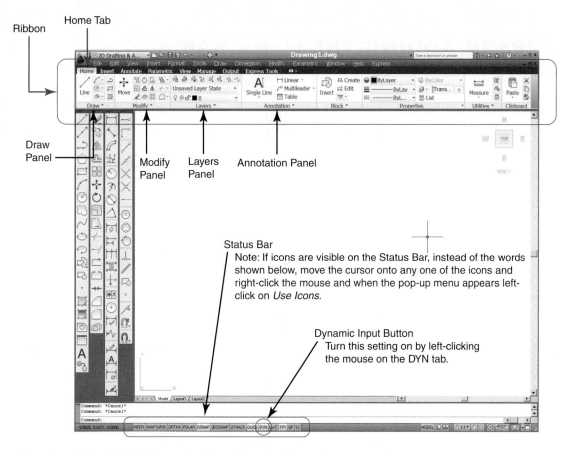

Draw
Panel

Modify
Panel

Layers
Panel

Annotation Panel

Status Bar
Note: If icons are visible on the Status Bar, instead of the words shown below, move the cursor onto any one of the icons and right-click the mouse and when the pop-up menu appears left-click on *Use Icons*.

Dynamic Input Button
Turn this setting on by left-clicking the mouse on the DYN tab.

4.2   AutoCAD 2011 Ribbon User Interface

NOTE

The instructions described in this text assume that *dynamic input* is turned on. When the **Dynamic Input** setting is on, dynamic prompts (windows containing command prompts or input windows relevant to the current command) will appear next to the cursor in the graphics window. Turn dynamic input on by left-clicking the mouse on the **DYN** button located on the status bar (when a setting on the status bar is *on*, its button will be displayed with a light blue background) or by pressing the **<F12>** function key located on the keyboard. Refer to Figure 4.2 for more information regarding the location of the status bar and the **DYN** button. Refer to Figure 4.6 to see examples of dynamic prompts and inputs associated with the **LINE** command.

4.3 ADDING TOOLBARS TO THE RIBBON INTERFACE

To make the ribbon environment easier to use for beginners, and more efficient for experienced users, the authors recommend the following changes to the interface:

Turn on the menu bar. The menu bar contains 13 drop-down menus that provide AutoCAD users easy access to many important commands and settings (see Figure 4.3). The **Format** and **Tools** menus are especially important to users of AutoCAD and are referred to later in this chapter.

Turn on the **Draw**, **Modify**, **Dimension**, and **Object Snap** toolbars. These four toolbars contain almost all the commands necessary to produce 2D multiview drawings with AutoCAD; and although most of these commands can also be found on the ribbon panels, it is often quicker to initiate a command from a toolbar than from a ribbon panel because only one mouse click is required, whereas many ribbon commands require two mouse clicks to open.

STEPS IN ADDING THE MENU BAR AND TOOLBARS TO THE RIBBON INTERFACE

STEP by STEP

1 Turn on the menu bar. Type **MENUBAR** on the command line at the bottom of the screen and press **<Enter>.** At the prompt type **1** and press **<Enter>.**When this step is complete, the menu bar shown near the top of the screen in Figure 4.3 will be visible.

2 Move the mouse cursor to the word **Tools** located on the menu bar and left-click. When the submenu drops down, left-click on the word **Toolbars**.

3 When the next submenu appears, left-click on the word **AutoCAD;** this will open the **Toolbar** menu. Move the mouse onto the word **Draw** and left-click; this will open the **Draw** toolbar.

> ── **NOTE** ──
> Once a toolbar has been opened, other toolbars can quickly be opened by right-clicking the mouse on the open toolbar and selecting from the list of toolbars located on the **Toolbar** menu.

4 Repeat the preceding steps to open the **Modify**, **Dimension**, and **Object Snap** toolbars. By left-clicking on the dark gray bars at either end of a toolbar and holding down the left-click button, you can drag the toolbar to the side of the screen and *dock* it as shown in Figure 4.3.

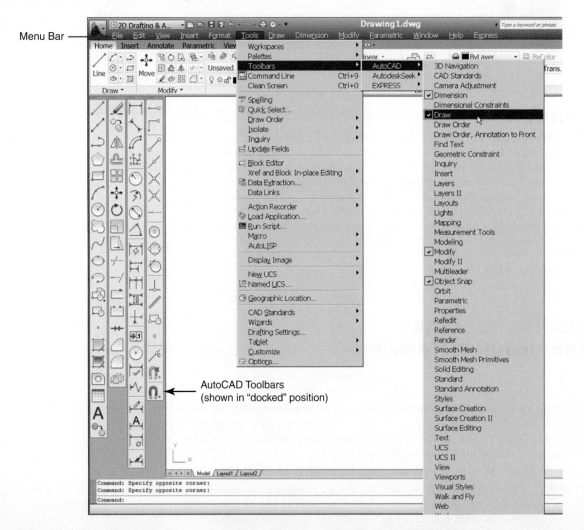

4.3   AutoCAD 2011 Ribbon User Interface with AutoCAD Toolbars Displayed

┌─ **JOB SKILLS** ───┐

In AutoCAD 2011, toolbars can also be opened by selecting the ribbon's **View**
tab and picking on the **Toolbars** tool located on the **Windows** panel. When the
drop-down list appears, click on the word **AutoCAD** and select the toolbars
from the list that appears in the toolbar menu.

└──┘

4.4 CREATING, OPENING, AND SAVING AUTOCAD DRAWING FILES

Locate the application button noted in Figure 4.4 (the red **A** in the upper left corner of the interface). By left-clicking on this button and choosing from the application menu, you can create a new drawing, open an existing drawing, save the
current drawing, or save a copy of the current drawing in a new location or with a
different drawing title.

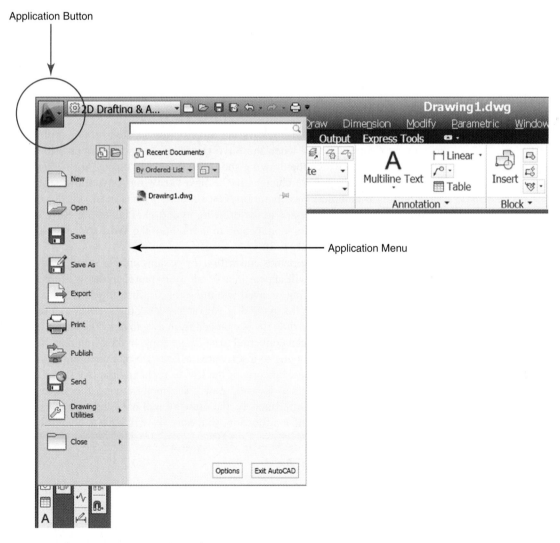

4.4 Application Button and Application Menu

Beginning a New Drawing

Left-clicking the **New** option from the application menu (see Figure 4.4) opens the **Select Template** window. You can choose from the list of template files (**dwt** file extension) displayed in this box, or by selecting the **Open** button, you can default to the **acad.dwt** template.

— NOTE —

In AutoCAD terminology, to *default* means that you accept the base setting offered by AutoCAD. As a new user of AutoCAD, you may find that you will often default to AutoCAD's base settings, but as your knowledge of AutoCAD grows you will become more comfortable with making changes to the AutoCAD environment.

After you have selected the **Open** button, a new drawing session will open. This drawing is automatically named **Drawing1.dwg**. This drawing title will also appear in the title bar at the top of the user interface (see Figure 4.1 for help in locating the title bar).

Opening an Existing Drawing

Left-clicking on the **Open** option from the application menu (see Figure 4.4) opens the **Select File** window. In this window, you can select the file name and location (the drive and folder) of the drawing file to be opened. After making these selections, select the **Open** button to open the file.

Saving a Drawing

To save a new drawing, left-click on the **Save** option located on the application menu (see Figure 4.4) and when the **Save Drawing As** window opens select the drive and folder in which the drawing should be saved and change the file name if desired. After making these changes in the **Save Drawing As** window, select the **Save** button to complete the operation. Once a drawing has been saved, you can continue to save changes made to the drawing by left-clicking on the **Save** option or by picking on the diskette icon located to the right of the **Workspace Switching** drop-down menu (see Figure 4.5).

AutoCAD drawing file names end with a *dwg* extension. For example, a drawing named **House Plan 1** will appear in a Windows Explorer folder as **House Plan 1.dwg**. Each time the drawing is saved two things occur: first, the dwg file is saved reflecting the most recent edits to the drawing, and second, the extension of the previously saved version of the drawing is changed from dwg to *bak*. The bak extension indicates that the file has been converted to a *backup* copy. In the event that the most recent drawing file is lost owing to a software or hardware malfunction (or user error), you can rename the backup copy of the file by replacing the *bak* in the extension with *dwg*. You may then open the newly renamed drawing file and resume working on the drawing. Unfortunately, the drawing will have lost any edits made between the last save and the malfunction, so these edits will have to be redone.

Performing a Save As

Save As is used to rename a current drawing and/or save the drawing to a new location. Left-clicking on the **Save As** option from the application menu (see Figure 4.4) opens the **Save Drawing As** window. In this window, you can select the drive and folder in which the drawing should be saved and change the file name as desired. After making the desired changes, select the **Save** button to complete the operation. The newly named drawing file will become the current drawing.

AUTOCAD'S CLASSIC WORKSPACE

AutoCAD's **Classic** workspace resembles the interface found in releases of AutoCAD that preceded the introduction of the ribbon in AutoCAD 2009 (see Figure 4.5). Although the ribbon interface is rapidly becoming the industry-wide standard, many engineering and architectural firms have elected to continue to use the **Classic** workspace, or a hybrid of the **Classic** and ribbon workspaces. For this reason, it is important for CAD technicians-in-training to know the differences between the two workspaces.

If your instructor prefers that you work in the **Classic** workspace mode, use the following steps to convert from the ribbon to the **Classic** workspace environment:

1 Left-click the down arrow in the **Workspace Switching** drop-down menu located to the right of the application button in the upper left corner of the user interface (see Figure 4.5).

2 From the **Workspace** drop-down menu, left-click the **AutoCAD Classic** workspace.

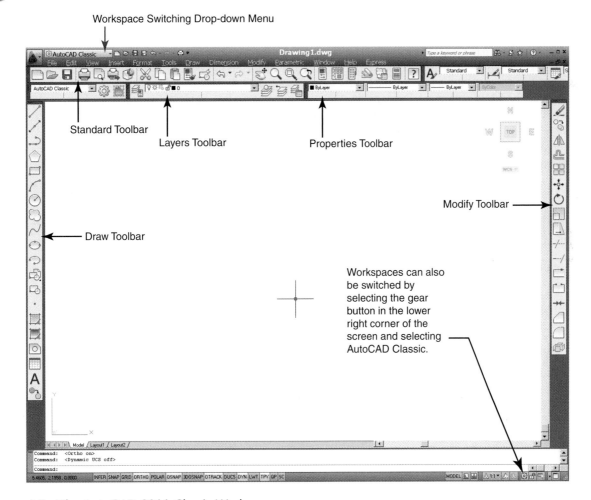

Workspace Switching Drop-down Menu

Standard Toolbar

Layers Toolbar

Properties Toolbar

Modify Toolbar

Draw Toolbar

Workspaces can also be switched by selecting the gear button in the lower right corner of the screen and selecting AutoCAD Classic.

4.5 The AutoCAD 2011 Classic Workspace

NOTE

If the menu bar shown in Figure 4.5 is not visible, type **MENUBAR** at the command line and press **<Enter>**, then type **1** and press **<Enter>**.

JOB SKILLS

Whenever you need help or information regarding a command or feature of the AutoCAD program, press the **<F1>** function key located on the keyboard. This will open AutoCAD's **Help** system window. Users can select from the options available in this window to search for help regarding commands or other AutoCAD specific concepts and techniques. You can also access the Help system by left-clicking on **Help** from the menu bar. In-depth information on accessing AutoCAD **Help** tools from the ribbon is included in Appendix E on page 438.

DRAWING YOUR FIRST LINE WITH AUTOCAD

1 Use the left-click button of your mouse to select the **Line** icon from the **Draw** toolbar, or select the **Line** icon from the **Draw** panel located on the ribbon's **Home** tab, or type **LINE** at the command line and press **<Enter>**.

2 Move the cursor into the graphics area and pick a point with the left-click button, then move the mouse to a new point and pick again. Congratulations, you've drawn your first line (see Figure 4.6)! By continuing to pick points, you can add to the line (note dynamic prompt and inputs shown in Figure 4.6). When you are finished, press the **<Esc>** (escape) key to end the **LINE** command. Drawing lines to random points in this way is easy; drawing lines to exact points is a little more complicated. For this, you'll need to understand *Cartesian coordinates*.

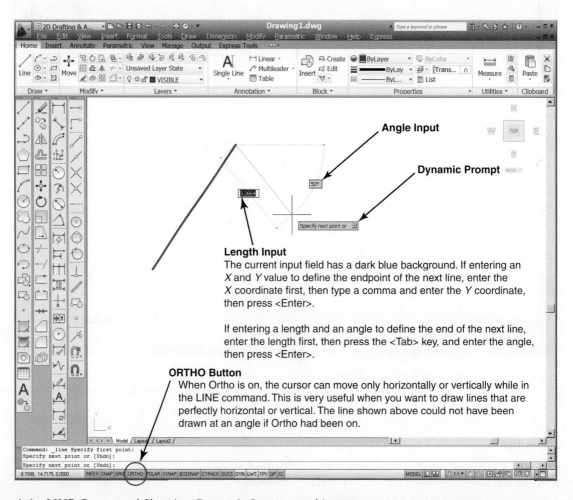

Angle Input

Dynamic Prompt

Length Input
The current input field has a dark blue background. If entering an X and Y value to define the endpoint of the next line, enter the X coordinate first, then type a comma and enter the Y coordinate, then press <Enter>.

If entering a length and an angle to define the end of the next line, enter the length first, then press the <Tab> key, and enter the angle, then press <Enter>.

ORTHO Button
When Ortho is on, the cursor can move only horizontally or vertically while in the LINE command. This is very useful when you want to draw lines that are perfectly horizontal or vertical. The line shown above could not have been drawn at an angle if Ortho had been on.

4.6 LINE Command Showing Dynamic Prompt and Inputs

STEP by STEP

> ┌─ **NOTE** ────────────────────────────────
> Information regarding the **ORTHO** button's effect on the **LINE** command is
> noted in Figure 4.6. Note that when the **LINE** command is in use, and **Ortho** is
> on, the cursor moves freely, but lines can be drawn only horizontally or vertically.
> This is very useful for drawing lines that are perfectly horizontal or vertical.
> **Ortho** is also useful with other commands like **MOVE** or **COPY** when it is
> desired to move or copy an object along a perfectly horizontal or vertical axis.
> **Ortho** can be turned on by picking the **ORTHO** button located on the status
> bar or by pressing the **<F8>** function key on the keyboard.

4.5 LOCATING POINTS ON THE CARTESIAN COORDINATE SYSTEM

AutoCAD employs the *Cartesian coordinate system* to define the exact location
of points in the graphics window. In the Cartesian coordinate system, a **0,0** (zero,
zero) point is established as the origin point. The first zero represents the start
point of measurements along the *X*-axis (horizontal), and the second zero represents the start point of measurements along the *Y*-axis (vertical). All other points
are located along the *X*- and *Y*-axes using 0,0 as the starting point. In Figure 4.7
the 0,0 point is located in the lower left corner. The coordinates of the other points
labeled on the grid refer to each point's location measured along the *X*- and *Y*-axes
relative to 0,0.

Locate the point labeled with the coordinates **1,2** in Figure 4.7. This point
is located on the grid by starting at the 0,0 origin in the lower left corner of the
grid and measuring 1 unit to the right along the *X*-axis and up 2 units along the
Y-axis. The *X*- and *Y*-values are separated with a comma. CAD drafters refer to
this point as 1,2.

Next, locate the point labeled with the coordinates **4,3** in Figure 4.7. This point
is found by starting at the 0,0 origin in the lower left corner of the grid and measuring 4 units to the right along the *X*-axis and up 3 units along the *Y*-axis. CAD
drafters refer to this point as 4,3. Lines drawn in two dimensions have a start and
an endpoint. Both points are defined by their respective *X*- and *Y*-coordinates.

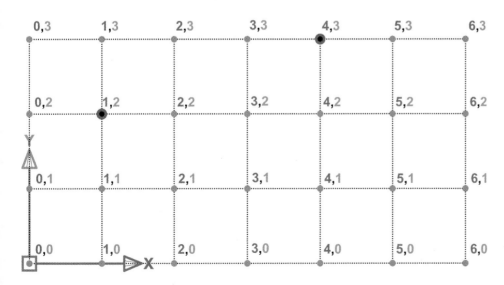

4.7   Points on the Cartesian Coordinate System

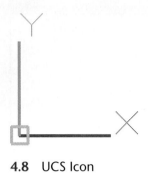

4.8   UCS Icon

The User Coordinate System (UCS) Icon

In AutoCAD the 0,0 point in the graphics window is represented in the lower left corner of the graphics window by the icon shown in Figure 4.8. This icon is called the *user coordinate system (UCS)* icon. The visibility of this icon can be controlled by typing **UCSICON** at the command line, pressing **<Enter>,** and selecting **On** or **Off** from the settings listed. This icon orients the CAD operator to AutoCAD's 0,0 point.

AutoCAD uses several types of coordinate systems to specify the location of points, although each system has its basis in Cartesian coordinates. In AutoCAD terminology these other coordinate systems are *absolute coordinates*, *relative coordinates*, and *polar coordinates*. AutoCAD drafters must be familiar with each system.

Absolute Coordinates

In AutoCAD terminology, points that are relative to point 0,0 (usually located in the lower left corner of the AutoCAD screen) are referred to as *absolute coordinates*. In Figure 4.9, a red line begins at absolute coordinates **2,2** and is drawn to coordinates **7,3**, then it is drawn to **10,6** and ends at the point with coordinates **4.5,7**. Because each of these points is located relative to 0,0 as measured along the *X*- and *Y*-axes, all these coordinates are considered absolute coordinates.

Drawing a Line with Absolute Coordinates

To draw the line shown in Figure 4.9 using absolute coordinates (assuming the **DYN** tab has been selected on the status bar), select the **LINE** command icon from the **Draw** toolbar and at the *Specify the first point*: prompt, type **2,2** and press **<Enter>**. At the *Specify the next point:* prompt, type **#7,3** and press **<Enter>**. To continue the line from **7,3** to absolute coordinates **10,6, type #10,6** and press **<Enter>.** To finish the line, type **#4.5,7** and press **<Enter>.** Pressing the **<Esc>** key will discontinue the **LINE** (or any other) command.

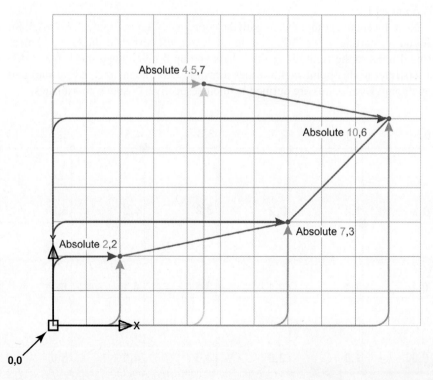

4.9   Absolute Coordinates

NOTE

When dynamic input is on and you have been prompted to *Specify the next point:*, you must type a # (pound) symbol before typing the *X*-coordinate value when entering an absolute coordinate value. However, when you are prompted to *Specify the first point:* of a line (or other entity), you do not need to type the # sign because it is assumed that the first point is an absolute coordinate.

TIP

When the **DYN** setting is *on,* typing the # sign before typing the *X*-coordinate value directs AutoCAD to locate points using absolute coordinates. To enter an absolute coordinate in releases of AutoCAD prior to Release 2006, or when drawing with the **DYN** setting *off* in newer releases, you do not need to type the # symbol before entering the *X*- and *Y*-coordinates.

STEPS IN DRAWING A LINE WITH ABSOLUTE COORDINATES

1 To draw the line shown in Figure 4.10, select the **LINE** command icon and at the *Specify the first point:* prompt, type **2,2** and press **<Enter>.**

2 At the *Specify the next point:* prompt, type **#8,7** and press **<Enter>.** Press **<Esc>** to end the command.

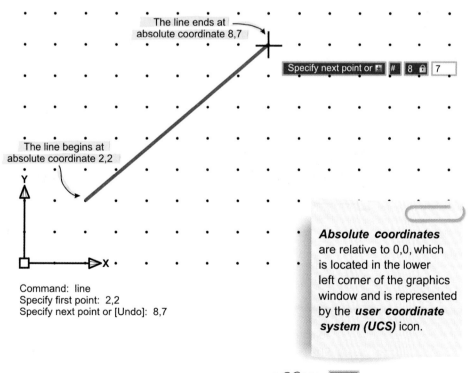

The line ends at absolute coordinate 8,7

Specify next point or [ ] # 8 🔒 7

The line begins at absolute coordinate 2,2

Command: line
Specify first point: 2,2
Specify next point or [Undo]: 8,7

Absolute coordinates are relative to 0,0, which is located in the lower left corner of the graphics window and is represented by the **user coordinate system (UCS)** icon.

LOOK➡ DYN Dynamic Input is ON.

4.10 Line Drawn by Entering Absolute Coordinates

STEP by STEP

Relative Coordinates

Relative coordinates are located relative to the last point defined. For example, in Figure 4.11, a line begins at the point with absolute coordinates **1,1** and is drawn to a second point located **5** units to the right along the *X*-axis and **0** units up along the *Y*-axis relative to the starting point. The line continues to a third point located **1** unit to the right along the *X*-axis and **2** units up along the *Y*-axis relative to the second point. The line continues to a fourth point located **0** units to the right along the *X*-axis and **2** units up along the *Y*-axis relative to the third point. The line continues in this fashion until it returns to the start point. With the exception of the start point of the first line, each point is located *relative* to the previously defined point.

NOTE

When defining a relative coordinate that is to the left of, or below, the previous point, it is necessary to enter a negative coordinate value. This is done by typing a minus sign (–) before the coordinate value. For example, typing **-3,-2** draws a line to a point **3** units to the left on the *X*-axis and **2** units below the point previously defined.

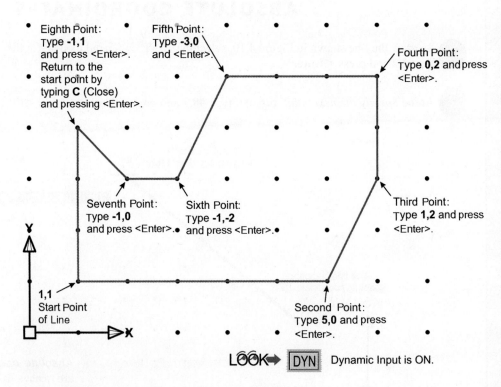

4.11   Lines Defined with Relative Coordinates

TIP

To enter relative coordinate values in releases of AutoCAD prior to Release 2006, or when drawing with the **DYN** setting off in newer releases, you must first type the **@** symbol before entering the *X* and *Y* distances. For example: typing **@6,5** draws a line to a point located **6** units to the right on the *X*-axis and **5** units up on the *Y*-axis relative to the last point entered.

STEPS IN DRAWING A LINE WITH RELATIVE COORDINATES

1 Select the **LINE** command icon and type **2,2** for the first point and press **<Enter>**. This will begin the line at the point with absolute coordinates **2,2** (see Figure 4.12).

2 At the *Specify the next point*: prompt, type **6,5** and press **<Enter>** again. The line will begin at the point with absolute coordinates **2,2** and be drawn to a point located **6** units along the *X*-axis and **5** units along the *Y* axis relative to **2,2** (see Figure 4.12).

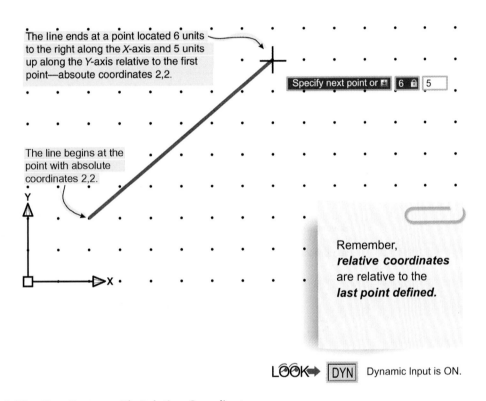

The line ends at a point located 6 units to the right along the *X*-axis and 5 units up along the *Y*-axis relative to the first point—absoute coordinates 2,2.

Specify next point or ☐ 6 🔒 5

The line begins at the point with absolute coordinates 2,2.

Remember, *relative coordinates* are relative to the *last point defined.*

LOOK➡ DYN   Dynamic Input is ON.

4.12   Line Drawn with Relative Coordinates

STEP by STEP

Polar Coordinates

To understand polar coordinates, you first have to understand two things about how AutoCAD measures angles:

1. *East* (as on a compass) is considered 0°.
2. Angles are measured *counterclockwise* (see Figure 4.13).

Polar coordinates are defined with a length *and* an angle and are located relative to the last point entered. When specifying a polar coordinate, it is necessary to type the length of the line, press the **<Tab>** key, and enter the desired angle. For example, entering **10 <Tab> 30** would draw a line **10** units long at a **30°** angle relative to the previous point defined (remember that AutoCAD measures angles counterclockwise, and East is 0°). Pressing **<Tab>** switches AutoCAD's coordinate entry mode from linear to angular. In Figure 4.14, the first line begins at

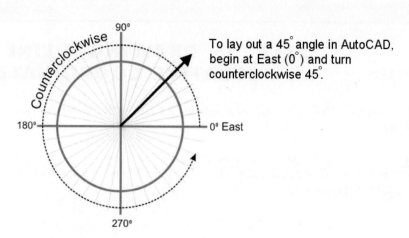

To lay out a 45° angle in AutoCAD, begin at East (0°) and turn counterclockwise 45°.

4.13 Angles in AutoCAD

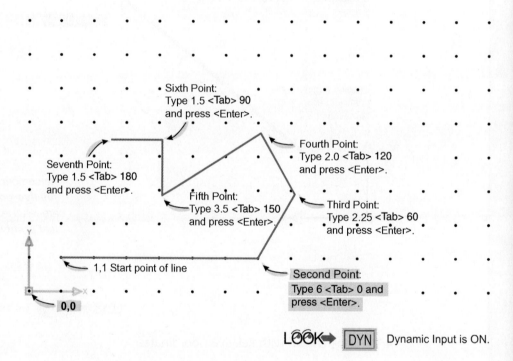

4.14 Lines Drawn with Polar Coordinates

absolute coordinate **1,1** and is drawn to a second point **6** units in length along a 0° angle (**6 <Tab> 0**). The second line begins at the last point and is drawn to a point **2.25** units in length at a **60°** angle (**2.25 <Tab> 60**). The third line is drawn **2** units in length at a **120°** angle (**2 <Tab> 120**). The line continues in this fashion until it ends at the seventh point.

> **— TIP —**
>
> To enter a polar coordinate value in releases of AutoCAD prior to Release 2006, or when drawing with the **DYN** setting off in newer releases, you must first type the **@** symbol to enter a polar coordinate value. Instead of pressing **<Tab>**, type the **<** (less than) symbol; for example, **@4<90.**

STEPS IN DRAWING A LINE
WITH POLAR COORDINATES

1 Select the **LINE** command icon and type **2,2** for the location of the first point and press **<Enter>** (see Figure 4.15).

2 At the *Specify the next point*: prompt, type **6 <Tab> 45** and press **<Enter>** again. This will result in a line beginning at absolute coordinate **2,2** that is drawn **6** units in length at a **45°** angle (see Figure 4.15).

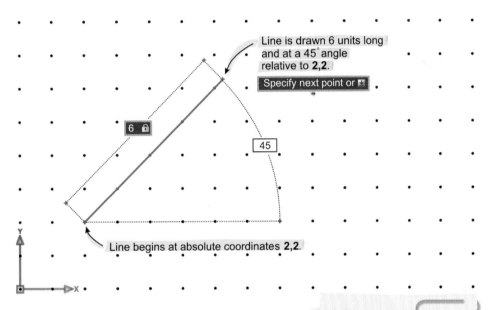

Line is drawn 6 units long and at a 45° angle relative to **2,2.**

Specify next point or ▣

6 🔒

45

Line begins at absolute coordinates 2,2.

Remember, the angle of **relative polar coordinates** is relative to **East,** *which is* **0°**.

LOOK➡ DYN Dynamic Input is ON.

4.15 Line Drawn with Polar Coordinates

4.6 DIRECT ENTRY METHOD
OF DRAWING LINES

Another method of drawing lines is by *direct entry*. This is the quickest and easiest way to draw horizontal and vertical lines. To use this method, turn on the **ORTHO** button located on the status bar. Next, begin the **LINE** command and type absolute coordinate values as the start point for the line. Then, move the mouse in the desired

X or *Y* (positive or negative) direction and type a value for the length of the line and press **<Enter>**. In Figure 4.16(a) the drafter turned **Ortho** on and began a line at **1,1,** then moved the cursor to the right (or positive *X*), typed in **2.5,** and pressed **<Enter>**. The resulting horizontal line was drawn 2.5 units to the right of the start point. In Figure 4.16(b) the drafter continued the line by moving the mouse in the positive *Y* direction (or up), typing **2,** and pressing **<Enter>**. The resulting line is 2 units long and vertical. This method can also be used to draw lines of defined lengths at preset angles by turning on the **POLAR** button located on the status bar.

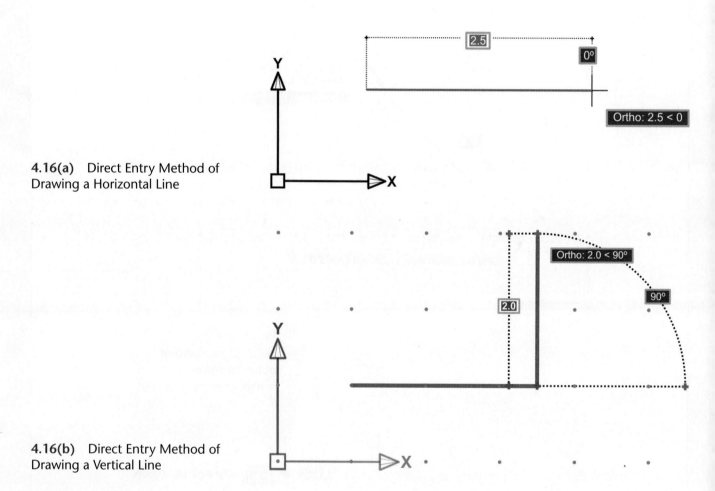

4.16(a) Direct Entry Method of Drawing a Horizontal Line

4.16(b) Direct Entry Method of Drawing a Vertical Line

Exercise 4.1

Begin a new AutoCAD drawing (default to the **acad.dwt** template). Using the **LINE** command and the coordinate entry methods described earlier, draw the object shown in Figure 4.17. Begin the bottom left corner of the object at absolute coordinates **2,2** and draw the first line in the positive X direction. Continue drawing lines until you are unable to continue owing to lack of coordinate information (21 contiguous lines total). At this point, begin a new line from absolute coordinates **2,2** and draw in the positive *Y* direction. Continue drawing lines in this manner until you are unable to continue owing to lack of coordinate information (4 contiguous lines total).

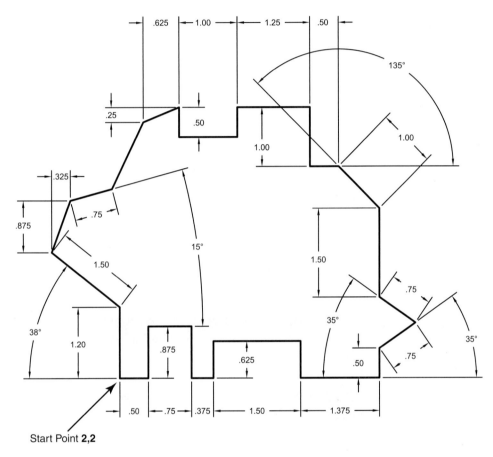

4.17   Exercise 4.1

To complete the drawing, draw a line connecting the endpoints of the two sets of lines. If you need assistance with this exercise, ask your instructor for help.

4.7 SETTING THE ENVIRONMENT FOR AUTOCAD DRAWINGS

Drawing Units

Before beginning an AutoCAD drawing, a drafter must first determine the appropriate *drawing units*, or units of measurement, for the type of drawing being created. For example, for architectural drawings, architectural units (feet and fractional inches) would be appropriate. For civil engineering drawings, engineering units (feet and decimal inches) would be appropriate; for mechanical engineering drawings, decimal units would be chosen.

STEP by STEP

SETTING DRAWING UNITS

1 Open the **Drawing Units** dialog box by choosing the **Format** pull-down menu and selecting **Units** (Figure 4.18) or by typing **UN** on the command line and pressing **<Enter>**.

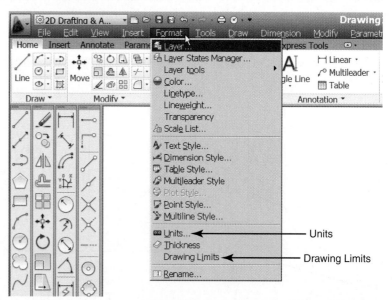

4.18 Selecting Drawing Units and Limits from the **Format** Menu

2 Select the type of units (decimal, engineering, architectural, fractional, or scientific) in **Length Type:** (Figure 4.19).

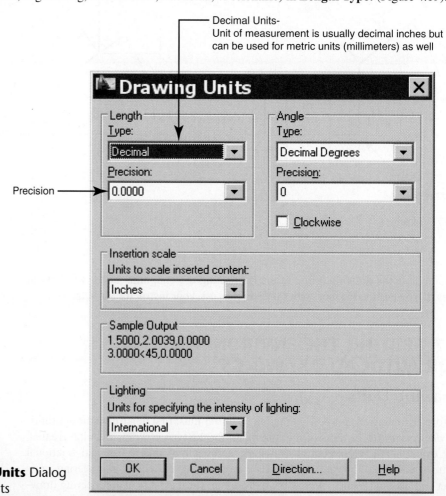

4.19 Drawing Units Dialog Box—Decimal Units

3 Select the level of precision (the number of decimal places or fractional precision) for entering units in **Precision:** below **Length Type:**.

In Figure 4.19, the drawing units are set to **Decimal,** which means that coordinates will be entered and displayed in decimal units. Precision for entering and displaying data is set to four decimal places.

In Figure 4.20, the drawing units are set to **Architectural**, which means that coordinates will be entered and displayed in feet and fractional inches. Precision for entering and displaying data is set to 1/16".

In Figure 4.21, the drawing units are set to **Engineering**, which means that coordinates will be entered and displayed in feet and decimal inches. Precision for entering and displaying data is set to four decimal places.

STEP by STEP

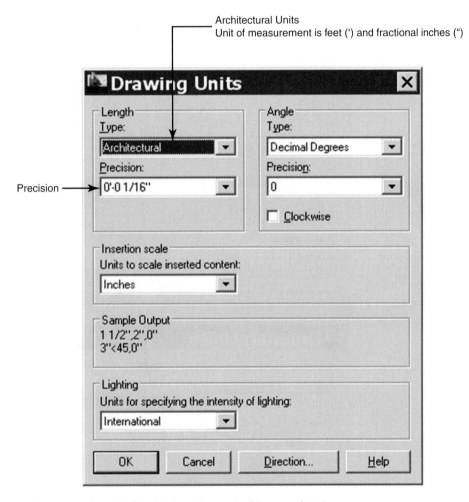

Architectural Units
Unit of measurement is feet (') and fractional inches (")

Precision

4.20 Drawing Units Dialog Box—Architectural Units

STEP by STEP

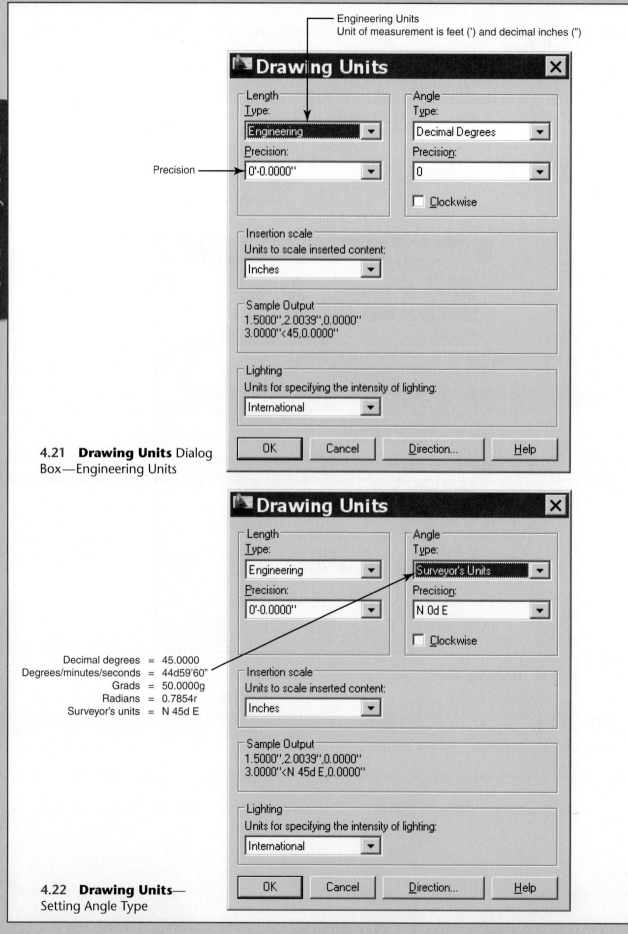

Engineering Units
Unit of measurement is feet (') and decimal inches (")

Precision

4.21 **Drawing Units** Dialog Box—Engineering Units

Decimal degrees = 45.0000
Degrees/minutes/seconds = 44d59'60"
Grads = 50.0000g
Radians = 0.7854r
Surveyor's units = N 45d E

4.22 **Drawing Units**— Setting Angle Type

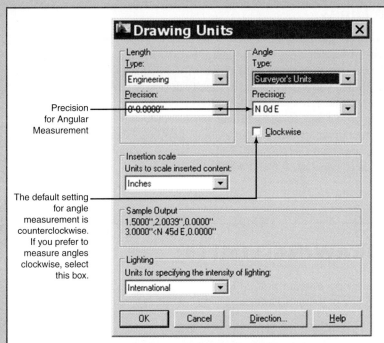

Precision for Angular Measurement

The default setting for angle measurement is counterclockwise. If you prefer to measure angles clockwise, select this box.

Setting Angle Type

After selecting the length type and precision, drafters select the angle type for the drawing. Several options are available: **Decimal Degrees**, **Degrees/Minutes/Seconds**, **Grads**, **Radians**, and **Surveyor's Units**.

1. In **Angle Type:** select from the options (decimal, deg/min/sec, grads, radians, or surveyor's units) (see Figure 4.22).

2. In **Precision:** select the measurement of angles (below **Angle Type:**) (see Figure 4.23).

4.23 **Drawing Units** Dialog Box—Setting Precision and Direction for Angular Measurement

Setting the Direction of Angle Measurement

Selecting the **Direction . . .** button in the **Drawing Units** dialog box opens the **Direction Control** dialog box (see Figure 4.24). The **Base Angle** setting affects the starting point for measuring angles, polar coordinates, and polar tracking. **East** (the default direction), is usually assigned as the base angle; however, a base angle other than East can be set as the direction for 0° by selecting either **North**, **West**, **South**, or **Other**.

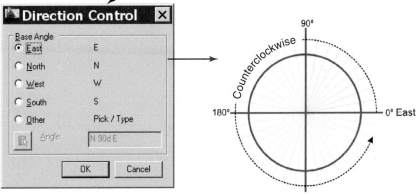

4.24 Setting Direction for Measuring Angles in AutoCAD

Drawing Limits

Setting the *drawing limits* defines the drawing area; this is comparable to selecting the sheet size for the drawing. Limits should be set *after* the units of the drawing have been set because the value for the limits will be displayed in the current units. When setting limits, you are prompted to specify the lower left and upper right corners of the drawing area. In most cases, the lower left corner is defaulted to 0,0, and the upper right corner is defined by typing in the coordinates of the corresponding sheet size. For example, if using decimal units, an A-size sheet limits are **0,0** and **12,9**; a B-size sheet limits are **0,0** and **17,11**; a C-size sheet limits are **0,0** and **22,17**; and a D-size sheet limits are **0,0** and **34,22**.

STEP by STEP

SETTING DRAWING LIMITS

1 Open the **Drawing Limits** dialog box by choosing the **Format** pull-down menu and selecting **Drawing Limits,** as shown in Figure 4.18, or by typing **LIMITS** and pressing **<Enter>**.

2 When prompted to *Specify lower left corner*: (the default limits 0,0 will be displayed as shown in Figure 4.25). Press **<Enter>** to accept 0,0 as the lower left limit.

```
Command: Limits
Reset Model space limits:
Specify lower left corner or [ON/OFF] <0.0000,0.0000>:

Specify upper right corner <12.0000,9.0000>:
```

4.25 Command Line Displaying Default Limits When Decimal Units Are in Effect

3 When prompted to *Specify upper right corner*: (the default limits **12,9** will be displayed as shown in Figure 4.25). Type the coordinates for a different sheet size, for example, **24,18,** and press **<Enter>** (see Figure 4.26).

```
Command: Limits
Reset Model space limits:
Specify lower left corner or [ON/OFF] <0.0000,0.0000>:
Specify upper right corner <12.0000,9.0000>: 24,18

Command:
```

4.26 Command Line Displaying Limits of 0,0 and 24,18

The drawing area will update to the new limits, but a **VIEW** command named **Zoom All** must be performed to see the new limits displayed in the graphics window. To perform a **Zoom All**, type **Z**, press **<Enter>,** and then type **A** and press **<Enter>.**

> **NOTE**
> Although it is possible to define coordinate values other than 0,0 as the lower left limit, it is seldom done.

The limits of a drawing are dependent on the units of measurement assigned to the drawing. Therefore, the limits assigned are based on the sheet sizes that are appropriate for drawings created with the assigned units. Tables 4.1, 4.2, and 4.3 show the **Limits** settings for various sheet sizes relative to the units of measurement for the drawing (decimal, architectural, or engineering).

Table 4.1 Limits Settings for Decimal and Metric Units

Limits Based on ASME Y14.1 Decimal Sheet Sizes
A Sheet Limits = 0,0 and 11,8.5
B Sheet Limits = 0,0 and 17,11
C Sheet Limits = 0,0 and 22,17
D Sheet Limits = 0,0 and 34,22
E Sheet Limits = 0,0 and 44,34
Limits Based on ASME Y14.1M Metric Sheet Sizes
A4 Sheet Limits = 0,0 and 297,210
A3 Sheet Limits = 0,0 and 420,297
A2 Sheet Limits = 0,0 and 594,420
A1 Sheet Limits = 0,0 and 841,594
A0 Sheet Limits = 0,0 and 1189,841

Table 4.2 Limits Settings for Architectural Units

Limits for Scale of: 1/4″ = 1′-0″
A Sheet Limits = 0′,0′ and 48′,36′
B Sheet Limits = 0′,0′ and 72′,48′
C Sheet Limits = 0′,0′ and 96′,72′
D Sheet Limits = 0′,0′ and 144′,96′
Limits for Scale of 1/8″ = 1′-0′
A Sheet Limits = 0′,0′ and 96′,72′
B Sheet Limits = 0′,0′ and 144′,96′
C Sheet Limits = 0′,0′ and 192′,144′
D Sheet Limits = 0′,0′ and 288′,192′

Table 4.3 Limits Settings for Engineering Units

Limits for Scale of: 1″ = 100′
A Sheet Limits = 0′,0′ and 1200′, 900′
B Sheet Limits = 0′,0′ and 1800′, 1200′
C Sheet Limits = 0′,0′ and 2400′, 1800′
D Sheet Limits = 0′,0′ and 3600′, 2400′

Layers

In AutoCAD drawings, lines and other entities are drawn on *layers*. Think of layers as sheets of clear glass layered one on top of the other. A layer can have its own color, linetype, or lineweight assigned to it.

When you begin an AutoCAD drawing from scratch, it contains only one layer, layer **0** (zero). If more layers are needed, they must be created.

STEP by STEP

STEPS INVOLVED IN CREATING NEW LAYERS

1 Click on the **Layer Properties Manager** icon located in the upper left corner of the **Layers** panel of the **Home** tab on the ribbon (see Figure 4.27).

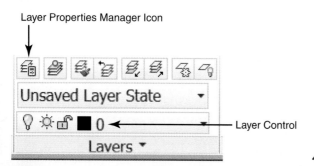

Layer Properties Manager Icon

4.27 **Layers** Panel Located on the **Home** Tab

2 When the **Layer Properties Manager** palette shown in Figure 4.28 opens, click the **New** button.

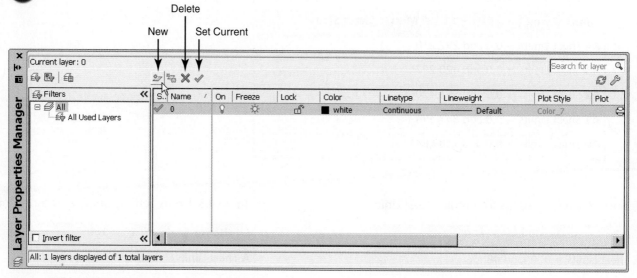

Delete

New   Set Current

4.28 **Layer Properties Manager** Palette

3 Select the new layer and replace its default name, **Layer 1**, with the new layer name.

4 Repeat Step 3 to create other layers. When all the new layers have been created, click **OK**. Figure 4.29 shows the layers created for a mechanical drawing.

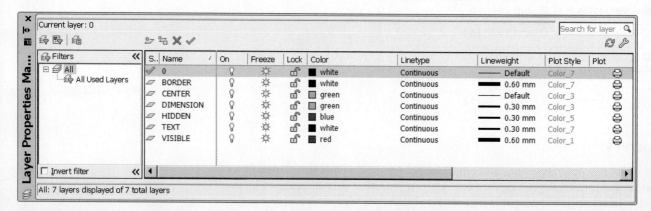

4.29 Layer Examples Shown in the **Layer Properties Manager** Palette

SETTING LAYER COLOR

1 Click on the **Layer Properties Manager** icon located in the upper left corner of the **Layers** panel of the **Home** tab on the ribbon (see Figure 4.30).

4.30   **Layer Properties Manager** Icon

2 Select the layer to which you want to assign a new color and click on the color assigned to the layer in the **Color** column in the dialog box as shown in Figure 4.31.

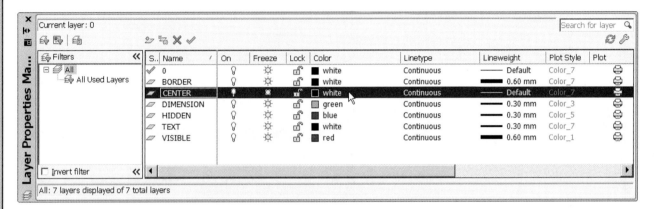

4.31   Assigning Color to a Layer in the **Layer Properties Manager** Palette

3 When the **Select Color** dialog box shown in Figure 4.32 opens, select the desired tile from the color palette and click **OK.**

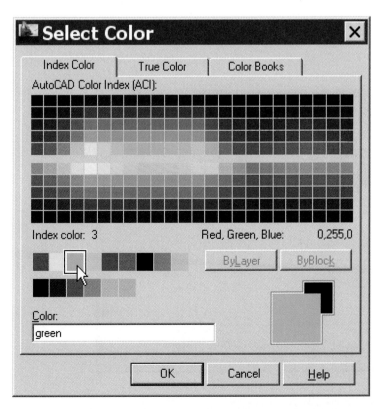

4.32   **Select Color** Dialog Box

SETTING LAYER LINETYPE

1 Click on the **Layer Properties Manager** icon located in the upper left corner of the **Layers** panel of the **Home** tab on the ribbon (see Figure 4.33).

4.33   Layer Properties Manager Icon

2 Select the layer to which you want to assign a new linetype and click on its linetype name in the **Linetype** column. See Figure 4.34.

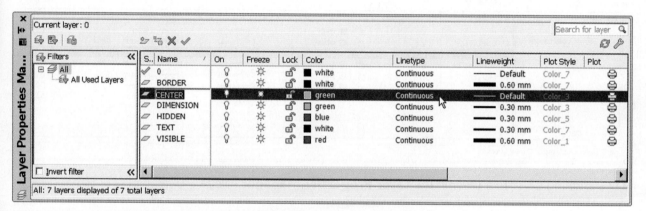

4.34   Assigning Linetype to a Layer in the **Layer Properties Manager Palette

3 The **Select Linetype** dialog box shown in Figure 4.35 will open. If you do not see the desired linetype listed, click the **Load . . .** button.

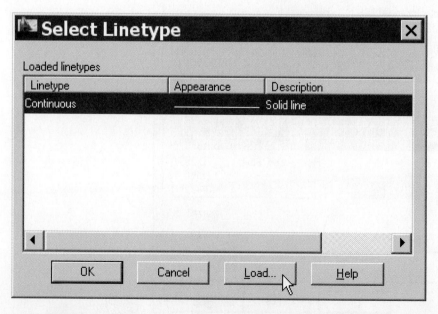

4.35   Select Linetype Dialog Box

4 The **Load or Reload Linetypes** dialog box shown in Figure 4.36 will open. Scroll through the linetypes. Select the linetype you wish to load and click **OK**.

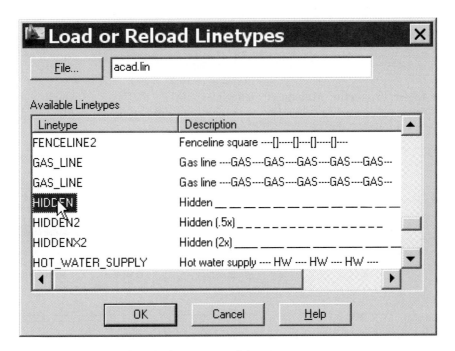

4.36 **Load or Reload Linetypes** Dialog Box

5 Select the newly loaded linetype from the **Select Linetype** dialog box and click **OK**. The new linetype will be assigned to the layer selected in Step 2 (see Figure 4.37).

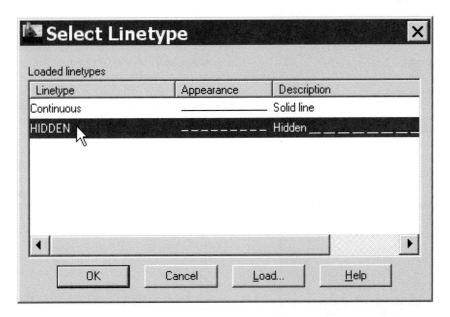

4.37 **Select Linetype** Dialog Box

SETTING LAYER LINEWEIGHT

1 Click on the **Layer Properties Manager** icon located in the upper left corner of the **Layers** panel of the **Home** tab the ribbon (see Figure 4.38).

4.38 Layer Properties Manager Icon

2 When the **Layer Properties Manager** palette opens, select the layer to which you want to assign a new lineweight and click on the lineweight setting in the **Lineweight** column (see Figure 4.39).

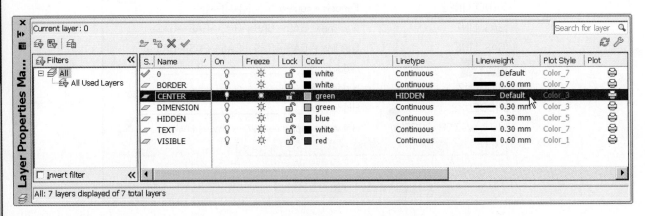

4.39 Assigning Lineweight to a Layer in the **Layer Properties Manager** Palette

3 When the **Lineweight** dialog box opens, scroll through and select the desired line thickness in which you want the layer to be printed and click **OK** (see Figure 4.40).

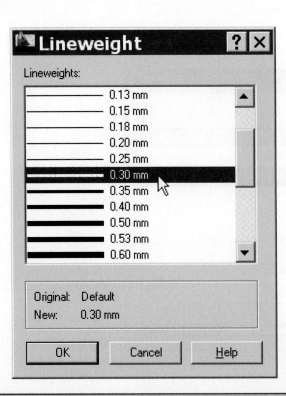

4.40 Lineweight Dialog Box

NOTE

The **LTSCALE** (*linetype scale*) command controls the spacing of the breaks and dashes in noncontinuous linetypes such as centerlines and hidden lines. Sometimes a noncontinuous line will appear to be a continuous line in the drawing window because its spaces are too small or too large. To change the linetype scale of all the noncontinuous lines in the drawing, type **LTS** and press **<Enter>** and change the default value (which is **1**) to a larger or smaller value. Settings like **LTS,** which affect every noncontinuous line in the drawing, are referred to as *global* settings.

STEP by STEP

Setting the Current Layer

In an AutoCAD drawing, you can draw only on the current layer. To set a different layer current, select the down arrow in the **Layer Control** window located in the **Layers** panel of the **Home** tab on the ribbon and left-click on the layer you want to make current from the list of layers shown (see Figure 4.41).

Controlling Layer Visibility

Visibility of a drawing's layers can be controlled in two ways: either turning the layers *off* or *freezing* them. This is particularly useful if you need an unobstructed

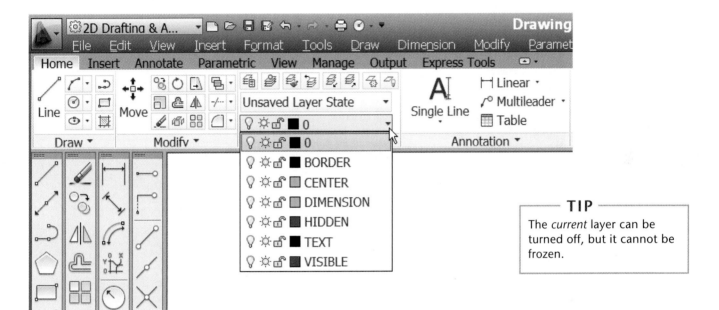

4.41   Layer Control Drop-Down Menu

view of an area of the drawing, or if you are working in detail on a particular layer or set of layers. Construction lines are often drawn on layers that are later turned off, or frozen, because entities on these layers are not plotted.

Turning Layers Off

Select the down arrow in the **Layer Control** window and turn a layer off by left-clicking the yellow lightbulb next to the layer name. Layers that are off will display the darkened lightbulb symbol (see Figure 4.41).

Freezing Layers

Select the down arrow in the **Layer Control** window and freeze a layer by clicking on the sun symbol next to its name. When the layer is frozen, the sun symbol will be replaced with a snowflake. Freezing, and *thawing* (unfreezing), layers takes a little more time than turning layers on and off because this operation causes the drawing to be regenerated.

4.8 ZOOM AND PAN COMMANDS

The **ZOOM** command allows you to view a drawing up close or far away. Zooming does not actually change the scale of entities in the drawing (this is accomplished with the **SCALE** command), just their magnification in the graphics window. The **PAN** command allows you to reposition the view of the drawing in the graphics window. Panning does not change the location of entities in the drawing (this is accomplished with the **MOVE** command), just the viewer's point of view. The **PAN** and **ZOOM** commands are located on the **View** tab on the ribbon in the **Navigate** panel. To see all the options for the **ZOOM** command, left-click on the down arrow next to **Extents** in the **Navigate** panel. For a detailed explanation of these important viewing tools, see Figure 4.42.

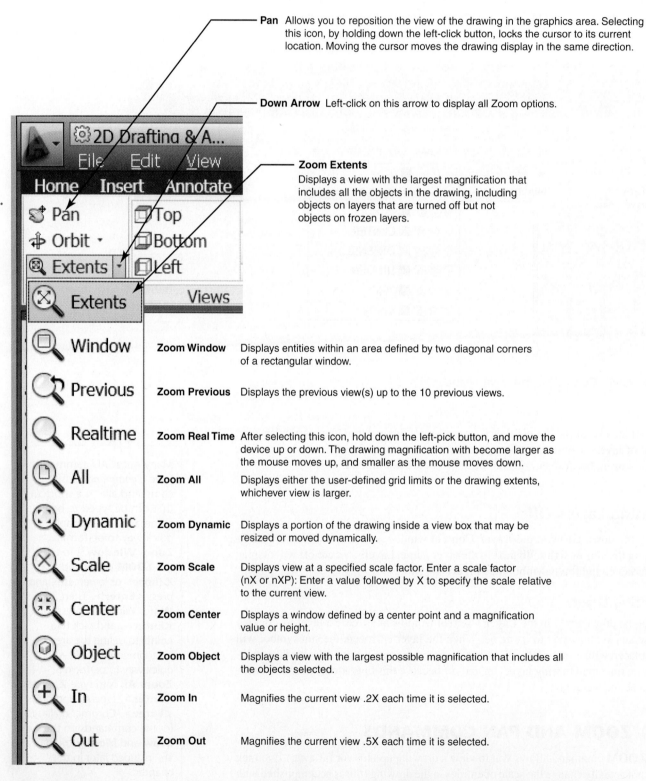

Pan Allows you to reposition the view of the drawing in the graphics area. Selecting this icon, by holding down the left-click button, locks the cursor to its current location. Moving the cursor moves the drawing display in the same direction.

Down Arrow Left-click on this arrow to display all Zoom options.

Zoom Extents
Displays a view with the largest magnification that includes all the objects in the drawing, including objects on layers that are turned off but not objects on frozen layers.

Zoom Window Displays entities within an area defined by two diagonal corners of a rectangular window.

Zoom Previous Displays the previous view(s) up to the 10 previous views.

Zoom Real Time After selecting this icon, hold down the left-pick button, and move the device up or down. The drawing magnification with become larger as the mouse moves up, and smaller as the mouse moves down.

Zoom All Displays either the user-defined grid limits or the drawing extents, whichever view is larger.

Zoom Dynamic Displays a portion of the drawing inside a view box that may be resized or moved dynamically.

Zoom Scale Displays view at a specified scale factor. Enter a scale factor (nX or nXP): Enter a value followed by X to specify the scale relative to the current view.

Zoom Center Displays a window defined by a center point and a magnification value or height.

Zoom Object Displays a view with the largest possible magnification that includes all the objects selected.

Zoom In Magnifies the current view .2X each time it is selected.

Zoom Out Magnifies the current view .5X each time it is selected.

4.42 Zoom and **Pan** Tools Located on the **Navigate** Panel of the **View** Tab

4.9 AUTOCAD TOOLBARS

AutoCAD commands can be invoked by choosing the appropriate icon from a panel on the ribbon, from command toolbars such as **Draw**, **Modify**, or **Dimension**, from a **menu bar** pull-down menu, or by typing the command's name or alias on the command line. The quickest way to open an AutoCAD toolbar is to right-click on any open toolbar. This will open a list of available toolbars, as shown in Figure 4.43. From this list, select the name of the toolbar that you wish to open by left-clicking on it.

Another way to open a toolbar when no toolbars are open is to left-click on the **Tools** menu located on the menu bar. When the submenu drops down, left-click on the word **Toolbars**. When the next submenu appears, left-click on the word **AutoCAD** and select the name of the toolbar from the **Toolbar** menu. In AutoCAD 2011, toolbars can also be opened by selecting the ribbon's **View** tab and picking on

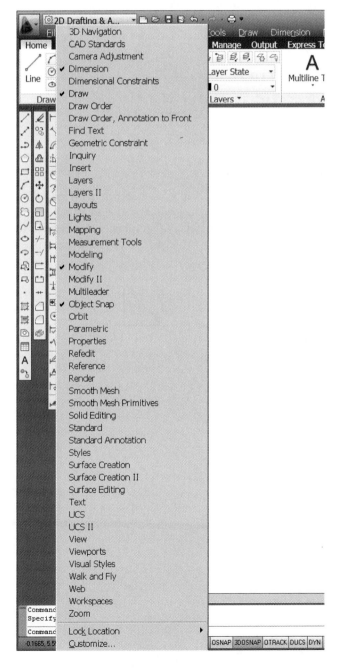

4.43 AutoCAD Toolbars

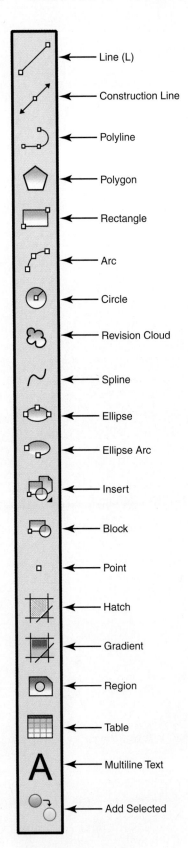

4.44 Autocad **Draw** Toolbar

the **Toolbars** tool located on the **Windows** panel. When the drop-down list appears, click on the word **AutoCAD** and select the toolbars from list that appears in the toolbar menu.

After the toolbar opens, you can drag it to a different location on the screen or dock the toolbar along the edges of the graphics window.

Draw Toolbar

The *Draw commands* on the AutoCAD **Draw** toolbar are shown in Figure 4.44. Some of the commands located on this toolbar, such as **Line**, **Circle**, **Arc**, and **Multiline Text**, are used more frequently than others; however, all the commands on this toolbar are useful, and you should familiarize yourself with each of them. Video tutorials for the commands on the **Draw** toolbar are located in the student data files at www.pearsondesigncentral.com. To access these tutorials, open the Pearson Design Central website and click on the *CAD Community* link, then select the *Click here to download student data files for our CAD titles* link. Next, click on the *Technical Drawing 101* link and select the *AutoCAD Tutorial Videos* zip file, then select the *Download* button and open (or save) the tutorials specified above.

- **TIP**
Press **<Esc>** to cancel an AutoCAD command. Pressing **<Enter>** will return you to the last AutoCAD command used.

LINE Command

The icon for the **LINE** command is shown in Figure 4.45(a). This command is used to draw lines in the graphics window. Lines can be drawn by using absolute coordinates (see Figure 4.10), relative coordinates (see Figures 4.11 and 4.12), or polar coordinates (see Figures 4.14 and 4.15), or by direct entry (see Figures 4.16a and 4.16b).

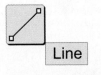

4.45(a) **Line** Icon

LINE COMMAND TUTORIAL

1 Select the **Line** icon from the **Draw** toolbar or the **Draw** panel of the **Home** tab.

2 When prompted to *Specify start point:*, define the start point of the line by left-clicking to select a point in the graphics window or by entering an absolute coordinate and pressing **<Enter>**.

3 When prompted to *Specify next point:*, define the next point of the line by left-clicking to select a point in the graphics window or by entering absolute, relative, or polar coordinates and pressing **<Enter>**. You can continue to define lines in this manner or end the command by pressing **<Esc>** or **<Enter>**. See Figure 4.45(b).

> ── TIP ─────────────────────
> The command alias for the **LINE** command is **L**.

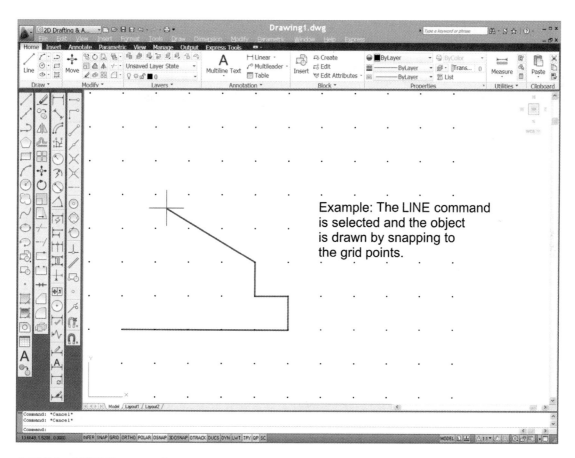

4.45(b)   LINE Command

Construction Line Command

The icon for the **Construction Line** command is shown in Figure 4.46(a). This command creates lines that extend to infinity that can be placed on a drawing to facilitate the construction of other objects.

4.46(a)   Construction Line Icon

CONSTRUCTION LINE COMMAND TUTORIAL

STEP by STEP

1 Select the **Construction Line** icon from the **Draw** toolbar or **Draw** panel of the **Home** tab.

2 When prompted to *Specify a point:*, type **H** and press **<Enter>** to place a horizontal construction line, type **V** and press **<Enter>** to place a vertical construction line, or type **A** and press **<Enter>** and an angle value at the *Enter angle of xline:* prompt to place a construction line at an angle. Press **<Enter>** after entering the value for an angle.

3 At the *Specify through point:* prompt, select a point on the screen through which the construction line is to be drawn. You can continue to pick points for placement of other construction lines or end the command by pressing **<Esc> or <Enter>.** See Figure 4.46(b).

TIP

The command alias for the **Construction Line** command is **XL**.

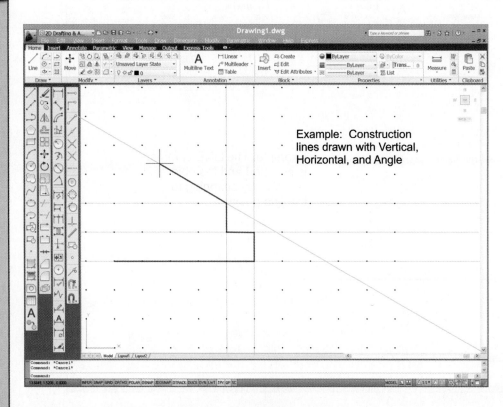

Example: Construction lines drawn with Vertical, Horizontal, and Angle

4.46(b)   Construction Line Command

The PLINE (Polyline) Command

The icon for the **Polyline** command is shown in Figure 4.47(a). This command creates continuous lines that may vary in width and shape.

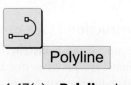

Polyline

4.47(a)   Polyline Icon

POLYLINE COMMAND TUTORIAL

1 Select the **Polyline** icon from the **Draw** toolbar or the **Draw** panel of the **Home** tab.

2 When prompted to *Specify start point:*, type absolute coordinates **1,8** and press **<Enter>**.

3 When prompted to *Specify next point or [Arc/Halfwidth/Undo/Width]:*, move your mouse to the right (with **Polar Tracking** turned on), type **4.5,** and press **<Enter>**. See Figure 4.47(b).

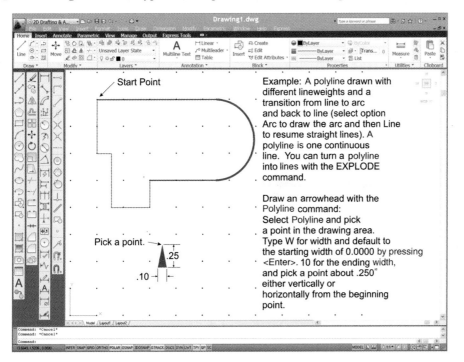

4.47(b) Polyline Command

4 When prompted to *Specify next point or [Arc/Halfwidth/Undo/Width]:*, type **A** for **Arc** and press **<Enter>**.

5 When prompted to *Specify endpoint of arc or [Angle/Center/Close/Direction/Halfwidth/Line/Radius/Undo/Width]:*, type **W** for **Width** and press **<Enter>**.

6 When prompted to *Specify starting width (0.0000):*, type **.06** and press **<Enter>**. When prompted to *Specify ending width <0.0600>:*, press **<Enter>** to accept the default lineweight. Notice that the lineweight has changed.

7 When prompted to *Specify endpoint of arc or [Angle/Center/Close/Direction/Halfwidth/Line/Radius/Undo/Width]:*, ensure that **Polar Tracking** is tracking at **270°** and type **2** for the distance and **<Enter>**.

8 When again prompted to *Specify endpoint of arc or [Angle/Center/Close/Direction/Halfwidth/Line/Radius/Undo/Width]:*, type **L** for **Line** and press **<Enter>**.

9 When prompted to *Specify next point or [Arc/Halfwidth/Undo/Width]:*, type **W** for **Width** and press **<Enter>**.

10 When prompted to *Specify starting width (0.0600):* type **0**. When prompted with *Specify ending width (0.0000):* press **<Enter>**.

11 Continue drawing polylines at either a 0 width or changing to different widths. Press **<Enter>** to end the command.

TIP

The command alias for the **Polyline** command is **PL**.

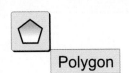

4.48(a) **Polygon** Icon

POLYGON Command

The icon for the **POLYGON** command is shown in Figure 4.48(a). This command is used to create multisided shapes with sides of equal length.

POLYGON COMMAND TUTORIAL

STEP by STEP

1 Select the **Polygon** icon from the **Draw** toolbar or the **Draw** panel of the **Home** tab.

2 When prompted to *Enter number of sides:*, enter a value and press **<Enter>**.

3 At the *Specify center of polygon:* prompt, select a point on the screen by left-clicking or typing coordinate values. See Figure 4.48(b).

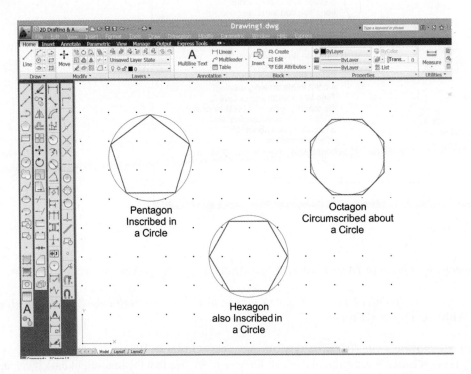

4.48(b) **POLYGON** Command

4 When prompted to *Enter an option [Inscribed in circle/Circumscribed about circle]:*, type either an **I** for inscribed or a **C** for circumscribed, and press **<Enter>**.

5 When prompted to *Specify radius of circle:*, enter a value for the radius of the circle in which the polygon will be inscribed inside or circumscribed about, and press **<Enter>**.

TIP
The command alias for the **POLYGON** command is **POL**.

RECTANGLE Command

The icon for the **RECTANGLE** command is shown in Figure 4.49(a). This command is used to create continuous-line rectangles.

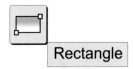

Rectangle

4.49(a)   Rectangle Icon

RECTANGLE COMMAND TUTORIAL

This tutorial presents the steps for drawing a rectangle that begins at the point with absolute coordinates **1,2** and has an *X*-value of **6** units and a *Y*-value of **2** units.

1 Select the **Rectangle** icon from the **Draw** toolbar or the **Draw** panel of the **Home** tab.

2 When prompted to *Specify first corner point or [Chamfer/Elevation/Fillet/Thickness/Width]:*, type **1,2** and press **<Enter>**. See Figure 4.49(b).

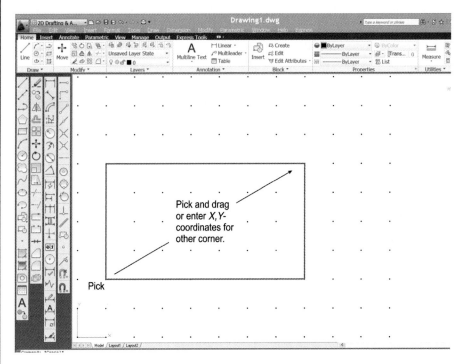

4.49(b)   RECTANGLE Command

3 When prompted to *Specify other corner point or [Area/Dimensions/Rotation]:*, type **6,2** (with dynamic input on), or **@6,2** and press **<Enter>**.

> ── TIP ──
> The command alias for the **RECTANGLE** command is **REC**.

ARC Command

The icon for the **ARC** command is shown in Figure 4.50(a). This command can create arcs using 11 different methods.

4.50(a)   **Arc** Icon

> — **NOTE** —
> Arcs are drawn counterclockwise.

ARC COMMAND TUTORIAL
(START, END, RADIUS METHOD)

This tutorial presents the steps for drawing an arc that begins at absolute coordinates **4,5** and ends at absolute coordinates **8,5** and has a radius of **3** units.

1 Select the **Draw** pull-down menu, highlight **Arc**, and pick **Start**, **End**, **Radius,** or select the **ARC** command from the **Draw** panel of the **Home** tab.

2 When prompted to *Specify start point of arc or [Center]:*, type **4,5** and press **<Enter>.**

3 When prompted to *Specify end point of arc:*, type **8,5** and press **<Enter>.**

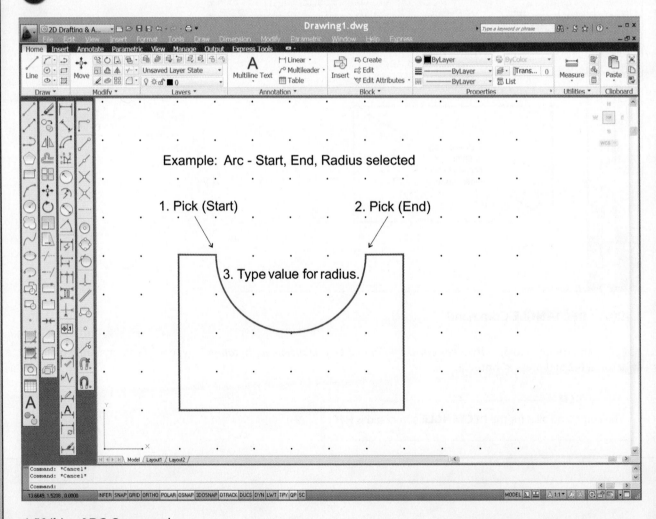

4.50(b)   **ARC** Command

4 When prompted to *Specify radius of arc:*, type **3** and press **<Enter>**. See Figure 4.50(b).

5 Try drawing another arc by typing **8,5** for the start and **4,5** for the end with a radius of **3**.

> **TIP**
> The command alias for the **ARC** command is **A**.

CIRCLE Command

The icon for the **CIRCLE** command is shown in Figure 4.51(a). This command is used to draw a circle after you are prompted to select (or enter) the center point and the radius or diameter.

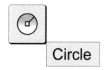

4.51(a)   Circle Icon

CIRCLE COMMAND TUTORIAL

1 Select the **Circle** icon from the **Draw** toolbar or the **Draw** panel of the **Home** tab.

2 When prompted to *Specify center point of circle or [3P/2P/Ttr (tan tan radius)]:*, type **2,7** and press **<Enter>**.

3 When prompted to *Specify radius of circle or [Diameter]:*, type **1** and press **<Enter>**. See Figure 4.51(b).

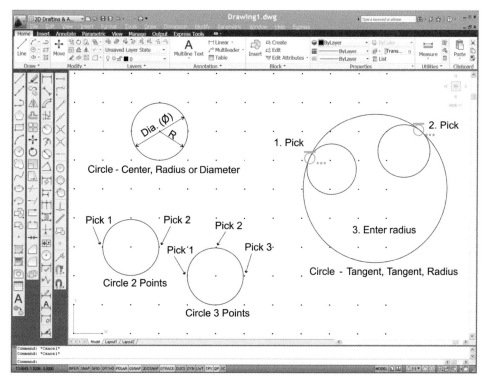

STEP by STEP

4.51(b)   CIRCLE
Command

④ Try it again except type **6,7** for the center and press **<Enter>.** When prompted to *Specify radius of circle or* [Diameter]:, type **D** for **Diameter.**

⑤ When prompted to *Specify diameter of circle <2.0000>*:, type **1** and press **<Enter>.**

TIP

The command alias for the **CIRCLE** command is **C**.

Revision Cloud

Revision Cloud (REVCLOUD) Command

The icon for the **Revision Cloud** command is shown in Figure 4.52(a). This command creates a cloud shape made of polyline arcs. Revision clouds are placed on drawings to draw attention to an area of the drawing.

4.52(a)   Revision Cloud Icon

STEP by STEP

REVISION CLOUD COMMAND TUTORIAL

① Select the **Revision Cloud** icon from the **Draw** toolbar or the **Draw** panel of the **Home** tab.

② When prompted to *Specify start point or [Arc length/Object/Style]*:, pick a point on the screen and draw the revision cloud either clockwise or counterclockwise. Selecting a point close to the beginning point will close the cloud. See Figure 4.52(b).

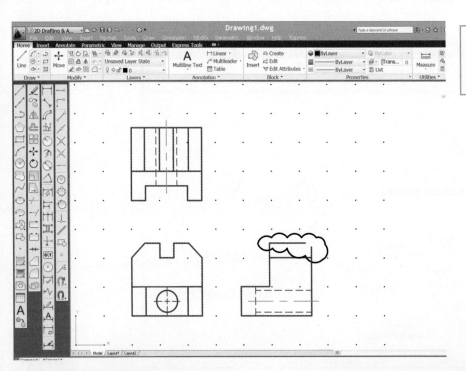

TIP

You can also find the **Revision Cloud** command in the **Draw** pull-down of the menu bar.

4.52(b)   REVCLOUD Command

SPLINE Command

The icon for the **SPLINE** command is shown in Figure 4.53(a). This command creates a nonuniform spline curve.

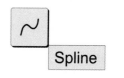

4.53(a)   **Spline** Icon

SPLINE COMMAND TUTORIAL

1 Select the **Spline** icon from the **Draw** toolbar or **Draw** panel of the **Home** tab.

2 When prompted to *Specify first point or [Object]:*, type **2,2** and press **<Enter>**.

3 When prompted to *Specify next point:*, type **4,5** and press **<Enter>**.

4 When prompted to *Specify next point:*, type **6,2** and press **<Enter>**.

5 When prompted to *Specify next point:*, type **8,5** and press **<Enter>**.

6 When prompted to *Specify next point:*, type **10,2** and press **<Enter>**.

7 When prompted to *Specify next point:*, press **<Enter>**.

8 When prompted to *Specify start tangent:*, press **<Enter>**.

9 When prompted to *Specify end tangent:*, press **<Enter>** to finish the spline curve. See Figure 4.53(b).

STEP by STEP

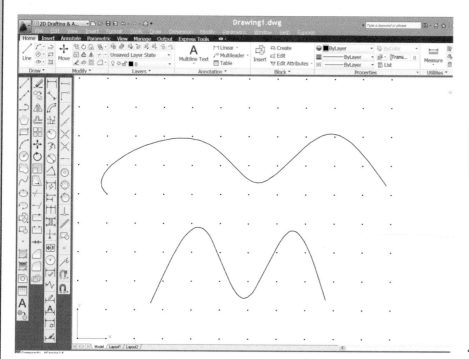

— **NOTE** —

You must press **<Enter>** three times to complete the **SPLINE** command.

— **TIP** —

The command alias for the **SPLINE** command is **SPL**.

4.53(b)   **SPLINE** Command

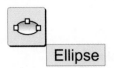

4.54(a)   Ellipse Icon

ELLIPSE Command

The icon for the **ELLIPSE** command is shown in Figure 4.54(a). This command is used to create an ellipse. An ellipse is defined by two axes: a long axis that defines its length (called the major axis) and a shorter axis that defines its width (called the minor axis).

ELLIPSE COMMAND TUTORIAL

1 Select the **Ellipse** icon from the **Draw** toolbar or the **Draw** panel of the **Home** tab.

2 At the *Specify axis endpoint of ellipse*: prompt, pick the start point of the major axis of the ellipse. See Figure 4.54(b).

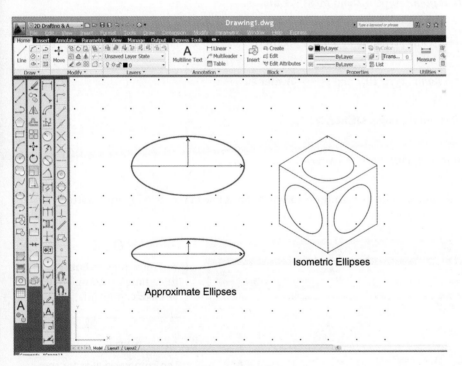

4.54(b)   ELLIPSE Command

3 At the *Specify other endpoint of axis*: prompt, pick the location of the endpoint of the major axis, or define the endpoint with coordinates, and press **<Enter>.**

4 At the *Specify distance to other axis*: prompt, drag the mouse in the direction desired for the minor axis and enter a distance for half the length of the minor axis and press **<Enter>.**

> **TIP**
> The command alias for the **ELLIPSE** command is **EL**.

Ellipse Arc Command

The icon for the **Ellipse Arc** command is shown in Figure 4.55(a). This command is used to draw an elliptical arc. An elliptical arc is defined by the length of its major axis and the endpoints of the break in the ellipse.

4.55(a)   Ellipse Arc Icon

ELLIPSE ARC COMMAND TUTORIAL

1 Select the **Ellipse Arc** icon from the **Draw** toolbar or the **Draw** panel of the **Home** tab (select the down arrow next to the **Ellipse** icon and choose from the drop-down list).

2 At the *Specify axis endpoint of elliptical arc*: prompt, pick the start point of the major axis of the ellipse. See Figure 4.55(b).

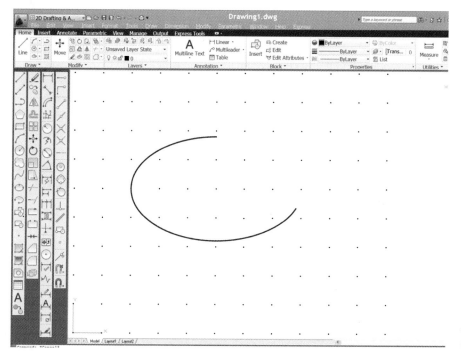

4.55(b)   Ellipse Arc Command

3 At the *Specify other endpoint of axis*: prompt, pick the location of the endpoint of the major axis, or define the end-point with coordinates, and press **<Enter>**.

4 At the *Specify distance to other axis*: prompt, drag the mouse in the direction desired for the minor axis and enter a distance equal to half the length of the minor axis and press **<Enter>**.

5 At the *Specify start angle*: prompt, enter an angle relative to the point defined in Step 4 where the elliptical arc should begin.

6 At the *Specify end angle*: prompt, enter an angle relative to the point defined in Step 5 where the elliptical arc should end.

> **TIP**
> Consulting the angle noted in the dynamic input window next to the cursor is helpful when defining the start and end angles for an elliptical arc.

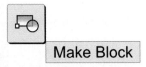

4.56   Insert Block Icon

Insert Block Command

The icon for the **Insert Block** command is shown in Figure 4.56. This command is used to place a named block, or a drawing, into the current drawing.

The steps involved in using the **Insert Block** command are presented in Chapter 10 of this text.

> ### TIP
> You can also find the **Insert Block** command in the **Block** panel of the **Home** tab. The command alias is **I**.

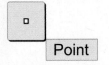

4.57   Block Icon

BLOCK Command

The icon for the **BLOCK** command is shown in Figure 4.57. A *block* is a named image defined within a drawing file that can be inserted into the drawing whenever it is needed. An example of this is a symbol for a door that is used multiple times in the creation of a floor plan.

The steps involved in using the **BLOCK** command are presented in Chapter 10 of this text.

> ### TIP
> You can also find the **BLOCK** command in the **Block** panel of the **Home** tab. The command alias is **B**.

4.58(a)   Point Icon

POINT Command

The icon for the **POINT** command is shown in Figure 4.58(a). This command places a single point on a drawing. The point style is defined by selecting the **Format** pull-down menu and selecting **Point Style**. When the **Point Style** dialog box opens, select the tile containing the desired style and click **OK**.

POINT COMMAND TUTORIAL

STEP by STEP

1. Select the **Point** icon from the **Draw** toolbar or **Draw** panel of the **Home** tab.

2. When prompted to *Specify a point*:, type **4.5,4.5** and press **<Enter>.** A point (a dot) will be placed at the point defined by the coordinates.

3. To change the point style, select the **Format** pull-down menu and select **Point Style**. See Figure 4.58(b).

4. When the **Point Style** dialog box opens, pick the tile whose symbol looks like a box with a center mark inside it and click **OK**. The original point will change to the new point style definition.

5. Select **Format**, **Point Style** and practice placing another point with a different style.

> ### TIP
> The command alias for the **POINT** command is **PO**.

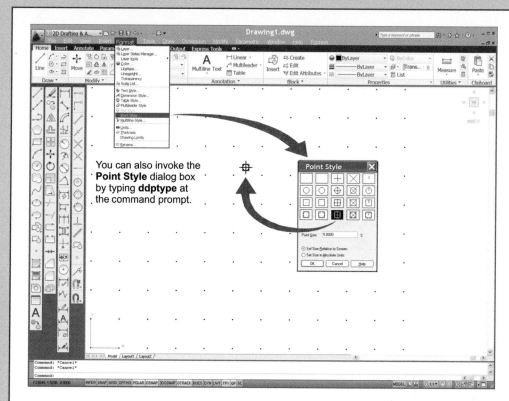

You can also invoke the **Point Style** dialog box by typing **ddptype** at the command prompt.

4.58(b)   **POINT** Command

HATCH Command

The icon for the **HATCH** command is shown in Figure 4.59. This command fills an enclosed area, or selected objects, with a hatch pattern, a solid fill, or a gradient fill.

The steps involved in using the **HATCH** command are presented in Chapter 8 of this text.

4.59   **Hatch** Icon

--- **TIP** ---

The command alias for the **HATCH** command is **H**.

GRADIENT Command

The icon for the **GRADIENT** command is shown in Figure 4.60(a). This command specifies a fill that allows a smooth transition from a darker color to a lighter one.

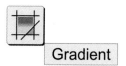

4.60(a)   **Gradient** Icon

STEP by STEP

STEP by STEP

GRADIENT COMMAND TUTORIAL

1 Draw a rectangle.

2 Select the **Gradient** icon from the **Draw** toolbar or the **Draw** panel of the **Home** tab.

3 Choose from the gradient styles shown in the **Pattern** panel of the **Hatch Creation** tab of the ribbon. See Figure 4.60(b).

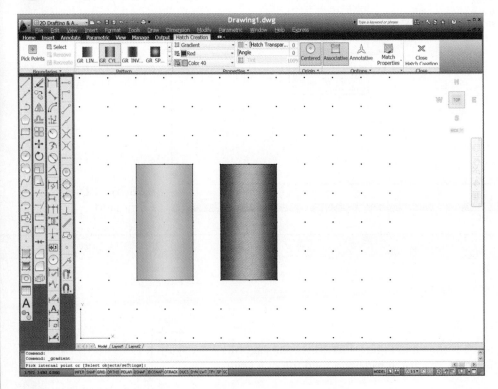

4.60(b) **GRADIENT** Command

4 Select the **Add: Pick points** button in the dialog box.

5 When prompted to *Pick internal point or [Select objects/remove Boundaries]:*, pick a point inside the rectangle and press **<Enter>**.

6 Click **OK**.

> ── **TIP** ──
> The command alias for the **GRADIENT** command is **GD**.

Region

4.61 **Region** Icon

REGION Command

The icon for the **REGION** command is shown in Figure 4.61. Regions are two-dimensional closed shapes or loops. Regions are often created with closed lines or polylines.

The steps involved in using the **REGION** command are presented in Chapter 13 of this text.

> ── **TIP** ──
> The command alias for the **REGION** command is **REG**.

TABLE Command

The icon for the **TABLE** command is shown in Figure 4.62(a). A table is an object that displays data in rows and columns.

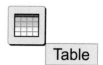

4.62(a)   Table Icon

TABLE COMMAND TUTORIAL

1 Select the **Table** icon from the **Draw** toolbar or the **Annotation** panel of the **Home** tab.

2 When the **Insert Table** dialog box opens, enter the number of columns and rows to be created, as well as their respective widths and heights, in the **Column & Row Settings** area. Click **OK** when these values have been entered.

3 At the *Specify insertion point*: prompt, select a point in the graphics window to insert the table. When the table appears, you will see the cursor blinking in the top cell. This indicates that text can be entered into this cell using the **Text Editor**. Content for other cells can be added or edited by double-clicking inside a cell with the left-click button of the mouse and using the options available in the **Text Editor** tab. Click the **Close Text Editor** tool on the **Text Editor** tab after entering the content. See Figure 4.62(b).

TIP

The command alias for the **TABLE** command is **TB**.

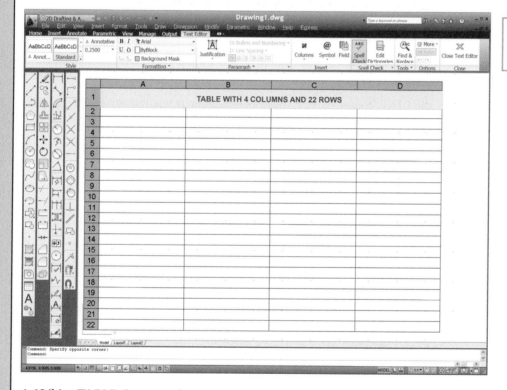

4.62(b)   TABLE Command

STEP by STEP

MTEXT (Multiline Text) Command

The icon for the **MTEXT** command is shown in Figure 4.63. This command is used to place one or more paragraphs of multiline text into the field of a drawing. Saved text from other formats can also be inserted into a drawing using this command.

The procedures involved in placing text with the **MTEXT** command are described later in this chapter.

4.63   Multiline Text Icon

─── **TIP** ───────────────────────────
You can also find the **MTEXT** command on the **Annotation** panel of the **Home** tab. The command alias is **T**.

Add Selected

4.64   Add Selected Icon

Add Selected Command

The icon for the **Add Selected** command is shown in Figure 4.64. This command allows you to initiate a drawing command by selecting an object that was created using that command. For example, selecting **Add Selected** and selecting an arc will open the **ARC** command.

─── **NOTE** ───────────────────────────
When you are using the **Add Selected** command, and select an object created with the **RECTANGLE** or **POLYGON** commands, the **Polyline** command will open.

STEP by STEP

ADD SELECTED COMMAND TUTORIAL

1 Select the **Add Selected** icon from the **Draw** toolbar.

2 Select an object in the graphics window, for example, a circle, and the **CIRCLE** command is invoked beginning with the *Specify the center point for the circle*: prompt.

Likewise, if the selected object is a line, the **LINE** command is invoked beginning with the *Specify the first point*: prompt.

Modify Toolbar

The *Modify commands* on the **Modify** toolbar are shown in Figure 4.65. Although you may find yourself using a few of the commands on this toolbar, such as **Move**, **Copy**, **Trim**, and **Offset**, much more frequently than some of the others, *all* the commands on this toolbar are useful, and you should familiarize yourself with each of them. Video tutorials for the commands on the **Modify** toolbar are located in the student data files at **www.pearsondesigncentral.com**. To access these tutorials, open the Pearson Design Central website and click on the *CAD Community* link, then select the *Click here to download student data files for our CAD titles* link. Next, click on the *Technical Drawing 101* link and select the *AutoCAD Tutorial Videos* zip file, then select the *Download* button and open (or save) the tutorials specified above.

─── **JOB SKILLS** ───────────────────────
There's a saying among experienced CAD drafters, "Never draw anything twice." What they mean by this is that drafters should use commands like **Copy**, **Move**, and **Rotate** to create technical drawings more quickly and efficiently. The **Modify** toolbar has many tools that speed up the drafting process.

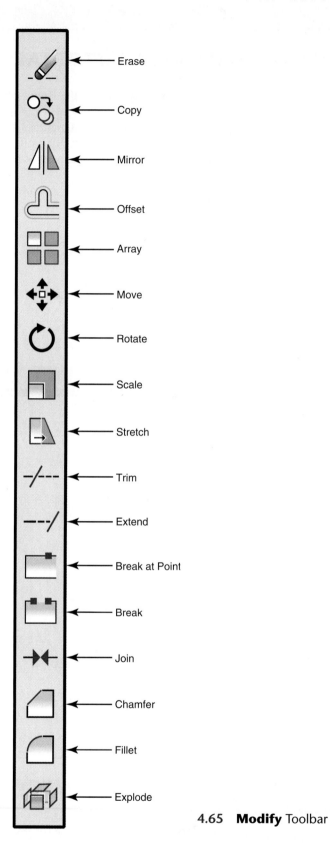

4.65   **Modify** Toolbar

ERASE Command

The icon for the **ERASE** command is shown in Figure 4.66(a). This command is used to remove objects from a drawing.

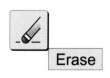

4.66(a)   **Erase** Icon

ERASE COMMAND TUTORIAL

1 Select the **Erase** icon from the **Modify** toolbar or the **Modify** panel of the **Home** tab.

2 When prompted to *Select objects:*, you can select them by left-clicking and selecting in the following ways: **Window** (picking left to right), **Crossing Window** (picking right to left), or by typing **Crossing Polygon** (type **CP**), and **Fence** (type **F**). When you are finished selecting the objects to erase, press **<Enter>** to complete the command. See Figure 4.66(b).

> **TIP**
> The **OOPS** command can be used to restore erased objects (just type **OOPS** on the command line and press **<Enter>**).

> **TIP**
> Objects can also be removed from a drawing by selecting them and pressing the **<Del>** key. You can also find the **ERASE** command in the **Modify** pull-down menu. The command alias is **E**.

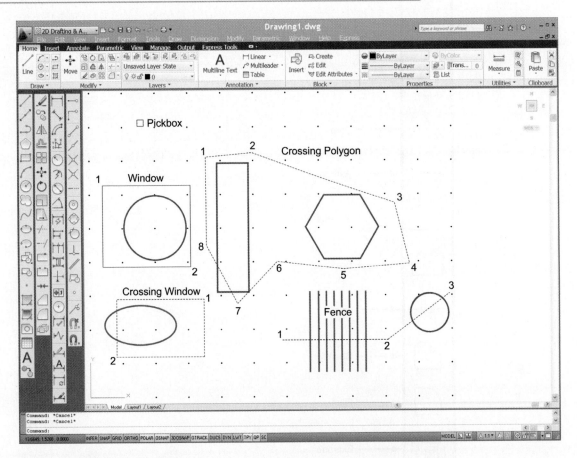

4.66(b) **ERASE** Command

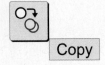

Copy

4.67(a) **Copy** Icon

COPY Command

The icon for the **COPY** command is shown in Figure 4.67(a). This command is used to create a copy of a selected object or objects.

COPY COMMAND TUTORIAL

1 Select the **Copy** icon from the **Modify** toolbar or the **Modify** panel of the **Home** tab.

2 When prompted to *Select objects:*, pick the objects you would like to copy by selecting them either individually or with a window and press **<Enter>.** See Figure 4.67(b).

3 When prompted to *Select the Base point:*, pick a point on the object. The base point can be thought of as a handle on the object to be copied.

4 When prompted to *define the Displacement:*, use the mouse to pick a point in the drawing window located at a specific distance from the base point of the original object, or enter absolute, relative, or polar coordinates, to define the point where you want to place the copy. You can continue to place copies by defining more points. Press **<Esc> or <Enter>** to end the command.

TIP

You can also find the **COPY** command in the **Modify** pull-down menu. The command alias is **CO**.

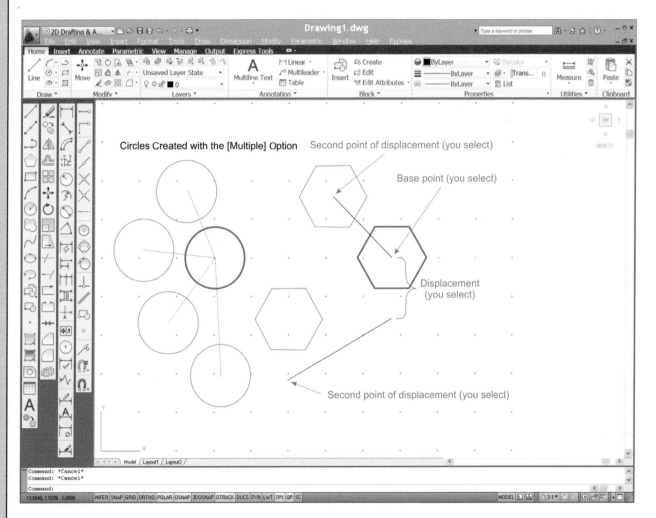

4.67(b) COPY Command

MIRROR Command

The icon for the **MIRROR** command is shown in Figure 4.68(a). This command is used to create a mirror image of an object around an axis called a *mirror line*.

4.68(a) **Mirror** Icon

STEP by STEP

MIRROR COMMAND TUTORIAL

1 Select the **Mirror** icon from the **Modify** toolbar or the **Modify** panel of the **Home** tab.

2 At the *Select objects*: prompt, pick the objects you would like to mirror by selecting them either individually, or with a window, and press **<Enter>.** See Figure 4.68(b).

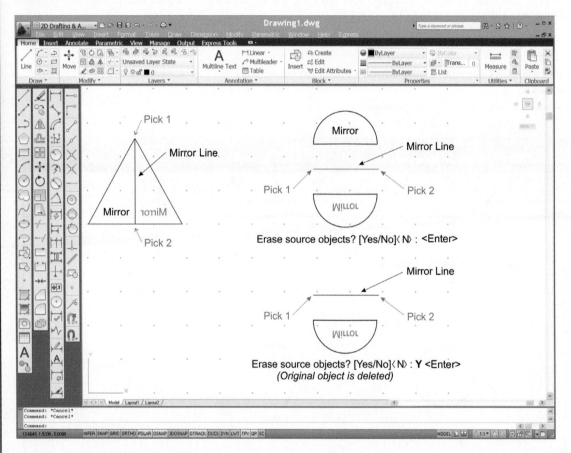

4.68(b) **MIRROR** Command

3 When prompted to *Specify first point of mirror line*:, define the first point of the mirror axis by selecting a point in the graphics window where you want the mirror axis to begin.

4 When you are prompted to *Select the second point of the mirror line*:, select a second point in the graphics window defining the other end of the mirror axis.

--- **TIP** ---

Set **Ortho** to on when defining a vertical or horizontal mirror line.

5 When prompted to *Erase source objects? [Y/N]*:, press **<Enter>** to retain the source object (the prompt's default is **No),** or type a **Y** and press **<Enter>** to erase the object being mirrored.

OFFSET Command

The icon for the **OFFSET** command is shown in Figure 4.69(a). The **OFFSET** command is used to create a new object whose shape parallels the shape of the selected object. Offsetting a circle or an arc creates a larger or smaller circle or arc (depending on which side you specify for the offset) that is concentric with the original circle or arc.

4.69(a)   **Offse**t Icon

OFFSET COMMAND TUTORIAL

1 Select the **Offset** icon from the **Modify** toolbar or the **Modify** panel of the **Home** tab.

2 When prompted to *Select the offset distance*:, type the value of the desired offset distance and press **<Enter>**.

3 When prompted to *Select object to offset:* select the object by left-clicking.

4 At the *Specify point on side to offset*: prompt, pick a point on the side of the object where you want the new object to be created. See Figure 4.69(b).

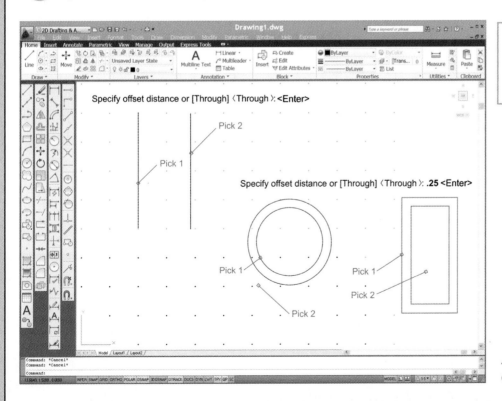

4.69(b)   **OFFSET** Command

S T E P by S T E P

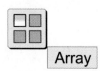

Array

4.70(a)   Array Icon

ARRAY Command

The icon for the **ARRAY** command is shown in Figure 4.70(a). This command is used to create multiple copies of objects in either a rectangular or a circular pattern. A circular array is referred to as a *polar array*.

ARRAY COMMAND TUTORIAL
(RECTANGULAR OPTION)

STEP by STEP

1 Select the **Array** icon from the **Modify** toolbar or the **Modify** panel of the **Home** tab.

2 From the **Array** dialog box, select **Rectangular Array**.

3 Select the **Select Objects** button and pick the objects to be arrayed. Press **<Enter>** when the objects to be arrayed have been selected.

4 Enter the number of rows (which run horizontally) and columns (which run vertically).

5 Enter the **Offset distance** between the rows and columns (*Note:* Negative values can be entered) and the **Angle of array** (the default angle is **0**).

6 Click **OK**. See Figure 4.70(b).

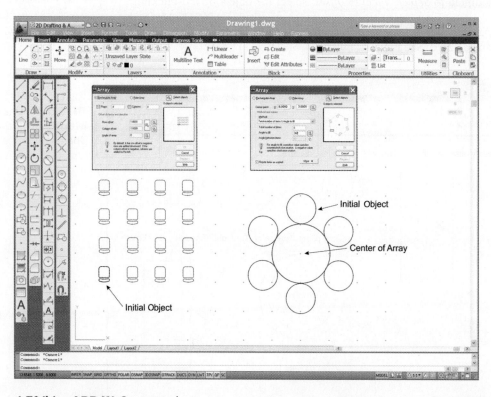

4.70(b)   ARRAY Command

ARRAY COMMAND TUTORIAL (POLAR OPTION)

1 Select the **Array** icon from the **Modify** toolbar or the **Modify** panel of the **Home** tab.

2 From the **Array** dialog box, select **Polar Array**.

3 Select the **Select Objects** button and pick the objects to be arrayed, and press **<Enter>**.

4 Define the **Center Point** for the array by entering X- and Y-coordinates, or by left-clicking a point in the graphics window.

5 Enter the **Total number of items** to be arrayed and the **Angle to fill** (to array in a full circle, enter **360**).

─ NOTE ─
Items are arrayed in a counterclockwise direction.

6 Check the box next to **Rotate objects as copied** if this is desired.

7 Click **OK**. See Figure 4.70(b).

─ TIP ─
You can also find the **ARRAY** command in the **Modify** pull-down menu.
The command alias is **AR**.

S T E P by S T E P

MOVE Command

The icon for the **MOVE** command is shown in Figure 4.71(a). This command is used to move existing objects to a new location.

4.71(a)   **Move** Icon

MOVE COMMAND TUTORIAL

1 Select the **Move** icon from the **Modify** toolbar or the **Modify** panel of the **Home** tab.

2 When prompted to *Select objects:*, pick the objects you would like to move by selecting them either individually or with a window, and press **<Enter>**.

3 When prompted to *Select the Base point:*, pick a point on the object. The base point is like a handle on the object to be moved.

S T E P by S T E P

STEP by STEP

4 When prompted to *define the Displacement:*, pick a point at a specific distance from the original object or enter absolute, relative, or polar coordinate values. See Figure 4.71(b).

> **TIP**
>
> You can also find the **MOVE** command in the **Modify** pull-down menu. The command alias is **M**.

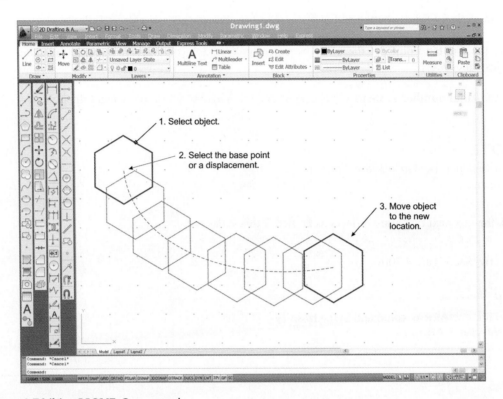

4.71(b) **MOVE** Command

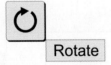

4.72(a) **Rotate** Icon

ROTATE Command

The icon for the **ROTATE** command is shown in Figure 4.72(a). This command is used to rotate objects about a base point. The rotation angle is based on the initial position of the object to be rotated and the selected base point. With **Ortho** on, rotations are limited to 90° angles only.

ROTATE COMMAND TUTORIAL

1 Select the **Rotate** icon from the **Modify** toolbar or the **Modify** panel of the **Home** tab.

2 When prompted to *Select objects:*, pick the objects you would like to rotate by selecting them either individually or with a window, and press **<Enter>.**

3 When prompted to *Select the Base point:*, select a point on the object. The base point is the pivot point around which the rotation will occur.

4 When prompted to *Specify the rotation angle:*, enter a value and press **<Enter>.** See Figure 4.72(b).

NOTE

Objects are rotated counterclockwise when positive rotation values are entered.

TIP

You can also find the **ROTATE** command in the **Modify** pull-down menu. The command alias is **RO**.

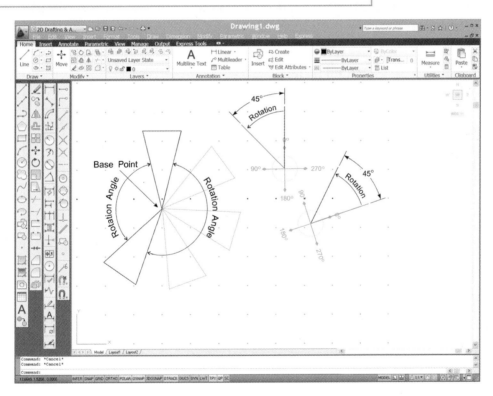

4.72(b)   ROTATE Command

SCALE Command

The icon for the **SCALE** command is shown in Figure 4.73(a). This command is used to change the size of objects.

You can scale up or down by either dragging or entering a scale factor. Scale factors are as follows: .5 = half size, 2 = twice the size, .75 = 3/4 size, and so on.

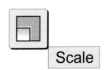

4.73(a)   Scale Icon

SCALE COMMAND TUTORIAL

STEP by STEP

1 Select the **Scale** icon from the **Modify** toolbar or the **Modify** panel of the **Home** tab.

2 When prompted to *Select objects:*, pick the objects you would like to scale by selecting them either individually or with a window, and press **<Enter>**.

3 When prompted to *Select the Base point:*, pick a point on the object. The objects that are scaled will expand or contract relative to this point.

4 When prompted to *Specify scale factor:*, enter a value (for example: .5 = half size, 2 = twice the size, .75 = 3/4 size) and press **<Enter>**. See Figure 4.73(b).

> **TIP**
> You can also find the **SCALE** command in the **Modify** pull-down menu.
> The command alias is **SC**.

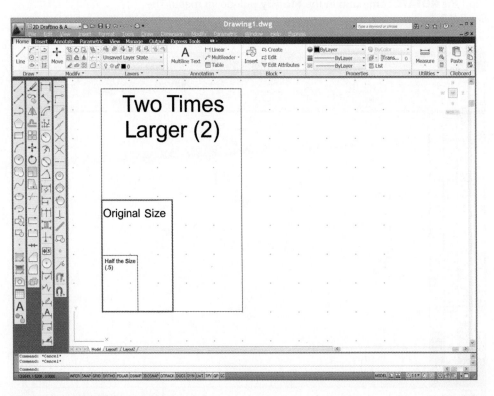

4.73(b) **SCALE** Command

Stretch

4.74(a) **Stretch** Icon

STRETCH Command

The icon for the **STRETCH** command is shown in Figure 4.74(a). This command can be used to lengthen or shorten objects. It can also distort objects. To stretch an object, you can either drag the base point to a new location or enter coordinates.

STRETCH COMMAND TUTORIAL

1 Select the **Stretch** icon from the **Modify** toolbar or the **Modify** panel of the **Home** tab.

2 When prompted to *Select objects:*, pick the objects you would like to stretch with a *crossing window* (define the window by picking from right to left) and press **<Enter>.**

3 When prompted to *Specify base point:*, select a point located on the object to be stretched.

4 When prompted to *Specify second point:*, define the point you wish the object to stretch to by picking a point with the mouse, or entering absolute, relative, or polar coordinate values. See Figure 4.74(b).

TIP

You can also find the **STRETCH** command in the **Modify** pull-down menu. The command alias is **S.**

STEP by STEP

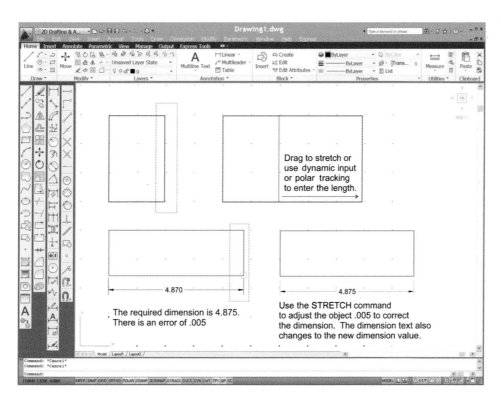

Drag to stretch or use dynamic input or polar tracking to enter the length.

4.870

4.875

The required dimension is 4.875. There is an error of .005

Use the STRETCH command to adjust the object .005 to correct the dimension. The dimension text also changes to the new dimension value.

4.74(b)   STRETCH Command

TRIM Command

The icon for the **TRIM** command is shown in Figure 4.75(a). This command is used to trim objects to an intersection or cutting edge defined by another object. Two trim methods are available: *quick trim* and *regular trim*.

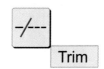

Trim

4.75(a)   Trim Icon

TRIM COMMAND TUTORIAL (QUICK TRIM OPTION)

1 Select the **Trim** icon from the **Modify** toolbar or the **Modify** panel of the **Home** tab.

2 When prompted to *Select cutting edges:*, press **<Enter>.** This will make every entity a cutting edge.

NOTE

Objects that intersect a cutting edge, *but do not extend beyond it,* cannot be trimmed. They should be erased instead.

TIP

Cutting edges can be selected individually with the mouse instead if you prefer. This is known as a *regular* trim.

3 When prompted to *Select object to trim:*, pick the object to be trimmed on the side of the cutting edge you want to trim to.

4 Press **<Enter>** to end the command. See Figure 4.75(b).

TIP

You can also find the **TRIM** command in the **Modify** pull-down menu. The command alias is **TR**.

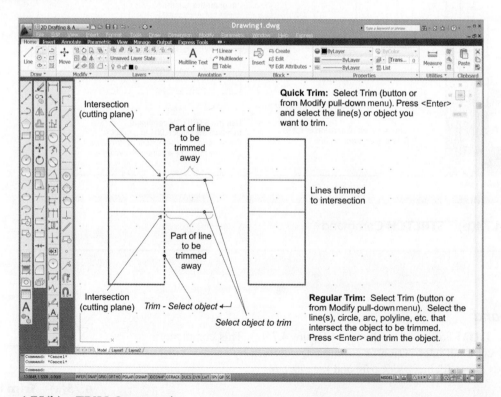

4.75(b) **TRIM** Command

EXTEND Command

The icon for the **EXTEND** command is shown in Figure 4.76(a). This command is used to extend a line or object to meet another object or line (called a *boundary edge*). Objects that can be extended are arcs, elliptical arcs, lines, polylines (2D and 3D), and rays.

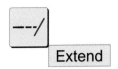

4.76(a)   Extend Icon

EXTEND COMMAND TUTORIAL

1 Select the **Extend** icon from the **Modify** toolbar or the **Modify** panel of the **Home** tab (select the down arrow next to the **Trim** icon and choose from the drop-down list).

2 When prompted to *Select boundary edge:*, press **<Enter>.** This will make all entities a boundary edge.

3 When prompted to *Select object to extend:*, select the object to be extended near the end that you would like to extend, and the object will be extended to the next boundary edge.

4 Press **<Esc>** or **<Enter>** to end the command. See Figure 4.76(b).

> **NOTE**
> Objects that do not intersect a boundary edge cannot be extended.

> **TIP**
> You can also find the **Extend** command in the **Modify** pull-down menu. The command alias is **EX**.

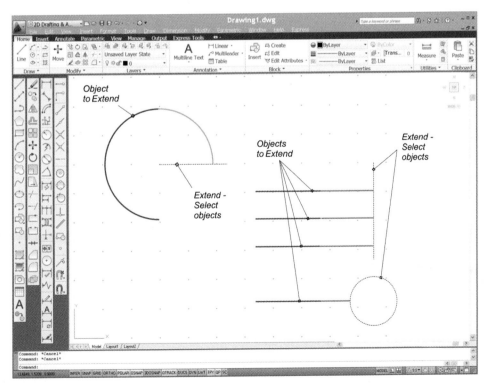

4.76(b)   EXTEND Command

S T E P by **S T E P**

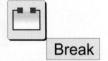

Break at Point Command

The icon for the **Break at Point** command is shown in Figure 4.77. This command is used to break a line into two separate but collinear lines at the selected point.

4.77 **Break At Point** Icon

BREAK AT POINT COMMAND TUTORIAL

1 Select the **Break at Point** icon from the **Modify** toolbar or the **Modify** panel of the **Home** tab.

2 When prompted to *Select object to break:*, select the line to be broken.

3 When prompted to *Select first break point:*, select the point on the line where you would like the break to occur.

BREAK Command

The icon for the **BREAK** command is shown in Figure 4.78(a). This command is used to break an object between two points.

4.78(a) **Break** Icon

BREAK COMMAND TUTORIAL

1 Select the **Break** icon from the **Modify** toolbar or the **Modify** panel of the **Home** tab.

2 When prompted to *Select object to break:*, select the object to be broken.

3 Type **F** for **First Point** and press **<Enter>**.

4 When prompted to *Select first break point:*, select the object to be broken at the start point of the desired break.

5 When prompted to *Select second break point:*, select the endpoint of the desired break. See Figure 4.78(b).

— TIP —
You can also find the **BREAK** command in the **Modify** pull-down menu. The command alias is **BR**.

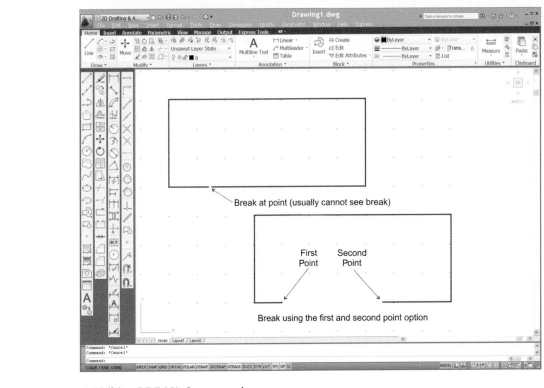

4.78(b)   BREAK Command

JOIN Command

The icon for the **JOIN** command is shown in Figure 4.79(a). This command is used to join objects (collinear lines, for example, can have a gap between them) into one object.

4.79(a)   Join Icon

JOIN COMMAND TUTORIAL

1 Select the **Join** icon from the **Modify** toolbar or the **Modify** panel of the **Home** tab.

2 When prompted to *Select source object*:, select the first line of a set of collinear lines.

3 When prompted to *Select lines to join to source*:, select the collinear line(s) that you would like to join to the source line. Press **<Enter>** to complete the command. See Figure 4.79(b).

— TIP —
You can also find the **JOIN** command in the **Modify** pull-down menu.
The command alias is **J**.

STEP by STEP

STEP by STEP

STEP by STEP

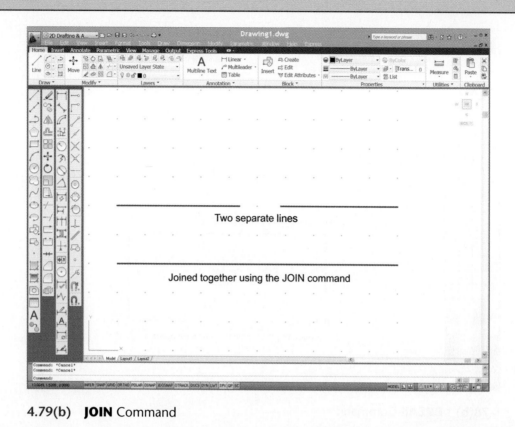

Two separate lines

Joined together using the JOIN command

4.79(b)   JOIN Command

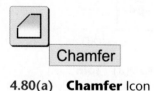

Chamfer

4.80(a)   Chamfer Icon

CHAMFER Command

The icon for the **CHAMFER** command is shown in Figure 4.80(a). This command is used to bevel the corners of objects and lines. The **Distance** option allows you to enter a chamfer distance for both sides of the beveled corner. The **Angle** option allows you to enter a distance and an angle for the beveled corner. The **Polyline** option will bevel the corners of the polyline.

CHAMFER COMMAND TUTORIAL

STEP by STEP

1 Select the **Chamfer** icon from the **Modify** toolbar or the **Modify** panel of the **Home** tab (select the down arrow next to the **Fillet** icon and choose from the drop-down list).

2 Type **D** (for distance) and press **<Enter>**.

TIP

To enter a distance and an angle for a chamfer, type **A** (for angle) instead of **D** and enter the desired chamfer distance and angle in response to the prompts.

---

3 When prompted to *Specify first chamfer distance:*, enter the distance to bevel the first edge and press **<Enter>**.

4 When prompted to *Specify second chamfer distance:*, enter the distance to bevel the second edge and press **<Enter>**.

5 When prompted to *Select first line:*, pick the first line to be beveled near the end to be beveled.

6 When prompted to *Specify second line:*, pick the second line to be beveled. See Figure 4.80(b).

TIP

You can also find the **CHAMFER** command in the **Modify** pull-down menu. The command alias is **CHA**.

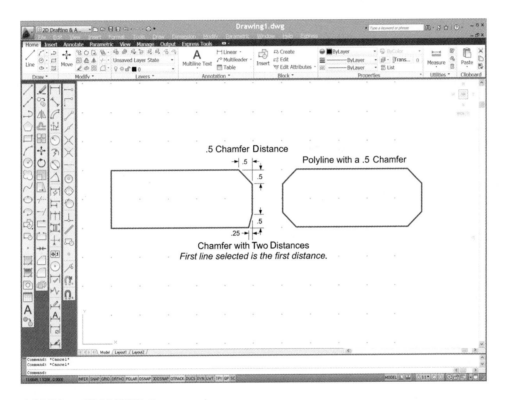

4.80(b)   CHAMFER Command

FILLET Command

The icon for the **FILLET** command is shown in Figure 4.81(a). This command is used to create fillets (rounded *inside* corners) and rounds (rounded *outside* corners) on objects. The **Polyline** option creates fillets and rounds on the corners of a polyline.

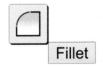

4.81(a)   Fillet Icon

FILLET COMMAND TUTORIAL

1 Select the **Fillet** icon from the **Modify** toolbar or the **Modify** panel of the **Home** tab.

2 Type **R** (for radius) and press **<Enter>.**

3 When prompted to *Specify fillet radius:*, enter the radius of the fillet and press **<Enter>.**

4 When prompted to *Select first object:*, pick the first line to be filleted near the end to be filleted.

5 When prompted to *Select second object:*, pick the second line to be filleted. See Figure 4.81(b).

TIP

You can also find the **FILLET** command in the **Modify** pull-down menu. The command alias is **F**.

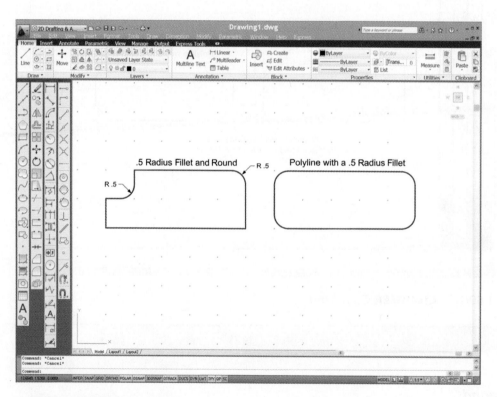

.5 Radius Fillet and Round   R .5

R .5

Polyline with a .5 Radius Fillet

4.81(b)   FILLET Command

Explode

4.82(a)   Explode Icon

EXPLODE Command

The icon for the **EXPLODE** command is shown in Figure 4.82(a). This command breaks compound objects, such as rectangles, polygons, polylines, and blocks, into separate entities—usually for the purpose of editing them.

EXPLODE COMMAND TUTORIAL

1 Select the **Explode** icon from the **Modify** toolbar or the **Modify** panel of the **Home** tab.

2 When prompted to *Select objects*:, select the object(s) to be exploded.

3 Press **<Enter>** to complete the command. See Figure 4.82(b).

TIP

You can also find the **EXPLODE** command in the **Modify** pull-down menu. The command alias is **X**.

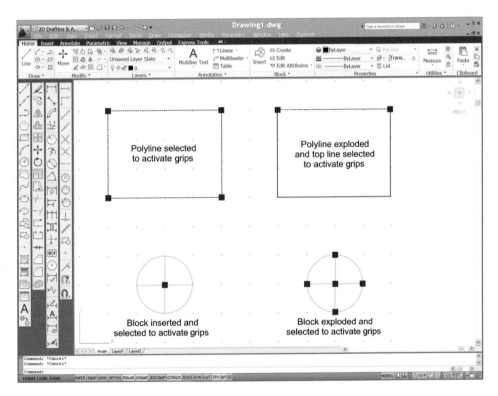

4.82(b) **EXPLODE** Command

Placing and Editing Text

There are two commands commonly used to place text in the field of a drawing, **MTEXT** (multiline text) and **DTEXT** (also called *single-line* or *dynamic* text). The **MTEXT** icon is the bold **A** located on the **Annotation** panel of the **Home** tab, as shown in Figure 4.83(a), and on the **Draw** toolbar, as shown in Figure 4.44. The **DTEXT** command can be found by selecting the down arrow located beneath the words **Multiline Text** in the **Annotation** panel and clicking on **Single Line** (see Figure 4.83(b)).

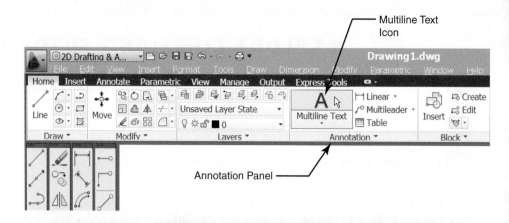

4.83(a) Location of the **Multiline Text** Icon in the **Annotation** Panel

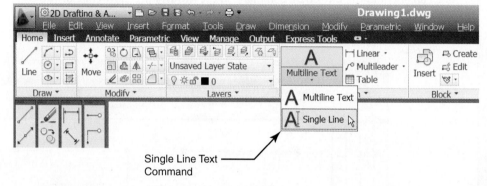

4.83(b) Location of fhe **Single Line Text** Command in the **Annotation** Panel

MTEXT COMMAND

Left-click on the **Multiline Text** icon located on the **Annotation** panel (see Figure 4.83a), or type **MTEXT** and press **<Enter>** to start the command. You will be prompted to *Specify the first and Opposite corner of a text box:*. By picking two points in the drawing window, you can define the width of the text box. After you have selected the two points defining the corners of the text box, a text box containing a blinking cursor will appear on the screen (see Figure 4.84). Simply type the desired text in the text box. If you would like to edit the properties of the text, such as the text height, font style, or justification, highlight the text by holding down the left-click button, and change the appropriate setting(s) in the panels of the **Text Editor** tab located above the drawing window (see Figure 4.84). To end the command, move the cursor outside the text box and press the left-click button on the mouse.

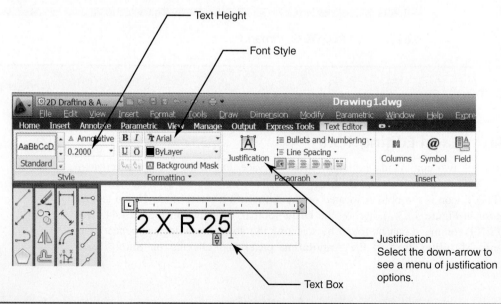

4.84 The **Multiline Text** Box and **Text Editor** Panel

DTEXT COMMAND

To start the command select on the down arrow located below the words **Multiline Text** in the **Annotation** panel and select **Single Line,** as shown in Figure 4.83(b), or type **DTEXT** or **TEXT** and press **<Enter>.** You will be prompted to select the text's start point, height, and rotation angle(these prompts appear in the dynamic prompts next to the cursor and on the command line. When you have defined all three text specifications, a cursor will appear in the drawing window. At the cursor, you can type the desired text. When you are finished entering the text you can end the command by pressing **<Enter>** twice, or you can continue to place text at a different location in the drawing window by left-clicking in the new location and entering text at the cursor.

STEP by **STEP**

NOTE

Unlike text placed with the **Multiline Text** command, it is not possible to edit the properties of **Single Line** text with the **Text Editor.**

EDITING MULTILINE TEXT

1. Use the mouse's left-click button to double-click on the annotation to be edited, or type **ED** and press **<Enter>** and select the text to be edited.

2. When the **Text Editor** box appears, highlight the text to be edited with the mouse's left-click button (by holding down the left-click button you can "swipe" the text to be edited), and make the desired changes. You can also change the setting(s) in the **Text Editor** (see Figure 4.84). When you completed the edit(s), move the cursor outside the text box and press the left-click button of the mouse.

STEP by **STEP**

> **NOTE**
>
> One advantage of **DTEXT** (or **Single Line Text**) over **Multiline Text** is that the former can be used to place text in multiple locations in the drawing window without having to restart the command each time. The properties of **DTEXT** however, are more complicated to edit, since the **Text Editor** does not work with **DTEXT**.

EDITING SINGLE-LINE TEXT

1 Use the mouse's left-click button to double-click on the annotation to be edited, or type **ED** and press **<Enter>** and select the text to be edited.

2 When the **Text Editor** box appears, move the cursor into the box and highlight the text to be edited with the mouse's left-click button, and enter the changes to the text (see Figure 4.85a). When you have completed the edit(s), left-click the mouse on a point located anywhere outside the text box and press **<Enter>** or **<Esc>**.

3 To edit the height, rotation, or style of text placed with **DTEXT**, select the text by left-clicking on it, then right-click the mouse and select **Properties** from the shortcut menu that appears. This will open the **Properties** palette (see Figure 4.85b). The selected text's properties can be changed by editing the values in the windows of the palette. Close the **Properties** palette when you have completed the desired edits by picking the **X** in the upper-left corner of the palette and press **<Esc>** to exit the command.

R. 25

4.85(a)   **Single Line Text Edit** Box

STEP by STEP

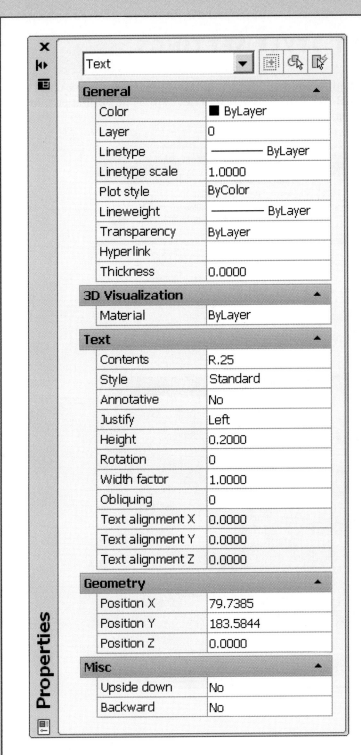

Properties

Text		
General		▲
Color	■ ByLayer	
Layer	0	
Linetype	———— ByLayer	
Linetype scale	1.0000	
Plot style	ByColor	
Lineweight	———— ByLayer	
Transparency	ByLayer	
Hyperlink		
Thickness	0.0000	
3D Visualization		▲
Material	ByLayer	
Text		▲
Contents	R.25	
Style	Standard	
Annotative	No	
Justify	Left	
Height	0.2000	
Rotation	0	
Width factor	1.0000	
Obliquing	0	
Text alignment X	0.0000	
Text alignment Y	0.0000	
Text alignment Z	0.0000	
Geometry		▲
Position X	79.7385	
Position Y	183.5844	
Position Z	0.0000	
Misc		▲
Upside down	No	
Backward	No	

4.85(b) **Properties Palette** Displaying the Properties of the Single Line Text Shown in Figure 4.85(b)

Controlling Text Style

The characteristics of text used in a drawing, such as font name, height, width factor, and oblique angle, are determined by the values set in the **Text Style** dialog box. You can choose to default to the settings of the **Standard** style, edit the **Standard** style, or create a new *text style.*

CHANGING TEXT STYLE SETTINGS

1 Left-click on the down arrow to the right of the word **Annotation** in the **Annotation** panel of the **Home** tab of the ribbon and select the **Text Style** icon as shown in Figure 4.86, or pick **Text Style . . .** from the **Format** pull-down menu of the menu bar. The **Text Style** dialog box will open, as shown in Figure 4.87.

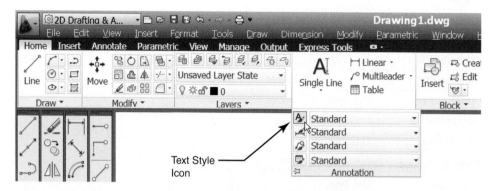

4.86   Location of the **Text Style** Icon in the **Annotation** Panel

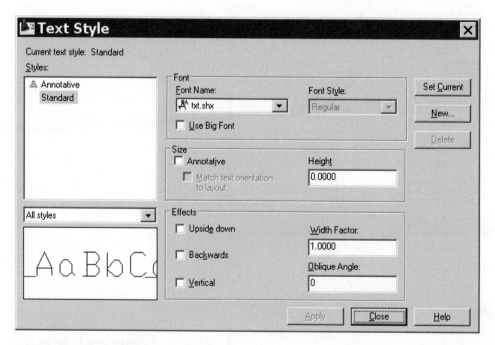

4.87   Text Style Dialog Box

2 Select the **Standard** style name in the **Styles** window or select the **New . . .** button if you wish to create a new text style.

3 To change the font, left-click the down arrow in the **Font Name** window (the default font name is **txt.shx**), and select the desired font from the list of font styles (see Figure 4.88). For mechanical drawings, a Gothic font, such as Arial, is appropriate. For architectural drawings, an architectural font, such as Stylus BT or City Blueprint, may be appropriate. The value for the height, width factor, and oblique angle can also be changed by editing the values in the appropriate window of the **Text Style** dialog box. After making the desired edits to the text style, select **Apply**. Select the **Set Current** button to set the new style as the current text style for the drawing. The new text style can also be assigned as the text used for dimensions by changing the **Text style** setting in the **Text** tab of the **Dimension Style Manager.**

┌─ **TIP** ───┐

If a desired font cannot be located in the drop-down list in the **Font Name**
window of the **Text Style** dialog box (see Figure 4.88) the organization's
computer systems administrator may need to install it. When creating a new text
style, it is best to leave the text height set to **0.0000**; otherwise, all text will
default to the height defined in the **Text Style** dialog box.

└──┘

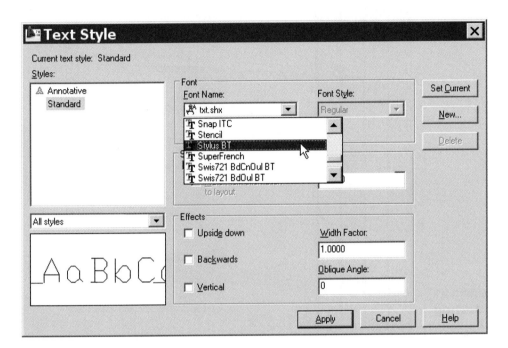

4.88   Selecting a New Font Name from the List in the **Text Style** Dialog Box

4.10 DRAFTING SETTINGS DIALOG BOX

Drafting settings are a group of drawing aids that can help you produce accurate
drawings more quickly. These drawing aids include **Grid**, **Snap**, **Polar Tracking**,
Running Object Snaps, **Dynamic Input**, **3D Object Snap**, **Quick Properties**,
and **Selection Cycling**.

Open the **Drafting Settings** dialog box by selecting **Drafting Settings** from
the **Tools** pull-down menu of the menu bar (see Figure 4.89), or by right-clicking
on the **Snap**, **Grid**, **Polar**, **Osnap**, **Otrack**, **LWT** (Show/Hide Lineweight), **QP**
(Quick Properties), or **SC** (Selection Cycling) button located on the status bar and
selecting **Settings**.

As you can see in Figure 4.90, the **Drafting Settings** dialog box has seven tabs
along its top edge, but this chapter focuses on four tabs: **Snap and Grid**, **Polar
Tracking**, **Object Snap**, and **Dynamic Input**.

Snap and Grid Tab

Grid is a drawing aid that displays a rectangular pattern of dots or lines in the drawing window. The spacing for the grid is defined in the **Grid X spacing** and **Grid Y
spacing** windows of the **Snap and Grid** tab (see Figure 4.91). The grid can be turned

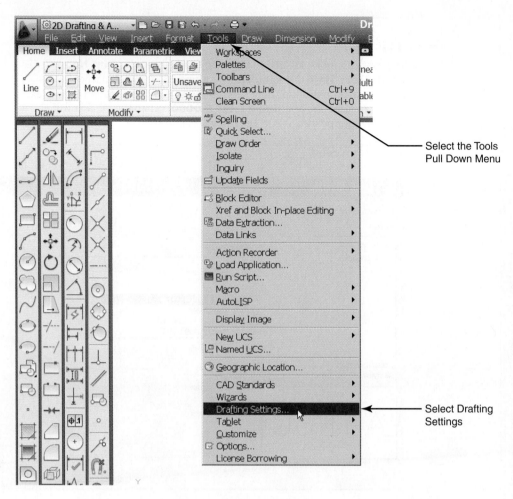

Select the Tools
Pull Down Menu

Select Drafting
Settings

4.89 Opening the
Drafting Settings
Dialog Box

Snap
and Grid
Tab

Polar
Tracking
Tab

Object
Snap
Tab

Dynamic
Input
Tab

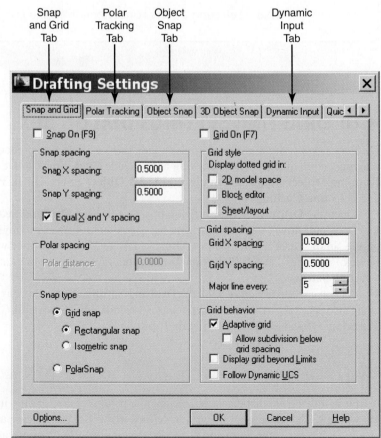

4.90 **Drafting Settings** Dialog Box

Snap On
Turns Snap mode on or off. You can also turn Snap mode on or off by clicking Snap on the status bar or by pressing <F9>.

Snap spacing
Creates a rectangular grid of snap locations that restricts cursor movement to the settings assigned in these boxes. Specifies the snap spacing in the Y and X directions. The value must be a positive real number.

Polar spacing
Polar distance sets the snap increment distance when PolarSnap is selected under Snap type. If this value is 0, the PolarSnap distance assumes the value for Snap X Spacing. The Polar distance setting is used in conjunction with polar tracking and/or object snap tracking. If neither tracking feature is enabled, the Polar distance setting has no effect.

Grid On
Turns the grid on or off. You can also turn Grid mode on or off by clicking Grid on the status bar or by pressing <F7>.

Grid spacing
Controls the display of a grid that reflects the drawing's limits. Specifies the grid spacing in the X and Y directions.

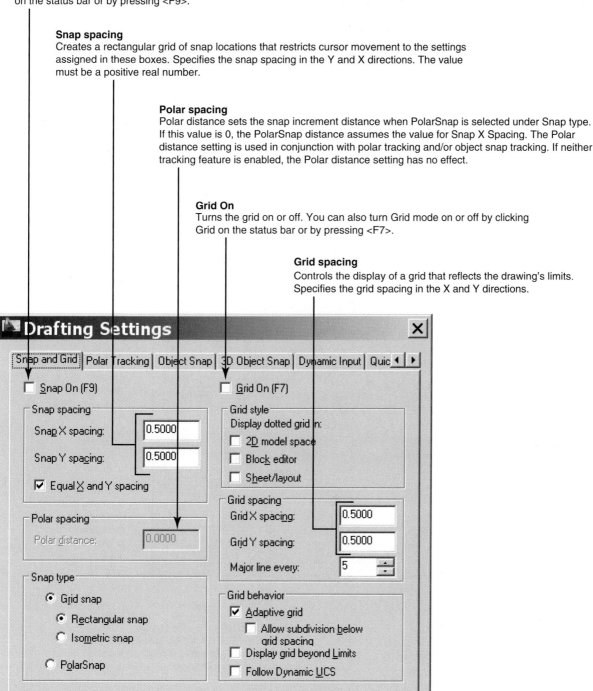

4.91 Snap and Grid Tab

on by left-clicking the **Grid** button located on the status bar or by pressing the **<F7>** key. In Figure 4.92 other settings that can affect the snap and grid drawing aids are shown.

Snap is a drawing aid that restricts the cursor's movement to the increments defined in the **Snap X spacing** and **Snap Y spacing** windows of the **Snap and Grid**

Grid snap Sets the snap type to grid. When you specify points, the cursor snaps along vertical or horizontal grid points.

Rectangular Snap Sets the snap style to standard rectangular snap mode. When the snap type is set to Grid snap and Snap mode is on, the cursor snaps to a rectangular snap grid.

Adaptive Grid Limits the density of the grid when zoomed out

Allow Subdivision Below Grid Spacing Generates additional, more closely spaced grid lines when zoomed in. The frequency of these grid lines is determined by the frequency of the major grid lines.

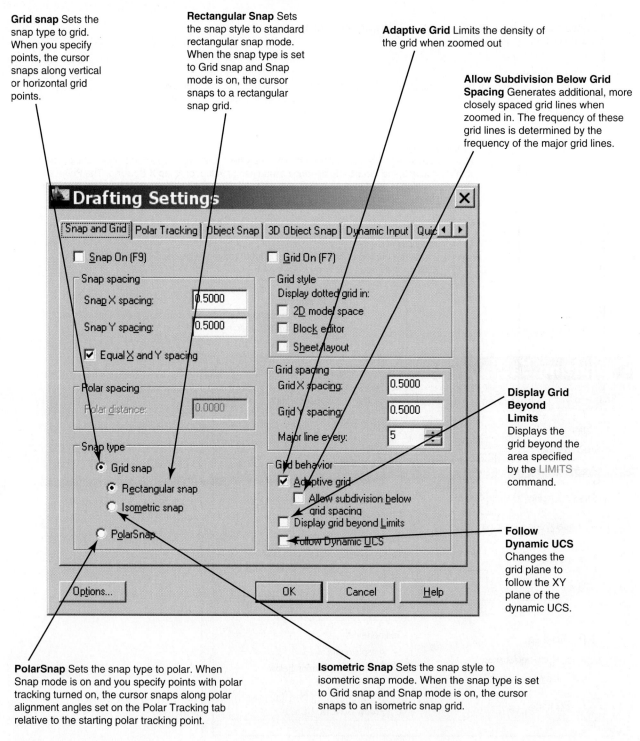

Display Grid Beyond Limits Displays the grid beyond the area specified by the LIMITS command.

Follow Dynamic UCS Changes the grid plane to follow the XY plane of the dynamic UCS.

PolarSnap Sets the snap type to polar. When Snap mode is on and you specify points with polar tracking turned on, the cursor snaps along polar alignment angles set on the Polar Tracking tab relative to the starting polar tracking point.

Isometric Snap Sets the snap style to isometric snap mode. When the snap type is set to Grid snap and Snap mode is on, the cursor snaps to an isometric snap grid.

4.92   Snap and Grid Tab

tab (see Figure 4.91). Snap increments can be set to the same increments as the grid spacing or they can be set to different values. **Snap** can be turned on by left-clicking the **Snap** button located on the status bar or by pressing the **<F9>** key.

Polar Tracking Tab

Polar tracking is a drawing aid that restricts the cursor's movement to specified increments along a polar angle. The user specifies the angle(s) by choosing an angle from the drop-down menu located next to the **Increment angle** window located

Increment Angle Sets the polar increment angle used to display polar tracking alignment paths. You can enter any angle or select a common angle of 90°, 45°, 30°, 22.5°, 18°, 15°, 10°, or 5° from the list.

Polar Tracking On Turns polar tracking on and off. You can also turn polar tracking on or off by pressing <F10>.

Track Orthogonally Only Displays only orthogonal (horizontal/vertical) object snap tracking paths for acquired object snap points when object snap tracking is on.

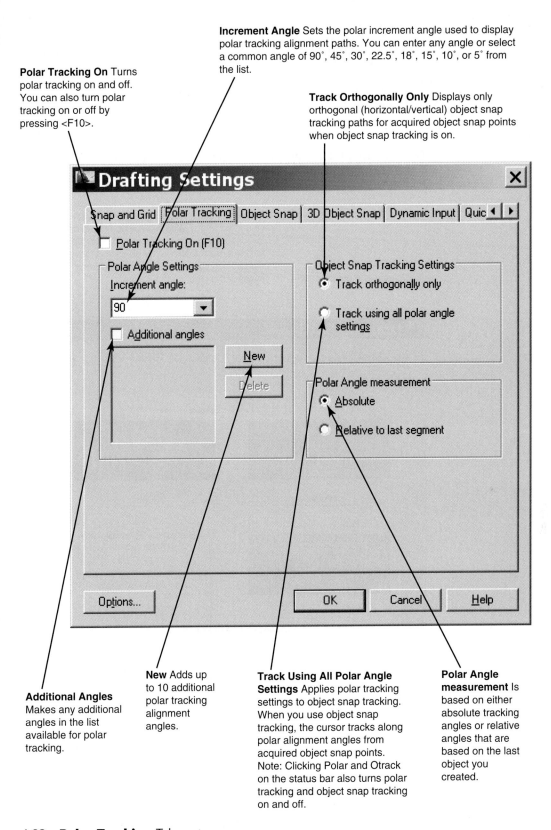

4.93 Polar Tracking Tab

Additional Angles Makes any additional angles in the list available for polar tracking.

New Adds up to 10 additional polar tracking alignment angles.

Track Using All Polar Angle Settings Applies polar tracking settings to object snap tracking. When you use object snap tracking, the cursor tracks along polar alignment angles from acquired object snap points. Note: Clicking Polar and Otrack on the status bar also turns polar tracking and object snap tracking on and off.

Polar Angle measurement Is based on either absolute tracking angles or relative angles that are based on the last object you created.

under the **Polar Tracking** tab (see Figure 4.93). Additional angles can be defined by checking the **Additional Angles** box and picking the **New** button. Polar tracking can be turned on by putting a check in the **Polar Tracking On** box of the tab, by left-clicking on the **Polar** button located on the status bar, or by pressing the <F10> key.

NOTE

The **Polar** and **Ortho** buttons of the status bar cannot both be on at the same time (when one is selected the other is automatically turned off).

Dynamic Input Tab

The **Dynamic Input** tab is divided into three panes: **Pointer Input**, **Dimension Input**, and **Dynamic Prompts** (see Figure 4.94).

Displays a dimension with tooltips for distance value and angle value when a command prompts for a second point or a distance. The values in the dimension tooltips change as you move the cursor. You can enter values in the tooltip instead of on the command line.

Turns pointer input on or off

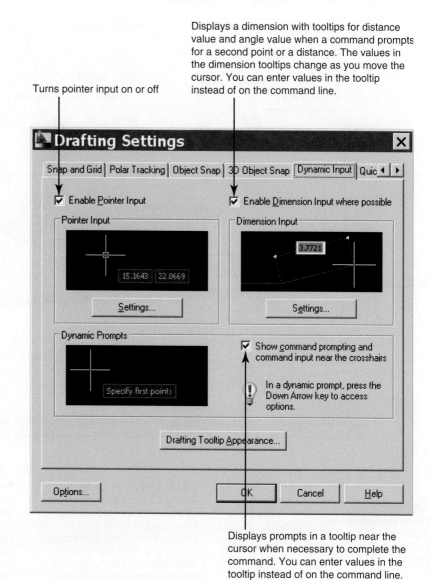

Displays prompts in a tooltip near the cursor when necessary to complete the command. You can enter values in the tooltip instead of on the command line.

4.94 Dynamic Input Tab

The Pointer Input Pane

Selecting the **Settings** button in the **Pointer Input** controls the format and visibility of the pointer input settings shown at the bottom left of Figure 4.95.

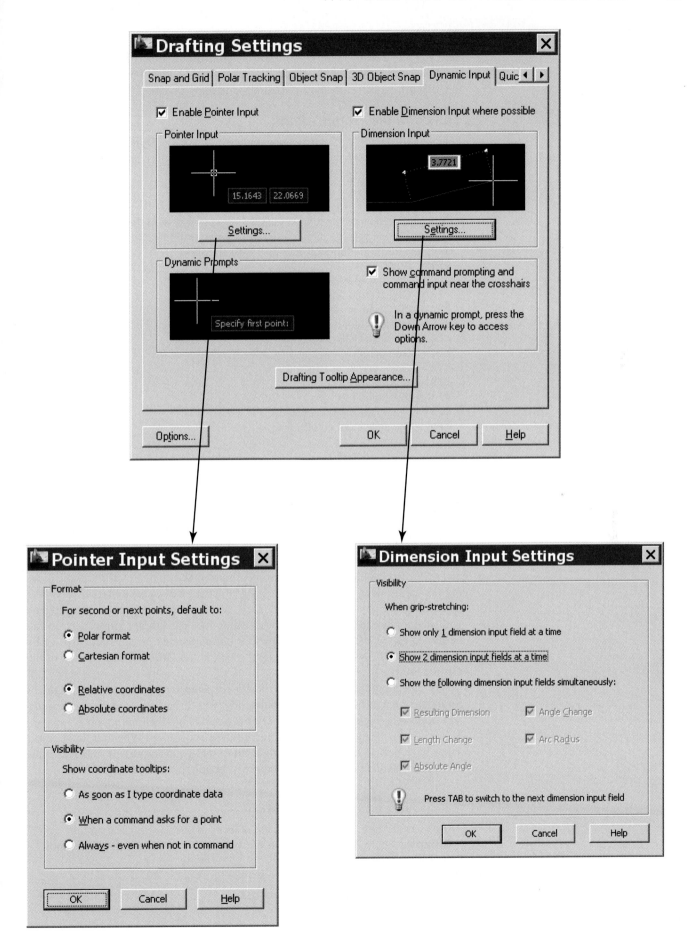

4.95 **Dynamic Input** Tab Settings

The Dimension Input Pane

Selecting the **Settings** button in the **Dimension Input** pane (Figure 4.94) controls the dimension settings shown at the bottom right of Figure 4.95 (it is recommended that this setting be set to show two dimension input fields).

The Dynamic Prompts Pane

Selecting the **Drafting Tooltip Appearance** button in the **Dynamic Prompts** pane (Figure 4.94) controls the color, size, and transparency of dynamic tooltips.

NOTE

Using the keyboard's function keys (**<F>** keys) to speed up the process of creating drawings is mentioned numerous times in this chapter. Here's a complete list of the function keys and what they do:

- **<F1>** AutoCAD Help
- **<F2>** Displays the AutoCAD text window
- **<F3>** Object snap on/off
- **<F4>** 3D Object snap on/off
- **<F5>** Isoplane toggle
- **<F6>** Dynamic UCS on/off
- **<F7>** Grid on/off
- **<F8>** Ortho on/off
- **<F9>** Snap on/off
- **<F10>** Polar on/off
- **<F11>** Osnap tracking on/off
- **<F12>** Dynamic input on/off

Object Snap Tab

Object snaps (also called *Osnaps*) are drafting aids that allow you to snap to exact points on an object, such as the *endpoint* or *midpoint* of a line, or the *center* of a circle, when an AutoCAD command has prompted you to select a point. For example, if the **Endpoint** object snap is on, and you used the **LINE** command to place the first point of a line and are being prompted to *Select next point:*, moving the cursor over, or near, the endpoint of a line will cause a marker to appear at the endpoint. If you left-click the mouse near the marked endpoint, the new line will snap to the exact endpoint of the existing line. The **Object Snap** function can be turned on by left-clicking the **OSNAP** button located on the status bar, or by pressing the **<F3>** key, or by putting a check in the **Object Snap On** box of the **Object Snap** tab.

By checking the boxes next to the *Object Snap settings* listed on the **Object Snap** tab of the **Drafting Settings** dialog box, you can set one or more *running object snaps* (see Figure 4.96). When **Object Snap** is on, the running object snap(s) will be active whenever you are prompted to select a point. When multiple object snaps have been selected in the **Object Snap** tab, you can press **<Tab>** to cycle through the available snap options before selecting the desired point.

NOTE

The quickest method to select running object snaps is to right-click on the **Osnap** button located on the status bar and select from the list of object snaps available on the pop-up menu.

4.11 OBJECT SNAP TOOLBAR

When an object snap is needed for a one-time selection (versus a running object snap), the appropriate **Osnap** icon can be selected from the **Object Snap** toolbar (see Figure 4.96). Selecting a single object snap while a command is active is referred to as using an *Osnap interrupt*. Follow the numbered steps shown in Figures 4.97 through 4.106 to see how object snaps are used to simplify drawing. Video tutorials for the commands of the **Object Snap** toolbar are located in the student data files at www.pearsondesigncentral.com. To access these tutorials, open the Pearson Design Central website and click on the *CAD Community* link, then select the *Click here to download student data files for our CAD titles* link. Next, click on the *Technical Drawing 101* link and select the *AutoCAD Tutorial Videos* zip file, then select the *Download* button and open (or save) the tutorials specified above.

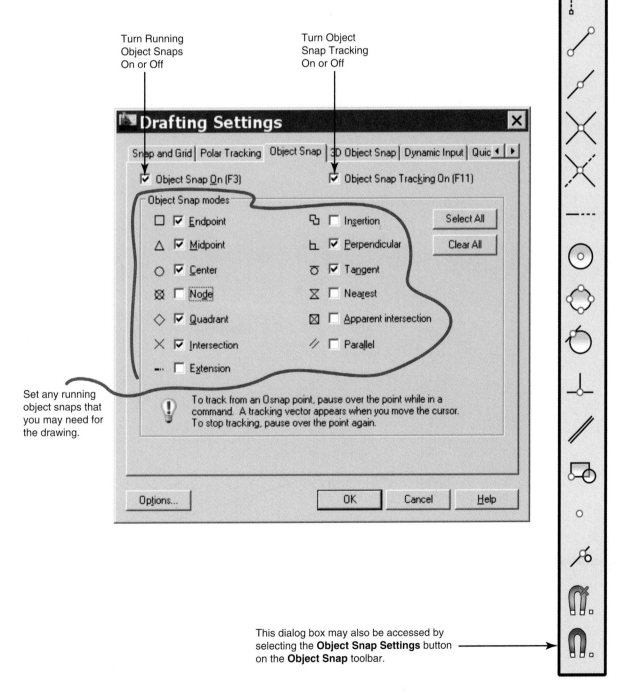

Turn Running Object Snaps On or Off

Turn Object Snap Tracking On or Off

Set any running object snaps that you may need for the drawing.

This dialog box may also be accessed by selecting the **Object Snap Settings** button on the **Object Snap** toolbar.

4.96   Object Snap Tab and Toolbar

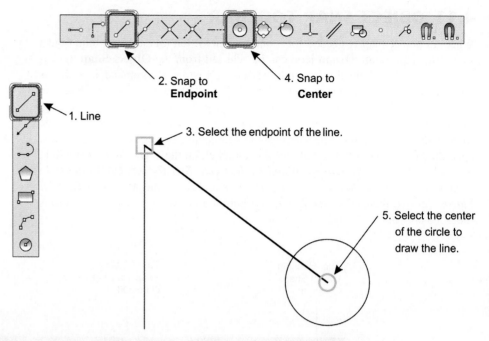

4.97 Steps in Drawing a Line from an Endpoint to a Center Point

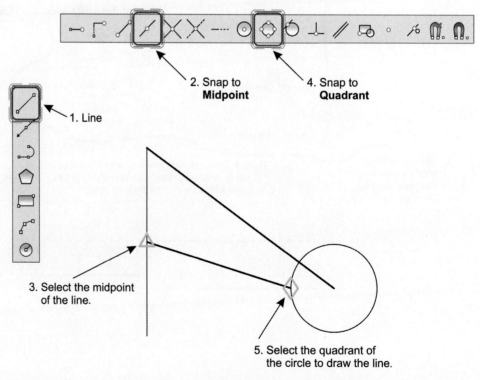

4.98 Steps in Drawing a Line from a Midpoint to a Quadrant

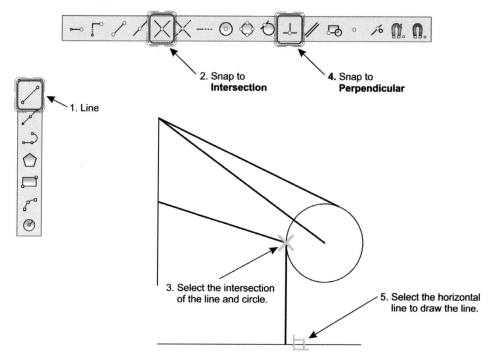

4.99 Steps in Drawing a Line from an Intersection That Is Perpendicular to Another Line

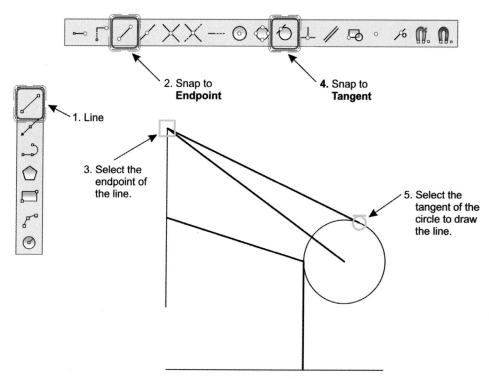

4.100 Steps in Drawing a Line from an Endpoint to a Tangency Point on a Circle

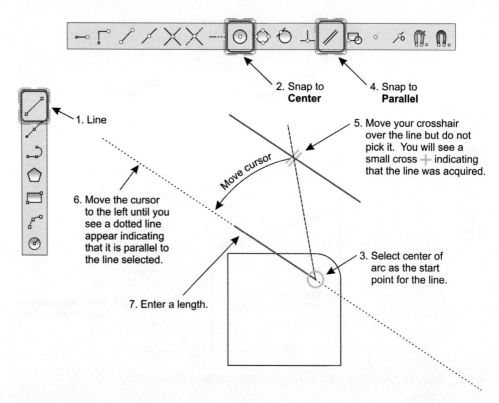

4.101 Steps in Drawing a Line Parallel to Another Line Using the **Parallel** Osnap Option

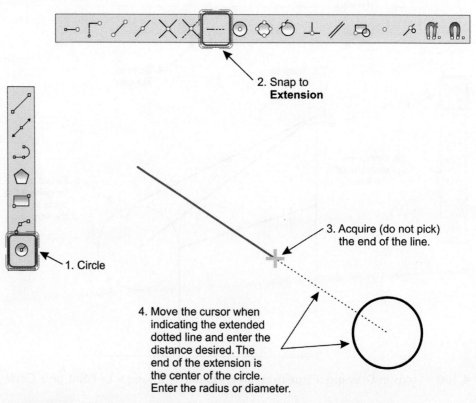

4.102 Steps in Defining the Center of a Circle Using the **Extension** Osnap Option

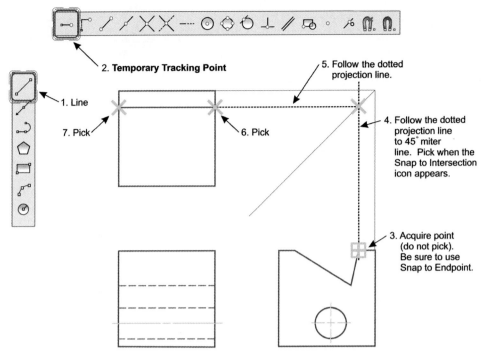

4.103 Steps in Using a Temporary Tracking Point to Project Information through a Miter Line

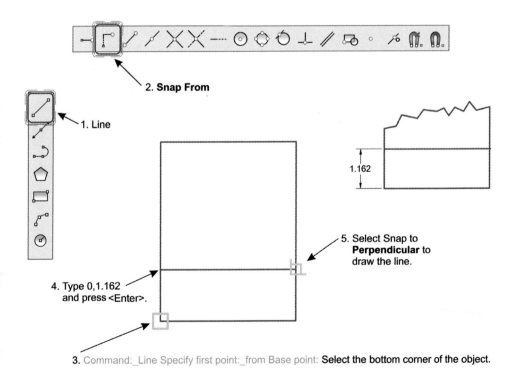

4.104 Steps in Drawing a Line Using the **Snap From** Osnap Option

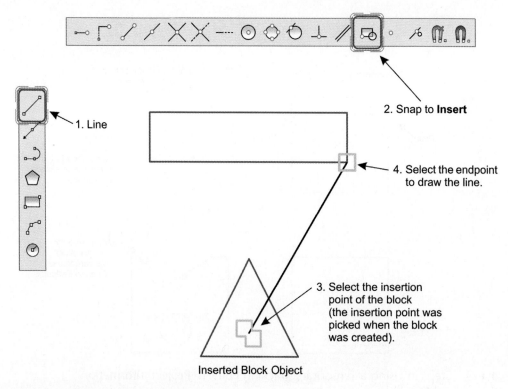

4.105 Steps in Drawing a Line from the Insertion Point of a Block Using the **Snap to Insert** Option

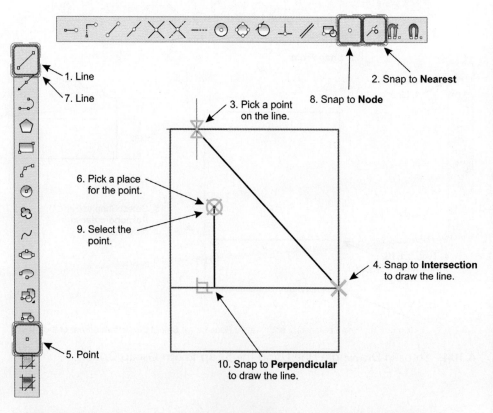

4.106 Drawing Lines Using the **Snap to Nearest** and **Snap to Node** Options

Open the **Object Snap** toolbar by right-clicking on any open toolbar and selecting the **Object Snap** toolbar with the left-click mouse button. Also, whenever you are in an AutoCAD command and have been prompted to select a point, if you hold down the **<Shift>** key and right-click you can select an object snap from the pop-up menu that appears next to the cursor.

> ┌─── **NOTE** ─────────────────────────────────────
> When using the object snap technique shown in Figure 4.103 to project a point in the side view through a miter line to the top view (or vice versa), the **Snap to Endpoint** and **Snap to Intersection** running object snaps must be turned on. The **Polar**, **Otrack**, and **Osnap** buttons found on the status bar must be turned on as well.

Exercise 4.2

Directions

1. Begin a new AutoCAD drawing (default to the **acad.dwt** template).
2. Set the upper right limit to **22,17** and the grid spacing to **1.00**. Make the following layers: **Visible**, **Hidden**, and **Center**. Assign a color to each layer and set the **Hidden** layer's linetype to **Hidden** and the **Center** layer's linetype to **Center**.
3. Set running osnaps for **Endpoint**, **Quadrant**, **Tangent**, **Perpendicular**, and **Intersection**.
4. Draw the front, top, and right-side views of the object shown in Figure 4.107(a). Begin the views at the absolute coordinates shown in Figure 4.107(a). Count the grids to determine the size of the object's features.
5. Save the drawing as Figure 4.107(a).
6. Repeat the preceding directions and draw the front, top, and right-side views of the objects shown in Figures 4.107(b) and 4.107(c). Save the drawings as Figure 4.107(b) and Figure 4.107(c), respectively.

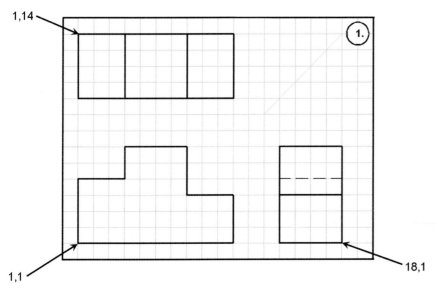

4.107(a) Exercise 4.2

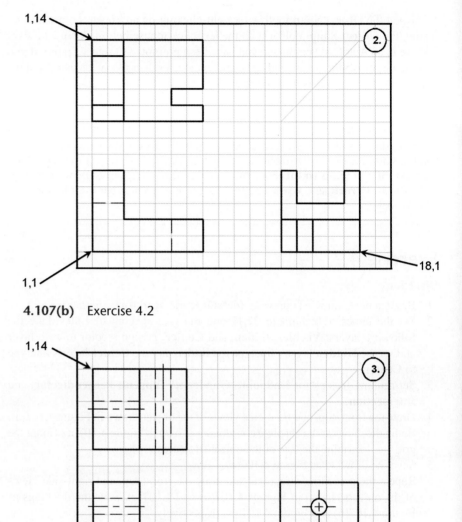

4.107(b) Exercise 4.2

4.107(c) Exercise 4.2

4.12 PROPERTIES COMMAND

The **PROPERTIES** command is used to display, or change, the *properties* of an object or group of objects, such as color, lineweight, layer, linetype, and linetype scale. This is a very useful feature of AutoCAD. Begin this command by choosing the arrow next to **Properties** at the bottom of the **Properties** panel of the **Home** tab of the ribbon (see Figure 4.108a), or by selecting the **Properties** icon from the **Palettes** panel of the **View** tab of the ribbon (see Figure 4.108b). Next, select an object in the drawing window and a **Properties** palette will open that displays the object's properties. In the example in Figure 4.109, the circle has been selected, and its properties are displayed in the **Properties** palette.

To change the properties of the circle, select the field in the palette next to the property to be changed. For example, the circle shown in Figure 4.109 is on the **VISIBLE** layer. Clicking on the field next to the **Layer** property displays a list of available layers. Selecting a different layer from the list moves the circle to the selected layer. The circle's other properties, such as lineweight, or linetype scale, can be changed in a similar fashion. Other information about the circle, such as its

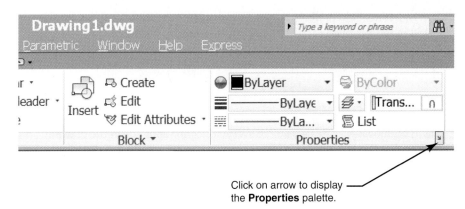

Click on arrow to display
the **Properties** palette.

4.108(a) Opening the **Properties** Palette from the **Home** Tab

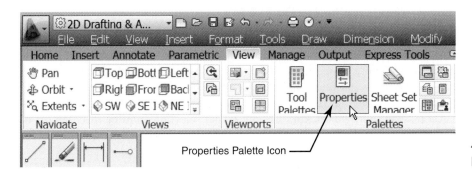

Properties Palette Icon

4.108(b) Opening the **Properties** Palette from the **View** Tab

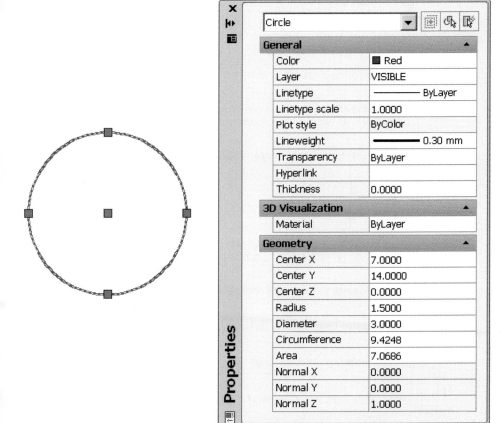

4.109 Properties Dialog Box Displaying the Properties of a Circle

diameter, radius, circumference, area, and center location, can be located or changed in the **Properties** palette under the **Geometry** heading.

To close the **Properties** palette, left-click the **X** in the upper left corner of the palette.

JOB SKILLS

Changing the linetype scale value of every noncontinuous line in the drawing by changing the **LTS** value to a larger or smaller value was discussed earlier in this chapter. Sometimes you may want to change the linetype scale of only one line. To do this, select the line, right-click, pick **Properties,** and change the **Linetype scale** value in the **Properties** palette.

4.13 INQUIRY TOOLBAR

The commands on the **Inquiry** toolbar are used to display information about Auto-CAD entities, such as the distance between two points, the coordinates of a single point, the area of a closed figure like a rectangle or circle, or the volume of a 3D object. The icons and functions of the commands on this toolbar are identified in Figure 4.110. Open the **Inquiry** toolbar by placing the cursor on any open Auto-CAD toolbar and right-clicking the mouse and selecting **Inquiry** from the list of toolbars.

NOTE

Many of the *Inquiry commands* can be accessed by picking on the down arrow under the word **Measure** located on the **Utilities** panel of the **Home** tab of the ribbon.

Select the down arrow in the corner of the icon to see all the Inquiry commands.

Region/Mass Properties Produces information about 3D objects such as volume and center of gravity

List Produces the properties of an object

Locate Point Displays *X, Y,* and *Z* coordinates of a selected point

Distance Measures distance between two selected points

Radius Calculates the radius of an arc or circle

Angle Calculates the angle

Area Calculates the area of a selected perimeter

Volume Calculates the volume of a selected 3D object

4.110 The **Inquiry** Toolbar

4.14 PLOTTING WITH AUTOCAD 2011

Select the **PLOT** icon from the **Plot** panel of the **Output** tab of the ribbon (see Figure 4.111), and the **Plot** dialog box shown in Figure 4.112 will open.

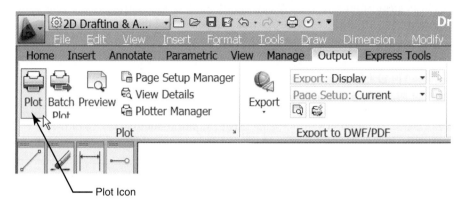

Plot Icon

4.111   Opening the Plot Command from the Output Tab

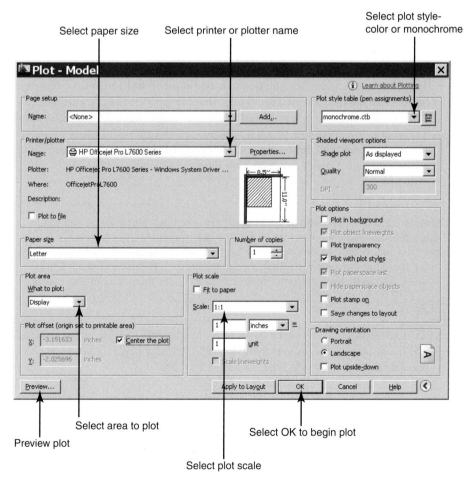

4.112   Plot Dialog Box

The options in the **Plot** dialog box allow you to do the following:

- Select the name of the printer/plotter where you want to send the plot. Pick the down arrow in the **Printer/plotter** window and select from the list of available printers and/or plotters (see Figure 4.112).

- Change the **Plot style table.** By changing the **Plot style table** settings, you can plot entities in a different color, lineweight, and linetype than what they appear in the drawing window. For example, entities that appear in color in the drawing window can be plotted in black by picking the down arrow in the **Plot style table** window and selecting **monochrome.ctb** from the list of available plot styles (see Figure 4.112). When you select the down arrow in the **Plot style table** window and pick **New** from the list, you are led through the prompts to define a new, custom plot style.

NOTE

Under **Plot style table**, select **acad.ctb** for color printing and plotting, or **monochrome.ctb** for black-and-white plots.

Selecting **acad.ctb** from the plot style list plots entities in the color they are assigned in the drawing.

- Select the paper size. Pick the down arrow in the **Paper size** window and select from the list of available paper sizes.

NOTE

Paper size is limited to the capabilities of the printer/plotter selected in the **Printer/Plotter** window (see Figure 4.112).

- Define the plot area. Pick the down arrow in the **What to plot** window and select from the list of available choices. **Display** prints the image currently visible in the drawing window, **Extents** prints to the extents of all entities placed in the drawing, **Window** prints a window defined by you, **Limits** prints the area defined by the **Limits** of the drawing, and **Layout** prints the page setup associated with a paper space tab (see Figure 4.112).

NOTE

Limits is available as a **What to Plot** option when printing from model space (basically, the area encompassed within the drawing limits), but **Layout** is a printing option only if printing from a **Layout** tab in paper space. **Layout** tabs and paper space are concepts that are usually presented in intermediate CAD courses, although your instructor may choose to cover them later in this course.

- Define the plot scale. Pick the down arrow in the **Scale** window and select from the list of plot scales, or select **Custom** and define a new plot scale, or check the **Fit to paper** box (see Figure 4.112).

TIP

Fit to paper is a **Plot scale** option, but the object will not be printed to an exact scale if this is selected, as the plot will probably be scaled up or down to fit the paper size. Select the down arrow in the window next to **Scale** to see a list of available plot scales.

- Preview the plot before printing. By previewing the plot before plotting, you can see whether settings you have chosen will result in the desired plot (see Figure 4.112).

When you have defined the preceding settings and you have previewed the plot to check for errors, select the **OK** button to send the plot to the printer or plotter.

4.15 CREATING A PAGE SETUP FOR PLOTTING

Creating a page setup for an AutoCAD project streamlines the process of plotting drawings. A *page setup* is a named set of predefined print/plot settings. When you wish to plot the project, you simply select the name of the page setup from the list in the **Plot** dialog box rather than redefining the plot settings each time.

STEPS IN CREATING A PAGE SETUP

Follow the steps below to create a page setup for a plot named **Cottage.**

1 Select the **Page Setup Manager** from the **Plot** panel of the **Output** tab of the ribbon. The **Page Setup Manager** dialog box opens, as shown in Figure 4.113.

4.113   **Page Setup Manager** Dialog Box

2 Select the **New. . .** button from the **Page Setup Manager** dialog box shown in Figure 4.113.

3 When the **New Page Setup** dialog box opens, type **Cottage** into the **New page setup name** window as shown in Figure 4.114 and click **OK**.

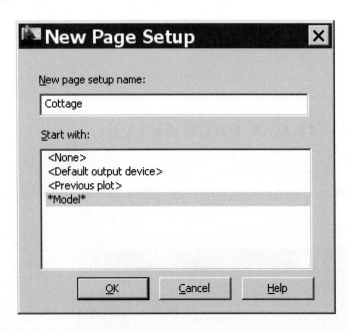

4.114   New Page Setup Dialog Box

4 When the **Page Setup** dialog box opens, enter the printer settings shown in Figure 4.115 (except select the printer associated with your computer).

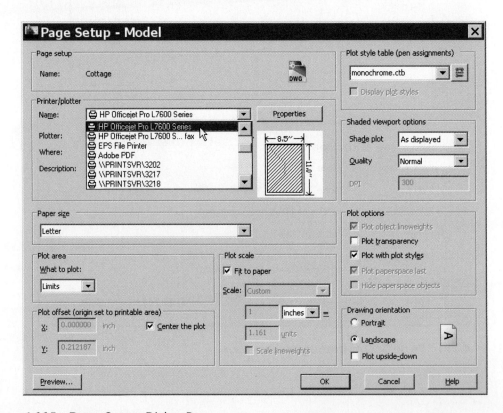

4.115   Page Setup Dialog Box

When the desired settings are in place, click **OK** to return to the **Page Setup Manager** dialog box, then click **Close** to return to your drawing.

5 To plot the page setup, select the **Plot** icon from the **Plot** panel of the **Output** tab of the ribbon (see Figure 4.111), and when the **Plot** dialog box opens, select the down arrow in the **Page Setup** window and select **Cottage** from the list, as shown in Figure 4.116. Click **OK** to send the drawing file to the plotter or printer.

TIP

It is sometimes necessary to adjust the settings in the **Page Setup** dialog box through trial and error until the desired plot settings are in place. Selecting the **Preview. . .** button allows you to see the settings and adjust accordingly.

Previewing the plot before selecting **OK** allows you to confirm that the settings in the page setup will result in the desired plot.

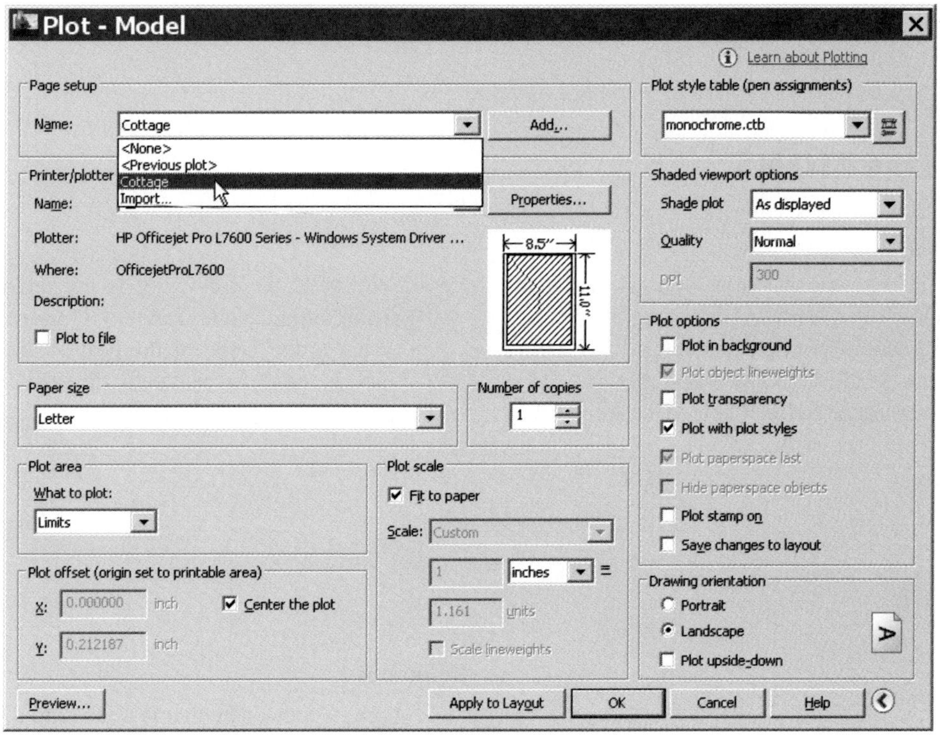

4.116 **Plot** Dialog Box

KEY WORDS

Absolute Coordinates

Cartesian Coordinate System

Draw Commands

Drawing Limits

Drawing Units

Inquiry Commands

Layers

Modify Commands

Object Snap Settings

Polar Coordinates

Properties

Relative Coordinates

Running Object Snaps

Text Style

User Coordinate System

CHAPTER SUMMARY

With each new software release, computer-aided design tools become more powerful, allowing CAD users to accomplish higher-level design and drafting tasks. However, as CAD software evolves, it also drives changes in how technical drawings are created, viewed, shared, and managed. Persons employed in the CAD field must be committed to the principle of life-long learning to keep up with the dynamic technology of this field.

REVIEW QUESTIONS

Short Answer

1. How is the point with coordinates 0,0 represented in the graphics window of an AutoCAD drawing?
2. What is the direction (North, South, East, or West) of the default **Base Angle** setting in AutoCAD?
3. What setting should be defined before the limits of an AutoCAD drawing are set?
4. Which of the following is *not* an AutoCAD **Object Snap** setting: **Node, Tangent, Quadrant,** or **Startpoint**?
5. What is the name of the tool on the **Inquiry** toolbar that is used to calculate the distance between two points?

Matching

Column A

a. **POLYGON**

b. **CHAMFER**

c. Polar

d. **Limits**

e. Absolute

f. **SCALE**

g. **RECTANGLE**

h. **Decimal**

i. **FILLET**

j. Relative

Column B

1. A type of coordinate that is relative to 0,0
2. **MODIFY** command used to change the size of an object
3. A type of coordinate that is relative to the last point defined
4. **Units** setting commonly used in mechanical drawings
5. **MODIFY** command used to round the corners of objects
6. **DRAW** command used to create a multisided object
7. A type of coordinate defined by a length and an angle
8. AutoCAD setting that defines the size of the drawing area
9. Command that requires you to define two diagonal points
10. **MODIFY** command used to bevel the corners of objects

CHAPTER EXERCISES

Exercise 4.3: Geoquick CAD Construction

Directions

1. Open the **Daily Work Prototype** drawing located in the student data files at www.pearsondesigncentral.com. To access this drawing, open the Pearson Design Central website and click on the ***CAD Community*** link, then select the ***Click here to download student data files for our CAD titles*** link. Next, click on the ***Technical Drawing 101*** link and select the ***Prototype Drawings*** zip file, then select the ***Download*** button and open (or save) the prototype drawing specified above.

2. Use **SAVE AS** to save the drawing to your **Home** directory and rename the drawing **GEOQUIK**.

3. Set the drawing units to **Decimal** and the limits to **0,0** for the lower left corner and **24,18** for the upper right corner.

4. Use the following steps to draw the object shown in Figure 4.117.

Step 1.   Draw a **2**"-diameter circle with a center point at absolute coordinates **4,5**. Draw another **1**"-diameter circle at the same center point (see Figure 4.118). Draw a second set of concentric circles at absolute coordinates **7,6**. One circle will have a radius of **.5** and the other **.25** (see Figure 4.118).

Step 2.   From the **Draw** pull-down menu of the menu bar, select the **CIRCLE** command and the **Tangent,Tangent, Radius** option, or select the **Circle** icon from the **Draw** toolbar and type **TTR** and press **<Enter>**. When prompted for the first and second tangency points, pick on the circles in the approximate locations shown in Figure 4.119. When prompted for the radius, type **3.** Your drawing should resemble Figure 4.120 when you have completed this step.

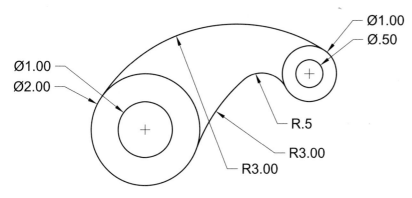

4.117   Geoquik Exercise with Dimensions

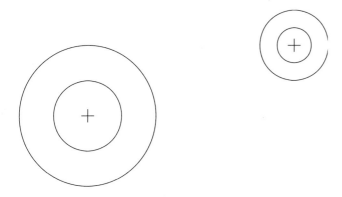

4.118   Circles Created in Step 1

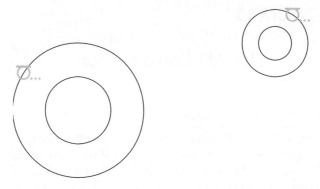

4.119 Location of Tangency Points for a Circle Drawn with the **Tangent, Tangent, Radius** Option

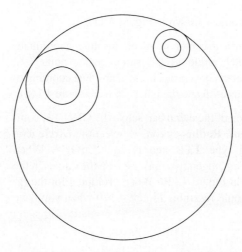

4.120 Geoquik Drawing Following Completion of Step 2

Step 3. Draw a second **3**"-diameter circle by choosing **CIRCLE** and **Tangent, Tangent, Radius** again. Pick the first and second tangent locations as shown in Figure 4.121. When prompted for the radius, type **3**. Your drawing should look like Figure 4.122 when you are finished.

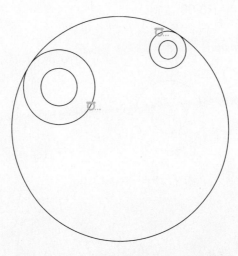

4.121 Location of Tangency Points for a Circle Drawn with the **Tangent, Tangent, Radius** Option

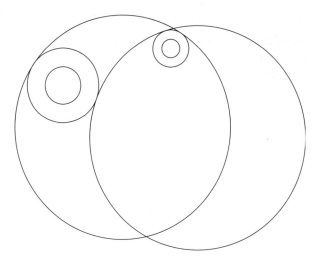

4.122 Geoquik Drawing Following Completion of Step 3

Step 4.   Choose **CIRCLE** and the **Tangent**, **Tangent**, **Radius** option again. Pick the first and second tangent locations as shown in Figure 4.123. When prompted for the radius, type **.5**. When you are finished, your drawing should look like the one in Figure 4.124.

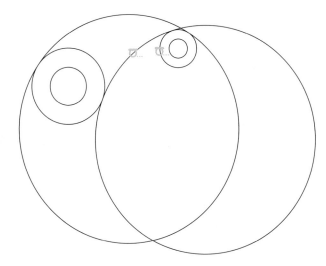

4.123   Location of Tangency Points for a Circle Drawn with the **Tangent, Tangent, Radius** Option

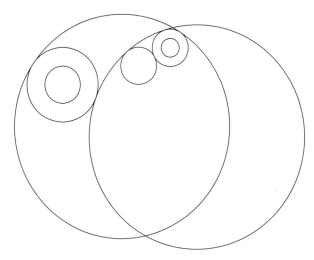

4.124   Geoquik Drawing Following Completion of Step 4

TIP

Pressing **<Enter>**
immediately after selecting
the **Trim** command causes
AutoCAD to recognize every
line as a **cutting edge**.

Step 5.   Select the **Trim** icon from the **Modify** toolbar and press **<Enter>.**

Select the circles in the locations shown in Figure 4.125 and begin to trim away the unnecessary construction lines. Continue to trim lines as shown in Figure 4.126.

After trimming all the unnecessary lines, your completed drawing should look like Figure 4.127.

Step 6.   Save and print the drawing as instructed by your teacher.

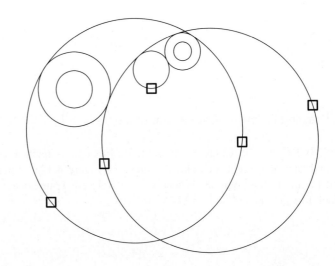

4.125 Location of Points for **TRIM** Command

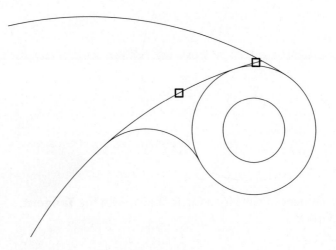

4.126 Location of Points for **TRIM** Command

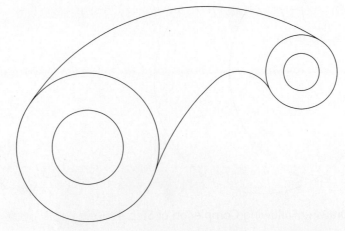

4.127 Geoquik Drawing Following Completion of Step 5

Exercise 4.4: Cam Construction

Directions

1. Select **File** and open the **GEOQUIK** drawing you created earlier.
2. Use the following steps to draw the object shown in Figure 4.128.

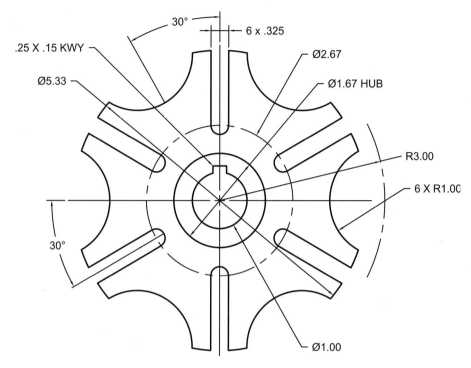

4.128 Cam

Constructing the Cam

Step 1. Draw two concentric circles with a center point at absolute coordinates **14,11**. Draw one circle with a **6"** diameter and the other with a **5.33"** diameter. Add a centerline to the circle (see Figure 4.129).

Step 2. Draw a circle **2"** in diameter in the position shown in Figure 4.130.

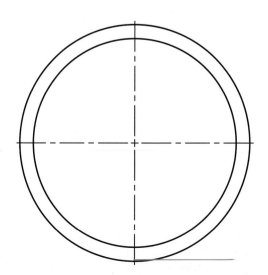

4.129 Concentric Circles

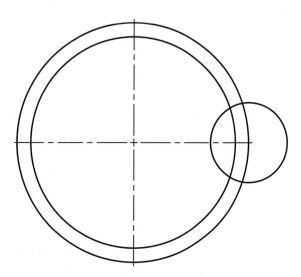

4.130 Adding 2" Circle

Step 3. Use the **ARRAY** command's **Polar** option to array **6** circles around the center of the cam to fill an angle of **360°** as shown in Figure 4.131.

Step 4. Erase the larger-diameter circle and trim the object to create the shape shown in Figure 4.132.

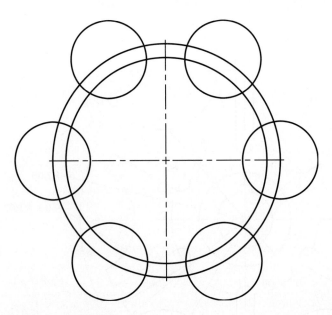

4.131   Polar Array

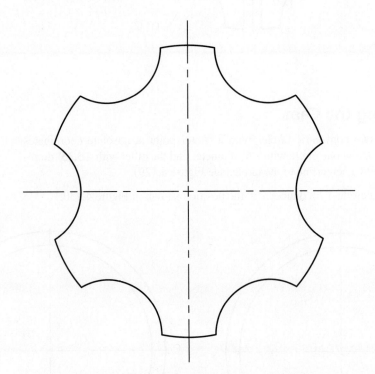

4.132   Erase And Trim

Step 5. To create the slot, first draw a circle with a diameter of **2.67"**. Using the point where the vertical centerline and this circle intersect as the center point, draw another circle with a diameter of **.325** as shown in Figure 4.133. Then, draw two lines vertical lines (turn **Ortho** on) starting from the quadrants on each side of the small circle as shown in Figure 4.133.

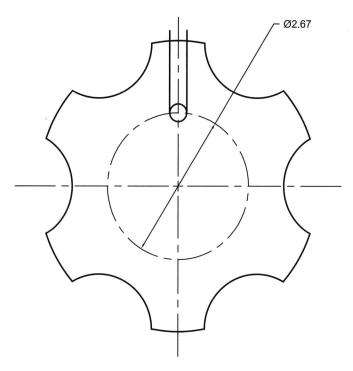

Ø2.67

4.133   Creating a Slot

Step 6.   Use **Polar Array** to array the slot created in Step 5. Pick the center of the
cam for the center of the array, and rotate **6** objects to fill an angle of **360°**,
rotating the objects as they are arrayed. Your cam drawing should look like
the object shown in Figure 4.134.

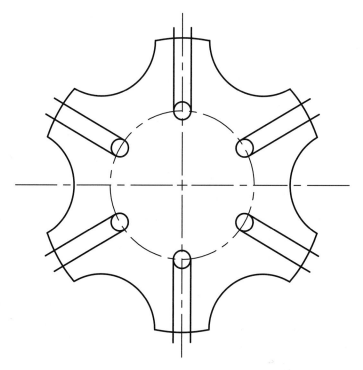

4.134   Polar Array of Slot

Step 7. Trim the slots as shown in Figure 4.135.

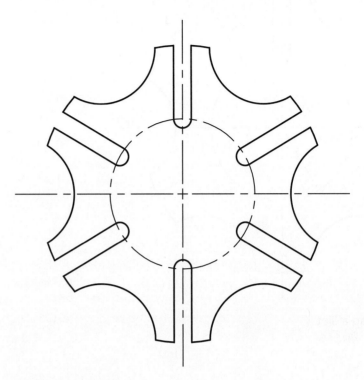

4.135 Trimmed Slots

Step 8. Add the hub and keyway to the cam. Draw two concentric circles, one with a diameter of **1.67**" and another with a diameter of **1.00**" to create the hub. Add a keyway to the top of the **1.00**" circle. The keyway is **.25**" wide and **.15**" tall. Trim the top of the **1.00** circle to open the keyway. See Figure 4.136.

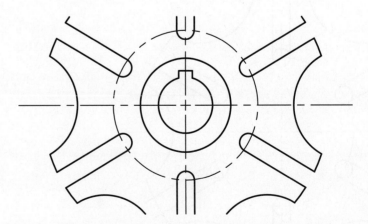

4.136 Adding the Keyway

This completes the cam construction (see Figure 4.137). Follow your instructor's directions to print the drawing. Be sure to save the drawing file before you close AutoCAD.

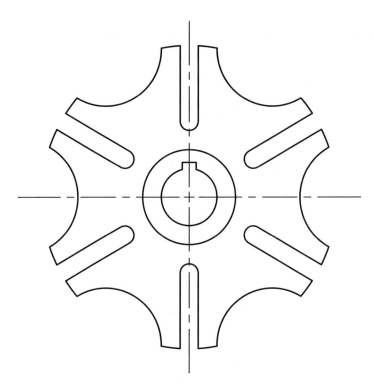

4.137   Completed Cam Drawing

CHAPTER PROJECTS

Project 4.1: Guest Cottage

In this project you will draw the floor plan of the guest cottage shown in the designer's sketch in Figure 4.138. In creating this drawing, you will be required to use many of the **Draw** and **Modify** tools that you learned about earlier in this chapter. Your instructor will guide you through this project, so do not hesitate to ask for help if you get stuck.

Directions

1. Open the **Cottage Prototype** drawing located in the student data files at **www .pearsondesigncentral.com**. To access this drawing, open the Pearson Design Central website and click on the *CAD Community* link, then select the *Click here to download student data files for our CAD titles* link. Next, click on the *Technical Drawing 101* link and select the *Prototype Drawings* zip file, then select the *Download* button and open (or save) the prototype drawing specified above.
2. Use **SAVE AS** to save the drawing to your **Home** directory and rename the drawing **GUEST COTTAGE**.
3. Set units to **Architectural** and precision to **1/16"**.

TIP

When architectural units are in effect, values will default to inches unless you enter a foot mark ('). For example, to enter the length of a line 5 feet 4 inches long, type **5'-4** (you do not need to type an inch mark after the 4 because AutoCAD defaults to inches).

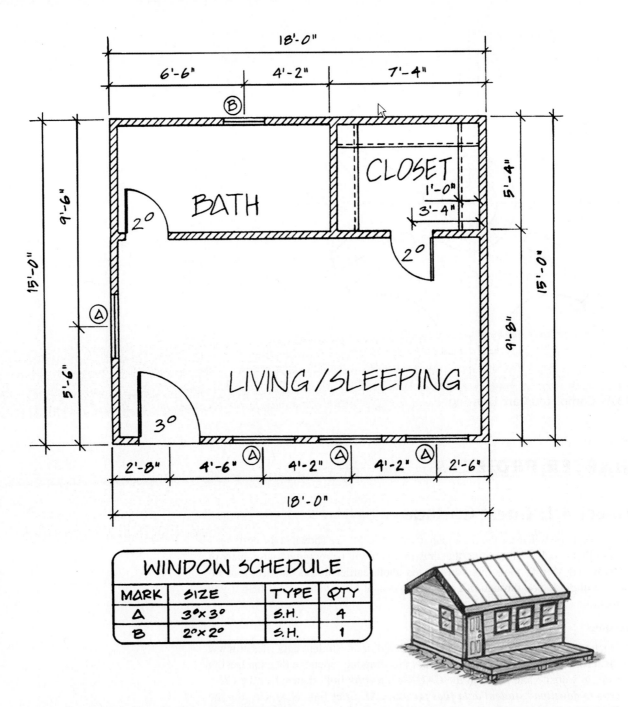

WINDOW SCHEDULE			
MARK	SIZE	TYPE	QTY
A	3⁰x3⁰	S.H.	4
B	2⁰x2⁰	S.H.	1

4.138 Designer's Sketch of the Guest Cottage

4. Set the upper right corner limits to **48',38'** and the grid to **4'**.

> **NOTE**
>
> If you neglect to include the foot mark (') when entering the drawing limits, the drawing limits for the upper right corner will default to inches and be set to **48",38"**.

5. Make the following layers: **Floor Plan, Windows, Doors, Labels, Text, Hatch, Clothes Rod,** and **Dimensions.** Assign a color to each layer and set the linetype of the Clothes Rod layer to **Dashed.**
   - In the **Text Style** dialog box, set **Stylus BT** as the font for the **Standard** text style.

- Set the following running object snaps: **Midpoint**, **Intersection**, **Endpoint**, and **Perpendicular**.
- Follow Steps 1 through 12 to create the floor plan.

Drawing the Cottage Floor Plan

Step 1.   To draw the exterior walls, set **Floor Plan** as the current layer. Use the **RECTANGLE** command to draw a rectangle **18' × 15'**. Begin the rectangle at absolute coordinates **10',12'** (see Figure 4.139). Use the **OFFSET** command to offset the rectangle **4"** to the inside. The two rectangles represent the exterior walls of the guest cottage. Explode both rectangles so that they can be edited.

4.139   Exterior Walls

Step 2.   To draw the interior walls, use the **OFFSET** command with the dimensions shown in Figure 4.140 to place the lines for the interior walls. Be careful to offset the wall to the side shown in the example.

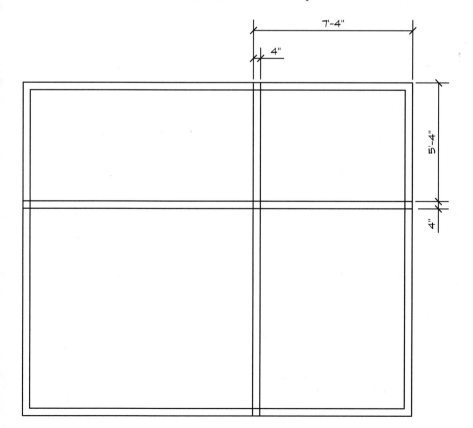

4.140   Interior Walls

Use the **TRIM** command to trim the offset lines as shown in Figure 4.141.

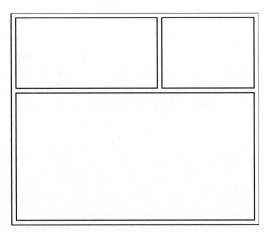

4.141 Trimmed Wall Openings

Step 3. To create the front door opening, offset the left outside wall line **2'8"** to the right to locate the center of the front door opening. Next, offset this line **1'6"** to both its right and left sides, as shown in Figure 4.142, to define the edges of an opening **3"-0"** wide.

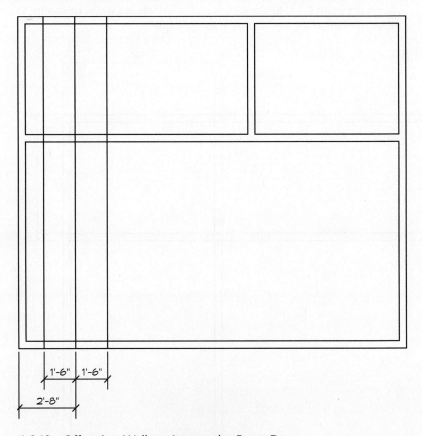

4.142 Offsetting Walls to Locate the Front Door

Trim the offset lines as needed to create the front door opening as shown in Figure 4.143.

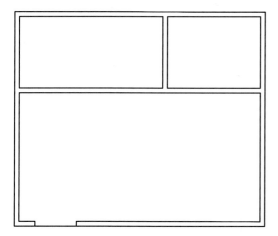

4.143   Trimming the Front Door Opening

Step 4.   To create the interior door openings, offset the walls as shown in Figure 4.144 to create the two **2'-0"** wide openings for the interior doors to the bath and closet.

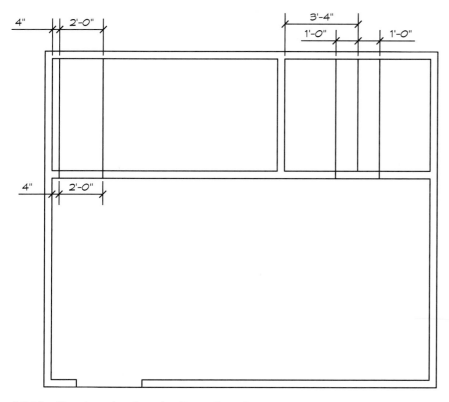

4.144   Constructing Interior Door Openings

Trim the offset lines to create the door openings as shown in Figure 4.145.

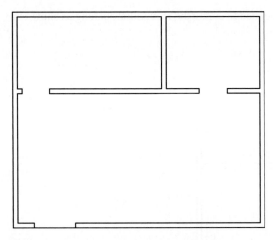

4.145   Trimming Interior Door Openings

Step 5.   To create and locate the windows, set **Windows** as the current layer. Next, offset the walls as shown in Figure 4.146(a) to locate the centers of the windows.

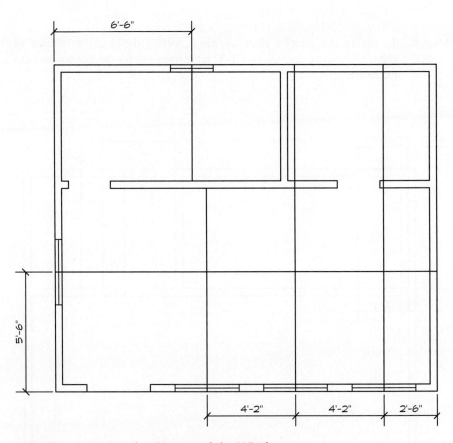

4.146(a)   Locating the Centers of the Windows

To make the windows, use the **RECTANGLE** command to draw two rectangles: one **36" × 4"**, as shown in Figure 4.146(b), and another **24" × 4"**. Draw a horizontal line through each rectangle from the midpoints of each vertical side as shown in Figures 4.146(c) and 4.146(d). Use **COPY** to make three copies of the larger window and then use the **MOVE** command to place these copies in their positions along the front wall of the cottage as in Figure 4.146(a).

4.146(b) Drawing a 36" × 4" Rectangle

4.146(c) Horizontal Line Drawn from Midpoint to Midpoint of the Vertical Sides of the Rectangle

4.146(d) 24" × 4" Window

Next, move the smaller window into position along the back wall. Finally, rotate the remaining window **90°** and move it to its place in the left side wall.

Step 6.   To create and locate the doors, set **Doors** as the current layer and use **RECTANGLE** to draw the three doors. Begin each rectangle at the corner of the door opening where the hinges would be attached (referred to as the *hinge jamb*) as shown in Figure 4.147(a) and use relative coordinates to define the door. The doors are drawn **1"** thick. For example, in Figure 4.147(a) the rectangle for the **3'-0"** front door starts at the top of the left inside corner of the door opening and then is drawn at a distance of **1"** along the X-axis and **36"** along the Y-axis. The other two interior doors are **1" × 24"** rectangles and are placed as in Figure 4.147(a).

TIP

Use **Object Snap** settings to move the window from its midpoint to the intersection of the offset line and the outside edge of the wall to facilitate the exact placement of the windows.

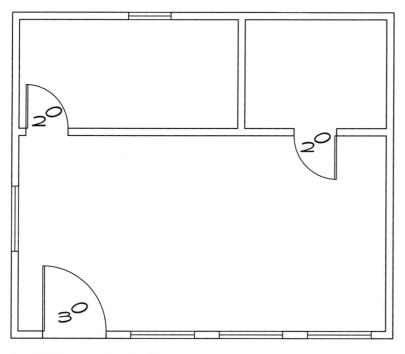

4.147(a) Creating the Doors

Use the **Start**, **Center**, **End** option of the **ARC** command to draw the door swings. For example, to draw the door swing for the front door, begin the **ARC** command and select the top corner of the door opening that is opposite the corner where the door hinge is attached as the arc's start point. Then type **C** (for center) and **<Enter>** and define the center of the arc by selecting the corner of the door opening where the door hinge is attached. Then, select the top right corner of the door to define the end of the arc. See Figure 4.147(b).

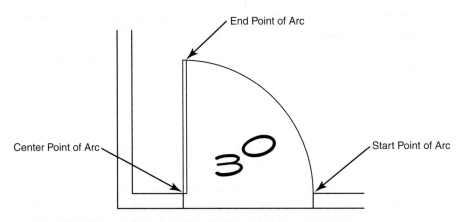

4.147(b) Drawing Door Swings with the **ARC** Command

NOTE

Because arcs are drawn counterclockwise, the order that the start, center, and end points are selected determines the orientation of the arc.

NOTE

The side of the door frame where the hinges are attached is referred to as the *hinge jamb*. The side of the door frame where the latching mechanism attaches is referred to as the *strike jamb*.

Step 7. To draw the closet shelves and clothes rods, set the **Floor Plan** layer current and add shelves to the closet by offsetting lines **12"** from the closet's inside walls (see Figure 4.148). Set the **Clothes Rod** layer current and add clothes rods to the closet by offsetting lines **10"** from the closet's inside walls (see Figure 4.148).

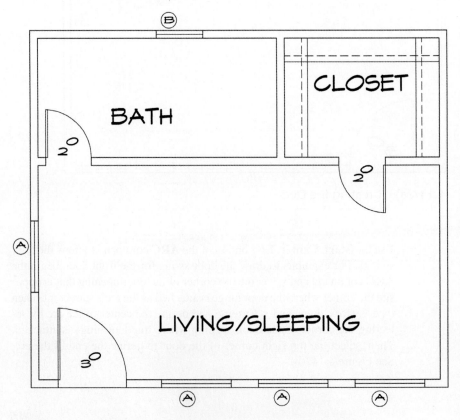

4.148 Closet Shelves and Clothes Rods

Step 8. To add room labels to the floor plan, set the **Text** layer current and use the **MTEXT** command to add the room names shown in Figure 4.148. The text height for room names should be **6"**. For door callouts, both numbers should be **4"**.

> **TIP**
> Place each of the numbers that make up the door callout as separate text entities using the **DTEXT** command. See Figure 4.83(b).

> **TIP**
> Use **Object Snap** settings to move the window from its midpoint to the intersection of the offset line and the outside edge of the wall to facilitate the exact placement of the windows.

Step 9. Window marks are used to identify each window in the floor plan. Create the window mark by drawing a circle that is **9"** in diameter and centering the letter **A** or **B** inside the circle (see Figure 4.149). Use **4"** text height for the letters. Place window marks next to each window as shown in the designer's sketch in Figure 4.138.

4.149   Window Mark

Step 10. Complete the window schedule by using **Text Edit** to change the placeholders in the schedule to the values shown in Figure 4.150. In the Window Schedule, the $3^0 \times 3^0$ label refers to a window that is **3'-0"** wide by **3'-0"** tall. The *S.H.* entries in the *TYPE* column indicate that the window type is single hung.

WINDOW SCHEDULE

MARK	SIZE	TYPE	QTY
A	$3^0 \times 3^0$	S.H.	4
B	$2^0 \times 2^0$	S.H.	1

4.150   Window Schedule

Step 11. To hatch the walls, set the **Hatch** layer current and use the **HATCH** command to place the pattern inside the walls. Select the **Net** pattern and set the scale to **10**, then use the **Pick Points** option to select inside the walls. After hatching, the plan should look like the one shown in Figure 4.151.

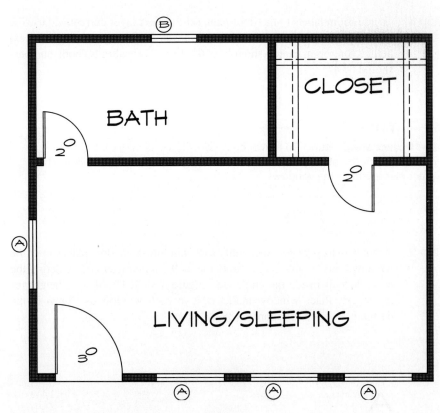

4.151 Walls with Hatch Pattern Applied

Step 12. Follow the steps presented earlier in this chapter to create a page setup for the cottage.

Plot the project by selecting the **Cottage** page setup from the **Plot** dialog box. Be sure to save the drawing file before closing AutoCAD.

Project 4.2: Bracket

Draw the front, top, and side views of the bracket shown in the designer's sketch in Figure 4.152.

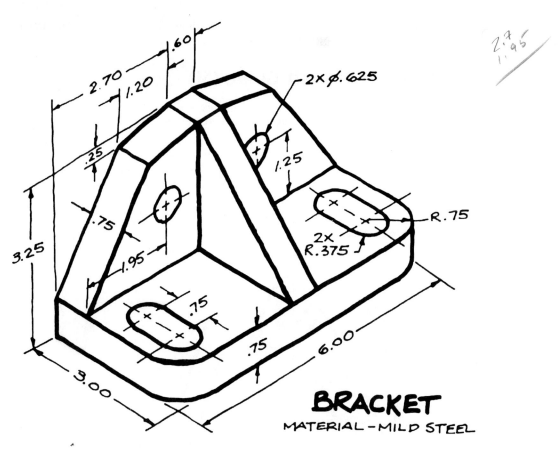

4.152 Designer's Sketch of Bracket

Directions

1. Open the **Daily Work Prototype** drawing located in the student data files at www. pearsondesigncentral.com. To access this drawing, open the Pearson Design Central website and click on the *CAD Community* link, then select the *Click here to download student data files for our CAD titles* link. Next, click on the *Technical Drawing 101* link and select the *Prototype Drawings* zip file, then select the *Download* button and open (or save) the prototype drawing specified above.

2. Use **SAVE AS** to save the drawing to your **Home** directory and rename the drawing **BRACKET**.

3. Make the drawing environment settings and create the following layers:
   a. Draw visible lines on the Visible layer.
   b. Draw hidden lines on the Hidden layer.
   c. Draw centerlines on the Center layer.
   d. Place text on the Text layer.

Drawing Environment Settings

Units:	Decimal
Units Precision:	0.000
Limits:	0,0–24,18
Text Style Font:	Arial

Layer Settings

Name	Color	Linetype	Lineweight
Visible	Red	Continuous	.50 mm
Hidden	Blue	Hidden	Default
Center	Green	Center	Default
Text	Green	Continuous	Default

Follow your instructor's directions to print the drawing. Be sure to save the drawing file before closing AutoCAD.

Project 4.3: Shaft Guide (SI)

Draw the front, top, and side views of the shaft guide shown in the designer's sketch in Figure 4.153. The units of measurement are millimeters.

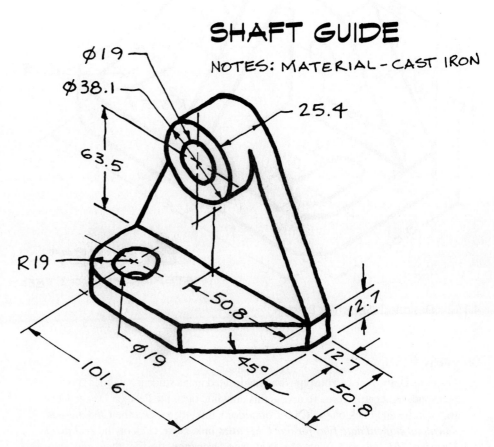

4.153 Designer's Sketch of Shaft Guide

Directions

1. Open the **Daily Work Metric Prototype** drawing located in the student data files at www.pearsondesigncentral.com. To access this drawing, open the Pearson Design Central website and click on the *CAD Community* link, then select the *Click here to download student data files for our CAD titles* link. Next, click on the *Technical Drawing 101* link and select the *Prototype Drawings* zip file, then select the *Download* button and open (or save) the prototype drawing specified above.
2. Use **SAVE AS** to save the drawing to your **Home** directory and rename the drawing **SHAFT GUIDE**.
3. Make the drawing environment settings and create the following layers:
   a. Draw visible lines on the Visiblelayer.
   b. Draw hidden lines on the Hidden layer.
   c. Draw centerlines on the Center layer.
   d. Place text on the Text layer.
4. Set **LTSCALE** to **25.4.**

— **NOTE** —

If dashes don't appear in noncontinuous lines with the **LTSCALE** set to 25.4, experiment with a smaller value until the dashes appear.

Drawing Environment Settings

Units:	Decimal
Units Precision:	0.0
Limits:	0,0–594,420 (Metric A2)
Text Style Font:	Arial

Layer Settings

Name	Color	Linetype	Lineweight
Visible	Red	Continuous	.50 mm
Hidden	Blue	Hidden	Default
Center	Green	Center	Default
Text	Green	Continuous	Default

Follow your instructor's directions to print the drawing. Be sure to save the drawing file before closing AutoCAD.

Project 4.4: Tool Holder

Draw the front, top, and side views of the tool holder shown in the designer's sketch in Figure 4.154.

Directions

1. Open the **Daily Work Prototype** drawing located in the student data files at www.pearsondesigncentral.com. To access this drawing, open the Pearson Design Central website and click on the *CAD Community* link, then select the *Click here to download student data files for our CAD titles* link. Next, click on the *Technical Drawing 101* link and select the *Prototype Drawings* zip file, then select the *Download* button and open (or save) the prototype drawing specified above.
2. Use **SAVE AS** to save your drawing to your **Home** directory and rename the drawing **TOOL HOLDER**.

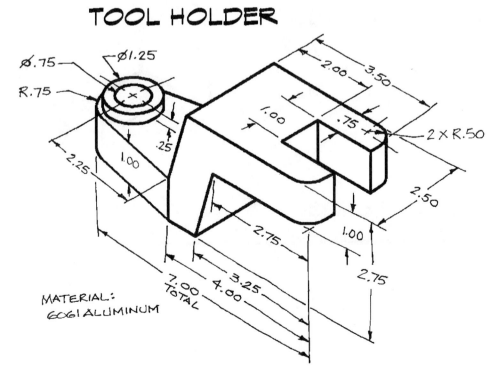

4.154 Designer's Sketch of Tool Holder

3. Make the drawing environment settings and create the following layers:
   a. Draw visible lines on the Visible layer.
   b. Draw hidden lines on the Hidden layer.
   c. Draw centerlines on the Center layer.
   d. Place text on the Text layer.

Drawing Environment Settings

Units:	Decimal
Units Precision:	0.000
Limits:	0,0–24,18
Text Style Font:	Arial

Layer Settings

Name	Color	Linetype	Lineweight
Visible	Red	Continuous	.50 mm
Hidden	Blue	Hidden	Default
Center	Green	Center	Default
Text	Green	Continuous	Default

Follow your instructor's directions to print the drawing. Be sure to save the drawing file before closing AutoCAD.

Project 4.5: Tool Slide

Draw the front, top, and side views of the tool slide shown in the designer's sketch in Figure 4.155.

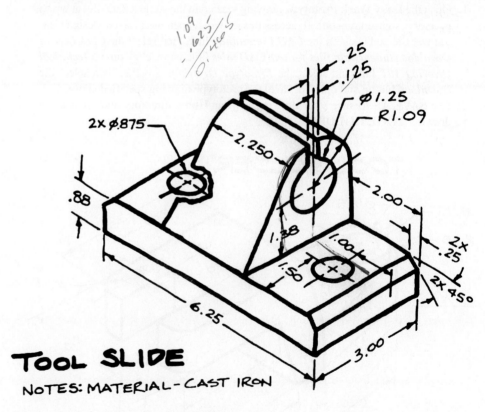

TOOL SLIDE
NOTES: MATERIAL - CAST IRON

4.155 Designer's Sketch of Tool Slide

Directions

1. Open the **Daily Work Prototype** drawing located in the student data files at **www .pearsondesigncentral.com.** To access this drawing, open the Pearson Design Central website and click on the ***CAD Community*** link, then select the ***Click here to download student data files for our CAD titles*** link. Next, click on the ***Technical Drawing 101*** link and select the ***Prototype Drawings*** zip file, then select the ***Download*** button and open (or save) the prototype drawing specified above.
2. Use **SAVE AS** to save the drawing to your **Home** directory and rename the drawing **TOOL SLIDE.**
3. Make the drawing environment settings and create the following layers:
   a. Draw visible lines on the Visible layer.
   b. Draw hidden lines on the Hidden layer.
   c. Draw centerlines on the Center layer.
   d. Place text on the Text layer.

Drawing Environment Settings

Units:	Decimal
Units Precision:	0.000
Limits:	0,0–24,18
Text Style Font:	Arial

Layer Settings

Name	Color	Linetype	Lineweight
Visible	Red	Continuous	.50 mm
Hidden	Blue	Hidden	Default
Center	Green	Center	Default
Text	Green	Continuous	Default

Follow your instructor's directions to print the drawing. Be sure to save the drawing file before closing AutoCAD.

OPTIONAL CHAPTER PROJECTS

Project 4.6: Offset Flange (SI)

Draw the front and side views of the offset flange shown in the designer's sketch in Figure 4.156. The units of measurement are millimeters.

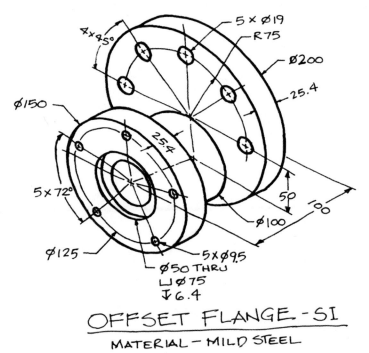

4.156   Designer's Sketch of the Offset Flange

Directions

1. Open the **Daily Work Metric Prototype** drawing located in the student data files at **www.pearsondesigncentral.com.** To access this drawing, open the Pearson Design Central website and click on the *CAD Community* link, then select the *Click here to download student data files for our CAD titles* link. Next, click on the *Technical Drawing 101* link and select the *Prototype Drawings* zip file, then select the *Download* button and open (or save) the prototype drawing specified above.

2. Use **SAVE AS** to save the drawing to your **Home** directory and rename the drawing **OFFSET FLANGE**.

3. Make the drawing environment settings and create the following layers:
   a. Draw visible lines on the Visible layer.
   b. Draw hidden lines on the Hidden layer.
   c. Draw centerlines on the Center layer.
   d. Place text on the Text layer.

4. Set **LTSCALE** to **25.4**.

NOTE

If dashes don't appear in noncontinuous lines with the **LTSCALE** set to 25.4, experiment with a smaller value until the dashes appear.

Drawing Environment Settings

Units:	Decimal
Units Precision:	0.0
Limits:	0,0–594,420 (Metric A2)
Text Style Font:	Arial

Layer Settings

Name	Color	Linetype	Lineweight
Visible	Red	Continuous	.50 mm
Hidden	Blue	Hidden	Default
Center	Green	Center	Default
Text	Green	Continuous	Default

Follow your instructor's directions to print the drawing. Be sure to save the drawing file when you close AutoCAD.

Project 4.7: Angle Stop (SI)

Draw the front, top, and side views of the angle stop shown in the designer's sketch in Figure 4.157. The units of measurement are millimeters.

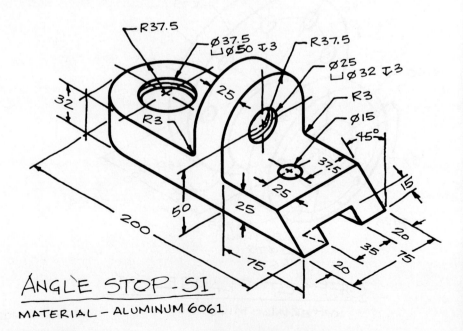

4.157 Designer's Sketch of the Angle Stop

Directions

1. Open the **Daily Work Metric Prototype** drawing located in the student data files at **www.pearsondesigncentral.com.** To access this drawing, open the Pearson Design Central website and click on the *CAD Community* link, then select the *Click here to download student data files for our CAD titles* link. Next, click on the *Technical Drawing 101* link and select the *Prototype Drawings* zip file, then select the *Download* button and open (or save) the prototype drawing specified above.
2. **SAVE AS** to your **Home** directory and rename the drawing **ANGLE STOP**.
3. Make the drawing environment settings and create the following layers:
   a. Draw visible lines on the Visible layer.
   b. Draw hidden lines on the Hidden layer.
   c. Draw centerlines on the Center layer.
   d. Place text on the Text layer.
4. Set **LTSCALE** to **25.4.**

> **── NOTE ──**
> If dashes don't appear in noncontinuous lines with the **LTSCALE** set to 25.4, experiment with a smaller value until the dashes appear.

Drawing Environment Settings		Layer Settings			
Units:	Decimal	**Name**	**Color**	**Linetype**	**Lineweight**
Units Precision:	0.0	Visible	Red	Continuous	.50 mm
Limits:	0,0–594,420 (Metric A2)	Hidden	Blue	Hidden	Default
Text Style Font:	Arial	Center	Green	Center	Default
		Text	Green	Continuous	Default

Follow your instructor's directions to print the drawing. Be sure to save the drawing file before closing AutoCAD.

Project 4.8: Swivel Stop

Draw the front, top, and side views of the swivel stop shown in the designer's sketch in Figure 4.158.

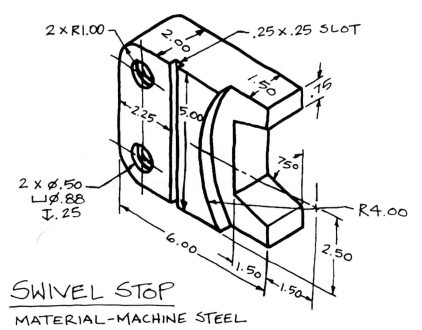

4.158 Designer's Sketch of the Swivel Stop

Directions

1. Open the **Daily Work Prototype** drawing located in the student data files at **www .pearsondesigncentral.com.** To access this drawing, open the Pearson Design Central website and click on the **CAD Community** link, then select the **Click here to download student data files for our CAD titles** link. Next, click on the **Technical Drawing 101** link and select the **Prototype Drawings** zip file, then select the **Download** button and open (or save) the prototype drawing specified above.

2. Use **SAVE AS** to save the drawing to your **Home** directory and rename the drawing **SWIVEL STOP**.

3. Make the drawing environment settings and create the following layers:
   a. Draw visible lines on the Visible layer.
   b. Draw hidden lines on the Hidden layer.
   c. Draw centerlines on the Center layer.
   d. Place text on the Text layer.

Drawing Environment Settings

Units:	Decimal
Units Precision:	0.000
Limits:	0,0–24,18
Text Style Font:	Arial

Layer Settings

Name	Color	Linetype	Lineweight
Visible	Red	Continuous	.50 mm
Hidden	Blue	Hidden	Default
Center	Green	Center	Default
Text	Green	Continuous	Default

Follow your instructor's directions to print the drawing. Be sure to save the drawing file before closing AutoCAD.

Project 4.9: Alignment Guide

Draw the front, top, and side views of the alignment guide shown in the designer's sketch in Figure 4.159.

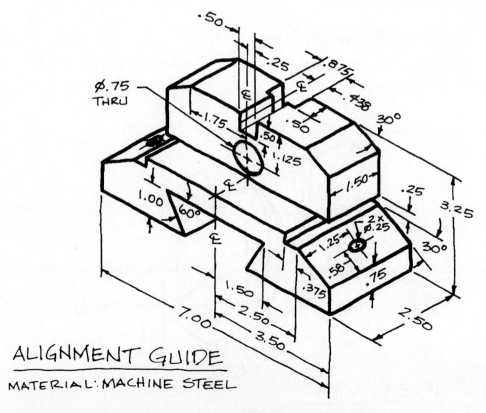

4.159 Designer's Sketch of the Alignment Guide

Directions

1. Open the **Daily Work Prototype** drawing located in the student data files at **www
   .pearsondesigncentral.com.** To access this drawing, open the Pearson Design
   Central website and click on the *CAD Community* link, then select the *Click here
   to download student data files for our CAD titles* link. Next, click on the *Technical
   Drawing 101* link and select the *Prototype Drawings* zip file, then select the
   Download button and open (or save) the prototype drawing specified above.
2. Use **SAVE AS** to save the drawing to your **Home** directory and rename the drawing **ALIGNMENT GUIDE**.
3. Make the drawing environment settings and create the following layers:
   a. Draw visible lines on the Visible layer.
   b. Draw hidden lines on the Hidden layer.
   c. Draw centerlines on the Center layer.
   d. Place text on the Text layer.

Drawing Environment Settings		Layer Settings			
Units:	Decimal	**Name**	**Color**	**Linetype**	**Lineweight**
Units Precision:	0.000	Visible	Red	Continuous	.50 mm
Limits:	0,0–24,18	Hidden	Blue	Hidden	Default
Text Style Font:	Arial	Center	Green	Center	Default
		Text	Green	Continuous	Default

Follow your instructor's directions to print the drawing. Be sure to save the drawing
file before closing AutoCAD.

Project 4.10: Flange #1105

Draw the front, top, and side views of Flange #1105 shown in the designer's sketch
in Figure 4.160.

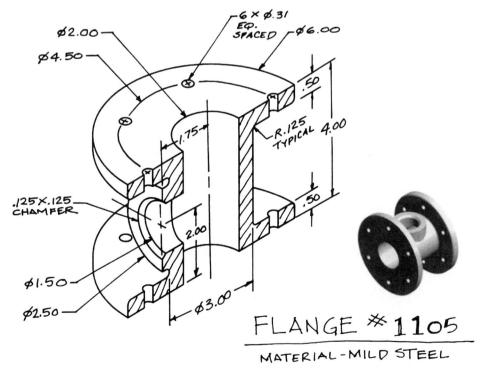

4.160 Designer's Sketch of Flange #1105

Directions

1. Open the **Daily Work Prototype** drawing located in the student data files at **www.pearsondesigncentral.com.** To access this drawing, open the Pearson Design Central website and click on the *CAD Community* link, then select the *Click here to download student data files for our CAD titles* link. Next, click on the *Technical Drawing 101* link and select the *Prototype Drawings* zip file, then select the *Download* button and open (or save) the prototype drawing specified above.

2. Use **SAVE AS** to save the drawing to your **Home** directory and rename the drawing **FLANGE 1105**.

3. Make the drawing environment settings and create the following layers:
   a. Draw visible lines on the Visible layer.
   b. Draw hidden lines on the Hidden layer.
   c. Draw centerlines on the Center layer.
   d. Place text on the Text layer.

Follow your instructor's directions to print the drawing. Be sure to save the drawing file before closing AutoCAD.

Drawing Environment Settings

Units:	Decimal
Units Precision:	0.000
Limits:	0,0–24,18
Text Style Font:	Arial

Layer Settings

Name	Color	Linetype	Lineweight
Visible	Red	Continuous	.50 mm
Hidden	Blue	Hidden	Default
Center	Green	Center	Default
Text	Green	Continuous	Default

CHAPTER FIVE

DIMENSIONING MECHANICAL DRAWINGS

OBJECTIVES

After studying the material in this chapter, you should be able to:

1. Define what dimensions are and explain the difference between size and location dimensions.

2. Describe the terminology associated with dimensioning.

3. Apply *ASME Y14.5-2009* standards when dimensioning machine parts.

4. List the dos and don'ts of dimensioning mechanical drawings.

5. Describe how dimensions are determined by designers.

6. Describe the importance of tolerances to the dimensioning process.

7. Calculate a fit between two simple parts.

8. Describe how ASME and ISO standards affect the creation of mechanical drawings.

9. Describe the role of drafters in the dimensioning process.

10. Use the commands on AutoCAD's **Dimension** toolbar.

11. Create and modify mechanical dimension styles with AutoCAD's **Dimension Style Manager**.

12. Add dimensions to mechanical engineering drawings.

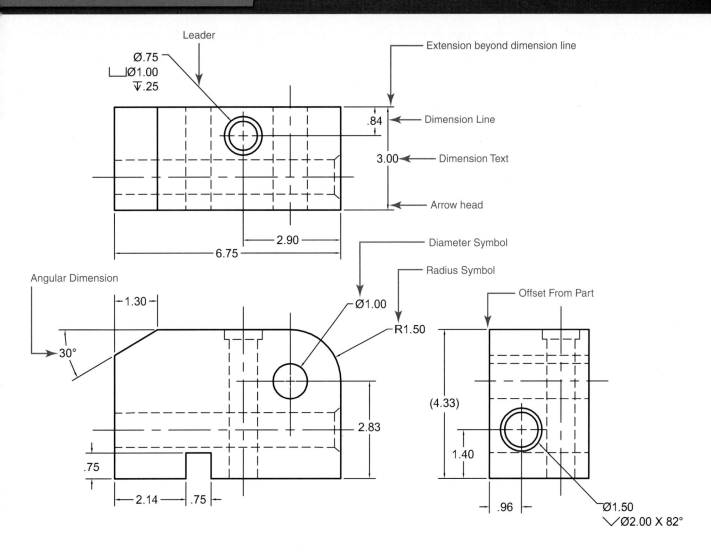

OVERVIEW

After the views necessary to describe the geometrical features of a machine part have been drawn, dimensions and notes—which fully describe the part—are added to the views. Dimensions communicate vital manufacturing information about the features of an object, for example, the diameter and location of a hole through a machine part. Designers and engineers carefully calculate the values of the dimensions included on their design inputs, and these values must be accurately reproduced, or the resulting part may not fit or function as intended. It is the drafter's responsibility to ensure that the dimensions and notes included on the designer's sketch (or other form of design input) are accurately represented on the finished mechanical drawing.

In Chapter 4 you created multiview drawings for machine parts by using the dimensional information presented on designer's sketches. The dimensions included on each sketch provided *all* the information that was needed to create the views of the part. In theory, if the designer's sketch contained 15 dimensions, all the drafter would need to dimension the part would be to add the 15 dimensions to the views of the object. However, in practice, it is a little more complicated than this, and here are several reasons why:

- The drafter must ensure that the value of each of the 15 dimensions is represented on the drawing with the exact precision (number of decimal places) shown on the designer's sketch. Each dimension must also reference the same **datum** shown on the designer's sketch. A datum is a theoretically perfect element (an edge, plane, axis, point, or other geometric feature) from which a dimension is placed. The features of finished parts are inspected by measuring the distance between the datums and the features described on the drawing. The use of datums will be presented in more detail later in this chapter.

- Before placing a dimension, the drafter must choose the view where the feature will most clearly be described by the dimension. For inexperienced drafters, this is sometimes a difficult decision to make.

- There are industry-wide guidelines for spacing and formatting of dimensions. Drafters must be familiar with these guidelines and know how to control the AutoCAD dimension settings necessary to comply with the guidelines.

Thus, there is much for beginners to learn before they can create properly dimensioned drawings. This chapter presents important information about the theory and practice of dimensioning drawings created for mechanical engineering, including the processes used by designers to calculate the values for dimensions. The dimensioning projects at the end of the chapter will give you the opportunity to create AutoCAD dimension styles that comply with industry-wide dimensioning guidelines and standards.

5.1 DIMENSIONING FUNDAMENTALS

Essentially, there are two types of dimensions: *size* and *location*. In Figure 5.1 the overall width and height of the part are size dimensions. The diameter of the hole through the part is also a size dimension, but the location of the center point of the hole is defined with location dimensions. Generally, the features of an object are located on the object with location dimensions and described with size dimensions.

Dimensional information may also include notes that provide information necessary to manufacture a machine part. For example, notes that specify the type of material from which the part is manufactured, or special processes to be performed on the part during manufacture (e.g., heat treating or polishing), are included in the field of the drawing. If the notes included on the designer's input are omitted from the technical drawing, the part may not be manufactured as the designer intended.

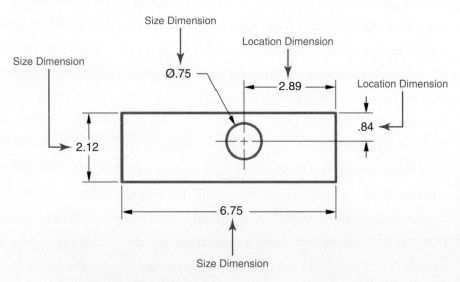

5.1   Size and Location Dimensions

Dimensioning Terminology

Figure 5.2 shows the terminology used to refer to the elements of dimensioning. Locate the *dimension* and *extension* lines noted in Figure 5.2. Extension lines extend out from the features of the object that are being dimensioned. Dimension lines are drawn between the extension lines and typically terminate in arrowheads that point to the extension lines. Dimension lines contain text that denotes the distance, or angle, between the extension lines. Now locate the *leader*, shown in Figure 5.2. Leaders point to the features of the part and are used in notations that describe the feature, like the diameter of a hole or the radius of an arc. Later in this chapter you will be required to relate the terminology shown in Figure 5.2 to the corresponding settings in AutoCAD's **Dimension Style Manager** dialog box to create an AutoCAD dimension style.

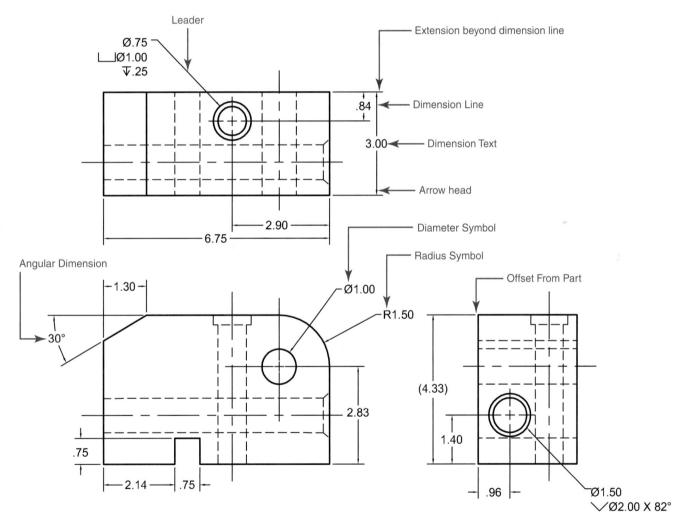

5.2   Dimensioning Terminology

Guidelines for Dimension Placement

Dimensions placed by the drafter on the multiviews of an object should be represented exactly as they are shown on the designer's sketch. For example, if a dimension on the sketch is shown at three decimal places of precision, for instance .625", it should be depicted with three decimal places on the drawing and not rounded to .63".

Dimensions should also be referenced from the same *datum* geometry indicated on the designer's sketch. This is because the designer may have designed a mating part that is intended to fit exactly in the space between the datum and the feature defined by the dimension. If the drafter references the dimension from a different datum than one used by the designer, the mating part may not fit.

Drafters are responsible for choosing the best placement of the dimensions on the views of the object. Drafters should use the following guidelines when determining the best location and placement of dimensions on a drawing:

1. Place dimensions on the *profile* view of the feature. For example, if you were trying to describe the length and angle of someone's nose, it would be best to show this information in a profile, or side, view rather than head-on. Conversely, the width of the nose and the distance between the eyes would best be described with a head-on view.
2. Avoid dimensioning to hidden lines or centerlines of hidden holes.
3. Whenever possible, group dimensions and place them between the views of the object.
4. Avoid drawing extension lines and leaders through dimension lines.
5. Avoid placing dimensions on the object unless it is absolutely necessary.

Figure 5.3 provides an example of a multiview drawing in which the preceding dimensioning guidelines were ignored. Can you find the mistakes? Compare this drawing with Figure 5.4. In Figure 5.4 the dimensions were placed following the guidelines. As a result, the dimensions in this figure are much better organized and easier to interpret than in Figure 5.3.

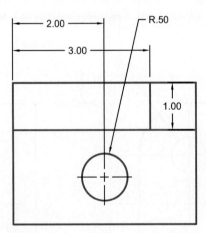

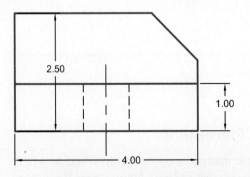
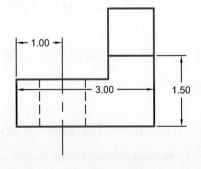

5.3   Poorly Placed Dimensions

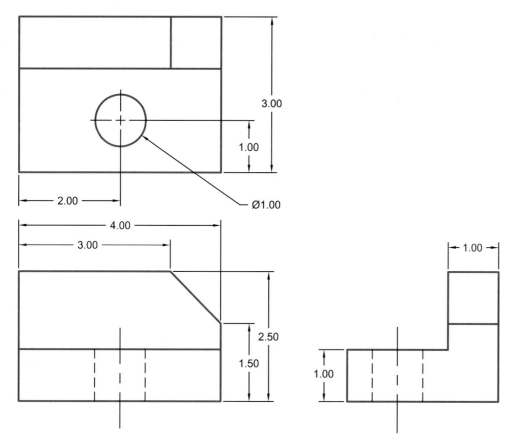

5.4   Dimensions Placed Following the Recommended Guidelines

5.2 DIMENSION STANDARDS FOR MECHANICAL DRAWINGS

Dimension standards define the rules and guidelines for the preparation of technical drawings. In the United States, the industry-wide standard for dimensioning machine parts is *ASME Y14.5-2009 Dimensioning and Tolerancing*, published by the American Society of Mechanical Engineers (ASME). According to ASME's website, "This standard establishes uniform practices for stating and interpreting dimensioning, tolerancing, and related requirements for use on engineering drawings."

ASME also publishes other standards concerning engineering drawing practices. These standards are available for purchase from the ASME. In the United States, standards of this type are created under the aegis of the *American National Standards Institute (ANSI)*. The *International Organization for Standardization (ISO)* also publishes drawing standards for the preparation of technical drawings including dimensioning. ANSI represents the United States as its delegate to ISO. The ISO dimensioning standard is very similar to the ASME dimensioning standard.

> ── **TIP** ──
> To find out more about ANSI/ASME and ISO standards, see Appendixes A and B.

Recommended Size and Spacing of Dimension Features

Figure 5.5 shows the recommended size and spacing of dimension features. The *ASME Y14.5-2009* standard specifies that the space between the part outline and the first dimension should not be less than .40" (10mm), and the spacing between succeeding parallel dimension lines should not be less than .25" (6mm). Dimension text height should not be less than .12" (3mm), and a good rule of thumb is to set the

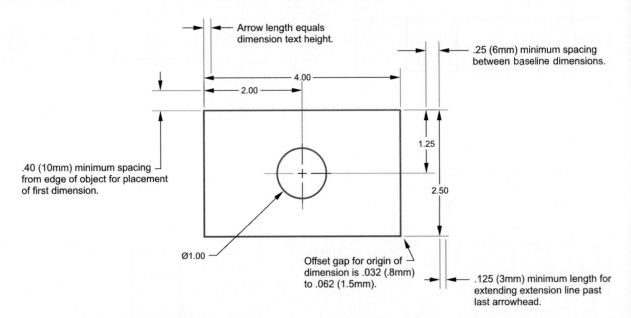

5.5   *ASME Y14.5-2009* Dimension Spacing

arrow length to match text height. There should be a short visible gap between the outline of the part and the beginning of an extension line. Usually, this gap is set to between .032" and .062" (.8 to 1.5mm). Extension lines should extend .1" to .12" (2 to 3mm) beyond the last arrowhead.

NOTE

The *ASME Y14.5* standard states that its recommendations for dimension spacing are "intended as guides only. If the drawing meets the reproduction requirements of the accepted industry or military reproduction specification, nonconformance to these spacing requirements is not a basis for rejection of the drawing."

TIP

In AutoCAD drawings, the recommended size and spacing for dimensions are assigned in the settings of the **Dimension Style Manager** dialog box. This dialog box and the steps involved in entering these settings are presented in detail later in this chapter.

Text Height and Style

When placing text on a technical drawing, legibility is the primary concern. The ASME standard governing text height and style on engineering drawings is *ASME Y14.2-2008 Line Conventions and Lettering*. This standard states that text used for titles and for denoting special characters, such as section view labels, should be no less than .24" (6mm). All other characters should have a minimum text height of .12" (3mm). Uppercase letters should be used unless lowercase letters are required. Single-stroke Gothic-style letters are recommended. Gothic characters do not have serifs at the ends of the strokes—serifs are the small flourishes found at the ends of the main strokes of characters in some font styles. Fonts without serifs are referred to as *sans serif* fonts.

Alignment of Dimension Text

The ASME standard for text states that text should face the bottom of the sheet. This is known as ***unidirectional text***. An example of unidirectional text is shown in Figure 5.6.

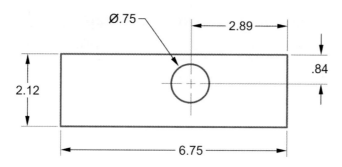

5.6   Unidirectional Text

Aligned text is aligned to dimension lines and may face the bottom and the right side of the sheet. This style is allowed on mechanical drawings prepared following the ISO standard but is not allowed on drawings employing the ASME dimensioning standard. An example of aligned text is shown in Figure 5.7.

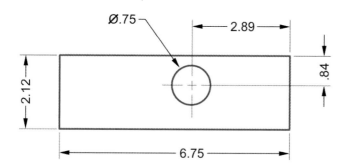

5.7   Aligned Text

Notating Holes and Arcs

When holes are dimensioned, the X- and Y- values to the center of the hole from the designer's datums should be provided and the hole's diameter specified. An arc should be described as a radius.

Figure 5.8 illustrates how leaders for small arcs and diameters are depicted. Figure 5.9 illustrates how leaders and notes are represented for large diameters and radii.

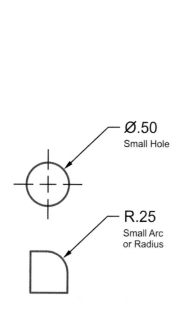

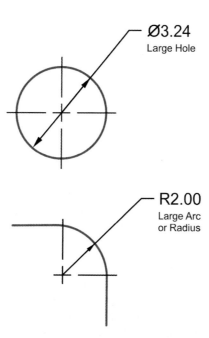

5.8   Dimensioning Small Holes and Arcs

5.9   Dimensioning Large Holes and Arcs

Dimensioning Cylindrical Shapes

ASME Y14.5-2009 specifies that cylinders and other outside diameters should be dimensioned in their profile (or side) view. The dimension should be preceded by the diameter symbol (see Figure 5.10).

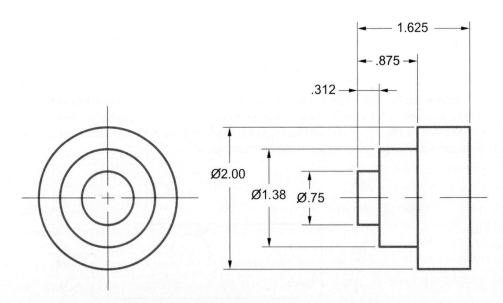

5.10   Dimensioning Cylindrical Shapes

Dimensioning Angles

An angle should also be dimensioned in its profile view, with the dimension value followed by the degree symbol (°) (see Figure 5.11). When greater accuracy for noting angles is desired, angles may be specified in degrees, minutes (′), and seconds (″). A minute equals 1/60th of one degree, and a second equals 1/60th of a minute (see Figure 5.12).

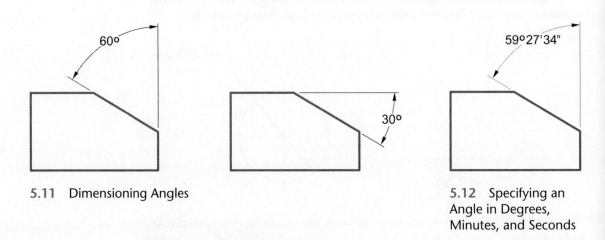

5.11   Dimensioning Angles

5.12   Specifying an Angle in Degrees, Minutes, and Seconds

Ordinate Dimensioning

In ordinate dimensioning a **0,0** (zero *X*, zero *Y*) datum point is defined on the object, and the object's features are located along the *X*- and *Y*-axes as referenced from the 0,0 datum point.

In the example in Figure 5.13 the 0,0 datum is at the lower left corner of the object, and the dimensions shown are all relative to this point. A table, like the one in Figure 5.14, is often placed on the drawing to describe hole diameters when ordinate dimensioning is employed.

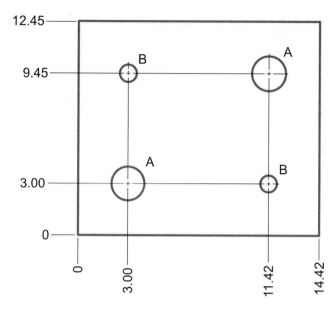

5.13   Ordinate Dimensioning

Hole Table	
Mark	Diameter
A	Ø2.00
B	Ø1.00

5.14   Hole Table

Ordinate dimensioning is useful for dimensioning parts that are to be manufactured by *computer-aided manufacturing (CAM)* machinery, such as a CAM drill press. The operator of the CAM drill press mounts the material to be drilled on the bed of the press and programs the location of the 0,0 point on the material. The operator then programs the location of holes along the *X*- and *Y*- coordinates. The drill bit moves along the *X*- and *Y*-axes relative to the 0,0 datum to drill holes in the material. (In some machines, the drill bit remains stationary, and the table on which the material is mounted moves to the bit instead.)

Notes for Drilling and Machining Operations

Notations for counterbored and countersunk holes are shown in Figure 5.15.
Because the computer keyboard lacks the characters for the geometric symbols that represent a counterbore (⎵), countersink (∨), or depth (⊤), AutoCAD's Geometric Dimensioning and Tolerancing (GDT) font is often used to place these symbols. In the

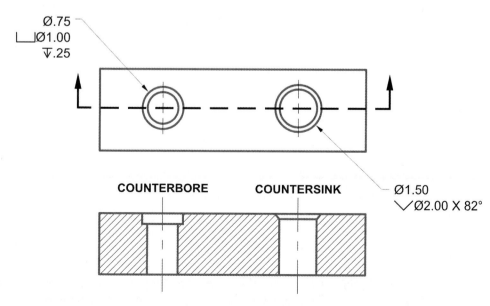

5.15   Notations for Counterbored and Countersunk Holes

GDT font, the lowercase alphabetical characters are replaced by the symbols and characters used in dimensioning and tolerancing notations. The lowercase alphabetical letter on the keyboard that corresponds to the dimensioning symbol in the GDT font is shown in Figure 5.16. For example, to insert the counterbore symbol into a notation for a hole, the drafter types a lowercase **v** into the note in place of the counterbore symbol and then highlights the **v** in the text window and changes it to the GDT font. The **v** is then replaced by the counterbore symbol in the note.

GDT SYMBOLS

Keyboard Character (lowercase)	GDT Symbol	Interpretation
V	⊔	Counterbored hole
W	∨	Countersunk hole
X	▽	Depth of hole

5.16   Lowercase Letters Corresponding to Symbols in AutoCAD's GDT Font

---

TIP

When you are using the **Text Editor** to edit a hole note, you can access the GDT characters needed to represent the counterbore, countersink, and depth symbols by selecting the **Symbol** tool located on the **Insert** panel of the ribbon. When the drop-down list appears, select **Other** from the bottom of the list. When the **Character Map** opens, select the GDT font, pick a symbol from the map, and click the **Select** button. Once you have selected all the required characters, click the **Copy** button, and close the **Character Map** by clicking on the **X** in the upper right corner. Then, right-click the mouse and select the **Paste** option from the shortcut menu. The GDT symbols will be pasted into the text window associated with the hole note.

NOTE

The symbols for degrees, plus/minus, and diameter can also be accessed by selecting the **Symbol** tool located on the **Insert** panel.

5.3 DOS AND DON'TS OF MECHANICAL DIMENSIONING (*ASME Y14.5-2009*)

Following the dimensioning guidelines listed here while creating a mechanical drawing will help ensure that the finished drawing is complete, orderly, and easy to interpret.

Dos

- Include every dimension and notation provided on the designer's sketch (or other form of input). If you have questions about the completeness of dimensions, consult the designer.

- Use the same precision (number of decimal places) identified by the designer when specifying dimension values.
- Use the datums identified on the designer's input when placing dimensions.
- Dimension to features in their profile (or most descriptive) view.
- Follow *ASME Y14.5-2009* spacing guidelines and dimension settings (see Figure 5.5).
- Place dimensions applying to two views between the views, but project extension lines from only one of the views.
- Describe a hole or cylinder (or other circular feature) with a diameter dimension (see Figures 5.8 and 5.9).
- Describe an arc with a radius dimension (see Figures 5.8 and 5.9).
- When dimensioning holes, provide the *X*- and *Y*-values of the center of the hole referenced from the datum features identified in the designer's input, and specify the diameter and depth of the hole.

NOTE

If the hole passes all the way through the part (referred to as a *through hole*) it is not necessary to specify a depth.

- Dimension cylinders and other outside diameters in their profile (side) view and include the diameter symbol (see Figure 5.10).
- Include all notes required to manufacture the part (material, scale, etc.).
- Use a single-stroke Gothic (sans serif) text style for dimensions and notes. Minimum dimension text height should be .12" (3mm). All text should be fully legible when plotted or printed.
- When dimension values are in decimal inches, place decimal points in line with the bottom of the dimension text.
- When dimension values are in millimeters, place a zero before the decimal point when dimension values are less than 1mm (e.g., 0.7mm).

Don'ts

- Don't overdimension. Features should be dimensioned only once. Do not include dimensions that were not on the designer's input without first consulting with the designer.
- Don't dimension to hidden lines or hidden features such as the centers of hidden holes.
- Don't cross dimension lines, or leaders, with extension lines (break the extension line).
- Don't run leaders through dimension lines if it can be avoided.
- Don't place dimensions on the object whenever possible.
- On drawings created with decimal inches, don't place a zero before the decimal point for a dimension value of less than 1" (suppress leading zeros).
- When dimension values are in millimeters, don't place a decimal point or a zero after a dimension that is a whole number (suppress trailing zeros).

5.4 ROLE OF DRAFTERS IN THE PREPARATION OF DIMENSIONED MECHANICAL DRAWINGS

The drafter's role in preparing a dimensioned drawing can be summarized as follows:

- In most cases, the drafter receives a design input—often a sketch—of the object to be drawn from a designer or engineer. The sketch will (or should) provide all the dimensions and other information necessary to fabricate the object. The drafter should ask for clarification from the designer if he or she feels that the sketch is missing a dimension or contains incorrect or unclear dimensions.

- The drafter determines which multiviews are necessary to describe the features of the object, as well as the sheet format and layout. The drafter then draws the views of the object.
- The drafter dimensions the views following the dimensions defined on the designer's sketch.
- The drafter is responsible for ensuring that the *ASME Y14.5-2009* (or other applicable) standard is followed with regard to the placement, spacing, and style of dimensions.

5.5 CHECKING DIMENSIONS ON THE FINISHED DRAWING

The finished dimensioned drawing should be compared carefully with the designer's input. To assure accuracy and completeness, the drafter should ask the following questions about the finished drawing:

- Does the drawing provide the multiviews necessary to describe the geometrical features of the object?
- Can each dimension and note included on the designer's input be accounted for on the final drawing?

TIP

An effective strategy for checking the sketch against the drawing is to use a yellow marker to highlight the dimensions on the sketch *and* the drawing, one by one, until all are accounted for.

- Have all applicable drafting and dimensioning standards been followed?
- Does the combination of the views, dimensions, and notes fully describe the object? Could this object be manufactured using *only* the views, dimensions, and notes provided on the drawing? (Novice drafters may find this difficult to answer, but as they gain experience with manufacturing processes and materials, it becomes easier.)

When the answers to all the questions posed are yes, the drawing is probably finished. However, in most offices, the final determination about whether a drawing is finished is made by an engineer, designer, or a *checker*.

Checkers are usually very experienced designer-drafters with expertise in manufacturing, drafting techniques, and dimensioning conventions. Often, there is an *Approved* box in the drawing's title block for the checker's initials. When a checker initials this box, it indicates that the drawing has passed the checker's review. It also means that the drafter is no longer the only one responsible for the accuracy of the drawing.

5.6 DESIGN BASICS: HOW DESIGNERS CALCULATE DIMENSIONS

Mechanical engineers and designers are responsible for calculating the dimensions of an object. They determine the dimensional values by carefully considering the form, fit, and function of the object they are designing. For example, the material from which the part is to be manufactured, how the object fits with other parts in an assembly, and the role it plays in the overall design are all factors that may affect the size and location of the features of a part. Sometimes, the dimensions define the aesthetic rather than the functional qualities of the finished object. The aesthetic qualities of an object refer more to the object's appearance than to its function.

Because the designer's dimensions are carefully calculated, it is very important that they are faithfully reproduced by the drafter during the preparation of an engineering drawing.

To appreciate how crucial it is that the designer's dimensions be accurately portrayed in a mechanical drawing, drafters must have an understanding of a very important concept of mechanical design: ***tolerances***.

5.7 TOLERANCES

Manufacturing a machine part to an extreme degree of precision is difficult *and* expensive; therefore, designers must decide how much the size and location of a part's features can deviate from the dimensions specified on the drawing and still perform their design function. This allowable variation in the location, or size, of a feature is called the *tolerance*. Once the acceptable tolerance for a feature has been determined, it is noted on the dimensioned drawing of the part.

> ### NOTE
> To underscore the importance of tolerances in the dimensioning process, the *ASME Y14.5* standard states as one of its fundamental rules: "Each dimension shall have a tolerance except those dimensions specifically identified as reference, maximum, minimum, or stock (commercial stock) size."

On engineering drawings, the dimension to which the tolerances are applied is referred to as the ***nominal size*** of the feature. For example, a designer may decide the allowable diameter of a hole is 1.00", with a tolerance of ±.01". In this example, 1.00" in diameter is the nominal size of the hole. By applying a tolerance of ±.01" to the nominal size of the hole, we can calculate that the hole could range in diameter from .99" to 1.01" and still fall within the acceptable size specified by the designer. The tolerance is the allowable difference between the hole's minimum and maximum size limits, so in this case the tolerance for this hole would be .02" (1.01 − .99 = .02).

The primary reason that designers calculate and specify tolerances on mechanical drawings is to control the size and location of the features of the part during the manufacturing process. After manufacture, the part is measured by quality control inspectors to verify that the features are within the allowable limits of size as defined by the tolerances on the drawing. Parts whose features measure within the allowable limits pass inspection. Parts whose features measure outside the limits are rejected.

Specifying tolerances on drawings has advantages for designers and manufacturers alike. The advantage for designers is that they can be confident that if the parts they design are manufactured within the tolerances specified on the drawing, their designs will fit and function as they intended. Manufacturers like toleranced parts because they can be confident that as long as the parts they make measure within the tolerances specified on the drawing, the client will purchase the parts.

Displaying Tolerances on Mechanical Drawings

Figures 5.17 and 5.18 show two examples of how tolerances may be specified for dimensions on a technical drawing. In Figure 5.17, the tolerance is shown beside the nominal dimension and noted with a plus/minus symbol (±). In Figure 5.18, the tolerance has been both added to and subtracted from the nominal size, and the allowable size limits are actually noted in the dimension.

Another method of specifying tolerances is to add notations in the field of the drawing or in the drawing's title block. Examples 1, 2, and 3 show three different

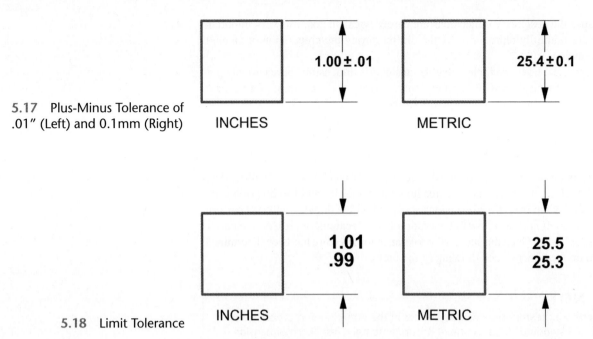

5.17   Plus-Minus Tolerance of .01″ (Left) and 0.1mm (Right)

5.18   Limit Tolerance

ways to depict tolerances with notations and include an interpretation of the specified tolerance.

Example 1 *General tolerances* may be labeled in the title block or given as notes in the field of the drawing.

> **.X ± .05**   Dimensions noted with one decimal place of precision on the drawing will have a tolerance of plus or minus .05″.
>
> **.XX ± .02**   Dimensions noted with two decimal places of precision on the drawing will have a tolerance of plus or minus .02″.
>
> **.XXX ± .003**   Dimensions noted with three decimal places of precision on the drawing will have a tolerance of plus or minus .003″.

Example 2 **Decimal Dimensions to Be ±.005″** A general tolerance of .005″ will apply to all dimensions labeled in decimal units.

Example 3 **Angular Tolerances ±1°** Dimensions on the drawing labeled as angles will have a tolerance of plus or minus 1°. For example, an angle labeled 30° on the drawing could measure between 29° and 31° on the manufactured part.

Interpreting Tolerances on Technical Drawings

Figures 5.19 and 5.20 show examples of a machine part in which the dimensions *do not* include tolerances.

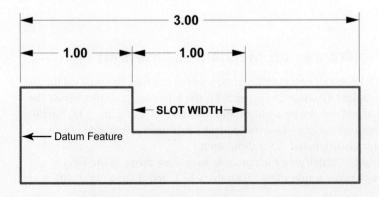

5.19   Part with Slot Dimensioned with a Continuous Dimension

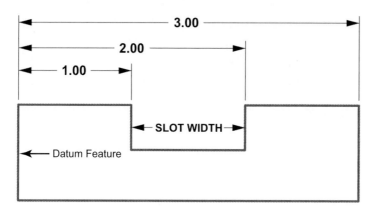

5.20 Part with Slot Dimensioned with a Baseline Dimension

In Figure 5.19, the width of the slot is dimensioned with a *continuous dimension*. A continuous dimension is referenced from the termination of the dimension that preceded it. The width of the slot in Figure 5.19 is 1.00".

In Figure 5.20, the width of the slot is dimensioned with *baseline dimensions*. Baseline dimensions are referenced from a common datum. In Figure 5.20, the datum feature is the left edge of the part. The width of the slot can be determined by calculating the difference between locations of the right and left sides of the slot. In this case, the width of the slot equals 1.00 (2.00 minus 1.00).

Because no tolerances are specified for the dimensions in Figures 5.19 and 5.20, the width of the slot will be 1.00" whether it is defined by a single continuous dimension or by two baseline dimensions.

Figure 5.21 shows a view of a part that includes dimensions *and* tolerances. The overall length of this part is labeled 3.00" ± .01". This means that when the part is manufactured, its overall length must measure between 2.99" and 3.01" to pass a quality control inspection.

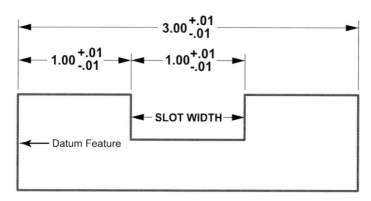

5.21 Part with Slot Dimensioned with a Toleranced Continuous Dimension

The left side of the slot in Figure 5.21 is located 1.00" ±.01" from the left edge of the part. This means that the location of the slot's left side must fall between .99" and 1.01" as measured from the left side of the part.

The width of the slot is dimensioned 1.00" ±.01", so as long as the width of the slot on the part measures between .99" and 1.01", it will pass inspection.

Comparison of Continuous Dimensioning and Baseline Dimensioning

Figure 5.22 shows a part that is dimensioned with three baseline dimensions that include plus or minus tolerances. Here, the left edge of the part serves as the datum feature for each of the three dimensions.

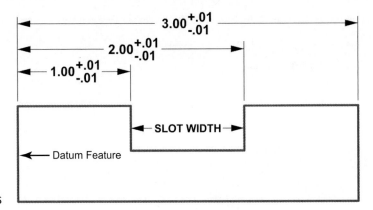

5.22   Part with Baseline Dimensions

The overall length of this part is labeled 3.00" ±.01", so when this part is manufactured, its overall length must measure between 2.99" and 3.01".

The width of the slot in Figure 5.22 is defined by two baseline dimensions instead of one continuous dimension, as in Figure 5.21. The location of the left side of the slot in Figure 5.22 must fall between .99" and 1.01" from the datum edge. The right side of the slot must be between 1.99" and 2.01" from the datum.

If the left edge of the slot is located .99" from the datum and the right edge is located 2.01" from the datum, the width of the slot will be 1.02".

If the left and right sides of the slot are located 1.01" and 1.99", respectively, from the datum edge, the width of the slot will measure .98".

Using baseline dimensions to define the slot could result in its width measuring between .98" and 1.02".

Dimensioning the slot with continuous dimensions as shown in Figure 5.21 resulted in its width measuring between .99" and 1.01".

As you can see from the comparison of the widths of the slots in Figures 5.21 and 5.22, the method used to dimension the slot (either baseline or continuous)—affects its size, after tolerances are factored in. In this case, the width of the slot defined with baseline dimensions may vary by as much as .04" (.98" to 1.02"), whereas defining the width with continuous dimensions results in its varying by .02" (.99" to 1.01").

The point of this comparison is not that either dimensioning technique—continuous or baseline—is inherently better or worse than the other but, rather, that the method used to define the widths of the slot in Figures 5.21 and 5.22 affects the slot's size after tolerances are applied. The designer chooses the dimensioning technique that will ensure that the part's features are manufactured within size limits to allow the part to function in its intended application.

This comparison was intended to help you understand the importance of applying the same dimensioning method (continuous or baseline) to the creation of an engineering drawing as is shown on the design input. Mechanical drafters who do not follow the same dimensioning method as the designer run the risk of inadvertently changing the intended size or location of a feature.

Tolerancing Terminology

The following terms are used frequently by designers when discussing tolerances. As a drafter-in-training, you should become familiar with each term so that you can communicate effectively with designers and engineers.

- *Feature:* A g ometric element that is added to the base part such as a slot, surface, or hole.
- *Nominal size:* A dimension used to describe the general size of the feature. Tolerances are applied to this dimension.
- *Tolerance:* The total permissible variation in a dimension value; the difference between the upper and lower size limits of a feature.
- *Limits:* The maximum and minimum sizes of a feature as defined by the toleranced dimension. For example, a hole dimensioned with a diameter of .50", with a tolerance of ±.02", has an upper limit of .52" and a lower limit of .48".
- *Allowance:* The minimum clearance or maximum interference between mating parts.
- *Datum:* A theoretically perfect element (an edge, plane, axis, point, or other geometric feature) from which dimensional information is referenced. Finished parts are inspected by measuring from the datum geometry identified on the drawing.
- *Actual size:* The measured size of a feature of a manufactured part. This size determines whether the part passes a quality control inspection.
- *Reference dimension:* A dimension without a tolerance that is provided only for information purposes. It is not used for manufacture or inspection of the part. A reference dimension is enclosed in parentheses.
- *Maximum material condition (MMC):* The condition of a feature when it contains the greatest amount of material. The MMC of an external feature, such as a shaft, is the upper limit of size. The MMC of an internal feature, such as a hole, is the lower limit of size.
- *Least material condition (LMC):* The condition of a feature when it contains the least amount of material. The LMC of an external feature is the lower limit. The LMC of an internal feature is the upper limit.

> **NOTE**
> The information provided later in the chapter will help clarify many of the terms presented here.

Interpreting Design Sketch 1

In the design sketch shown in Figure 5.23, the designer has provided the dimensions required to define the nominal sizes of the diameter (.98") and the length (2.00") of a cylinder. The designer has also specified a plus or minus tolerance of .01".

Analyzing Design Sketch 1

Applying the tolerance to the cylinder's nominal dimensions results in a range for its *diameter* between a minimum of .97" (.98" minus .01") and a maximum of .99" (.98" plus .01"). Applying the same sort of calculation to the *length* of the cylinder results in a range between a minimum of 1.99" (2.00" minus .01") and a maximum of 2.01" (2.00" plus .01").

The designer has calculated the size of the cylinder so that it should be able to perform as intended as long as its features fall within the allowable size limits.

Calculating Maximum Material Condition (MMC) for Design Sketch 1

Applying the plus tolerance to the cylinder's nominal dimensions will define the MMC of the cylinder's diameter and length. According to this calculation, the MMC for the cylinder's diameter is .99" (.98" plus .01"), and the MMC for the length of the cylinder is 2.01" (2.00" plus .01").

Calculating Least Material Condition (LMC) for Design Sketch 1

Applying the minus tolerance to the cylinder's nominal dimensions will define the cylinder's LMC. According to this calculation, the LMC of the cylinder's diameter is .97" (.98" minus .01"), and the LMC for the length of the cylinder is 1.99" (2.00" minus .01").

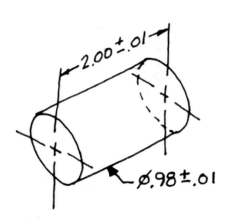

5.23   Design Sketch 1

Interpreting Design Sketch 2

In the design sketch shown in Figure 5.24, the designer has provided the coordinate (*X* and *Y*) dimensions required to locate the center of the hole from the left side and bottom edge of the object. These sides will be used as *datum features* for referencing dimensions on the drawing and later for inspecting the finished part.

The designer has also noted a tolerance range of plus or minus one hundredth of an inch ($\pm$ .01") that is to be applied to each nominal dimension.

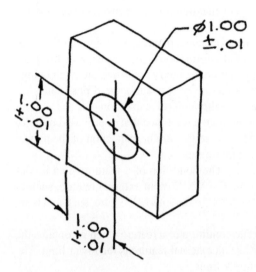

5.24 Design Sketch 2

Analyzing Design Sketch 2

When this part is manufactured, the location of the center of the hole, as well as the diameter of the hole, must comply with the conditions noted in Figure 5.25.

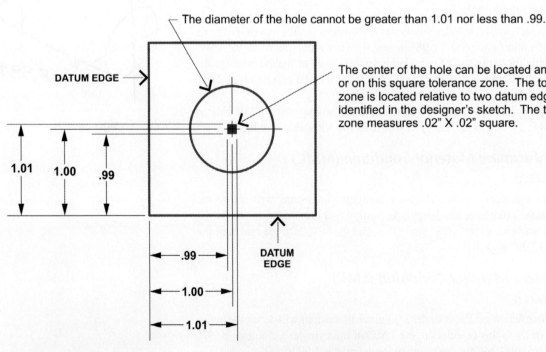

5.25 Design Sketch 2 Analysis

> **NOTE**
>
> Square tolerance zones are often considered a shortcoming of coordinate dimensioning.
>
> Geometric dimensioning and tolerancing (GD&T) techniques (which will be discussed later) allow designers to avoid this problem.

Otherwise, the part will be out of tolerance and may be rejected during a quality-assurance inspection check. When the part is inspected, the inspector will make measurements from the same datum features that are defined by the dimensions in the technical drawing.

Calculating Maximum Material Condition (MMC) for the Hole in Design Sketch 2

Subtracting the *minus* tolerance from the hole's nominal dimension will define its MMC. The nominal size of the hole is 1.00" in diameter, and the minus tolerance is .01", so in this case the MMC for the diameter of the hole is .99".

Calculating Least Material Condition (LMC) for the Hole in Design Sketch 2

Adding the plus tolerance to the hole's nominal dimension will define its LMC. The hole's nominal diameter is 1.00", and the plus tolerance is .01", so in this case the LMC for the hole's diameter is 1.01".

Calculating the Fit between the Parts in Design Sketches 1 and 2

Suppose the designer of the parts in Design Sketches 1 and 2 (see Figure 5.26) intended that the parts be assembled after they were manufactured. During the design of each part, the designer would have needed to analyze the possible limits of size of the cylinder in Part 1 and the hole in Part 2 to see if an interference could exist that would prevent the parts from being assembled.

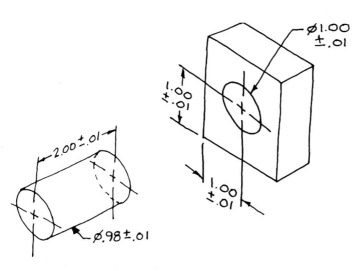

5.26   Assembling Parts 1 and 2

Best-Case Scenario for Assembly

If the cylinder in Design Sketch 1 is manufactured at its LMC, or smallest allowable diameter (.97"), and the hole in Design Sketch 2 is manufactured at its LMC, or largest allowable diameter (1.01"), the clearance between the two at LMC will be .04". With a clearance of .04", these parts can easily be assembled.

Worst-Case Scenario for Assembly

The worst-case scenario for assembly exists if the cylinder in Design Sketch 1 is manufactured at its MMC, or largest allowable diameter (.99"), and the hole in Design Sketch 2 is manufactured at its MMC, or smallest allowable diameter (.99"). At first it might seem that having the same diameter would cause interference when the parts are assembled, but this is not the case. The resulting fit would, however, be very tight, which would make assembling them more difficult.

If the designer desired a looser fit at MMC of both parts, the nominal diameter specified for the cylinder could be reduced to .97", or the nominal diameter of the hole could be enlarged to 1.01". Either would result in a clearance fit between the parts at MMC.

Reference Dimensions

Figure 5.27 shows an example of a machine part with an overall dimension of 3.00" labeled inside parentheses and a chain of three continuous dimensions, each labeled 1.00" ±.01". The dimension in parentheses is a *reference dimension*. A reference dimension is an untoleranced dimension that is provided only for informational purposes and is not used to manufacture or to inspect the part.

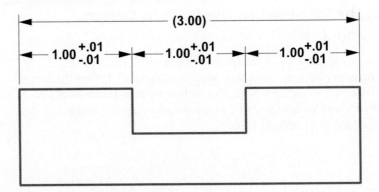

5.27   Reference Dimension

Because the reference dimension is not used to make the part in Figure 5.27, the overall length of the part will be a product of the cumulative effects of the three dimensions labeled 1.00" plus or minus their tolerances. Thus, the overall length of the part could range between 2.97" (.99" times 3) to 3.03" (1.01" times 3). This phenomenon, in which the sizes of toleranced features have a cumulative effect on the overall length, is called a *tolerance accumulation*.

In Figure 5.27 if the overall length dimension had been labeled 3.00" ±.01" (instead of as a reference dimension), it would be impossible to reconcile its allowable limits (2.99" to 3.01") with the limits allowed by applying a tolerance to each of the dimensions labeled 1.00" (2.97" to 3.03").

In contrast, if the chain of 1.00" dimensions was broken by removing one of them, the overall dimension would no longer be a reference dimension and would need to have a tolerance.

Confirming the Tolerances of Manufactured Parts

It is important to confirm that after the part is manufactured, it falls within the allowable size limits defined by the dimensions and tolerances noted on the drawing. This step in the manufacturing cycle is performed during a *quality control inspection*. Quality control (QC) inspectors use precise measuring (metrology) equipment to determine the actual size of the part. QC inspectors compare the actual size of the part with the dimensions noted on the technical drawing. Parts that measure within the allowable size limits will pass the QC inspection, whereas parts that measure outside the limits will be rejected.

Tolerance Costs

Designers must consider cost when determining the tolerances for a feature, because as tolerances become tighter, the cost of manufacturing a part may increase. One reason is that as tolerance allowances become stricter, it may take longer to manufacture the part. Another reason is that due to tighter tolerances, fewer parts may pass a quality control inspection. The designer walks a fine line between the desired accuracy of the part and the cost of manufacturing the part within the budget constraints of the project.

Although tight tolerances usually add to the cost of a project, a type of tolerancing known as *geometric dimensioning and tolerancing (GD&T)*, may actually lower the costs of producing a part. GD&T tolerances control the *form* (flatness, straightness, circularity, and cylindricity), *orientation* (perpendicularity, angularity, parallelism), or *position* of a part's features. By using GD&T, the odds that parts will pass a quality control inspection rise, and fewer rejected parts results in lower production costs. The *ASME Y14.5-2009* standard covers the application of GD&T to technical drawings.

5.8 DIMENSIONING WITH AUTOCAD

The AutoCAD **Dimension** toolbar, containing all the commands necessary to add dimensions to a drawing, is shown in Figure 5.28. These commands are also located in the **Dimensions** panel of the **Annotate** tab of the ribbon. In Figure 5.28 each *dimension command* icon is labeled with its function. An explanation of each icon is presented on the following pages.

Video tutorials for the commands on the **Dimension** toolbar are located in the student data files at **www.pearsondesigncentral.com.** To access these tutorials, open the Pearson Design Central website and click on the *CAD Community* link, then select the *Click here to download student data files for our CAD titles* link. Next, click on the *Technical Drawing 101* link and select the *AutoCAD Tutorial Videos* zip file, then select the *Download* button and open (or save) the tutorials specified above.

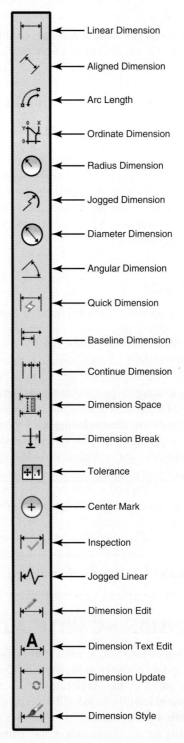

Linear Dimension

Aligned Dimension

Arc Length

Ordinate Dimension

Radius Dimension

Jogged Dimension

Diameter Dimension

Angular Dimension

Quick Dimension

Baseline Dimension

Continue Dimension

Dimension Space

Dimension Break

Tolerance

Center Mark

Inspection

Jogged Linear

Dimension Edit

Dimension Text Edit

Dimension Update

Dimension Style

5.28 AutoCAD **Dimension** Toolbar

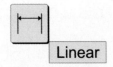

5.29(a) Linear Dimension Icon

Linear Dimension Command

The icon for the **Linear** dimension command is shown in Figure 5.29(a). This command displays the linear distance between two selected points. This option is used to dimension both vertical and horizontal features, as shown in Figure 5.29(b).

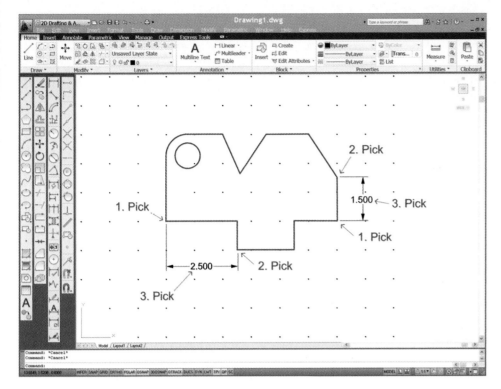

5.29(b) **Linear** Dimension Command

— NOTE —

Whenever a dimension is placed on an AutoCAD drawing, AutoCAD automatically creates a new layer named **Defpoints** and places objects called *definition points* (defpoints) on this layer. The definition points reflect the points chosen by the user to define the dimension and are used by AutoCAD to calculate the value for the dimension. A special property of the Defpoints layer is that it does not print when the drawing is plotted, so don't be alarmed when you see the Defpoints layer appear in the list of layers shown in the **Layer Properties Manager** dialog box. Of course, since this layer does not print, it is probably not a good idea to set it current and create your drawing on it either.

Aligned Dimension Command

The icon for the **Aligned** dimension command is shown in Figure 5.30(a). This command is used to display the length of an angled line, as shown in Figure 5.30(b).

Arc Length Command

The icon for the **Arc Length** command is shown in Figure 5.31(a). This command is used to denote the length dimension of an arc or a polyline arc segment, as shown in Figure 5.31(b).

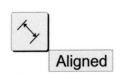

5.30(a) **Aligned** Dimension Icon

Ordinate Dimension Command

The icon for the **Ordinate** dimension command is shown in Figure 5.32(a). This command is used to denote distances along *X*- and *Y*-axes relative to a defined origin point (usually labeled 0,0), as shown in Figure 5.32(b).

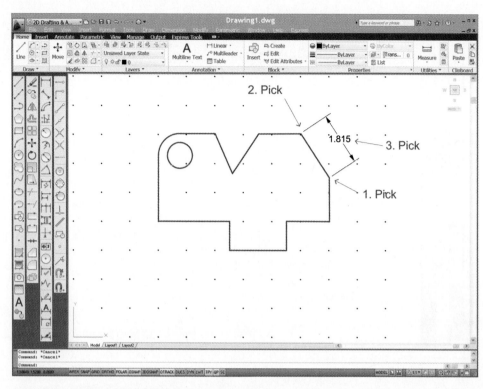

5.30(b)   **Aligned** Dimension Command

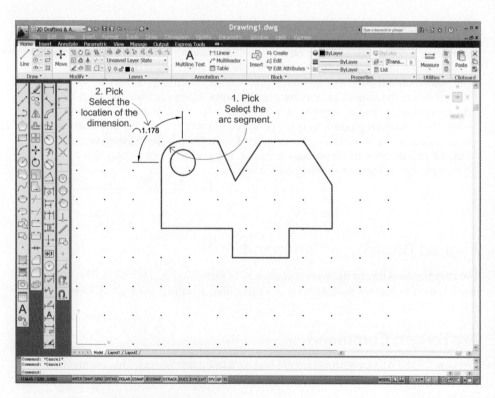

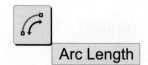

Arc Length

5.31(a)   **Arc Length** Icon   5.31(b)   **Arc Length** Command

Radius Dimension Command

The icon for the **Radius** dimension command is shown in Figure 5.33(a). This command is used to denote the radius of an arc, as shown in Figure 5.33(b).

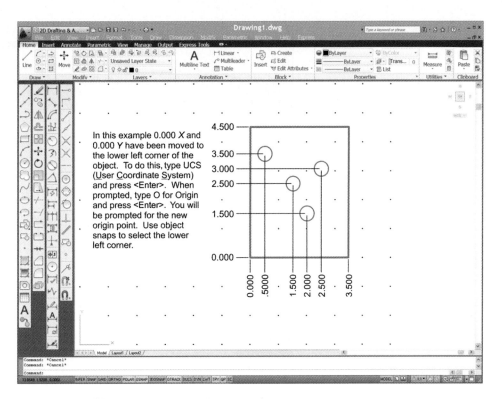

5.32(b) **Ordinate** Dimension Command

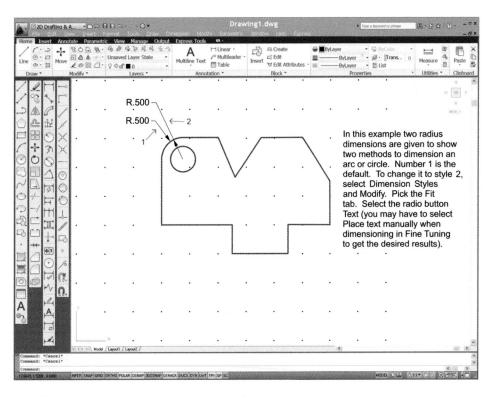

5.33(a) **Radius** Dimension Icon

5.33(b) **Radius** Dimension Command

Jogged Dimension Command

The icon for the **Jogged** dimension command is shown in Figure 5.34(a). This command is used to create a jogged radius or diameter when dimensioning a large arc or circle whose center is outside the drawing area, as shown in Figure 5.34(b).

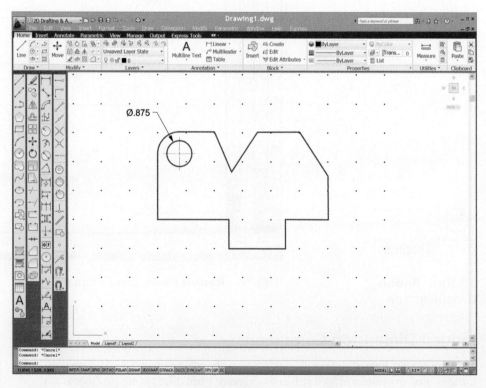

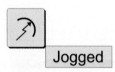

5.34(a) Jogged
Dimension Icon

5.34(b) **Jogged** Dimension Command

Diameter Dimension Command

The icon for the **Diameter** dimension command is shown in Figure 5.35(a). This command is used to denote the diameter of a circle, as shown in Figure 5.35(b).

5.35(a) **Diameter**
Dimension Icon

5.35(b) **Diameter** Dimension Command

Angular Dimension Command

The icon for the **Angular** dimension command is shown in Figure 5.36(a). This command is used to denote the angle between two features of an object, as shown in Figure 5.36(b).

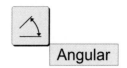

5.36(a)   **Angular** Dimension Icon

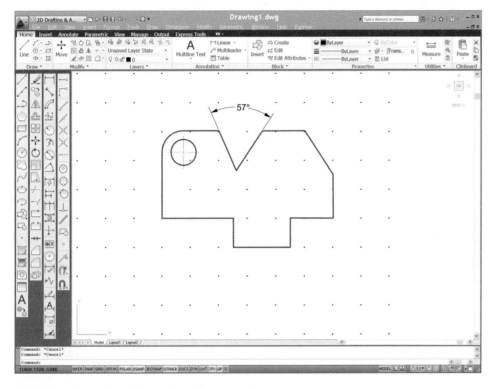

5.36(b)   **Angular** Dimension Command

Quick Dimension Command

The icon for the **Quick Dimension** command is shown in Figure 5.37(a). This command is used to create a group of dimensions quickly. You can either pick features on the object individually with the mouse or use a crossing window to select an area of the object to be dimensioned, as shown in Figure 5.37(b). Several options are available: **Continue, Staggered, Baseline, Ordinate, Radius,** and **Diameter**.

Baseline Dimension Command

The icon for the **Baseline** dimension command is shown in Figure 5.38(a). This command is used to create a series of dimensions measured from the same baseline (datum). The first extension line of the first dimension placed (using the **Linear** dimension command) becomes the default first extension line for dimensions placed after the **Baseline** option is selected, as shown in Figure 5.38(b).

Continue Dimension Command

The icon for the **Continue** dimension command is shown in Figure 5.39(a). This command is used to create a string of continuous dimensions. The first dimension in the string is placed using the **Linear** dimension option. After the **Continue** option is selected, subsequent dimensions begin at the second extension line of the previously defined dimension, as shown in Figure 5.39(b). This dimensioning method is also called *chain dimensioning*.

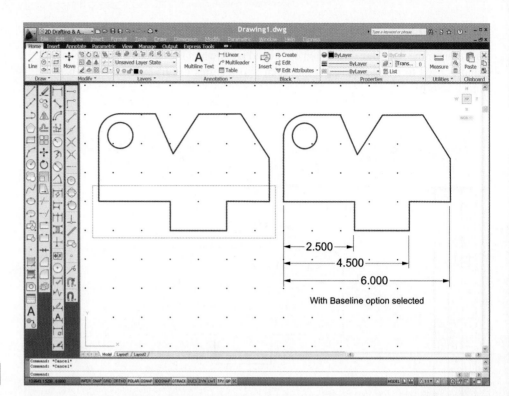

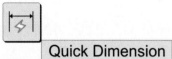

Quick Dimension

**5.37(a) Quick
Dimension** Icon

5.37(b)   Quick Dimension Command

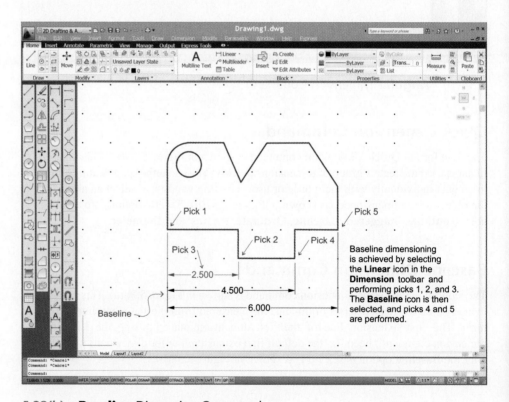

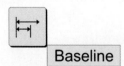

Baseline

5.38(a) Baseline
Dimension Icon

5.38(b)   Baseline Dimension Command

Dimension Space Command

The icon for the **Dimension Space** command is shown in Figure 5.40(a). This command adjusts the space between parallel linear dimensions to match a defined distance, as shown in Figure 5.40(b).

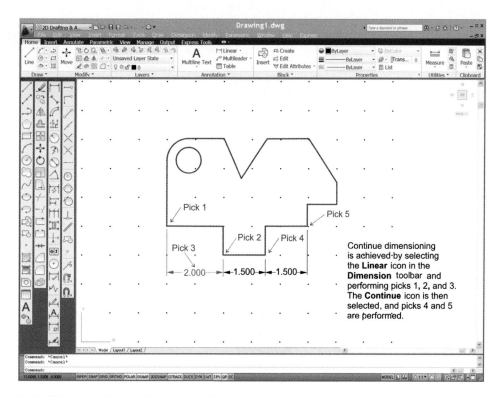

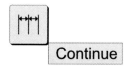

5.39(a) Continue
Dimension Icon

5.39(b)   Continue Dimension Command

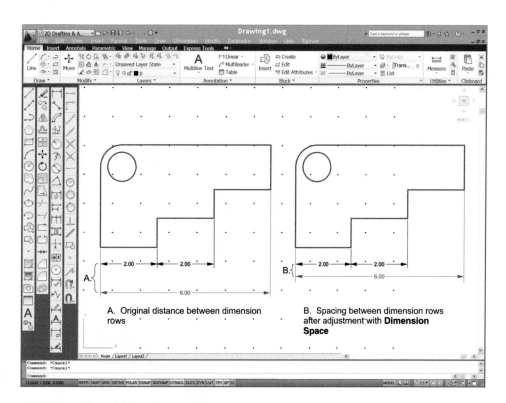

5.40(a) Dimension Space Icon

5.40(b) Dimension Space Command

Dimension Break Command

The icon for the **Dimension Break** command is shown in Figure 5.41(a). This command is used to break dimension or extension lines where they overlap other lines, as shown in Figure 5.41(b).

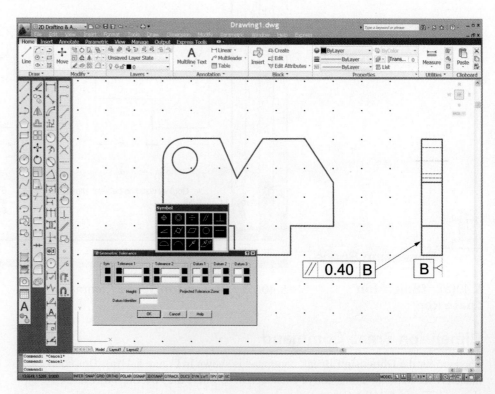

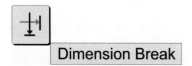

Dimension Break

**5.41(a)   Dimension
Break** Icon

5.41(b)   Dimension Break Command

Tolerance Command

The icon for the **Tolerance** command is shown in Figure 5.42(a). This command is used to specify the symbols and values for geometric dimensioning and tolerancing, as shown in Figure 5.42(b).

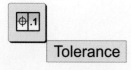

Tolerance

5.42(a)   Tolerance
Icon

5.42(b)   Tolerance Command

Center Mark Command

The icon for the **Center Mark** command is shown in Figure 5.43(a). This command is used to create center marks or centerlines on circles and arcs, as shown in Figure 5.43(b). The option for centerlines or center marks can be found in the **Dimension Styles** dialog box in the **Symbols and Arrows** tab.

Center Mark

5.43(a)   **Center Mark** Icon

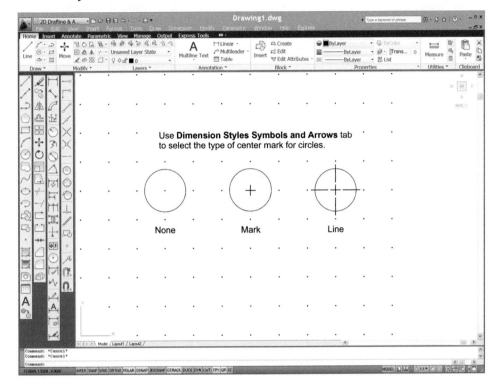

5.43(b)   **Center** Mark Command

Inspection Command

The icon for the **Inspection** command is shown in Figure 5.44(a). This command creates a dimension inside a frame that is used to provide inspection information about the feature, as shown in Figure 5.44(b).

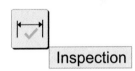

Inspection

5.44(a)   **Inspection** Icon

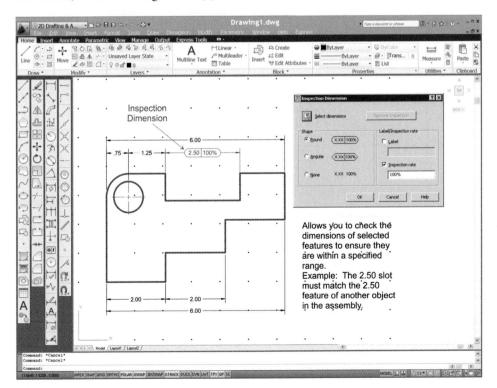

5.44(b)   **Inspection** Command

Jogged Linear Command

The icon for the **Jogged Linear** command is shown in Figure 5.45(a). This command is used to create a jog in a linear dimension line when the feature is not drawn full size, as shown in Figure 5.45(b).

Jogged Linear

5.45(a)   **Jogged Linear** Icon

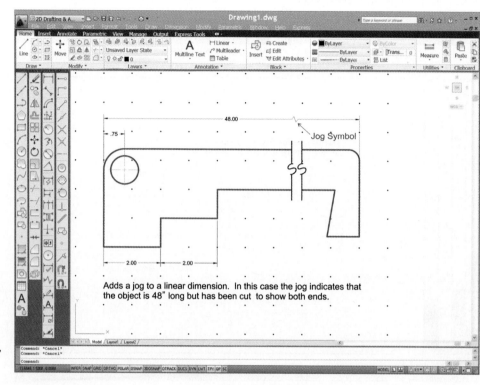

5.45(b)   **Jogged Linear** Command

Dimension Edit Command

The icon for the **Dimension Edit** command is shown in Figure 5.46(a). This command is used to edit existing dimensions, as shown in Figure 5.46(b). Options in this command

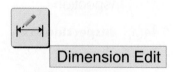

Dimension Edit

5.46(a)   **Dimension Edit** Icon

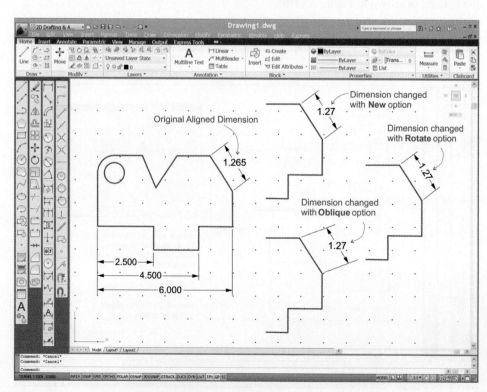

5.46(b)   **Dimension Edit** Command

include **Home**, which changes rotated dimensions back to the default position; **New**, which changes dimension text with the **Multiline Text Editor**; **Rotate**, which rotates dimension text; and **Oblique**, which changes extension lines to oblique angles.

Dimension Text Edit Command

The icon for the **Dimension Text Edit** command is shown in Figure 5.47(a). This command is used to move and rotate dimension text, as shown in Figure 5.47(b).

5.47(a)   **Dimension Text Edit** Icon

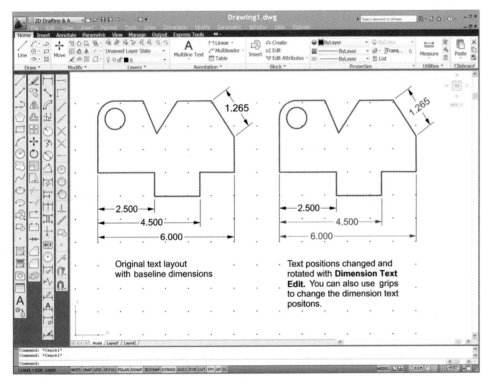

5.47(b)   **Dimension Text Edit** Command

Dimension Update Command

The icon for the **Dimension Update** command is shown in Figure 5.48(a). This command is used when selecting the individual dimensions that will be *updated* by dimension style overrides defined in the **Dimension Style Manager** dialog box (this is discussed later in this chapter). See Figure 5.48(b).

Dimension Style Command

A *dimension style* is a named set of values that define the appearance and format of dimensions, such as text height, precision, and arrowhead length. These values are assigned to the dimension style by entering them in the **Dimension Style Manager** dialog box. To open the **Dimension Style Manager** dialog box, click on the **Dimension Style** icon shown in Figure 5.49(a). The **Dimension Style Manager** dialog box is shown in Figure 5.49(b).

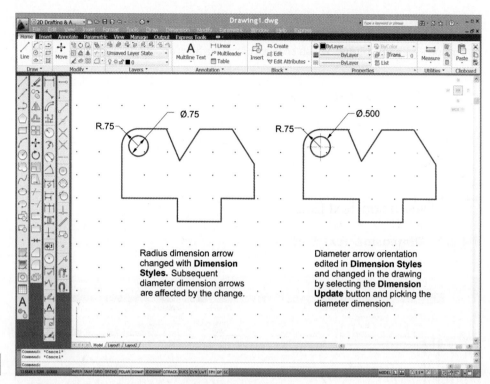

Radius dimension arrow changed with **Dimension Styles.** Subsequent diameter dimension arrows are affected by the change.

Diameter arrow orientation edited in **Dimension Styles** and changed in the drawing by selecting the **Dimension Update** button and picking the diameter dimension.

Dimension Update

5.48(a) Dimension Update Icon

5.48(b)   Dimension Update Command

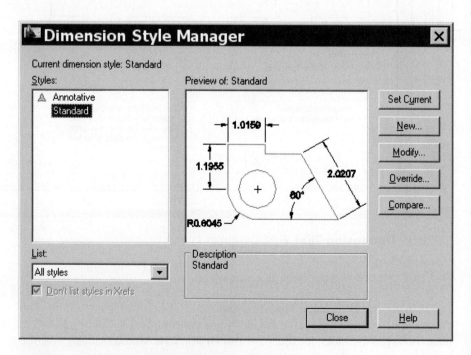

Dimension Style

5.49(a) Dimension Style Icon

5.49(b)   Dimension Style Manager Dialog Box

5.9 DEFINING DIMENSION SETTINGS WITH THE DIMENSION STYLE MANAGER

Before adding dimensions to an AutoCAD drawing, the drafter must set the values in the **Dimension Style Manager** that control the appearance and format of the dimensions. For example, entering the *ASME Y14.5-2009* dimensioning standard's spacing, size, and formatting values (see Figure 5.5) in the **Dimension Style Manager** dialog box *before* dimensioning the drawing, will ensure that when dimensions are added to the drawing they will automatically comply with the ASME standard.

The **Dimension Style Manager** dialog box, shown in Figure 5.49(b), can be opened either by selecting the **Dimension Style** icon located on the **Dimension** toolbar, by picking on the arrow in the lower right corner of the **Dimensions** panel of the **Annotate** tab of the ribbon, or by typing **DIMSTYLE** and pressing <**Enter**>. By choosing from the buttons located on the right side of the **Dimension Style Manager** dialog box, shown in Figure 5.49(b), it is possible to create a new dimension style, modify or override the current dimension style, set a different dimension style current, or compare the settings of two dimension styles. Figure 5.50 provides detailed information about the functions of each of the buttons in this dialog box.

Selecting the **Compare** button on the **Dimension Style Manager** dialog box will open the **Compare Dimension Styles** dialog box. Selecting two different dimension styles in the **Compare** and **With** windows of this dialog box will display a comparison of the dimension style settings assigned to each of the dimension styles (see Figure 5.51).

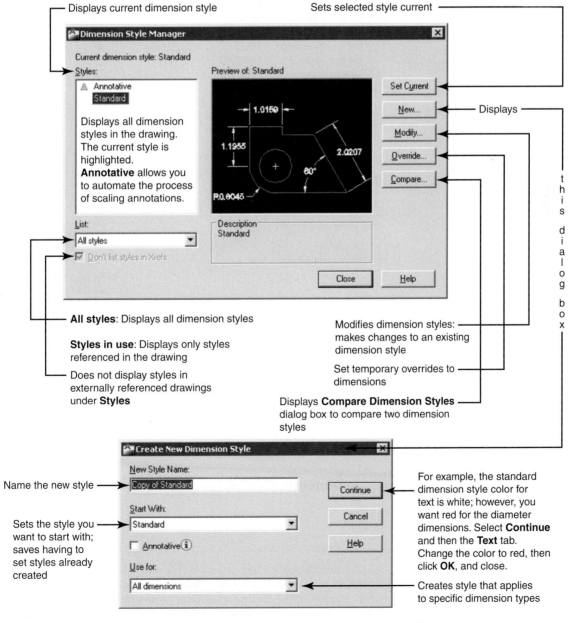

5.50   Detail of Buttons Located in the **Dimension Style Manager** Dialog Box

Displays and sets <u>first</u> dimension style for comparison.

Displays <u>second</u> dimension style for comparison
If set to **None**, displays all settings for the style

All Properties
Description - dimension style property
Variable - system variable that controls property
Standard - system variable style properties

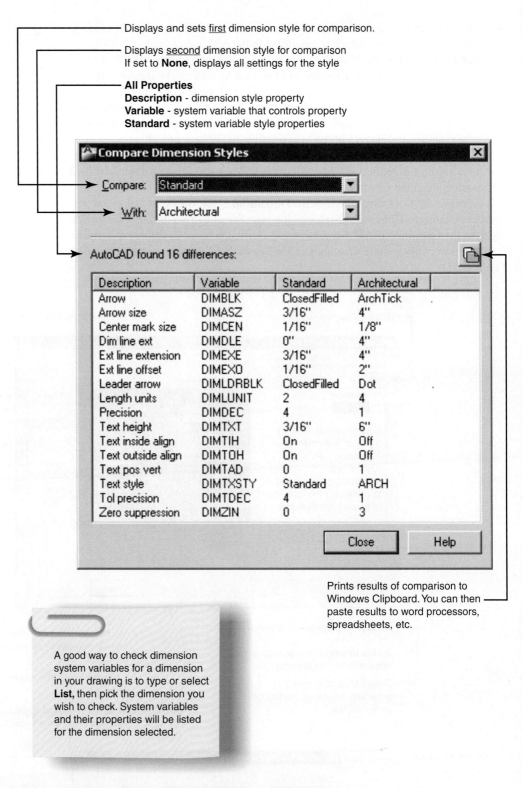

Prints results of comparison to
Windows Clipboard. You can then
paste results to word processors,
spreadsheets, etc.

A good way to check dimension
system variables for a dimension
in your drawing is to type or select
List, then pick the dimension you
wish to check. System variables
and their properties will be listed
for the dimension selected.

5.51   Compare Dimension Styles Dialog Box

TIP

A quick way to check a dimension's system variables is select the dimension,
right-click your mouse, and select **Properties.** The **Properties** palette will
open, displaying the dimension settings for the dimension. Many of these
settings can be edited by changing the values shown in the **Properties** palette.

CREATING A NEW DIMENSION STYLE

Use the following steps to create a new dimension style:

1 Select the **Dimension Styles** icon, and when the **Dimension Style Manager** dialog box opens, select the **New** button.

2 When the **Create New Dimension Style** box opens (see Figure 5.52), enter a name for the new dimension style in the **New Style Name** window. In Figure 5.52, **ASME Y14.5-2009** has been entered as the name of the new style.

Create New Dimension Style

New Style Name:
ASME Y14.5-2009

Start With:
Standard

☐ Annotative ⓘ

Use for:
All dimensions

Continue
Cancel
Help

> **NOTE**
>
> Selecting a style in the **Start With** window that already has some of the desired dimension settings in place can speed up the process of creating a new style. The **Start With** style defaults to the settings in AutoCAD's **Standard** dimension style unless a different text style is chosen from the drop-down list in this window.

5.52 **Create New Dimension Style** Dialog Box

3 Locate the **Start With** window in Figure 5.52. AutoCAD uses the settings of the style shown in this window as a *template* for creating the new style.

4 Select the **Continue** button, and when the **New Dimension Style** dialog box opens select from among the **Lines**, **Symbols and Arrows**, **Text**, **Fit**, **Primary Units**, **Alternate Units**, and **Tolerances** tabs (these tabs are explained in detail on pages 242–248) and enter values for dimension features such as text height, arrowhead style and size, and dimension spacing. Refer to Figures 5.54 through 5.61(b) to see the settings included on each of these tabs. When you have completed making these settings, click **OK,** and the **Dimension Style Manager** dialog box will reappear.

5 Set the new dimension style current by selecting the **ASME Y14.5-2009** style from the styles shown in the **Styles** pane of the **Dimension Style Manager** dialog box and click the **Set Current** button, shown in Figure 5.53. Pick the **Close** button to close the dialog box. When dimensions are added to the drawing, their settings will reflect the new dimension style.

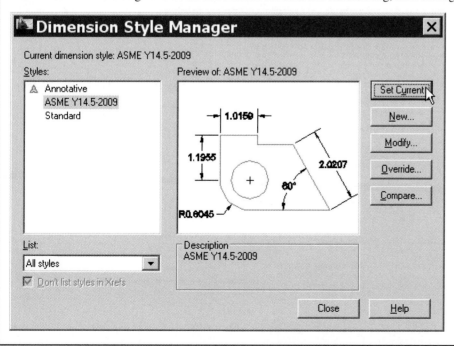

5.53 Setting a New Dimension Style Current

Tabs of the New Dimension Style Dialog Box

Step 4 of the *Creating a New Dimension Style* section instructs you to select from among the **Lines**, **Symbols and Arrows**, **Text**, **Fit**, **Primary Units**, **Alternate Units**, and **Tolerances** tabs of the **New Dimension Style** dialog box to enter the values for the dimension features of the new dimension style. The settings for each of these tabs are described next.

Lines Tab

The **Lines** tab controls settings such as the distance an extension line is offset from the object or extends past an arrowhead. This tab also controls the space between baseline dimensions. The settings of this tab that are affected by the suggested size and spacing guidelines of the *ASME Y14.5-2009* standard are noted in Figure 5.54.

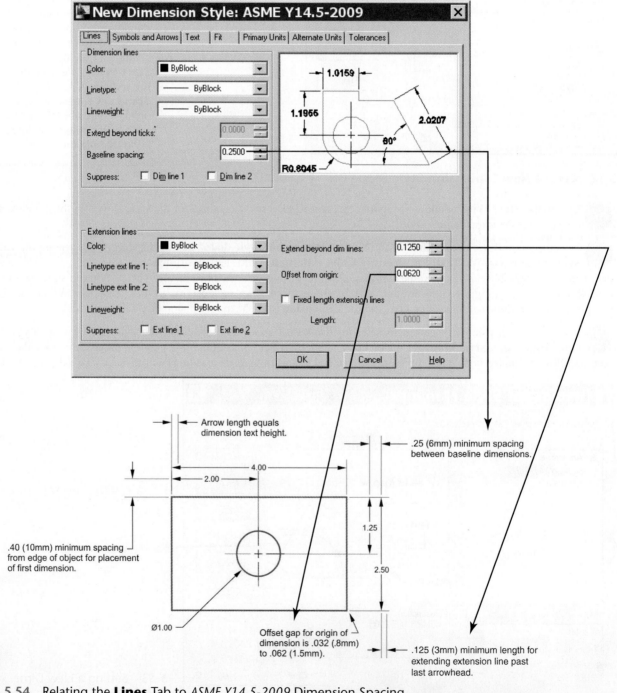

5.54   Relating the **Lines** Tab to *ASME Y14.5-2009* Dimension Spacing

Symbols and Arrows Tab

The **Symbols and Arrows** tab controls the size and type of arrowheads, including architectural tick marks, and the style of center marks used to dimension circles and arcs. The settings of this tab that are affected by the suggested size and spacing guidelines of the *ASME Y14.5-2009* standard are noted in Figure 5.55.

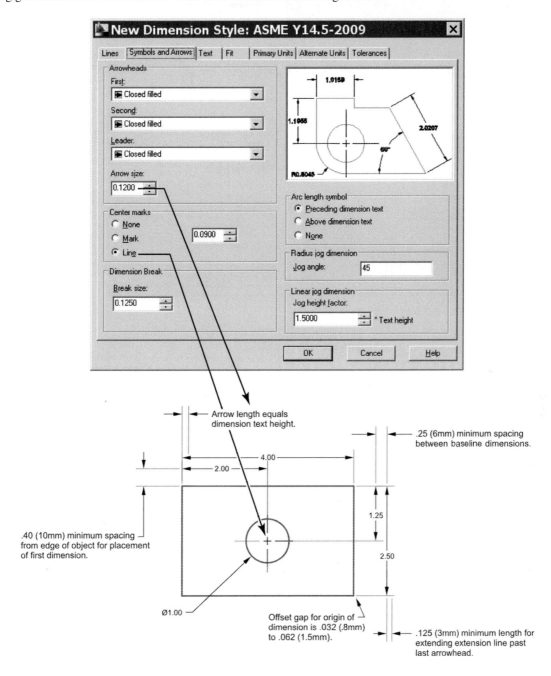

5.55 Relating the **Symbols and Arrows** Tab to *ASME Y14.5-2009* Dimension Spacing

Text Tab

The **Text** tab controls the text style, height, placement, and alignment of dimension text. The text style is based on the text properties defined in the **Text Style** dialog box. See Figure 5.56.

TIP

Text height for dimensions should not measure less than .12" (3mm) to comply with ASME standards for text height.

STEP by STEP

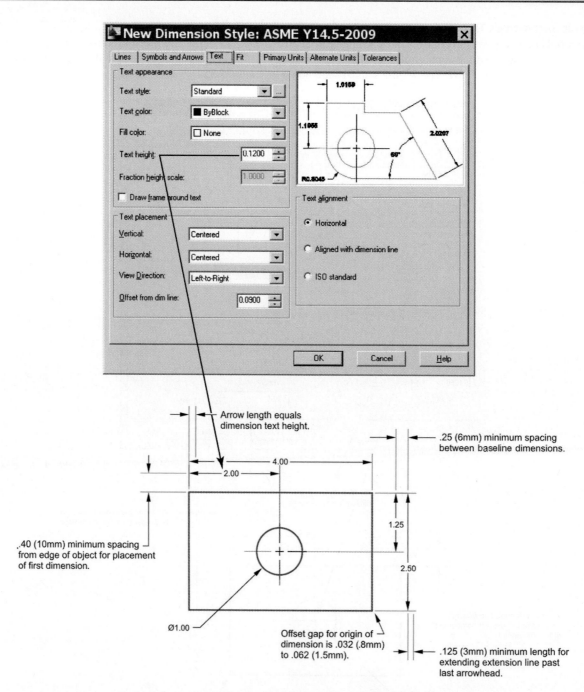

5.56 Relating the **Text** Tab to *ASME Y14.5-2009* Dimension Spacing

Fit Tab

The **Fit** tab controls the placement of text and the orientation of arrows on dimensions. Different combinations of settings from this tab can be used to force text between arrows or to force an arrow outside, for example. Study the examples in Figures 5.57(a) through 5.57(d) to see how different combinations result in different leader arrow placement and format.

Primary Units Tab

The **Primary Units** tab controls the format of units (decimal, architectural, engineering, etc.) and the precision (the number of decimal places or fractional round-off) of dimensions. Checking the **Leading** box in the **Zero suppression** pane will suppress the leading zero on decimal dimensions less than 1.00 unit in size. The setting in the **Scale**

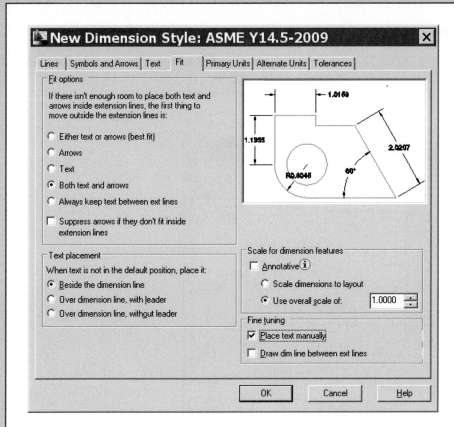

5.57(a)   **Fit** Tab Settings for Controlling Arrow Orientation on Small Circles and Radii

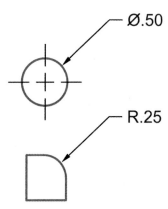

5.57(b)   Arrow Orientations Resulting from Settings Shown in Figure 5.55(a)

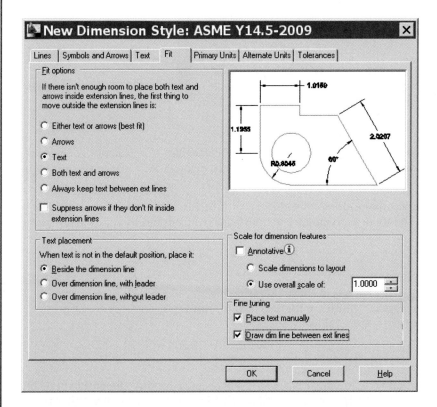

5.57(c)   **Fit** Tab Settings for Controlling Arrow Orientation on Large Circles and Radii

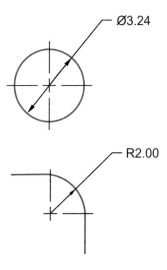

5.57(d)   Arrow Orientations Resulting from Settings Shown in Figure 5.55(c)

STEP by STEP

factor window located in the **Measurement scale** pane determines the numeric scale factor of the dimension display (see Figure 5.58). For example, if you add dimensions to a (model space) view that has been scaled to half-size (.5X), the dimensions will be displayed at half their full-scale value. By setting the **Scale factor** to 2 in the **Primary Units** tab, the numeric value for the dimensions will be multiplied by a factor of two and the view's full-size dimensions will be displayed. Likewise, if the view has been scaled to double-size (2X), setting the **Scale factor** to **.50** will display the dimension values at full size.

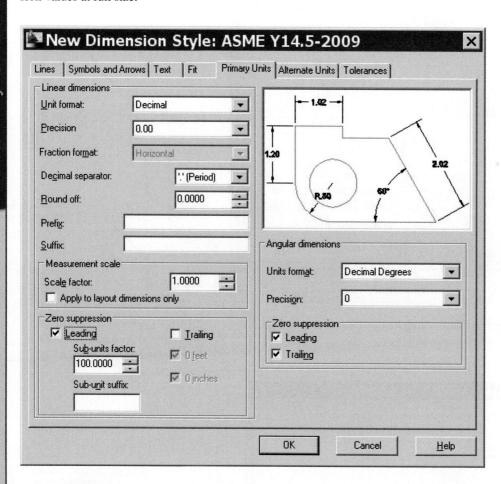

5.58   **Primary Units** Tab

Alternate Units Tab
The **Alternate Units** tab allows dual dimensions to be shown side by side on the drawing—for example, decimal units shown along side metric units. The alternate unit will be placed inside brackets. See Figure 5.59.

Tolerances Tab
The **Tolerances** tab allows tolerances to be incorporated into dimension text. Tolerances may be shown as **Limits** by applying the settings in Figures 5.60(a) and 5.60(b), or as **Symmetrical** (plus/minus) dimensions by applying the settings shown in Figures 5.61(a) and 5.61(b).

> **── NOTE ──**
> To change the dimension style of a dimension that has already been placed on the drawing, double-click on the dimension and when the **Properties** palette opens, left-click in the field next to **Dim Style,** and pick on the down arrow and select a different dimension style from the drop-down list.

Modifying a Dimension Style
Selecting the **Modify** button from the **Dimension Style Manager** dialog box will open the **Modify Dimension Style** box. Like the **New Dimension Style** dialog box, this dialog box contains the **Lines**, **Symbols and Arrows**, **Text**, **Fit**, **Primary Units**, **Alternate Units**, and **Tolerances** tabs. The settings included in these tabs are exactly the same as the ones presented

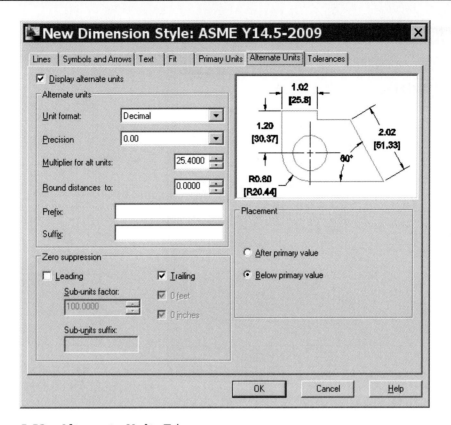

5.59 **Alternate Units** Tab

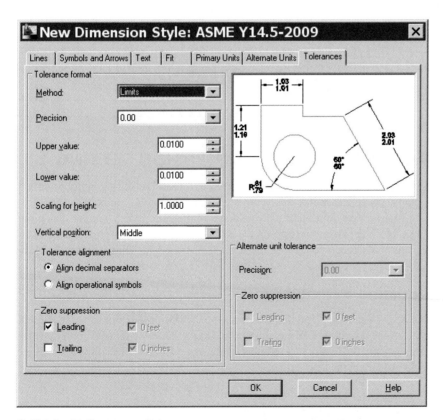

5.60(a) **Tolerances** Tab

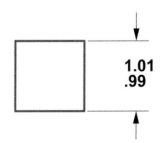

5.60(b) Example of Limits Dimensions

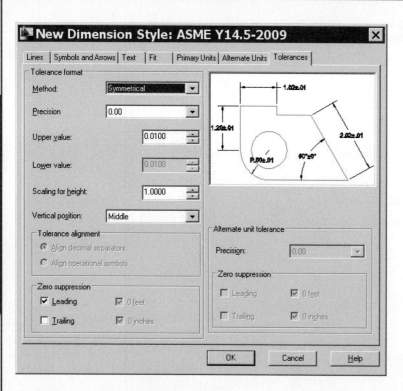

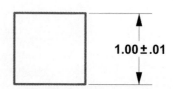

5.61(b)   Example of Plus or Minus (Symmetrical) Dimensions

5.61(a)   The **Tolerances** Tab Settings for Symmetrical Dimensions

earlier in the *Tabs of the New Dimension Style Dialog Box* section. Refer to Figures 5.52 through 5.59(b) to see the settings included on each of these tabs. When the desired settings have been entered into the tabs, click the **OK** button in the **Modify Dimension Style** box and when the **Dimension Style Manager** dialog box appears, click **Close**.

TIP

Most experienced CAD users choose to create a new dimension style with custom settings rather than modify the settings of the **Standard** dimension style.

5.10 OVERRIDING A DIMENSION SETTING

Sometimes it is necessary to have a different dimension setting apply to only a few dimensions. In a case like this, a dimension style override can be performed.

To override a dimension style, open the **Dimension Style Manager** dialog box and select the **Override** button (see Figure 5.62). Next, select the appropriate tab(s) and assign the new setting(s),click **OK**, then click **Close** to exit the **Dimension Style Manager**.

Updating a Dimension

Select the **Dimension Update** icon located on the **Dimension** toolbar or the **Dimensions** panel of the **Annotate** tab) (see Figure 5.63), and select the dimension(s) to which you want to apply the overridden setting(s) and press <**Enter**>. The dimension's style will update to reflect the new setting(s).

NOTE

The new settings defined in the dimension style override will not go into effect until a **Dimension Update** command is performed on the dimensions to be changed.

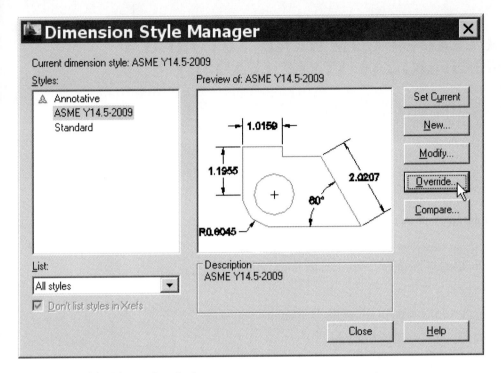

5.62 Override Dimension Style

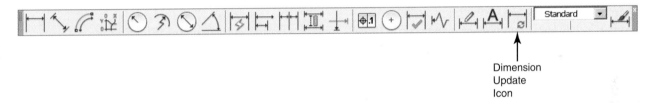

Dimension
Update
Icon

5.63 Location of **Dimension Update** Icon on **Dimension** Toolbar

5.11 ADDING A LEADER TO A DRAWING

A leader is an annotation created by drawing a line (or a spline) with an arrowhead at one end and text at the other end. Figure 5.64(a) shows a leader created for a mechanical engineering drawing including the three components of a leader: the arrowhead (which can be assigned a symbol other than an arrowhead), the leader line, and the landing line. Leaders are place in drawings using either the **Quick Leader** or **Multileader** command.

```
─── TIP ───
The landing line is also referred to as the shoulder of a leader.
```

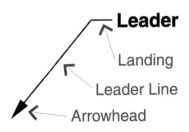

5.64(a) Leader Terminology

QUICK LEADER COMMAND TUTORIAL
(MECHANICAL STYLE LEADER)

STEP by STEP

1 Type **QLEADER** on the command line and press <**Enter**>.

--- **TIP** ---

The alias for **QLEADER** is **LE**.

2 At the **Specify first leader point:** prompt, select the point for the arrowhead to begin.

3 At the *Specify next point:* prompt, select the point for the leader line to end.

4 At the *Specify next point:* prompt, select the point where the landing line should end.

--- **TIP** ---

Turn **Ortho** on to draw a horizontal landing line.

5 At the *Specify text width:* prompt, either press <**Enter**>, or type a width value and press <**Enter**>.

6 At the *Enter first line of annotation text*: prompt, enter the text for the first line of the leader annotation in the **Text** box and press <**Enter**>.

7 At the *Enter next line of annotation*: prompt, enter the text for the next line or, to end the command, press <**Enter**>.

--- **NOTE** ---

To change the settings of a **Quick Leader**, begin the command, and when prompted for the first leader point, type **S** (for Settings) and <**Enter**>, this will open the **Leader Settings** dialog box, which contains three tabs—**Annotation, Leader Line & Arrow**, and **Attachment**. By selecting the **Leader Line & Arrow** tab, and choosing from the available options, you can change the leader line from straight to spline and/or change the arrowhead style. When you have selected the desired settings in the dialog box, select the **OK** button and follow the prompts to complete the command. To change the properties of a leader that has already been placed in the drawing, double-click on the leader line and edit the fields in the **Properties** palette. To change the text of an existing leader, double-click on the text and make the changes inside the **Text** box.

STEP by STEP

MULTILEADER COMMAND TUTORIAL

1 Type **MLEADER** (or **MLD**) on the command line and press <**Enter**>, or select the **Multileader** tool from either the **Annotation** panel of the **Home** tab of the ribbon or from the **Leaders** panel of the **Annotate** tab. See Figure 5.64(b).

> ## TIP
> The alias for **MLEADER** is **MLD**.

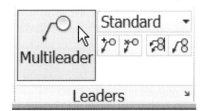

5.64(b)   **Multileader** Tool Located on the **Leaders** Panel of the **Annotate** Tab

2 At the *Specify first leader point:* prompt, select the point for the arrowhead to begin.

3 At the *Specify leader landing location:* prompt, select the point for the leader line to end.

4 When the **Text** box opens, enter the desired text; to end the command, pick a point in the drawing window outside the **Text** box.

MODIFYING OR CREATING A MULTILEADER STYLE

The **Multileader** tool defaults to the settings in effect for the **Standard** multileader style found in the **Multileader Style Manager** dialog box. These settings include leader format (straight or spline), arrowhead type and size, and text height. However, it is possible to modify the **Standard** style settings or to create a new style(s) by changing the settings in this dialog box. Creating multiple styles allows drafters to utilize leaders with different style settings within the same drawing.

To modify an existing multileader style, or create a new style, follow these steps:

1 Select the arrow icon next to the word **Leaders** on the **Leaders** panel of the **Annotate** tab of the ribbon. See Figure 5.64(b).

2 When the **Multileader Style Manager** dialog box opens, select the **Modify** button to modify the **Standard** style, or the **New** button to define a new style. Selecting either button opens a new dialog box containing three tabs. Make the desired changes in the windows of these tabs and select the **OK** button.

3 If you are modifying the *current* style, select the **Close** button, and the new settings will apply the next time the **Multileader** command is activated. If you created a new style in Step 2, left-click on the new style name in the **Styles** window then select the **Set Current** button and click the **Close** button. The new settings will apply the next time the **Multileader** tool is activated,

STEP by STEP

> ## NOTE
> Another way to change the settings of a multileader is to select the **Multileader** tool and type **O** (for Options) and press <**Enter**> and choose a settings option from the pop-up list. For example, if you choose the **Leader type** option, you can choose either **straight** (for mechanical notes), or **Spline** (for architectural notes). After selecting the desired options, choose **eXit options** and follow the prompts to complete the **Multileader** command. To change the properties of a leader that has already been placed in the drawing, double-click on the leader and edit the fields in the **Properties** palette.

KEY WORDS

Aligned Text

American National Standards Institute (ANSI)

Baseline Dimensions

Checker

Computer Aided Manufacturing (CAM)

Continuous Dimension

Datum

Dimension Standards

Geometric Dimensioning and Tolerancing (GDT)

International Standards Organization (ISO)

Nominal Size

Quality Control Inspection

Tolerances

Unidirectional Text

CHAPTER SUMMARY

Dimensions communicate important information about the size and location of the features of an object. In the United States, an industry-wide standard for dimensioning mechanical drawings is published by the American Society of Mechanical Engineers. This standard is known as *ASME Y-14.5-2009*. This standard guides the format, style, and placement of dimensions. Drafters who are employed by organizations that adopt the ASME standard are responsible for dimensioning objects in accordance with its guidelines.

Mechanical engineers and designers are responsible for calculating the dimensions to be included on a technical drawing, but drafters are responsible for creating drawings that accurately reflect the designer's intentions. In the mechanical engineering field, drafters must ensure that each dimension on the drawing reflects the exact dimensional value, including the exact degree of precision (the number of decimal places), as the designer's input. Drafters must also ensure that the dimensions on the drawing reference the same datum geometry that the designer specified in the input. If the drafter fails to portray the designer's input faithfully, the manufactured part may not fit or function as the designer intended. Also, parts that do not pass a quality control inspection may have to be scrapped, thus hampering the organization's ability to produce the product in the desired timeframe, or worse, prevent the organization from profitably manufacturing the product.

Drafters must not only be familiar with dimensioning theory and standards, but they must also be able to manipulate the dimension tools and style settings of the CAD program they are using to create the drawing.

REVIEW QUESTIONS

Short Answer

1. What is a tolerance?
2. What does ISO stand for?
3. What is a datum?
4. Who is responsible for calculating tolerances on an engineering drawing?
5. Is the diameter of a hole a *size* or a *location* dimension?
6. In the United States, what is the name of the organization that publishes a dimensioning standard for engineering drawings?
7. What does the term CAM stand for?
8. What is a reference dimension?
9. What is meant by nominal size?
10. Which method of labeling text complies with the ASME standard: unidirectional or aligned?

Matching

Column A

a. **Primary Units**

b. **Lines**

c. **Text**

d. **Fit**

e. **Symbols and Arrows**

Column B

1. The **Dimension Style Manager** tab where dimension arrow size is defined

2. The **Dimension Style Manager** tab where dimension height is defined

3. The **Dimension Style Manager** tab where dimension precision is defined

4. The **Dimension Style Manager** tab where the orientation of arrowheads on circles and arcs is defined

5. The **Dimension Style Manager** tab where center mark style is defined

CHAPTER PROJECTS

Dimensioning Project 5.1

Open the **Bracket** drawing you created in Chapter 4. Create a new layer named **Dimensions** and set it current. Add dimensions and notations to the views of the bracket (see Figure 5.65). Follow the dimensioning rules presented earlier in this chapter.

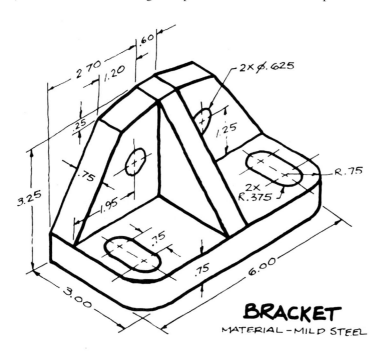

BRACKET
MATERIAL – MILD STEEL

5.65 Designer's Sketch of the Bracket

In the **Dimension Style Manager** dialog box, create a new dimension style named **ASME Y14.5** that contains the following dimension style settings (do not enable the settings of the **Alternate Units** or **Tolerances** tabs), and set the new style current.

Text height:	.125
Arrow size:	.125
Center marks:	Line
Extend beyond dim lines:	.125
Precision:	Varies—match precision of dimensions on sketch
Zero suppression:	Leading
Offset from origin:	.062

Follow your instructor's directions to print the drawing when you are finished placing the dimensions.

Dimensioning Project 5.2

Open the **Shaft Guide** drawing you created in Chapter 4. Create a new layer named **Dimensions** and set it current. Add dimensions and notations to the views of the shaft guide (see Figure 5.66). Follow the dimensioning rules presented earlier in this chapter.

> ── NOTE ──────────────────
> Because the shaft guide is an SI drawing, the following dimension variables are in millimeters.

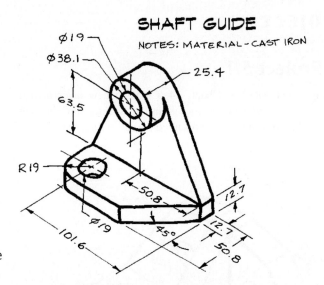

SHAFT GUIDE
NOTES: MATERIAL-CAST IRON

5.66 Designer's Sketch of the Shaft Guide

In the **Dimension Style Manager** dialog box, create a new dimension style named **ASME Y14.5-Metric** that contains following dimension style settings (do not enable the settings of the **Alternate Units** or **Tolerance**s tabs), and set the new style current (values shown are in millimeters).

Text height:	3
Arrow size:	3
Center marks:	Line
Center mark size:	2
Extend beyond dim lines:	3
Precision:	0.0
Zero suppression:	Trailing
Offset from origin:	1.5
Offset from dim line:	1.5

Follow your instructor's directions to print the drawing when you are finished placing the dimensions.

Dimensioning Project 5.3

Open the **Tool Holder** drawing that you created in Chapter 4. Create a new layer named **Dimensions** and set it current. Add dimensions and notations to the views of the tool holder (see Figure 5.67). Follow the dimensioning rules presented earlier in this chapter.

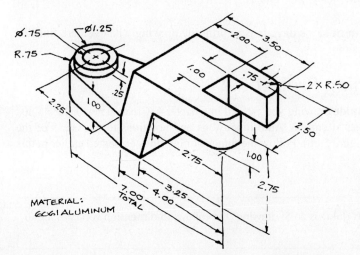

MATERIAL:
6061 ALUMINUM

5.67 Designer's Sketch of the Tool Holder

In the **Dimension Style Manager** dialog box, create a new dimension style named **ASME Y14.5** that contains the following dimension style settings (do not enable the settings of the **Alternate Units** or **Tolerances** tabs), and set the new style current.

Text height:	.125
Arrow size:	.125
Center marks:	Line
Extend beyond dim lines:	.125
Precision:	0.00
Zero suppression:	Leading
Offset from origin:	.062

Follow your instructor's directions to print the drawing when you are finished placing the dimensions.

Dimensioning Project 5.4

Open the **Tool Slide** drawing you created in Chapter 4. Create a new layer named **Dimensions** and set it current. Add dimensions and notations to the views of the tool slide (see Figure 5.68). Follow the dimensioning rules presented earlier in this chapter.

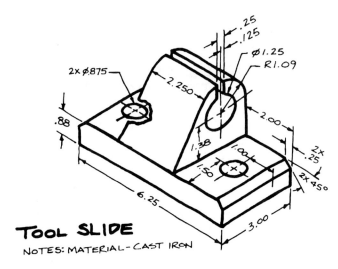

5.68 Designer's Sketch of the Tool Slide

In the **Dimension Style Manager** dialog box, create a new dimension style named **ASME Y14.5** that contains the following dimension style settings (do not enable the settings of the **Alternate Units** or **Tolerances** tabs) and set the new style current.

Text height:	.125
Arrow size:	.125
Center marks:	Line
Extend beyond dim lines:	.125
Precision:	Varies—match precision of dimensions on sketch
Zero suppression:	Leading
Offset from origin:	.062

Follow your instructor's directions to print the drawing when you are finished placing the dimensions.

OPTIONAL CHAPTER PROJECTS

Dimensioning Project 5.5

Open the **Offset Flange** drawing you created in Chapter 4. Create a new layer named **Dimensions** and set it current. Add dimensions and notations to the views of the offset flange (see Figure 5.69). Follow the dimensioning rules presented earlier in this chapter.

NOTE

Because the offset flange is an SI drawing, the dimension variables are in millimeters.

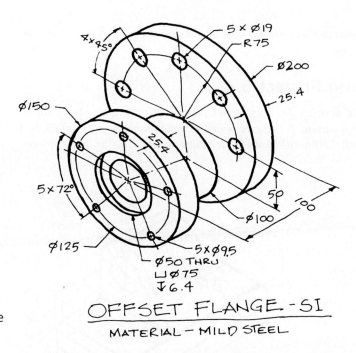

5.69 Designer's Sketch of the Offset Flange

In the **Dimension Style Manager** dialog box, create a new dimension style named **ASME Y14.5-Metric** that contains the following dimension style settings (do not enable the settings of the **Alternate Units** or **Tolerance**s tabs), and set the new style current (values are in millimeters).

Text height:	3
Arrow size:	3
Center marks:	Line
Center mark size:	2
Extend beyond dim lines:	3
Precision:	0.0
Zero suppression:	Trailing
Offset from origin:	1.5
Offset from dim line:	1.5

Follow your instructor's directions to print the drawing when you are finished placing the dimensions.

Dimensioning Project 5.6

Open the **Angle Stop** drawing you created in Chapter 4. Create a new layer named **Dimensions** and set it current. Add dimensions and notations to the views of the angle stop (see Figure 5.70). Follow the dimensioning rules presented earlier in this chapter.

NOTE

Because the angle stop is an SI drawing, the dimension variables are in millimeters.

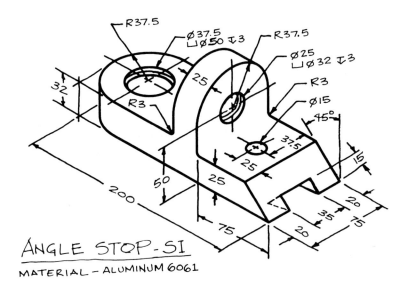

5.70   Designer's Sketch of the Angle Stop

In the **Dimension Style Manager** dialog box, create a new dimension style named **ASME Y14.5-Metric** that contains the following dimension style settings (do not enable the settings of the **Alternate Units** or **Tolerances** tabs), and set the new style current (values are in millimeters).

Text height:	3
Arrow size:	3
Center marks:	Line
Center mark size:	2
Extend beyond dim lines:	3
Precision:	0.0
Zero suppression:	Trailing
Offset from origin:	1.5
Offset from dim line	1.5

Follow your instructor's directions to print the drawing when you are finished placing the dimensions.

Dimensioning Project 5.7

Open the **Swivel Stop** drawing you created in Chapter 4. Create a new layer named **Dimensions** and set it current. Add dimensions and notations to the views of the swivel stop (see Figure 5.71). Follow the dimensioning rules presented earlier in this chapter.

In the **Dimension Style Manager** dialog box, create a new dimension style named **ASME Y14.5** that contains the following dimension style settings (do not

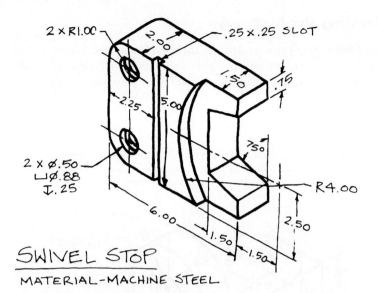

5.71 Designer's Sketch of the Swivel Stop

enable the settings of the **Alternate Units** or **Tolerances** tabs), and set the new style current.

Text height:	.125
Arrow size:	.125
Center marks:	Line
Extend beyond dim lines:	.125
Precision:	0.00
Zero suppression	Leading
Offset from origin:	.062

Follow your instructor's directions to print the drawing when you are finished placing the dimensions.

Dimensioning Project 5.8

Open the **Alignment Guide** drawing you created in Chapter 4. Create a new layer named **Dimensions** and set it current. Add dimensions and notations to the views of the alignment guide (see Figure 5.72). Follow the dimensioning rules presented earlier in this chapter.

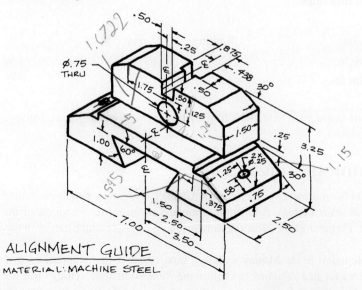

5.72 Designer's Sketch of the Alignment Guide

In the **Dimension Style Manager** dialog box, create a new dimension style named **ASME Y14.5** that contains the following dimension style settings (do not enable the settings of the **Alternate Units** or **Tolerances** tabs), and set the new style current.

Text height:	.125
Arrow size:	.125
Center marks:	Line
Extend beyond dim lines:	.125
Precision:	Varies—match precision of dimensions on sketch
Zero suppression:	Leading
Offset from origin:	.062

Follow your instructor's directions to print the drawing when you are finished placing the dimensions.

Dimensioning Project 5.9

Open the Flange #1105 drawing you created in Chapter 4. Create a new layer named **Dimensions** and set it current. Add dimensions and notations to the views of the flange #1105 (see Figure 5.73). Follow the dimensioning rules presented earlier in this chapter.

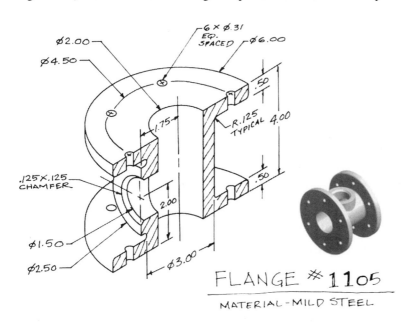

5.73   Designer's Sketch of Flange #1105

In the **Dimension Style Manager** dialog box, create a new dimension style named **ASME Y14.5** that contains the following dimension style settings (do not enable the settings of the **Alternate Units** or **Tolerances** tabs), and set the new style current.

Text height:	.125
Arrow size:	.125
Center marks:	Line
Extend beyond dim lines:	.125
Precision:	Varies—match precision of dimensions on sketch
Zero suppression:	Leading
Offset from origin:	.062

Follow your instructor's directions to print the drawing when you are finished placing the dimensions.

CHAPTER SIX

DIMENSIONING ARCHITECTURAL DRAWINGS

OBJECTIVES

After studying the material in this chapter, you should be able to:

1.   Explain how dimensions are determined on architectural drawings.

2.   Describe standards that affect the creation of architectural drawings.

3.   List the guidelines for adding dimensions to architectural drawings.

4.   Use the commands on AutoCAD's **Dimension** toolbar.

5.   Create and modify architectural dimension styles with AutoCAD's **Dimension Style Manager**.

6.   Add dimensions and notes to a floor plan.

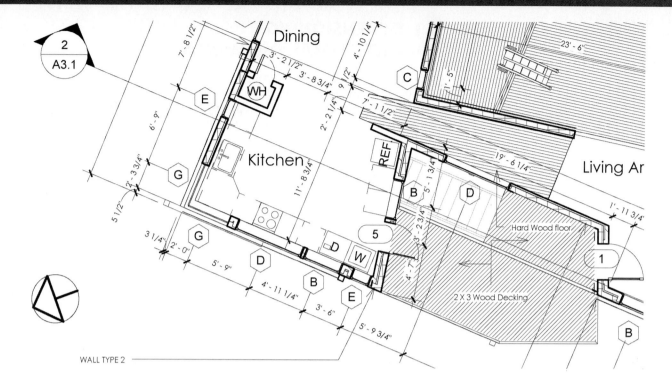

OVERVIEW

In preparing a set of architectural plans, drafters add dimensions to floor plans, elevations, and construction details. Drafters are responsible for accurately transferring dimensions from the designer's input to the finished drawing. A mistake on an architectural drawing could lead to a costly revision on a construction site or, even worse, the failure of a structural system.

This chapter presents the theory and practice of dimensioning architectural drawings and the use of AutoCAD's dimensioning tools and settings for architectural design.

6.1 DIMENSIONING ARCHITECTURAL DRAWINGS

As with mechanical drawings, drawing and dimensioning standards apply to the creation of architectural drawings. Often, the standard is described in an in-house drafting manual that has been developed by the designers, architects, and drafters of the firm. This manual is used to guide placement and spacing of dimensions, text height for dimensions and notations, and naming conventions for the title block and layers.

Increasingly, however, national standards are being adopted by architectural design firms, especially those that bid on publicly funded projects such as schools and government buildings. At present, the ***United States National CAD Standard (NCS)*** is gaining acceptance by the building design and construction industry. The NCS is being developed by experts from the fields of architecture, engineering, and the construction industry to standardize building design data and improve communication among owners, designers, and construction professionals. The NCS defines standards for drafting conventions, CAD layer naming conventions (based on *AIA CAD Layer Guidelines*), dimensioning, drawing sheets, schedules, drawing sets, terms and abbreviations, graphic symbols, notations, and plotting.

Advances in CAD modeling and linking of digital information are driving another paradigm in design, construction, and building management called the ***Building Information Model (BIM)***. Projects incorporating BIM technologies will move away from 2D drawings that do not have intelligence built into them toward a linked database that all users of the system can access. This standard, the *National Building Information Model Standard (NBIMS),* is being developed by the National Institute for Building Sciences (NIBS). The NIBS website describes the mission of the NBIMS standard as an attempt to "improve the performance of facilities over their full life cycle by fostering common and open standards and an integrated life-cycle information model for the A/E/C & FM (Architectural/Engineering/ Construction & Facilities Management) industry."

BIM covers all aspects of the project, from information management to the design, construction, and operation of the facility. BIM is not intended to compete with the NCS standard.

— TIP —

To learn more about the United States National CAD Standard, see Appendix C. To learn more about the National Building Information Model Standard, visit the National Institute for Building Sciences website: www.nibs.org.

6.2 DETERMINING DIMENSIONS ON ARCHITECTURAL DRAWINGS

Architectural designers determine the dimensions and notes that will go into the design of a building and use this information to create a design input. Often, the design input comes to the drafter as a sketch showing placement of walls, doors, windows, and other features of the building. Drafters use the design input to draw the building's features and add the dimensions and notes necessary to build the project.

6.3 ARCHITECTURAL DRAFTING CONVENTIONS

Dimensioning conventions for architectural drawings differ from those for mechanical drawings. For example, the very small tolerances commonly noted on mechanical drawings are usually much less critical in architectural drawings—although sometimes a dimension may be marked *clear,* which indicates that after construction the actual dimension between finished surfaces may never be less than the clear dimension. Another difference is that either arrowheads or **tick marks** (short diagonal lines that NCS refers to as a *slashes*) can be used to show the termination of dimensions.

In the *drafting conventions* section of the NCS, three methods for dimensioning walls and partitions are presented: dimensioning from an exterior wall face to the face of stud walls or masonry units, dimensioning from an exterior wall face to the centerlines of walls (and from centerline to centerline of interior partitions), and dimensioning to the faces of *finished* walls (however, this requires the builder to know exactly what the final finish of walls will be during the layout of the wall). Windows and doors are dimensioned to the centers of their openings. The standard also states that dimension fractions should not be given in increments of less than 1/16".

In the detail of the floor plan shown in Figure 6.1, note how dimensions are given from the outside edges of framed exterior walls to the face of interior walls; doors and windows are dimensioned to their centers; and, unlike in mechanical drawings, unbroken chains of dimensions are the norm.

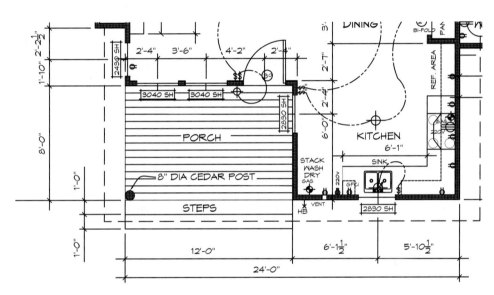

6.1   Detail from a Floor Plan

The NCS specifies that text used on architectural drawings should be **sans serif** (meaning without *serifs*). Serifs are the small flourishes found at the ends of the main strokes of characters in some font styles. Minimum text height should be not less than 3/32" (2.5mm), and all notations should be capitalized. Italicized, underlined, or bold fonts should be avoided.

TIP

AutoCAD comes loaded with several architectural-style fonts that resemble hand-lettered text. Many architects and designers like the traditional look that these fonts lend to their drawings (although these fonts may become less popular as architectural drawing conventions become more standardized). AutoCAD's architectural fonts include CityBlueprint, CountryBlueprint, and Stylus BT.

Dimensions and notations are also added to the elevation drawings of the project. These dimensions may include floor heights, overhangs of eaves, roof pitches, and building materials. It is helpful for architectural designers and drafters to have an understanding of construction processes, particularly framing, to determine the best placement of dimensions.

6.4 ALIGNMENT OF DIMENSION TEXT

Aligned text is used on architectural drawings. Aligned text faces the bottom and the right side of the drawing sheet. Unlike in mechanical drawing, the text is placed above the dimension line on architectural drawings. Examples of aligned text are shown on the dimensions in Figure 6.1.

6.5 ARCHITECTURAL DIMENSIONING GUIDELINES

The following is a review of architectural dimensioning guidelines:

- Dimensions are placed from the outside face of framing of exterior walls.
- The first line of dimensions locates interior walls and the centers of doors and windows.
- The second line of dimensions denotes distances between outside walls and interior walls.
- The third line of dimensions denotes the overall distance between outside walls.
- Interior dimensions usually locate interior walls and other features from edges of outside walls.
- Dimensions should be aligned with dimension lines and read from the bottom and right side of the sheet.
- Dimensions should be centered above dimension lines.
- The space between the outside edge of the building and the first dimension line (9/16″ minimum) should be consistently applied throughout the drawing (see Figure 6.2).

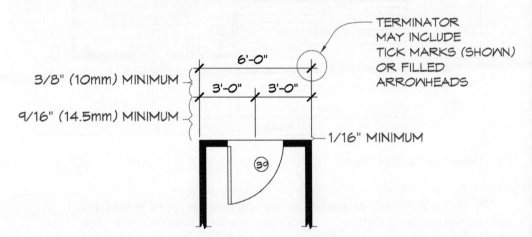

6.2 NCS Minimum Dimension Spacing Guidelines for Architectural Drawings

- The spacing between succeeding parallel dimension lines (3/8″ minimum) should be consistent throughout the drawing (see Figure 6.2).
- Dimensions may terminate in tick marks or arrowheads. Tick marks should be parallel.
- Dimension text height should not be less than 3/32″ on CAD drawings (1/8″ on hand-drafted plans).
- Dimension font style should be sans serif, and all notations should be capitalized. Italicized, underlined, or bold fonts should be avoided.

6.6 ARCHITECTURAL DIMENSION SPACING

Minimum suggested spacing for architectural dimensions is shown in Figure 6.2. The spacing values shown apply to the plotted drawing. These spacings are entered into AutoCAD's **Dimension Style Manager** before dimensions are applied to the drawing.

6.7 ADDING A LEADER TO A DRAWING

Figure 6.3 shows an example of a leader that is appropriate for an architectural drawing. These leader styles can be created using either the **Quick Leader** or **Multileader** command.

6.3   Architectural Leader Style

QUICK LEADER COMMAND TUTORIAL

To create a quick leader with a curved (spline) leader line use the following steps:

1   Type **QLEADER** (or **LE**) the command line and press **<Enter>**.

2   At the *Specify first leader point:* prompt, type **S** (for Settings) and press **<Enter>**.

3   When the **Leader Settings** dialog box opens, select the **Leader Line & Arrow** tab and choose the **Spline** option for the **Leader Line** setting and click **OK**.

4   At the *Specify first leader point:* prompt, select the point for the arrowhead to begin.

5   At the *Specify next point:* prompt, select the point for the leader line to end.

6   At the *Specify next point:* prompt, select the point where the landing line should end.

7   At the *Specify text width:* prompt, either press **<Enter>** or type in a width value.

8   At the *Enter first line of annotation text:* prompt, enter the text for the first line of the leader annotation and press **<Enter>**.

9   At the *Enter next line of annotation:* prompt, enter the text for the next line or press **<Enter>**.

STEP by STEP

STEP by STEP

MULTILEADER COMMAND TUTORIAL

To create a mulitleader leader with a curved (spline) leader line use the following steps:

1 Type **MLEADER** (or **MLD**) on the command line and press **<Enter>**, or select the **Multileader** tool from either the **Annotation** panel of the **Home** tab of the ribbon or the **Leaders** panel of the **Annotate** tab. See Figure 5.64(b).

2 At the *Specify leader arrowhead location:* prompt type **O** (for Options) and click the **Leader Type** tab, the **Spline** option, then **eXit Options** and follow the prompts to complete the **Multileader** command.

KEY WORDS

Building Information Model (BIM)

Sans Serif

Tick Marks

United States National CAD Standard (NCS)

CHAPTER SUMMARY

Architectural drafters are responsible for creating dimensioned drawings that are used by construction professionals to locate walls, windows, doors, and other features of the building project. Drafters are responsible for ensuring that the dimensions on the drawing accurately reflect the dimensions provided on the designer's input. Drafters must be familiar with architectural drawing and dimensioning standards and the appropriate dimension style settings for the preparation of CAD drawings.

REVIEW QUESTIONS

Short Answer

1. Who is responsible for determining dimensions on architectural drawing?
2. In the United States, what is the name of the organization that publishes a drawing standard for architectural drawings?
3. How are the locations of doors and windows defined with dimensions on architectural drawings?
4. What termination symbol is often used on architectural dimensions?
5. Which direction(s) does aligned text face?

Matching

Refer to Figures 6.5(a) - (e) to determine the answers to the following questions.

Column A

a. **Primary Units**

b. **Lines**

c. **Text**

d. **Fit**

e. **Symbols and Arrows**

Column B

1. The **Dimension Style Manager** tab where the size of tick marks (slashes) is defined
2. The **Dimension Style Manager** tab where the distance that dimension lines should extend beyond tick marks is defined
3. The **Dimension Style Manager** tab where the format for dimension units is defined
4. The **Dimension Style Manager** tab where placing text above vertical dimension lines is defined
5. The **Dimension Style Manager** tab where the overall scale of dimension features is defined

CHAPTER PROJECT

Project 6.1: Dimensioning the Guest Cottage

In this project, you will open the **Guest Cottage** drawing that you created in Chapter 4 and apply the dimensions shown in Figure 6.4. Follow the rules of dimensioning outlined earlier in this chapter.

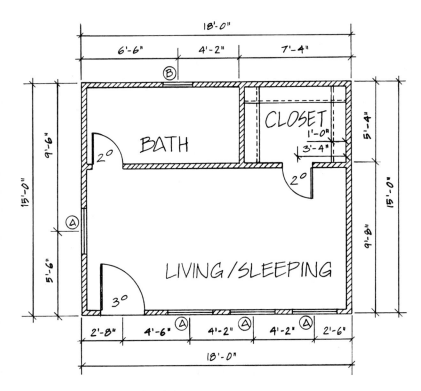

6.4   Designer's Sketch of the Guest Cottage

Before dimensioning the cottage, create a new dimension style named **ARCH48** and assign the dimension style settings shown in Figures 6.5(a)–(e) and set the new style current (refer to the *Creating a New Dimension Style* section of Chapter 5 (page 241) if you need help creating a new dimension style). Set the **Dimensions** layer current and use the **Linear Dimension** tool to place the first dimension of the first row of dimensions, then use the **Continue** dimension tool to place the rest of the dimensions that make up the first row. The first rows of dimensions should be spaced a minimum of **2′-3″** from the outside walls of all four sides of the cottage. The second rows of dimensions should be spaced **1′-6″** from the first rows. Dimension spacing should be consistent on each side of the floor plan.

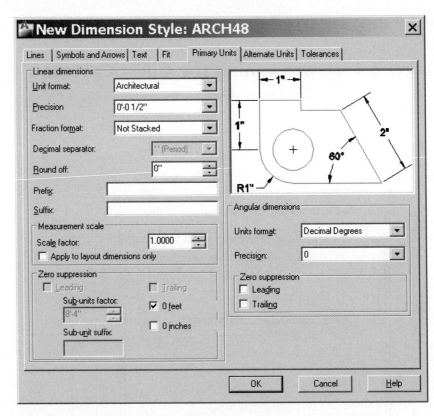

6.5(a)   Dimension Settings for **Primary Units** Tab of ARCH48
Dimension Style

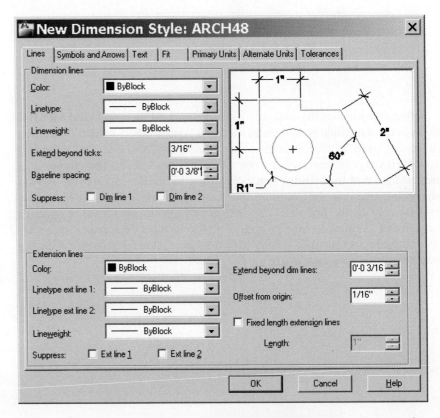

6.5(b)   Dimension Settings for **Lines** Tab of ARCH48 Dimension Style

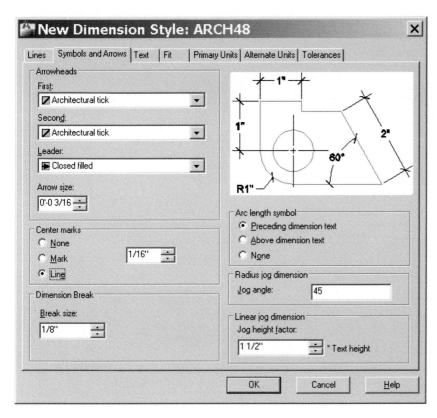

6.5(c) Dimension Settings for **Symbols And Arrows** Tab of ARCH48 Dimension Style

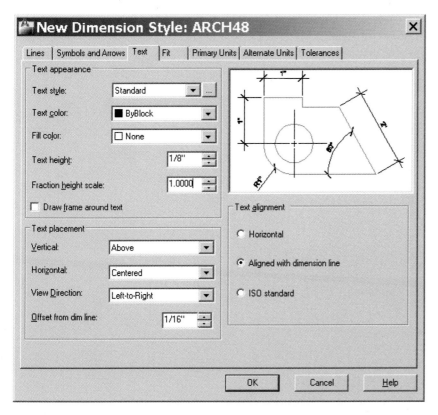

6.5(d) Dimension Settings for **Text** Tab of ARCH48 Dimension Style

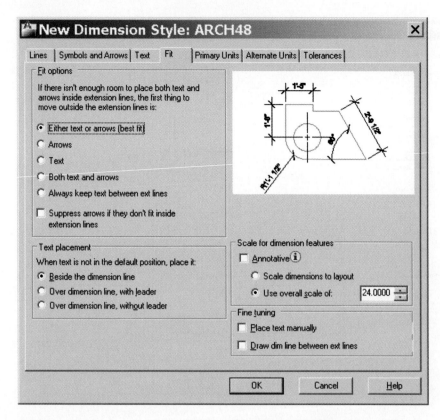

6.5(e)   Dimension Settings for **Fit** Tab of ARCH48 Dimension Style

Follow the directions in the plotting section of Chapter 4 (page 171) to create a page setup named **Cottage.** To plot the page setup, select the **Plot** icon from the **Plot** panel of the **Output** tab of the ribbon (see Figure 4.111), and when the **Plot** dialog box opens, select the down arrow in the **Page Setup** window and select **Cottage** from the list, shown in Figure 4.116. Click **OK** to send the print to the plotter or printer.

Save the drawing file before closing AutoCAD.

CHAPTER SEVEN

ISOMETRIC DRAWINGS

OBJECTIVES

After studying the material in this chapter, you should be able to:

1. Define the term *isometric drawing*.

2. Correctly orient lines, ellipses, fillets, and rounds in isometric drawings.

3. Construct inclined planes in isometric drawings.

4. Construct isometric drawings with AutoCAD.

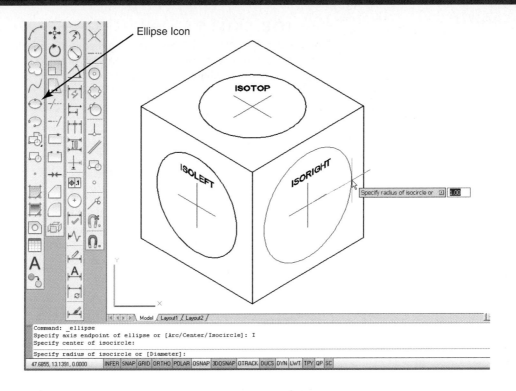

Ellipse Icon

OVERVIEW

An *isometric drawing* is a type of drawing known as a *pictorial drawing*. In a pictorial drawing, an object appears to be three-dimensional; that is, it appears to have width, height, and depth. However, unlike a 3D model, a pictorial drawing is constructed using 2D drawing techniques. The type of drawing discussed in this chapter—isometric drawing—is generally used for drawing machine parts pictorially. Figure 7.1(a) shows an isometric drawing of a cube. In this drawing, the box appears to have width, depth, and height, but this drawing was constructed using only *X*- and *Y*- coordinates, so it is considered a 2D drawing.

In the architectural field, pictorial drawings are created using *perspective drawing* techniques. In a perspective drawing, lines appear to recede toward a vanishing point, whereas in an isometric drawing, the receding lines are drawn parallel. Figure 7.1(b) shows an example of a perspective

drawing. Study the differences in the two types of pictorial drawings—isometric and perspective—shown in Figures 7.1(a) and (b).

In many modern CAD applications, a drafter can construct a 3D model of an object and use it to generate a pictorial image instead of using isometric or perspective drawing techniques.

7.1(a)   Isometric Drawing   **7.1(b)**   Perspective Drawing

7.1 ORIENTATION OF LINES IN ISOMETRIC DRAWINGS

In an isometric drawing, an object's horizontal lines are drawn at 30° angles relative to the horizon, and its vertical lines are drawn at a 90° angle relative to the horizon (in other words, the object's vertical lines are drawn vertically), as shown in Figure 7.2. When isometric lines meet at their ends to define a regular (not inclined) plane, the plane is classified in AutoCAD terminology as *isoright*, *isoleft*, or *isotop*, as shown in Figure 7.2.

──── **TIP** ────

Even though isometric planes are described in AutoCAD terms as *isoright, isoleft,* and *isotop,* drafters may also refer to these planes as *right vertical, left vertical,* and *horizontal planes,* respectively.

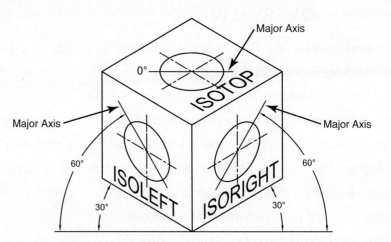

7.2   Orientation of Isometric Lines and Ellipses

7.2 ORIENTATION OF ELLIPSES IN ISOMETRIC DRAWINGS

Another characteristic of isometric drawings is that round shapes, such as circles and cylinders, appear as ellipses. For the drawing to look natural, however, an isometric ellipse must be aligned correctly along its *major axis*. Figure 7.2 shows the correct orientation of isometric ellipses on their respective planes. Note that although horizontal isometric lines are drawn at 30° angles, the major axes of ellipses located on isoright and isoleft planes are aligned along 60° angles. The major axis of an isometric ellipse on an isotop plane is aligned along a horizontal (0°) line. Study the differences in the orientation of the major axes of the isoright, isoleft, and isotop planes as shown in Figure 7.2.

CONSTRUCTING AN ISOMETRIC DRAWING USING THE BOUNDING BOX TECHNIQUE

One of the easiest ways for beginners to construct an isometric drawing is to start by creating an isometric *bounding box*. A bounding box is a box drawn along isometric axes that can completely enclose the object. The bounding box is constructed using the overall width, depth, and height dimensions of the object. After drawing the bounding box, you can reference measurements from its corners to locate the object's features.

The steps in creating an isometric drawing of the object shown in Figure 7.3 using a bounding box are shown in Figures 7.4 through 7.6. These steps illustrate how to locate the object's features by measuring from the corners of the bounding box.

1 Construct an isometric bounding box using height, width, and depth dimensions taken from Figure 7.3. The completed bounding box is shown in Figure 7.4.

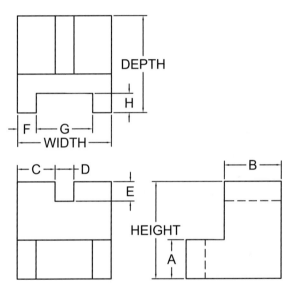

7.3 Multiview Drawing of an Object to Be Drawn Isometrically

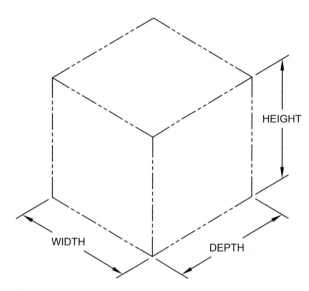

7.4 Isometric Bounding Box

2 Transfer distances *A* and *B* from Figure 7.3 to the isometric drawing by measuring from the corners of the bounding box. Add lines as needed to construct the view shown in Figure 7.5.

3 Transfer distances *C* through *H* from Figure 7.3 to locate the two slots. Trim and add lines as needed to complete the view as shown in Figure 7.6.

STEP by STEP

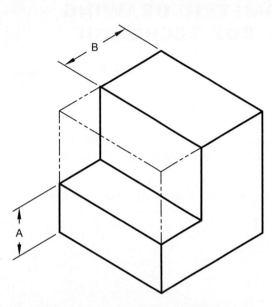

7.5 Transferring Distances A and B to the Bounding Box

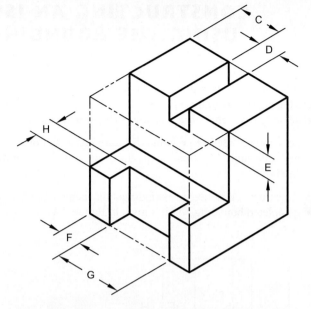

7.6 Transferring Distances C through H to the Bounding Box to Locate the Slots

CONSTRUCTING INCLINED PLANES IN ISOMETRIC DRAWINGS

The angle of an inclined plane cannot be measured directly in an isometric drawing. You must instead locate the start and end-points of the corners of the inclined plane by using measurements taken from a multiview drawing and connecting the points to define the angled plane. The bounding box technique discussed earlier is also helpful for locating the corners of inclined planes.

The object shown in Figure 7.7 contains an inclined plane. The steps in creating an isometric drawing of this object, including the construction of the inclined plane, are illustrated in Figures 7.8 through 7.10.

1   Construct an isometric bounding box using height, width, and depth dimensions taken from Figure 7.7. The completed bounding box is shown in Figure 7.8.

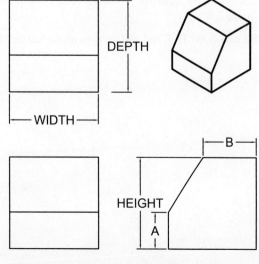

7.7 Multiview Drawing of Object to Be Drawn Isometrically

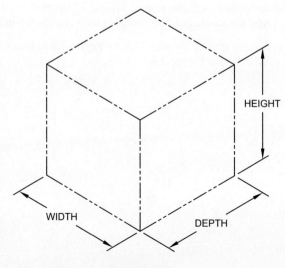

7.8 Isometric Bounding Box

2 Transfer distances *A* and *B* from Figure 7.7 by measuring from the corners of the bounding box. Add lines as needed to construct the view shown in Figure 7.9.

3 Connect the points that define the inclined plane to complete the view as shown in Figure 7.10.

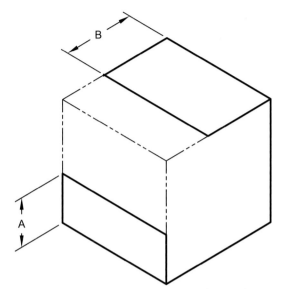

7.9 Transferring Distances A and B to the Bounding Box

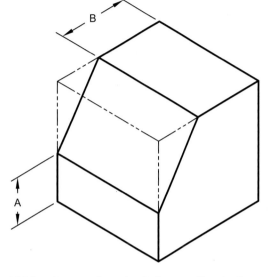

7.10 Connecting the Points to Create the Inclined Plane

7.3 CREATING ISOMETRIC DRAWINGS WITH AUTOCAD

The first step in creating an isometric drawing is to set AutoCAD's snap type from rectangular to isometric. You do this by left-clicking on the **Tools** pull-down menu on the menu bar and selecting **Drafting Settings** or by right-clicking on the **Snap**, **Grid**, **Polar**, **Osnap**, **Otrack**, **LWT** (Show/Hide Lineweight), **QP** (Quick Properties), or **SC** (Selection Cycling) button located on the status bar and clicking on **Settings.** When the **Drafting Settings** dialog box opens, click the **Snap and Grid** tab and check the button next to **Isometric snap** (see Figure 7.11), and then click the **OK** button.

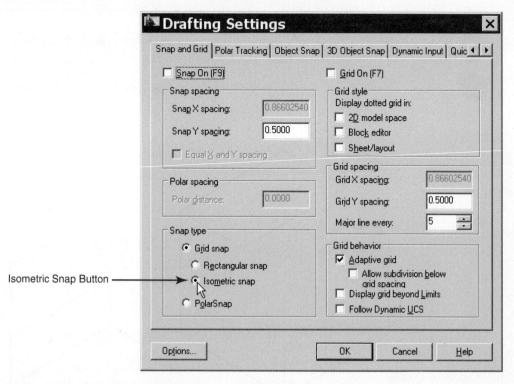

7.11 Setting Isometric Snap

After changing the snap type from rectangular to isometric, you will notice that the crosshairs of the cursor are oriented at isometric angles. When **Ortho** is on, and the **LINE** command has been selected, lines are automatically limited to the isometric axes displayed by the angles of the lines in the cursor. To draw lines along different isometric axes than the ones displayed by the cursor, you must change the orientation of the cursor, either by pressing the **<F5>** key or by pressing the **<Ctrl>** and **<E>** keys simultaneously. Each time you press the **<F5>** key the orientation of the cursor's crosshairs, or *isoplane*, will change, cycling between the isotop, isoleft, and isoright isoplanes.

NOTE

The current isoplane setting will also be displayed on the command line each time you press **<F5>**.

TIP

When **Drafting Settings** are set to **Isometric snap**, and **Ortho** mode is turned on, lines drawn in an isometric drawing are automatically aligned along isometric axes. Toggling the **<F5>** key allows you to quickly change the isometric orientation between the isotop, isoleft, and isoright orientations. To draw lines that are not aligned to an isometric angle, you must turn **Ortho** off.

In an isometric drawing, horizontal isometric lines are drawn at 30° relative to the horizon. Creating an isometric drawing with AutoCAD, however, requires that the angle of isometric lines be converted to polar coordinates (where East equals 0°).

In Figure 7.12 the possible isometric angles for the lines of the object are noted on each corner (this example depicts the angles with **Dynamic Input** on). The angle of each line is determined by the position of its start point and its direction relative to East. Note that the angle of the inclined plane does not fall on an isometric angle and therefore would need to be drawn using the technique described in Figures 7.8 through 7.10.

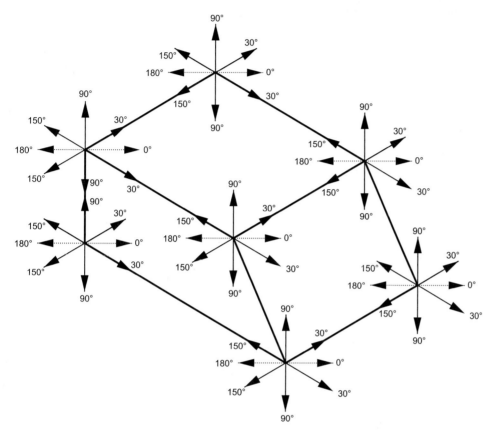

7.12   Isometric Angles

An example of the principal isometric axes for isometric lines using AutoCAD polar coordinates is shown in Figure 7.13. Some examples of polar coordinates for isometric lines (assuming **Dynamic Input** is on) are **6 <Tab> 30, 4 <Tab> 90, 7 <Tab> 150,** and **6 <Tab> 180.**

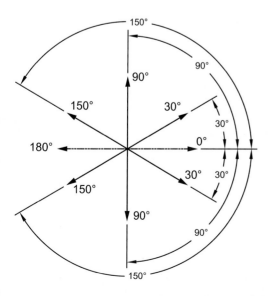

7.13   Isometric Axes

DRAWING ISOMETRIC ELLIPSES WITH AUTOCAD

Figure 7.14 shows an isometric box with three isometric ellipses. Notice that each ellipse in Figure 7.14 is oriented differently from the others. This is because each ellipse was drawn on a different isoplane—isotop, isoright, or isoleft. AutoCAD refers to ellipses that are oriented on isometric planes as *isocircles*.

To place an isocircle in an isometric drawing, first determine the orientation of the isoplane on which the ellipse is to be drawn (isotop, isoright, or isoleft) by referring to Figure 7.14. Then, toggle to the appropriate isoplane by pressing **<F5>**. Next, select the **Ellipse** tool from the **Draw** toolbar or the **Draw** panel (**Axis End** option), type **I** for **Isocircle,** and press **<Enter>**. Next, specify the center of the ellipse and its radius and press **<Enter>** to complete the command.

> ─ **NOTE** ─────────────────────────────
> The **Isocircle** option **of the ELLIPSE** command is available only when **Snap type** has been set to **Isometric snap** in the **Snap and Grid** tab of the **Drawing Settings** dialog box.

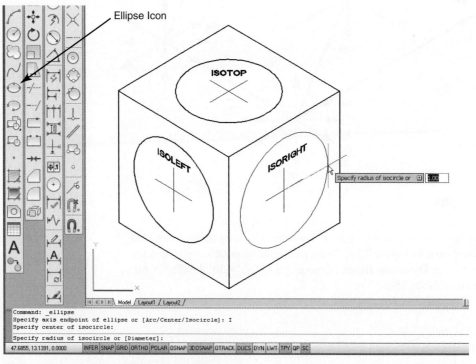

7.14 Autocad Isocircles and Isoplanes

The steps in constructing an isometric cylinder are shown in Figures 7.15(a)–(c).

1 Draw an ellipse (isocircle) at the desired diameter and orientation of the cylinder. Copy the ellipse along an isometric angle the desired length of the cylinder as shown in Figure 7.15(a).

2 Draw lines from the quadrants of the front ellipse to the corresponding quadrants of the back ellipse as shown in Figure 7.15(b).

3 Trim the back ellipse to complete the cylinder as shown in Figure 7.15(c).

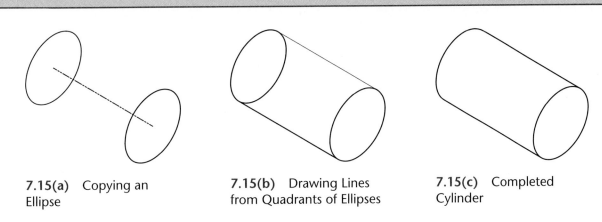

7.15(a) Copying an Ellipse

7.15(b) Drawing Lines from Quadrants of Ellipses

7.15(c) Completed Cylinder

Possible orientations for horizontal and vertical cylinders are shown in Figure 7.16.

Isocircles can be used to create counterbored, countersunk, and through holes in isometric drawings, as shown in Figure 7.17.

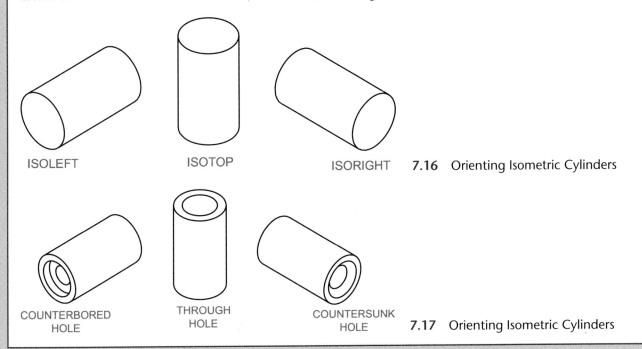

ISOLEFT

ISOTOP

ISORIGHT   **7.16** Orienting Isometric Cylinders

COUNTERBORED HOLE

THROUGH HOLE

COUNTERSUNK HOLE   **7.17** Orienting Isometric Cylinders

CONSTRUCTING ISOMETRIC ARCS AND RADII (FILLETS AND ROUNDS)

In technical drawing, the terms *fillet* and *round* refer to a rounded inside and outside corner, respectively. On a multiview drawing, AutoCAD's **FILLET** command can be used to create fillets and rounds at an object's corners, but the **FILLET**. Therefore, drafters must use steps similar to the ones illustrated in Figures 7.18 through 7.22 to add isometric fillets and rounds to an object. In these examples the objective is to add a rounded edge with a **1″** radius to corners A–D of the object shown in Figure 7.18.

1 Copy edges **1** through **6** along isometric axes **1″** inside the edges of the part as shown in Figure 7.19.

2 Using the intersections of the lines copied in Step 1 for center points, draw four **2″**-diameter ellipses (isocircles) as shown in Figure 7.20.

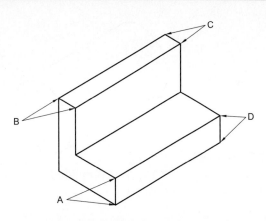

7.18 Adding a 1" Radius to Corners A, B, C, and D of Object

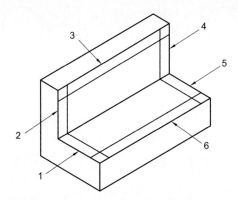

7.19 Copying Edges 1–6 along Isometric Axes

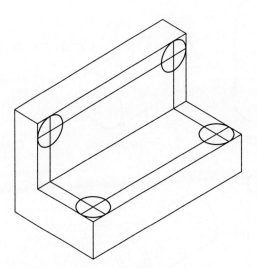

7.20 Adding Ellipses at Intersections of Copied Lines

3 Trim the ellipses to create a round for each corner, and copy the rounds along isometric axes (turn **Ortho** on) to the corresponding corner as shown in Figure 7.21.

4 Erase and edit construction lines as needed to complete the view as shown in Figure 7.22.

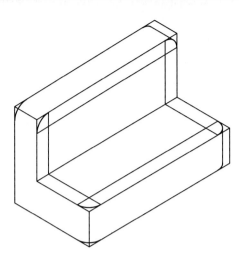

7.21 Trimming Ellipses to Create Rounded Corners

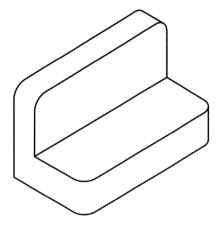

7.22 The Finished Isometric Drawing

STEP by STEP

KEY WORDS

Fillet

Isometric Drawing

Perspective Drawing

Pictorial Drawing

Round

CHAPTER SUMMARY

Pictorial drawings appear to be three-dimensional but are constructed using only *X*- and *Y*-coordinates, so they are actually a form of two-dimensional drawing. To create isometric drawings in AutoCAD, drafters must master the concept of polar coordinates, be able to orient correctly the major axes of isometric ellipses, and be able to use the techniques needed to construct inclined planes.

Pictorial views created from 3D CAD models are replacing isometric and perspective drawings in many fields of technical graphics. However, the ability to create freehand pictorial sketches quickly to facilitate communication of design ideas remains an important job skill for designers and drafters and one that students seeking to become employable in this field should strive to develop.

REVIEW QUESTIONS

Multiple Choice

1. In which field of technical drawing are isometric techniques most often used to create a pictorial image?

    a. Archaeological
    b. Architectural
    c. Mechanical
    d. Civil

2. What is the angle of an object's horizontal lines in an isometric drawing?

    a. 60°
    b. 180°
    c. 30°
    d. None of the above

3. What is the angle of an object's vertical lines in an isometric drawing?
   a. 90°
   b. 45°
   c. 30°
   d. 60°

4. On which tab in the **Drafting Settings** dialog box is the **Rectangular snap** button located?
   a. **Snap and Grid** tab
   b. **Polar Tracking** tab
   c. **Dynamic Input** tab
   d. **Object Snap** tab

5. At what angle is the major axis of an ellipse drawn on an isoright plane?
   a. 90°
   b. 45°
   c. 30°
   d. 60°

True or False

1. *True or False*: Angles of inclined planes can be measured directly in an isometric drawing.
2. *True or False*: Pressing **<F5>** or **<Ctrl>+E** are the two ways to change the orientation of the crosshairs in an isometric drawing created with AutoCAD.
3. *True or False*: When drawing an isometric ellipse, a drafter must select **Isoplane** after beginning AutoCAD's **ELLIPSE** command.
4. *True or False*: It is not important for drafters and designers to understand isometric drawing techniques.
5. *True or False*: In an isometric drawing the lines appear to recede toward a vanishing point.

CHAPTER PROJECTS

Project 7.1: Tee Connector Isometric

Directions

Create an isometric drawing of the tee connector shown in Figure 7.23.

1. Open the **Daily Work Prototype** drawing located in the student data files at **www .pearsondesigncentral.com.** To access this drawing, open the Pearson Design Central website and click on the *CAD Community* link, then select the *Click here to download student data files for our CAD titles* link. Next, click on the *Technical Drawing 101* link and select the *Prototype Drawings* zip file, then se- lect the *Download* button and open (or save) the prototype drawing specified above.
2. Use **SAVE AS** to save the drawing to your **Home** directory, and rename the drawing **TEE CONNECTOR**.
3. Set the units to **Decimal** and the upper right corner of the drawing limits to **24,18**.

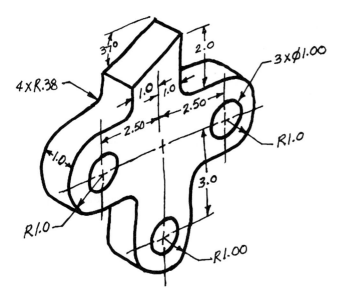

7.23   Designer's Sketch of the Tee Connector

4. Set AutoCAD's snap type to **Isometric snap** in the **Snap and Grid** tab of the **Drawing Settings** dialog box and turn **Ortho** on.

Steps in Constructing the Tee Connector

Step 1.   Draw the horizontal and vertical isometric lines shown in Figure 7.24.

Step 2.   Draw a **1″** diameter and a **2″** diameter ellipse (isocircle) at the three end- points as shown in Figure 7.25.

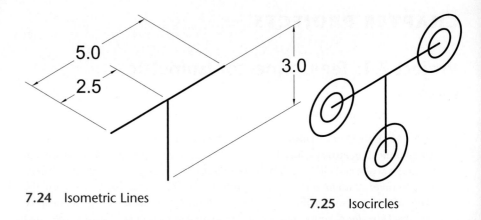

7.24 Isometric Lines

7.25 Isocircles

Step 3.   Draw tangency lines connecting the ellipses as shown in Figure 7.26.

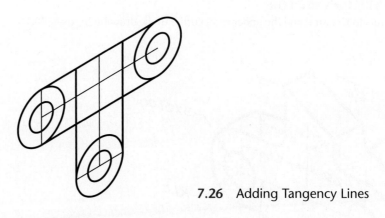

7.26 Adding Tangency Lines

> ─── **TIP** ───
> You may need to add construction lines from the center points of the isocircles
> drawn in Step 2 to find snap points tangent to the ellipses.

Step 4.   To construct the **37°** angle shown in the designer's sketch, you will need to
create an orthographic front view of the top part of the object to find distance **A** as shown in Figure 7.27(a). Change the snap type in the **Drafting
Settings** dialog box from **Isometric** to **Rectangular snap** to construct the

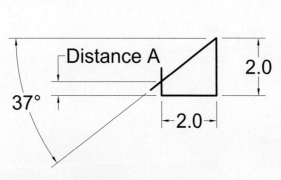

7.27(a)   Orthographic View Drawn to
Determine Distance A

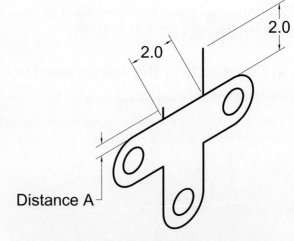

7.27(b)   Transferring Distance A to the
Isometric Drawing

view shown in Figure 7.27(a). Transfer distance **A** from the orthographic drawing to the isometric construction as shown in Figure 7.27(b), and set the **Snap type** in the **Drafting Settings** dialog box back to **Isometric** from **Rectangular snap**.

Step 5.   Connect the endpoints of the lines drawn in Step 4 and trim any unnecessary construction lines. Following completion of this step, your drawing should resemble the object shown in Figure 7.28.

Step 6.   With **Ortho** on, copy construction lines **.38″** from the inside corners of the object and draw **.76″** (.38″ × 2) diameter ellipses (isocircles) at the intersections of these lines as shown in Figure 7.29.

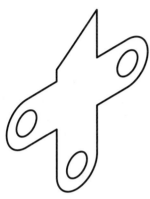

7.28   Front Surface of the Tee Connector

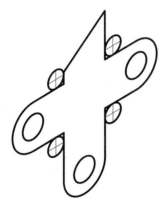

7.29   Adding Fillets

Step 7.   Trim the **.38″** diameter ellipses to create the fillets at the inside corners of the tee connector and then copy the object **1″** behind the first object at an angle of **150°** as shown in Figure 7.30.

Step 8.   Trim any unnecessary lines and add isometric lines connecting the front edge of the tee connector to the back edge as shown in Figure 7.31 to complete the construction.

Step 9.   Follow your instructor's directions to plot the drawing. Be sure to save the drawing file when you close AutoCAD.

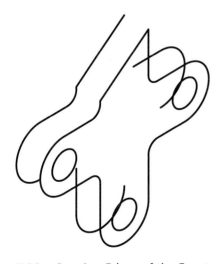

7.30   Copying Edges of the Front Face Back 1″ at a 150° Angle

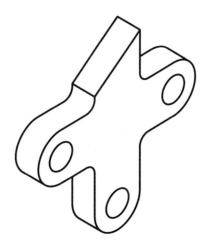

7.31   Finished Project

Project 7.2: Tool Holder Isometric

Directions

Open the drawing titled **Tool Holder** that you created in Chapter 4 and use the following steps to create an isometric drawing from the sketch shown in Figure 7.32. Construct the isometric view in the space located to the right of the drawing's border, but move the finished isometric drawing inside the upper right corner of the sheet (to the right of the top view and above the right view). Set AutoCAD's **Snap type** to **Isometric snap** in the **Snap and Grid** tab of the **Drawing Settings** dialog box and turn **Ortho** on. When you are finished with this project, this drawing will include both the isometric drawing of the tool holder as well its dimensioned multiviews.

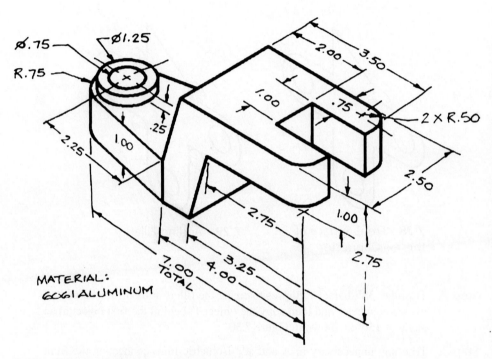

7.32 Designer's Sketch of the Tool Holder

Steps in Constructing the Tool Holder Isometric Project

Step 1. Create a **7.00″ × 2.50″ × 2.75″** bounding box that can contain the tool holder as shown in Figure 7.33.

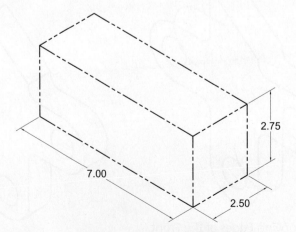

7.33 Bounding Box for the Tool Holder

Step 2.   Construct the basic shape of the front of the tool holder within the bounding box and add fillets to the front corners using the dimensions shown in Figure 7.34.

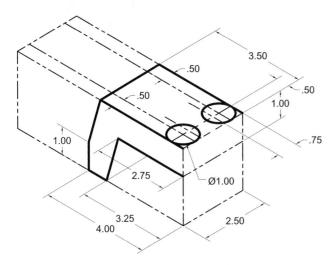

7.34   Constructing the Front Part of the Tool Holder

Step 3.   Copy the filleted corners created in Step 2, down 1.00″ along the *Y*-axis and add the slot using the dimensions shown in Figure 7.35.

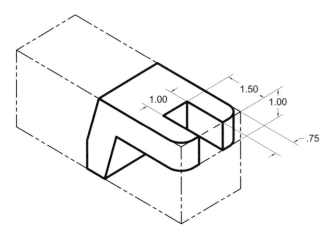

7.35   Completed Construction of the Front Part of the Tool Holder

Step 4.   Locate the two **1.50″** diameter ellipses at the back of the object and add tangency lines between the ellipses as shown in Figure 7.36. (The front part of the tool holder has not been shown in Figure 7.36 for clarity.)

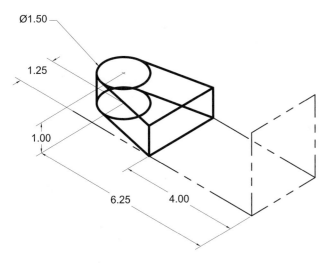

7.36   Constructing the Back Part of the Tool Holder

Step 5. Trim the lines drawn in Step 4 so that your drawing resembles the one shown in Figure 7.37.

Step 6. Add two **1.25″** diameter ellipses **.25″** apart to form the raised cylinder (also referred to as a *boss*) shown in Figure 7.38. Next, add a **.75″** diameter ellipse at the top of the boss as shown in Figure 7.38. Trim the lines as needed to complete the boss as shown in Figure 7.39.

Step 7. Trim any unneeded lines to finish the isometric view of the tool holder. Your drawing should resemble the one shown in Figure 7.40.

Step 8. Follow your instructor's directions to plot the drawing. Be sure to save the drawing file when you close AutoCAD.

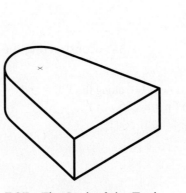

7.37 The Back of the Tool Holder after Trimming Ellipses

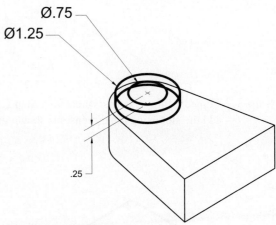

7.38 Constructing the Boss

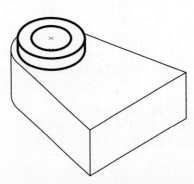

7.39 Completed Construction of the Back Part of the Tool Holder

7.40 Completed Isometric Drawing of the Tool Holder

CHAPTER EIGHT

SECTIONS

OBJECTIVES

After studying the material in this chapter, you should be able to:

1. Define what section views are.

2. Describe how section views are used in technical drawings.

3. Provide the names and descriptions of the different types of sections and the terminology associated with section views.

4. Use AutoCAD to create section views, including properly placing cutting plane lines and hatch patterns.

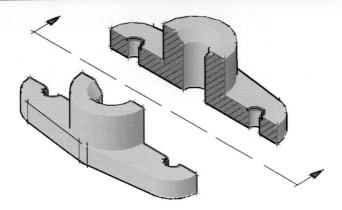

OVERVIEW

A *section* view is a type of drawing in which part of an object's exterior is removed to reveal its interior features. For example, in mechanical engineering drawings, sections are used to show interior features of machine parts that would not be clearly represented by hidden lines. In architectural drawings, sections are used to reveal the interior details of walls, roofs, and foundations.

In creating a section view, an imaginary *cutting plane* is used to slice through the object to reveal its interior features. In mechanical drawings, the sectioned areas are usually filled with diagonal *section lines* (also called *cross-hatching*), which indicate where the cutting plane line passes through the part. In architectural drawings, the sectioned areas may be filled with hatch patterns that represent building materials such as concrete or insulation.

8.1 SECTIONS IN MECHANICAL DRAWINGS

In Figure 8.1, an object with five machined holes is shown as it would look if it were cut in half to show its inside detail. The heavy dashed line shown between the views is called a *cutting plane line*. The cutting plane line defines the line along which the object is cut. The arrows on the ends of the cutting plane line indicate the direction in which the viewer is observing the sectioned object. The diagonal lines drawn on the plane created by cutting the part in half are the *section lines*.

The principal reason for using section views in mechanical drawings is to define the complex interior features of an object by replacing hidden lines with visible lines in a view. This allows the drafter to dimension to interior features without dimensioning to hidden lines.

Figure 8.2 shows the front and top views of the object shown in Figure 8.1. The heavy dashed line running through the center of the top view is the cutting plane line. This line defines the line along which the object is cut. The upward-pointing arrows on the ends of the cutting plane line indicate the direction in which the viewer is observing the sectioned object. The diagonal lines shown on the front, or sectioned, view in Figure 8.1 indicate that the view is a section. The profile edges of the machined holes, which would have been represented by hidden lines in a regular multiview drawing, are represented by visible lines in the section view.

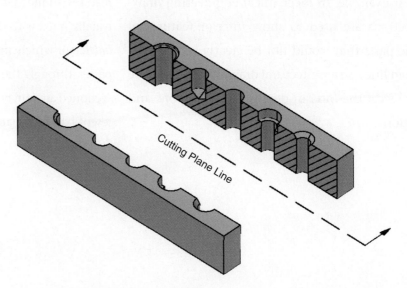

8.1   Section View of a 3D Object

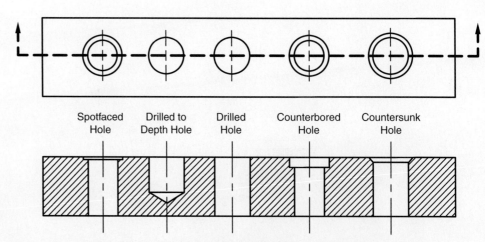

8.2   Top View and Sectioned Front View of an Object

8.2 SECTIONS IN ARCHITECTURAL DRAWINGS

In architectural drawings, sections are often included on foundation plans to show details through beams and footings, as shown in the designer's sketch in Figure 8.3. A CAD drafter might work from a sketch of this type to create a technical drawing.

Wall sections are prepared in architectural drawings to specify the composition of a wall, as shown in Figure 8.4. Often, a wall section of a building must be included in a set of architectural plans before a building permit will be granted for a project. Study Figure 8.4 and note the hatch patterns used to represent the insulation and concrete as well as the earth around the foundation.

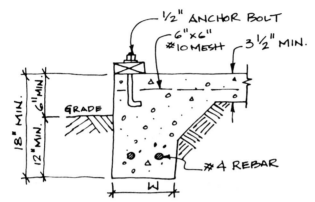

MONOLITHIC SLAB DETAIL
WITH INTEGRAL FOOTING
1.) TWO #4 REBAR @ 4"O.C.
2.) 6"X6" - #10 MESH IN FLOOR SLAB
3.) 1/2" ANCHOR BOLTS @ 6'-0" O.C.
4.) FOOTING WIDTH, W = 10" MIN.

8.3 Architectural Designer's Sketch of a Foundation Section Detail

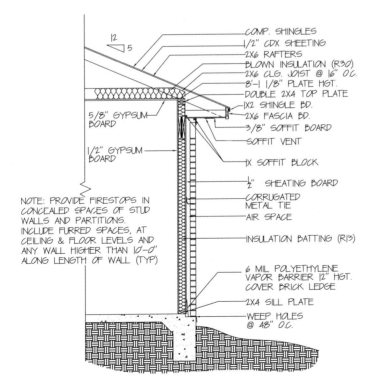

ONE STORY DETAIL
3/8" = 1'-0"

8.4 Architectural Wall Section

8.3 TYPES OF SECTIONS

Common section view types are *full, half, broken-out, revolved, removed,* and *offset*. Drafters decide on the type of section view to draw based on which one most clearly represents the necessary features.

Full Sections

A full section shows the object as if it has been cut in half. Figures 8.5 and 8.6 show the front and side views of an apple. The knife blade in the front view (Figure 8.5) represents the cutting plane line. In the side view (Figure 8.6), the apple appears as it would if it were sliced in half along the cutting plane line. This view represents a full section.

8.5 Knife Blade Represents the Cutting Plane Line in Front View

8.6 Side View Shown as a Full Section

In Figures 8.7 and 8.8 the front and side views of a machine part are shown. The thick dashed lines with the arrows pointing to the left in the front view represent the cutting plane line (see Figure 8.7). The view shown in Figure 8.8 represents a full

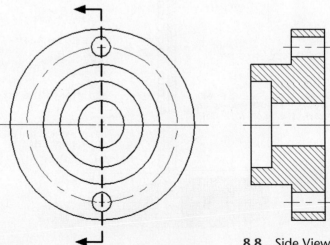

8.7 Front View with the Cutting Plane Line for a Full Section

8.8 Side View Drawn as a Full Section

section. This view is drawn as it would appear if the part of the object in the front view that lies behind the cutting plane line had been removed. The diagonal lines shown in the side view are the section lines.

> ─── **TIP** ───
> Cutting plane lines take precedence over centerlines. When a cutting plane line is used as the centerline, show the cutting plane line only.

Half Sections

A *half section* shows the object as if one fourth of it has been removed. In Figures 8.9 and 8.10 the top and front views of an apple are shown. The knife blades in the top view (Figure 8.9) represent the cutting plane line. In the front view (Figure 8.10) the apple appears as it would if the part of the apple framed by the knife blades in the top view had been removed. This view represents a half section.

In Figures 8.11 and 8.12 the top and front views of a machine part are shown. The thick dashed line with the arrow pointing up in the top view represents the cutting plane line (see Figure 8.11). The view in Figure 8.12 represents a half section. This view is drawn as it would appear if the part of the object in the top view framed by the cutting plane line had been removed.

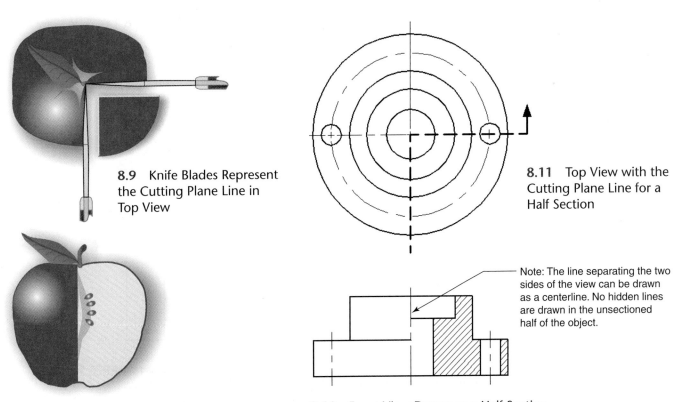

8.9 Knife Blades Represent the Cutting Plane Line in Top View

8.11 Top View with the Cutting Plane Line for a Half Section

Note: The line separating the two sides of the view can be drawn as a centerline. No hidden lines are drawn in the unsectioned half of the object.

8.10 Front View of an Apple Shown as a Half Section

8.12 Front View Drawn as a Half Section

> ─── **TIP** ───
> In a half section, it is not necessary to draw hidden lines in the unsectioned half of the view.

In Figures 8.13 and 8.14 the front and side views of an apple are shown. The knife blades in the front view (Figure 8.13) represent the cutting plane line. In the side view (Figure 8.14), the apple appears as it would if the part of the apple inside the knife blades in the front view had been removed. This view represents a half section.

In Figures 8.15 and 8.16 the front and side views of a machine part are shown. The thick dashed line with the arrow pointing toward the left in the front view represents the cutting plane line (see Figure 8.15). The view in Figure 8.16 represents a half section. This view is drawn as it would appear if the part of the object in the front view framed by the cutting plane line had been removed.

8.13 Knife Blades Represent the Cutting Plane Line in Front View

8.14 Side View of Apple Shown as a Half Section

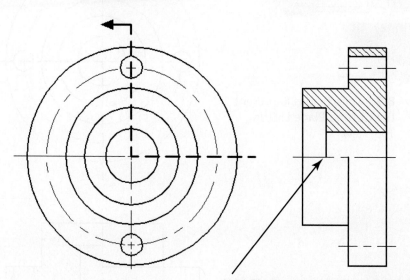

8.15 Front View with the Cutting Plane Line for a Half Section

Note: The line separating the two sides of the sectioned view is drawn as a centerline and no hidden lines are drawn in the unsectioned half of the object.

8.16 Side View Drawn as a Half Section

Broken-Out Sections

A *broken-out section* is used when only a small portion of the object needs to be sectioned. Figure 8.17 shows the front and side views of an apple. In the side view, a piece of the apple has been broken out to show the worm on the inside.

TIP
A cutting plane line is not necessary on a broken-out section.

8.17 Front and Side Views of Apple with a Broken-Out Section Shown in the Side View

Figure 8.18 shows the front and top views of a machine part. The front view is drawn as it would appear if a small part of the object has been removed, or broken out, to reveal the desired interior feature. The broken line is drawn as a visible line, and diagonal section lines are added to the sectioned areas. The front view in Figure 8.18 represents a broken-out section.

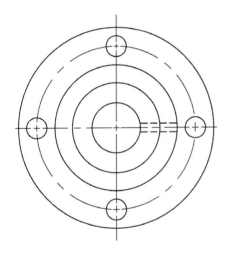

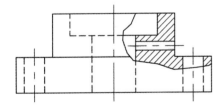

8.18 Front and Top Views with a Broken-Out Section in the Front View

Revolved Sections

In a ***revolved section*** the cross-sectional view of the object is drawn on the object as shown in Figures 8.19 and 8.20. Drafters can place dimensions directly on the revolved section.

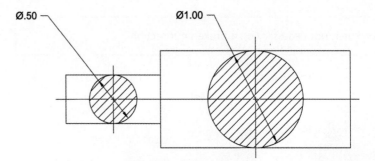

8.19 Revolved Section

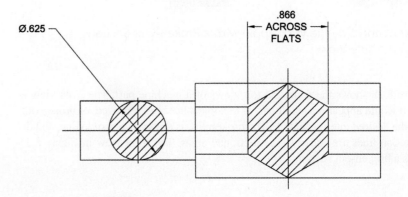

8.20 Revolved Section

Removed Sections

In a ***removed section*** the view created by the cutting plane line is not drawn in its normal "projected" position but is drawn somewhere else on the sheet. In Figure 8.21, two cutting planes lines are shown; one is labeled *A-A*, and the other is labeled *B-B*. Figure 8.22 shows the removed section of the object that results when the object is viewed through the cutting plane line labeled *A-A*. The section is labeled *SECTION A-A* to show its relationship to cutting plane *A-A*. Figure 8.23 shows the removed section that results when the object is viewed through the cutting plane labeled *B-B*. This view is labeled *SECTION B-B* to correspond to cutting plane *B-B*. Drafters must ensure that the cutting plane line *and* the resulting removed section view are labeled alike to avoid confusion when using this technique.

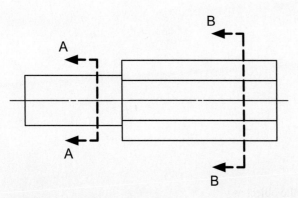

8.21 Cutting Plane Lines for Removed Sections
A-A and B-B

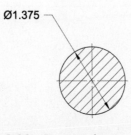

8.22 Removed
Section A-A

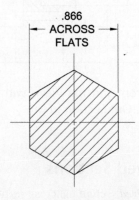

8.23 Removed Section B-B

Offset Sections

Offset sections allow a drafter to create a section with features that would not lie on the path of a straight cutting plane line (see Figure 8.24). In an offset section, the cutting plane line is offset at 90° angles to allow it to pass through the features that the drafter would like to be shown in the resulting section view (see Figure 8.25).

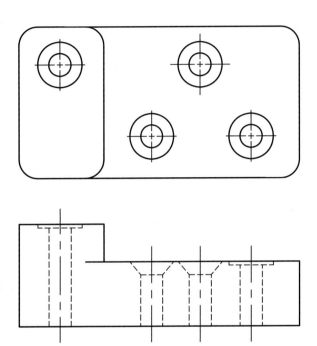

8.24 Front and Top Views of a Mechanical Part with Hidden Lines Shown

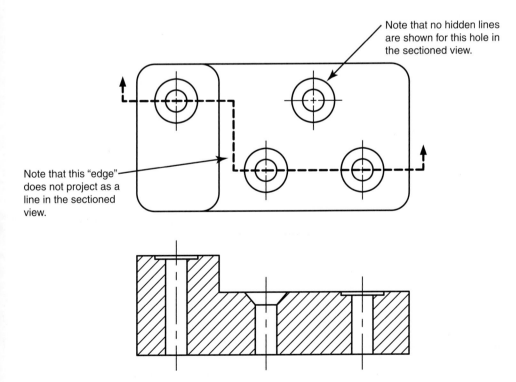

Note that no hidden lines are shown for this hole in the sectioned view.

Note that this "edge" does not project as a line in the sectioned view.

8.25 Offset Section View

STEPS IN CREATING A SECTION VIEW

The steps involved in creating a full section view of the object shown in Figure 8.26 are as follows:

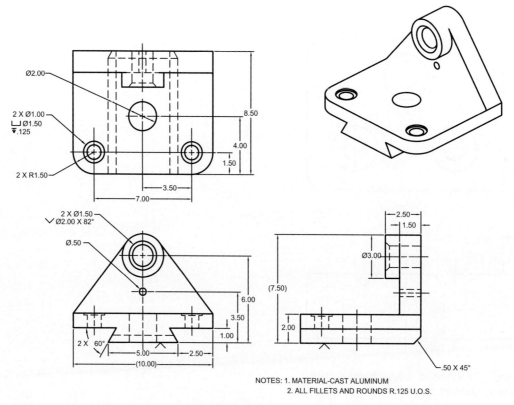

8.26   Multiview Drawing to Be Sectioned

NOTES: 1. MATERIAL-CAST ALUMINUM
2. ALL FILLETS AND ROUNDS R.125 U.O.S.

1   Determine the view to be sectioned and the location of the cutting plane line. In this case, the cutting plane line will be located on the front view (see Figure 8.27). The placement of the cutting plane line on the object's front view, along with the direction of the cutting plane line's arrows, indicates that the right-side view of the object will be drawn as a full section.

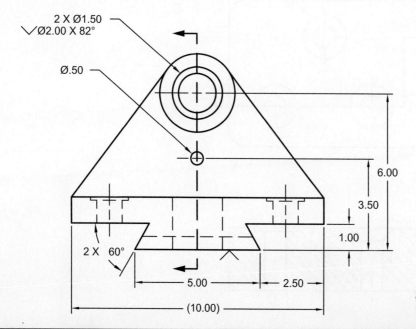

TIP

The **Polyline** command can be used to make the large arrowheads needed at the ends of cutting plane lines. This is done by drawing a short polyline (about .25" long) that has a starting width of 0 (zero) and an ending width of .10. See Figure 4.44(b).

8.27   Placing the Cutting Plane Line on the Front View

2 Study the right-side view (see Figure 8.28) and determine which of the object's hidden lines will become visible after it has been sectioned. Convert these hidden lines to visible lines as shown in Figure 8.29.

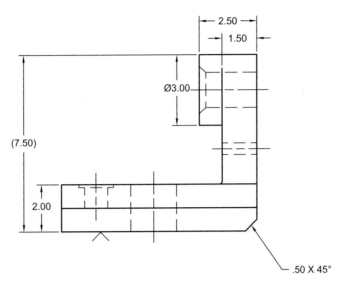

8.28   View Showing Hidden Lines

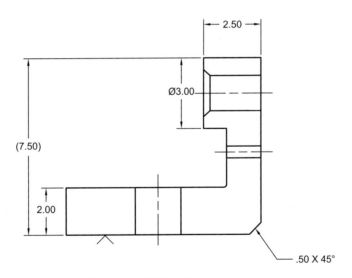

8.29   View Showing Visible Lines

3 Place section lines inside the areas created by the cutting plane line's passing through the object. In an AutoCAD drawing, the **HATCH** command is used to place section lines or other hatch patterns into a sectioned area.

NOTE

Two conditions must exist before a hatch pattern can be inserted into a drawing:
1. The objects that define the borders of the area to receive the pattern must create a *closed boundary* (closed boundaries do not have gaps in their boundary objects).
2. No part of the hatch boundary may lie outside the drawing window's display. For this reason, you may need to adjust the display window's size so that the entire hatch boundary is visible before beginning the **HATCH** command.

STEP by STEP

Using the HATCH Command

Select the **HATCH** command icon shown in Figure 8.30(a) from the **Draw** toolbar or the **Draw** panel of the **Home** tab of the ribbon. The **Hatch Creation** tab shown in Figure 8.30(b) will open (replacing the **Home** tab). This tab contains six panels: **Boundaries**, **Pattern**, **Properties**, **Origin**, **Options**, and **Close**; however, the most important panels for beginners to master are the first three. These panels are explained next.

The Boundaries Panel

Left-clicking the **Pick Points** button in this panel [see Figure 8.30(b)] allows you to define the boundary area(s) to be hatched by picking points inside existing objects (such as circles, rectangles, polygons, and closed polylines) that form a closed boundary around the pick point. If the selected area is not a closed boundary, the **Hatch-Boundary Definition Error** dialog box will open and offer some assistance with solving the problem.

Picking the **Select** button in the **Boundaries** panel [see Figure 8.30(b)] rather than **Pick Points** allows you to define a hatch boundary by selecting the objects that form the closed boundary.

The Pattern Panel

This panel displays predefined hatch patterns that can be assigned when using the **HATCH** command. These patterns are represented in the panel by swatches that show a preview of the pattern. You can scroll through the swatches by picking the up or down arrows on the right side of the panel. Left-click on the swatch you wish to assign as the current hatch pattern style.

The Properties Panel

Because this is a fundamentals text, we will focus on only two settings from this panel, the **Hatch Angle** setting and the **Hatch Pattern Scale** setting.

The value assigned in the **Hatch Angle** window defines the angle for the hatch pattern relative to the *X*-axis of the current **UCS**. The default angle setting is **0°**.

NOTE

The lines in the **ANSI31** pattern shown in Figure 8.30(b) will automatically be inserted at **45°** even though the default **Angle** of the pattern is set to **0°**. The angle settings for other predefined hatch patterns may follow this convention as well.

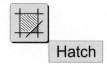

Hatch

8.30(a) **Hatch** Icon

Pick Points · Swatch · Hatch Angle · Select Objects · Hatch Scale

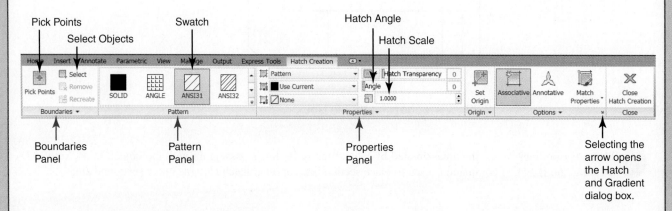

Boundaries Panel · Pattern Panel · Properties Panel · Selecting the arrow opens the Hatch and Gradient dialog box.

8.30(b) **Hatch Creation** Tab Settings

The value assigned in the **Hatch Pattern Scale** window enlarges or reduces the size of a predefined (or custom) hatch pattern. The default scale setting is **1**. In metric and architectural drawings this setting must often be increased to a very large value or else the hatch pattern may appear so dense in the drawing that it may seem to be a solid fill.

To place the hatch pattern in the section view shown in Figure 8.31, you would select the **Hatch** icon to access the **Hatch Creation** tab on the ribbon, then select **ANSI31** from the **Pattern** panel, and accept the default settings for **Hatch Angle** and **Hatch Pattern Scale** in the **Properties** panel. Next, you would select the **Pick Points** button from the **Boundaries** panel and pick inside the areas where the hatch pattern should be applied. When finished you would press **<Enter>**, and the hatch pattern would fill the areas defined by the pick points.

Figure 8.31 shows the side view with the ANSI31 hatch pattern applied. Note that no hidden lines are shown in this view.

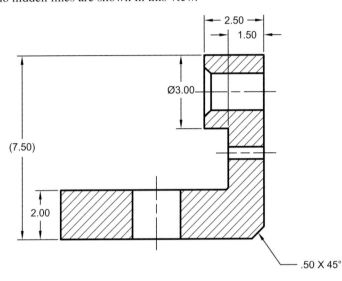

8.31 Sectioned Side View

Figure 8.32 shows the finished drawing with the right-side view replaced with a full section view. The full section provides a clear portrayal of the part's interior features.

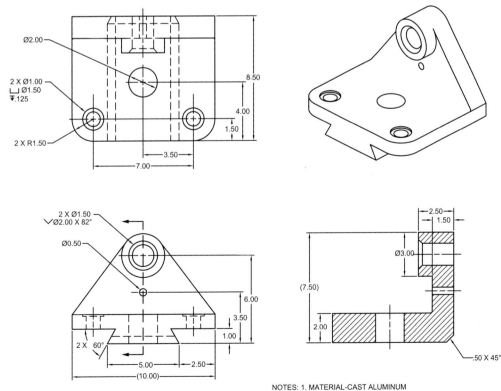

NOTES: 1. MATERIAL-CAST ALUMINUM
2. ALL FILLETS AND ROUNDS R.125 U.O.S.

8.32 Drawing with Sectioned Side View Shown

KEY WORDS

Broken-Out Section

Cutting Plane

Full Section

Half Section

Offset Section

Removed Section

Revolved Section

Section

Section Lines

CHAPTER SUMMARY

Interpreting an object's complex interior features is often difficult, especially when the features are represented by hidden lines in a front, top, or side view. By creating a section view of the object, the drafter can clarify the interior details by replacing the hidden lines with visible lines.

Because dimensioning to hidden lines should be avoided in technical drawings, creating a section view also facilitates the placement of dimensions by making complex interior features visible.

To create and interpret section views, drafters and designers must be familiar with the different types of sections and the CAD techniques used to create them.

Before drawing a section view of an object, a drafter must imagine what the object will look like after it has been sliced along a cutting plane line. The ability to visualize section views is a skill that beginners can develop and improve with practice.

REVIEW QUESTIONS

Multiple Choice

1. What are the diagonal lines in a section view called?
   a. Section lines
   b. Cutting plane lines
   c. Horizontal plane lines
   d. Straight plane lines

2. In an offset section, the cutting plane line is offset at what angle?
   a. 45°
   b. 35°
   c. 90°
   d. 25°

3. Where is a removed section placed on a drawing?
   a. On another sheet
   b. Somewhere else on the sheet
   c. Deleted from the sheet
   d. On another tab

4. What do the arrows on a cutting plane line indicate?
   a. Direction in which section is viewed
   b. Placement of centerlines
   c. The top of the sheet
   d. None of the above

5. What is the name of the **HATCH** setting that controls the density of the hatch pattern?
   a. **Volume**
   b. **Scale**
   c. **Hue**
   d. **All the above**

Matching

Column A

a. Half

b. Removed

c. One fourth

d. Revolved

e. Offset

Column B

1. Section view that requires a label

2. Percentage of an object removed to create a half section

3. The type of section on which a cutting plane line is not necessary

4. Percentage of an object removed to create a full section

5. Section that cuts through features that do not lie on a straight line

CHAPTER PROJECTS

Project 8.1: Tool Holder Sectioning

In this project, you will open the **Tool Holder** drawing you created in Chapter 4 and convert its front view to a full section.

Studying Figure 8.33 will help you visualize the tool holder after it has been cut along the cutting plane line. Figure 8.34 shows the location of the cutting plane line in the top view.

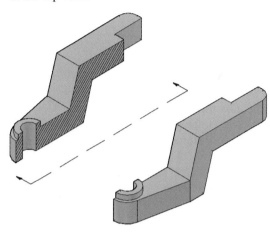

8.33   3D Sketch of the Tool Holder Shown as a Full Section

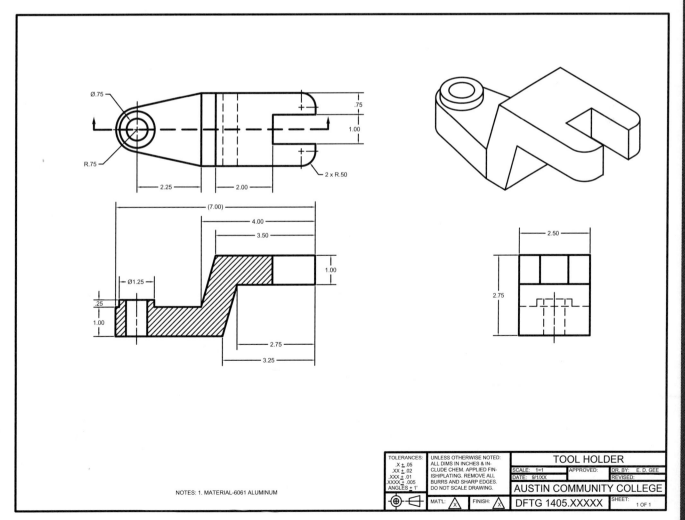

TOLERANCES:	UNLESS OTHERWISE NOTED:	TOOL HOLDER		
X ± .05	ALL DIMS IN INCHES & IN-			
.XX ± .02	CLUDE CHEM. APPLIED FIN-	SCALE: 1=1	APPROVED:	DR. BY: E. D. GEE
.XXX ± .01	ISH/PLATING. REMOVE ALL	DATE: 9/1/XX		REVISED:
.XXXX ± .005	BURRS AND SHARP EDGES.	AUSTIN COMMUNITY COLLEGE		
ANGLES ± 1'	DO NOT SCALE DRAWING.			
	MAT'L:	FINISH:	DFTG 1405.XXXXX	SHEET: 1 OF 1

NOTES: 1. MATERIAL-6061 ALUMINUM

8.34   Completed Tool Holder Drawing with Full Section

Directions

1. Open the **Tool Holder** drawing you created in Chapter 4 and make two new layers named **Cutting Plane** and **Hatch Pattern**.
2. Set the linetype for the **Hatch Pattern** layer to **Continuous** and the lineweight to **Default**. Use the **ANSI31** hatch pattern to draw the section lines.
3. Set the linetype for the **Cutting Plane** layer to **DashedX2** and set the lineweight to **.60mm**.

Project 8.2: Flange Bearing Sectioning

Directions

1. Open the **MechC1-1** drawing located in the student data files at **www.pearsondesigncentral.com/**. To access this drawing, open the Pearson Design Central website and click on the *CAD Community* link, then select the *Click here to download student data files for our CAD titles* link. Next, click on the *Technical Drawing 101* link and select the *Prototype Drawings* zip file, then select the *Download* button and open (or save) the prototype drawing specified above.
2. Use **SAVE AS** to save the drawing to your **Home** directory and rename the drawing **FLANGE BEARING**.
3. Refer to the designer's sketch in Figure 8.35 and draw the front and top views of the flange bearing, but draw the top view as a full section.

NOTE

The front view should be the view that depicts the holes in the flange bearing as circles, and the cutting plane line should run horizontally through this view with its arrows pointing down.

If you need help visualizing the sectioned view, refer to Figure 8.36.

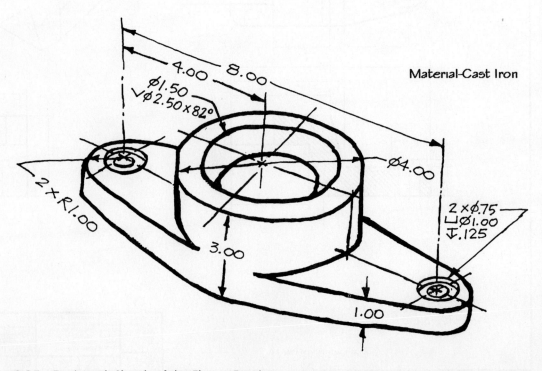

8.35 Designer's Sketch of the Flange Bearing

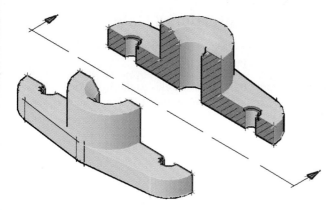

8.36   3D Flange Bearing

In the **Dimension Style Manager** dialog box, create a new dimension style named **ASME Y14.5** that contains the following dimension style settings, and set the new style current:

Text height:	.125
Arrow size:	.125
Center marks:	Line
Extend beyond dim lines:	.125
Precision:	Varies—match precision of dimensions on sketch
Zero suppression:	Leading
Offset from origin:	.062

Add dimensions to the views, including any necessary notes. When you are finished, follow your instructor's directions to print the drawing.

The notations and construction of the geometry for the countersunk and counterbored holes shown in Figure 8.35 are explained next.

Interpreting the Counterbored Hole Note

Before you can draw a counterbored hole, you must first be able to interpret the annotation and symbology used in notating the hole. An explanation of the note attached to the leader pointing to the counterbored hole in Figure 8.37 follows.

Line 1: A **.75″**-diameter hole passes all the way through the part.
Lines 2 and 3: A **1.00″**-diameter, flat-bottomed hole (a counterbore) is to be bored into the part to a **depth** of **.125″**. The symbols for notating *counterbore* and *depth* in technical drawings are ⌴ and ⤓, respectively.

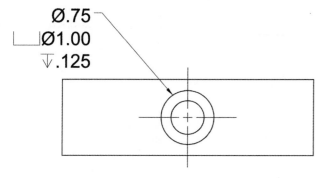

8.37   Counterbored Hole Specification

Steps in Constructing a Counterbored Hole

Step 1.   Begin the construction by drawing two concentric circles in the top view, .75" diameter and **1.00**" diameter, respectively.

Step 2.   Project lines from the quadrants of these circles to the front view to construct the hidden lines for the through hole and **.125** deep counterbore as shown in Figure 8.38.

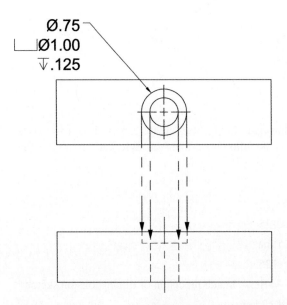

8.38   Multiview Drawing of Counterbored Hole

Adding Annotation to a Counterbored Hole

The following steps describe how to annotate a counterbored hole. The desired notation is shown in Figure 8.39.

Step 1.   Select the **Diameter** dimension icon from the **Dimension** toolbar (see Figure 8.40) and place a diameter dimension on the larger circle.

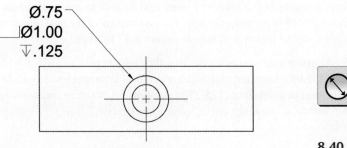

8.39   Counterbored Hole Note

8.40   Diameter Dimension Icon

─NOTE─

To enter the symbol for diameter, click on the **Symbol** icon located on the **Insert** panel of the **Text Editor** tab of the ribbon, and select **Diameter** from the drop-down list. See Figure 8.41(b).

Step 2.   Select the diameter dimension created in Step 1, type **ED** (to open the **Text Editor**), and press **<Enter>**. Make edits inside the **Text Editor** box to create the three lines of text shown in Figure 8.41(a).

Step 3.   Highlight the **v** and pick on the down arrow in the **Font** window located on the **Formatting** panel and change the font to **gdt** (geometric dimensioning and tolerancing (see Figure 8.42). When the font is changed, the **v** will be replaced by the **counterbore** symbol (⌴). Repeat this step for the **x,** and it will be replaced by the **depth** symbol (⊤̄).

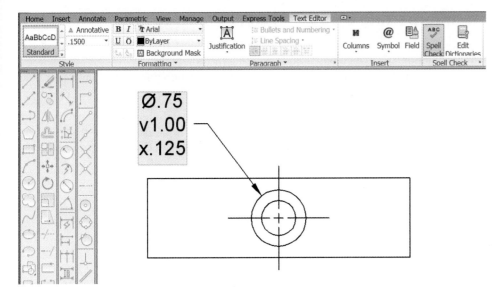

8.41(a)   Entering Text for
the Counterbored Hole

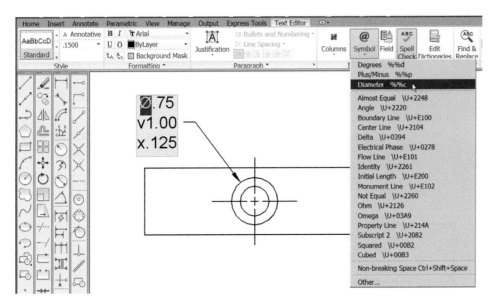

8.41(b)   Adding a Diameter
Symbol to the Notation of
the Counterbored Hole

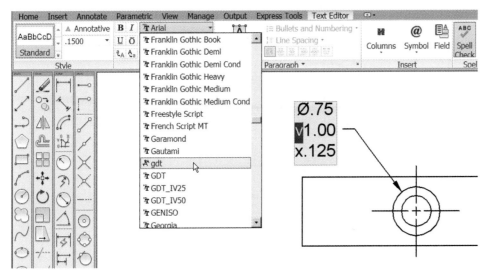

8.42   Converting an Arial
Font Character to gdt Font in
the Notation of the
Counterbored Hole

Interpreting a Countersunk Hole Note

Before you can draw a countersunk hole, you must first be able to interpret the annotation and symbology used in notating the hole.

An explanation of the note attached to the leader pointing to the countersunk hole in Figure 8.43 follows.

Line 1: A **1.50**"-diameter hole passes all the way through the part.
Line 2: A **2.50**"-diameter countersunk hole is to be drilled into the part. The angle between the sloping sides of the countersink is **82°**. The symbol for notating a countersink on a technical drawing is ∨.

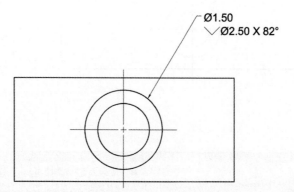

8.43 Countersunk Hole Specification

Steps in Constructing a Countersunk Hole

Step 1. Begin the construction by drawing two concentric circles in the front view, **1.50**" diameter and **2.50**" diameter, respectively. Project construction lines from the quadrants of these circles to the top view as shown in Figure 8.44.

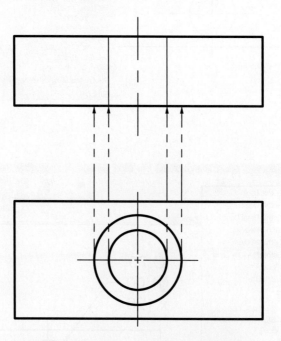

8.44 Constructing a Countersunk Hole

Step 2.   From the lines projected from the circle quadrants in the front view, construct the **82°** angled sides of the countersunk hole and the sides of the through hole in the top view (see Figure 8.45). For help constructing the angles, see Figures 8.46 through 48.

Use the protractor in Figure 8.46 to determine countersink angles. Once you have determined the beginning points of the countersunk diameter, draw lines by using either polar coordinates or polar tracking with the required angles added in as illustrated in Figures 8.47 and 8.48. Do not be concerned with the length of the lines; concentrate on the angle. If the lines are too short, use **EXTEND** to extend them to the vertical (or horizontal) lines. If they overlap, use **TRIM** to trim back to the vertical (or horizontal) lines.

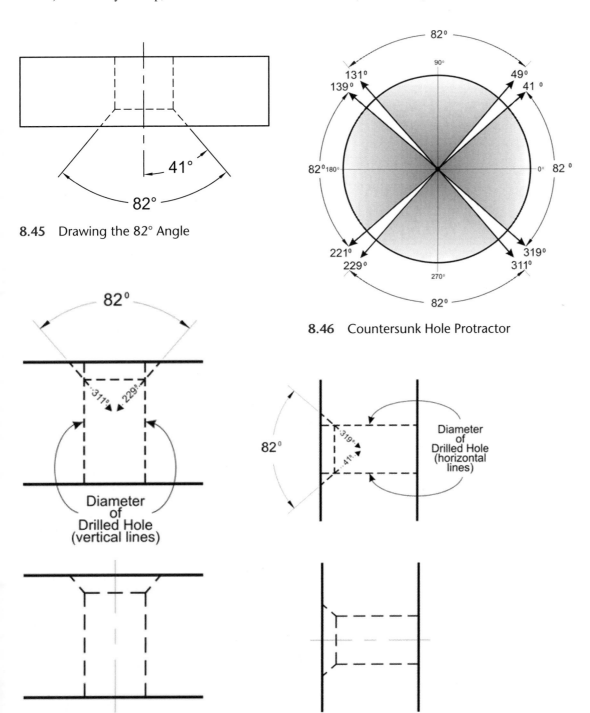

8.45   Drawing the 82° Angle

8.46   Countersunk Hole Protractor

8.47   Constructing a Vertical Countersunk Hole

8.48   Constructing a Horizontal Countersunk Hole

The completed front and top views of the countersunk hole are shown in Figure 8.49.

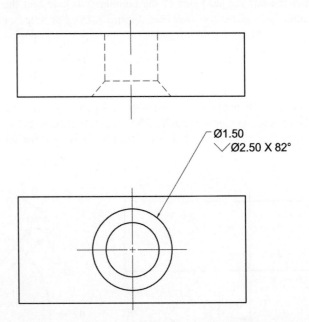

Ø1.50
Ø2.50 X 82°

8.49   Completed Multiviews of the Countersunk Hole

Adding Annotation to a Countersunk Hole

The steps required to annotate a countersunk hole are as follows. The desired notation is shown in Figure 8.50.

Step 1.   Select the **Diameter** dimension icon from the **Dimension** toolbar (see Figure 8.51) and place a diameter dimension on the larger circle.

Step 2.   Select the diameter dimension created in Step 1, type **ED** (to open the **Text Editor**), and press **<Enter>**. Make edits inside the **Text Editor** box to create the two lines of text shown in Figure 8.52.

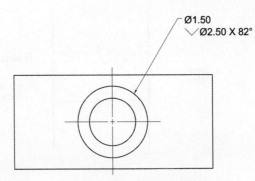

Ø1.50
Ø2.50 X 82°

8.50   Countersunk Hole Specification

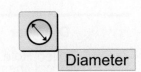

Diameter

8.51   **Diameter** Dimension Icon

NOTE

To enter the symbol for degrees, click on the **Symbol** icon located on the **Insert** panel of the **Text Editor** tab of the ribbon, and select **Degrees** from the drop-down list. See Figure 8.41(b).

TIP

When entering text with AutoCAD's **Text Editor**, typing **%%C** will produce a diameter symbol, and typing **%%d** will produce a degree symbol.

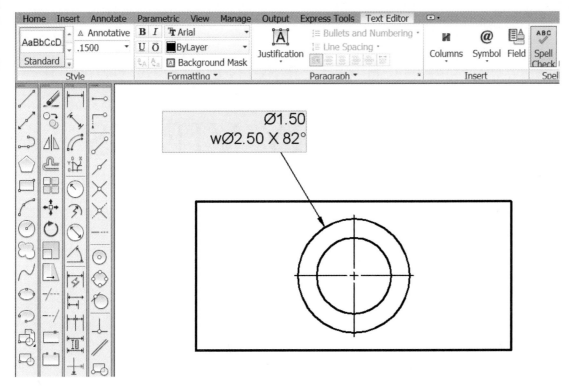

8.52   Entering Text for the Countersunk Hole

Step 3.   Highlight the **w** and pick on the down arrow in the **Font** window located on the **Formatting** panel and change the font to **gdt** (see Figure 8.53). When the font is changed, the **w** will be replaced by the countersink symbol (∨).

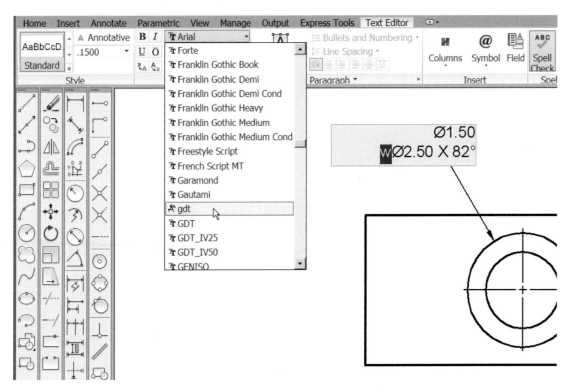

8.53   Converting an Arial Font Character to gdt Font in the Notation of the Countersunk Hole

CHAPTER NINE

AUXILIARY VIEWS

OBJECTIVES

After studying the material in this chapter, you should be able to:

1. Define what auxiliary views are and how they are used in technical drawings.

2. Explain the glass box theory of visualizing an auxiliary view.

3. Use AutoCAD to create a primary auxiliary view for an inclined surface.

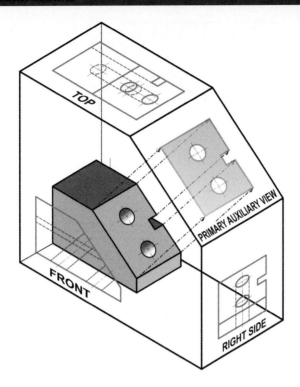

OVERVIEW

In some instances, such as when an object has features on an inclined plane, the regular multiviews may not describe these features in their true size or shape. In Figure 9.1, the holes and slot located on the inclined plane labeled *A* are not shown in true shape in either the top or right-side view because the plane is foreshortened in both views. This situation may present problems when a drafter is attempting to dimension these features.

In such cases, the drafter may decide to draw an auxiliary view of the inclined plane. The auxiliary view is drawn as if the viewer's line of sight were perpendicular to the inclined plane. The features of the inclined plane will appear true size and shape in the auxiliary view.

If the drafter is working from a 3D CAD model of the object, preparing an auxiliary view is a relatively easy process of rotating the model until the inclined plane is parallel to the plane of projection.

If the drafter is working with 2D geometry, the process of creating an auxiliary view is more complicated. This chapter discusses the techniques used to add an auxiliary view to a 2D multiview drawing.

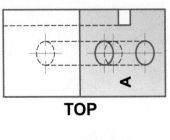

TOP

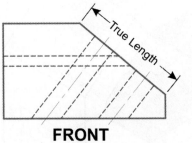

FRONT

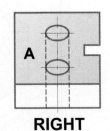

RIGHT

9.1 Multiview Drawing of an Object Including Inclined *Plane A*

9.1 VISUALIZING AN AUXILIARY VIEW

In Figure 9.2 the object shown in Figure 9.1 has been placed inside a glass box. The box has a projection plane labeled ***primary auxiliary view***. This projection plane is parallel to the object's inclined plane.

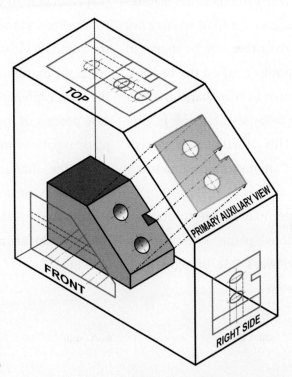

9.2 Glass Box with an Auxiliary View of *Plane A*

Viewed through this projection plane, the inclined surface is true size and shape. This is because its features are projected perpendicular to the projection plane.

In Figure 9.3 the projection planes of the glass box are unfolded. In the resulting views, you can see the position of the auxiliary view relative to the other views.

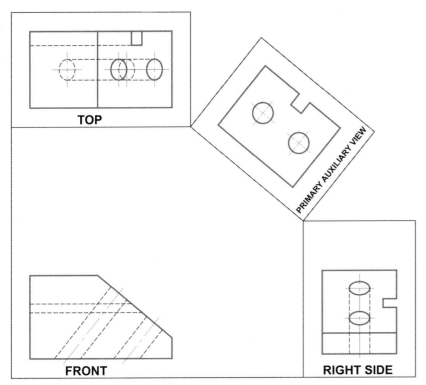

9.3 Glass Box Unfolded to Show the Primary Auxiliary View

The view in Figure 9.3 is called a primary auxiliary view because it is adjacent to, and aligned with, a principal view of the object.

A *secondary auxiliary view* would be adjacent to, and aligned with, a primary auxiliary view.

— **TIP** —
The auxiliary view is in-line with the inclined plane.

TUTORIAL 9.1: CONSTRUCTING A PRIMARY AUXILIARY VIEW—DESCRIPTIVE GEOMETRY METHOD

In this project you will use AutoCAD and the principles of descriptive geometry to create a primary auxiliary view for the object shown in Figure 9.3.

Directions

1. Open the **Auxiliary View Prototype** drawing located in the student data files at **www.pearsondesigncentral.com.** To access this drawing, open the Pearson Design Central website and click on the *CAD Community* link, then select the *Click here to download student data files for our CAD titles* link. Next, click on the *Technical Drawing 101* link and select the *Prototype Drawings* zip file, then select the *Download* button and open (or save) the prototype drawing specified above.
2. Use **SAVE AS** to save the drawing to your **Home** directory, and rename the drawing **AUXILIARY VIEW PROJECT**.
3. Follow Steps 1 through 33 to create a primary auxiliary view of the inclined plane.

1 Create two new layers named **Reference** and **Projections**. Assign the **Phantom** linetype to the **Reference** layer. On the Reference layer, you will draw two reference lines from which distances are measured. You will use the Projections layer for laying out construction lines. The prototype drawing already contains layers 0, Center, Hidden, and Visible.

2 At the command line, type **SNAP** and press **<Enter>.** When prompted with *Specify snap spacing or [ON/OFF/Aspect/Style/Type]* <0.5000>:, type **R** for **ROTATE,** and press **<Enter>.**

3 When prompted with *Specify a base point:*, select the top end of the line in the front view labeled *Plane A* (see Figure 9.4).

STEP by STEP

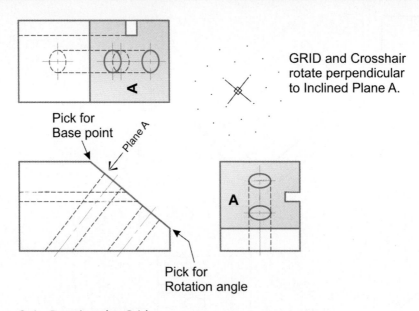

GRID and Crosshair
rotate perpendicular
to Inclined Plane A.

Pick for
Base point

Plane A

A

Pick for
Rotation angle

9.4   Rotating the Grid

4   When prompted with *Specify rotation angle:*, select the bottom end of the line labeled *Plane A*. The grid and crosshairs will rotate and be perpendicular to *Plane A*. The grid and cursor should be turned as in Figure 9.4.

5   Set the **Projections** layer current, turn **Ortho** on, and draw two **12"** lines extending from each endpoint of inclined *Plane A* as shown in Figure 9.5.

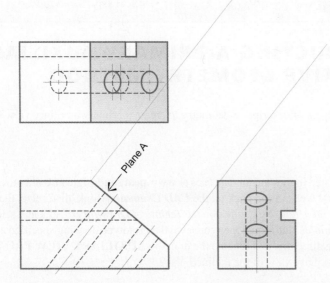

Plane A

9.5   Extending Lines from *Plane A*

6   Set the **Reference** layer current. Draw a line parallel to inclined *Plane A* as shown in Figure 9.6. An easy way to do this is by drawing a line from *midpoint* to *midpoint* of the two construction lines drawn in Step 5. This line will be referred to as *Reference line 1*.

7   Turn **Ortho** off, and draw a second line on the left edge of the right-side view as shown in Figure 9.6. This line will be referred to as *Reference line 2*.

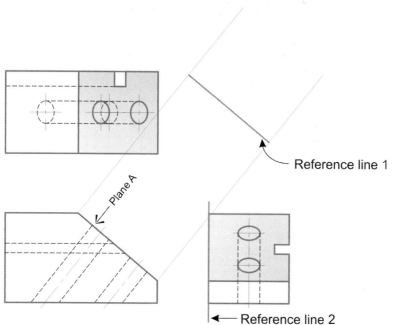

9.6 Adding *Reference Line 1* and *Reference Line 2*

8 Use the **Distance** command to measure the distances from *Reference line 2* to the points labeled *a* and *b* on the right-side view in Figure 9.7 by selecting the **Distance** button from the **Inquiry** toolbar (see page 168) or typing **DI**, at the command prompt. When prompted with *_dist Specify first point:*, select point *1* on the right-side view where the object intersects *Reference line 2*.

9 When prompted with *Specify second point:*, select point *a* on the right-side view. The **Distance** command determines that the distance between these points, measured along the *X*-axis, equals **2.75**.

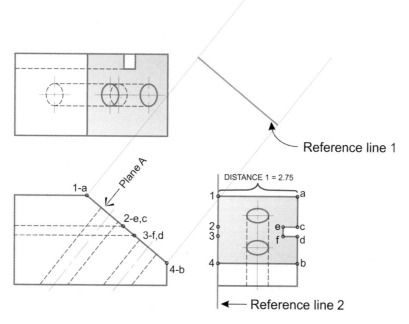

9.7 Measuring Distance between *Point 1* and *Point a*

10 Use the **Distance** command to measure the distance between point *4* and point *b* in the right-side view, as you did in Step 9.

11 To add lines *1-a* and *4-b* to the auxiliary view as shown in Figure 9.8, set the **Visible** layer current. Transfer the distance found between point *1* and point *a* in Step 8 by drawing a line **2.75"** in length from the top point of *Reference line 1* along the angled projection line constructed in Step 6.

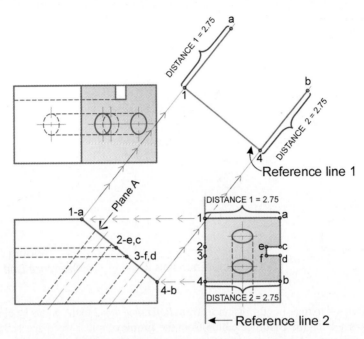

9.8   Transferring Distances *1-2* and *4-b*

12 Draw another line **2.75"** in length from the bottom point of *Reference line 1* along the other angled projection line to represent the distance between point *4* and point *b* (see Figure 9.8).

13 To locate the top and bottom edges of the slot in the auxiliary view (see Figure 9.9), set the **Projections** layer current, turn **Ortho** on, and project construction lines from the points in the front view labeled *2-e, c* and *3-f, d*, as described in Steps 14 and 15.

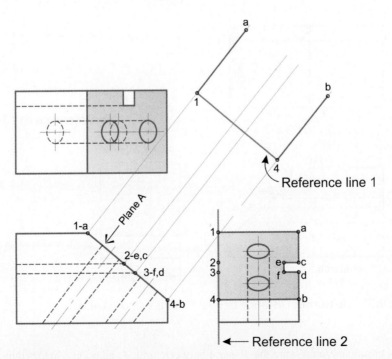

9.9   Extending Lines from *Point 2-e, c* and *Point 3-f, d*

14 Draw a construction line **12"** long from the point labeled *2-e, c* in the front view that is perpendicular to *Reference line 1*.

15 Draw a construction line **12"** long from the point labeled *3-f, d* in the front view that is perpendicular to *Reference line 1*.

16 Use the **POINT** command and the **Snap From** object snap setting to locate the points labeled *c* and *d* on the angled construction lines in Figure 9.10. Set the **Reference** layer current, and follow Steps 17 through 24.

17 Select **Point Style** from the **Format** pull-down menu. When the **Point Style** dialog box opens, select the **X** point style (fourth from the right on the top row), select the **Set Size in Absolute Units** button, set the **Point Size** to **.125**, and click **OK**.

18 Turn on the following **Osnaps**: **Endpoint, Midpoint, Center, Node,** and **Intersection. Dynamic Input** should also be on. Refer to Figure 9.10 and note that the distance in the right-side view from point *2* to point *c* is the same distance as measured earlier between point *1* and point *a* (**2.75"**). This is true of the distance between point *3* and point *d* as well.

19 Open the **Object Snap** toolbar and select the **POINT** command from the **Draw** toolbar. When prompted with *Specify a point:*, select the **Snap From** icon (see Figure 4.104) on the **Object Snap** toolbar and select the point where the angled line drawn from point *2-e, c* in the front view intersects *Reference line 1*. When prompted with *from Base point:*, move the cursor to the top end of the angled projection line until the **Endpoint** object snap lights up (do not select the point), type **2.75**, and press **<Enter>**.

20 Repeat the **POINT** command as in Step 19, except this time, when prompted with *Specify a point:*, select the **Snap From** icon on the **Object Snap** toolbar and select the point where the angled line drawn from point *3-f, d* in the front view intersects *Reference line 1*. When prompted with *from Base point:*, move the cursor to the top end of the angled projection line until the **Endpoint** object snap lights up (do not select the point), type **2.75**, and press **<Enter>**.

21 Using the **POINT** command and the **Snap From** object snap setting, locate the points labeled *e* and *f* on the angled construction lines as shown in Figure 9.11.

22 Use the **Distance** command to find the distance between point *2* and point *e* in the right-side view.

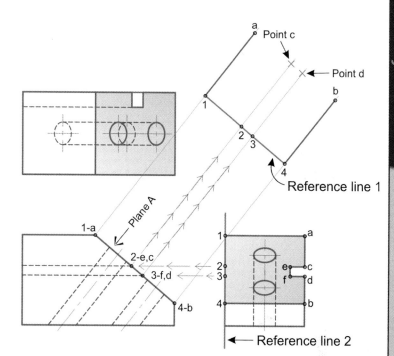

9.10 Locating *Point c* and *Point d* in Auxiliary View

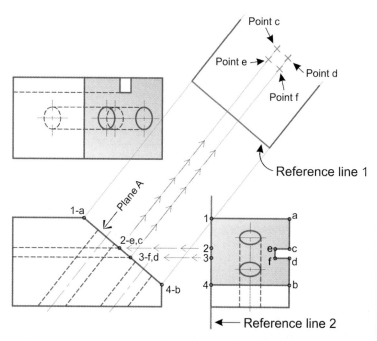

9.11 Locating *Point e* and *Point f* in Auxiliary View

STEP by STEP

23 Select the **POINT** command from the **Draw** toolbar. When prompted with *Specify a point:*, select the **Snap From** icon on the **Object Snap** toolbar and select the point where the angled line drawn from point *2-e, c* in the front view intersects *Reference line 1*. When prompted with *from Base point:*, move the cursor to the top end of the angled projection line until the **Endpoint** object snap lights up (do not select the point), type the distance between point *2* and point *e* in the right-side view, and press **<Enter>**.

24 Repeat the **POINT** command as in Step 23, except this time, when prompted with *Specify a point:*, select the **Snap From** icon on the **Object Snap** toolbar and select the point where the angled line drawn from point *3-f, d* in the front view intersects *Reference line 1*. When prompted with *from Base point:*, move the cursor to the top end of the angled projection line until the **Endpoint** object snap lights up (do not select the point), type the distance between point *2* and point *e* in the right-side view, and press **<Enter>**.

25 Set the **Visible** layer current and use the **LINE** command to connect points *a, c, e, f, d,* and *b* in the auxiliary view as shown in Figure 9.12. Change *Reference line 1* to the **Visible** layer. This completes the true shape profile of inclined *Plane A*.

26 To locate the centers of holes marked *g* and *h* on the right-side view in Figure 9.13 to their positions in the auxiliary view, set the **Projections** layer current.

27 Draw a construction line **12"** long from the point labeled *5-g* in the front view that is perpendicular to *Reference line 1* as shown in Figure 9.13.

28 Repeat Step 27, but this time, draw a construction line **12"** long from the point labeled *6-h* in the front view that is perpendicular to *Reference line 1* as shown in Figure 9.13.

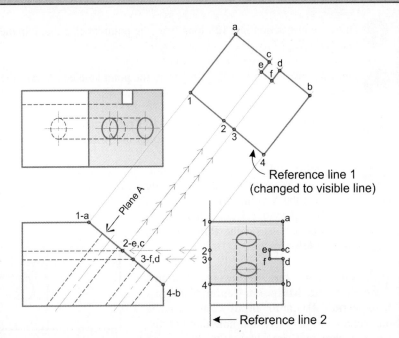

9.12 Connecting Points *a, c, e, f, d* and *b* in Auxiliary View

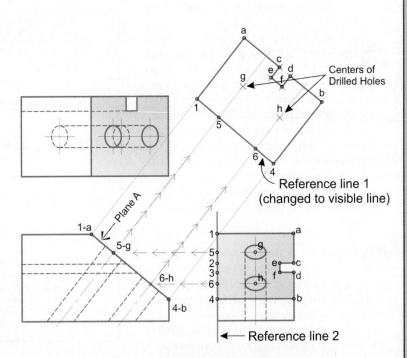

9.13 Locating Points *g* and *h* in Auxiliary View

29 Use the **Distance** command to find the horizontal distance between *Reference line 2* and point *g* in the right-side view.

30 Select the **POINT** command from the **Draw** toolbar. When prompted with *Specify a point:*, select the **Snap From** icon on the **Object Snap** toolbar and select the point where the angled line drawn from point *5-g* in the front view intersects *Reference line 1*. When prompted with *from Base point:*, move the cursor to the top end of the angled projection line until the **Endpoint** object snap lights up (do not select the point), type the distance between *Reference line 2* and point *g* in the right-side view, and press **<Enter>**.

31 Repeat the **POINT** command as in Step 30, except this time, when prompted with *Specify a point:*, select the **Snap From** icon on the **Object Snap** toolbar. Select the point where the angled line drawn from point *6-h* in the front view intersects *Reference line 1*. When prompted with *from Base point:*, move the cursor to the top end of the angled projection line until the **Endpoint** object snap lights up (do not select the point), type the horizontal distance between *Reference line 2* and point *h* in the right-side view (this distance is the same as between *Reference line 2* and point *g*), and press **<Enter>**.

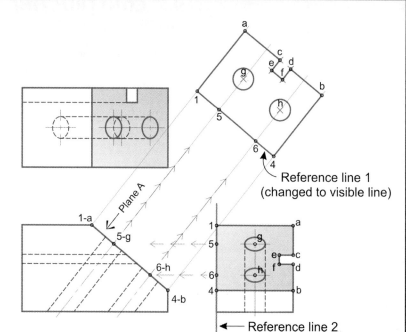

9.14   Drawing Circles at Points *g* and *h* in Auxiliary View

32 Set the **Visible** layer current and draw two circles **.75"** in diameter at the points identified in Steps 26–31 for *g* and *h* as shown in Figure 9.14.

33 Turn off the **Reference** and **Projections** layers. Add centerlines to the holes in the auxiliary view. Complete the view by adding centerlines between the front view and the holes in the auxiliary view as shown in Figure 9.15.

Technically, the view shown in Figure 9.15 would be considered a ***partial auxiliary view*** because the other planes of the object are not shown in this view. If the drafter wished, broken lines could be added to the view to show more of the object, as in Figure 9.16.

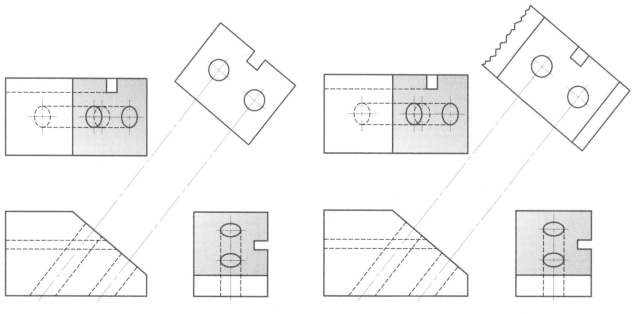

9.15   The Completed Auxiliary View of *Plane A*

9.16   Partial Auxiliary View Showing Broken Lines

9.2 CONSTRUCTING AN AUXILIARY VIEW WITH THE OFFSET COMMAND

A simpler, and quicker, way to construct an auxiliary view takes advantage of AutoCAD's **OFFSET** and **TRIM** commands. Also, instead of the **Distance** command, the **Linear** dimension command is used to measure distances in the right-side view.

The tutorial accompanying Project 9.2 shows how to quickly create an auxiliary view using these CAD commands.

TUTORIAL 9.2: CONSTRUCTING A PRIMARY AUXILIARY VIEW—QUICK CAD METHOD

In this project you will use the quick CAD method to create the primary auxiliary view for the object shown in Figure 9.3.

Directions

1. Open the **Auxiliary View Prototype** drawing located in the student data files at **www.pearsondesigncentral.com.** To access this drawing, open the Pearson Design Central website and click on the *CAD Community* link, then select the *Click here to download student data files for our CAD titles* link. Next, click on the *Technical Drawing 101* link and select the *Prototype Drawings* zip file, then select the *Download* button and open (or save) the prototype drawing specified above.

2. Use **SAVE AS** to save the drawing to your **Home** directory, and rename the drawing **QUICK AUXILIARY VIEW PROJECT**.

3. Follow Steps 1 through 10 to create a primary auxiliary view of the inclined plane.

1. Create a new layer named **Projections** and set the **Visible** layer current. Select the **OFFSET** command and when prompted to *Specify offset distance:*, type **6.5** and press **<Enter>**. Select the line marked *Plane A* in the front view as the object to offset and press **<Enter>**. Pick a point above the right-side view when prompted to *specify point on side to offset:*. The resulting line represents the left edge of the auxiliary view (see Figure 9.17).

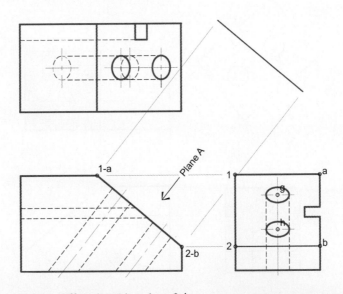

9.17   Offsetting Line *1-a, 2-b*

2 Use the **Linear** dimension tool to place the three dimensions shown on the right-side view of Figure 9.18. As you can see from the dimensions in Figure 9.18, the width of the object in the right-side view is **2.75"**. Select the **OFFSET** command and enter **2.75** as the offset distance. Select the line created in Step 1 and offset it to the right side. The resulting line represents the right edge of the auxiliary view as shown in Figure 9.18.

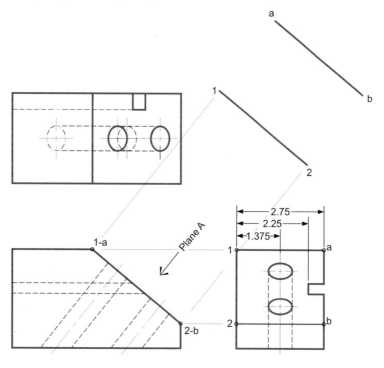

9.18 Offsetting Line *1, 2* to Create Line *a, b*

3 Draw a line connecting point *1* and point *a* in the auxiliary view as shown in Figure 9.19. Draw another line connecting point *2* and point *b*.

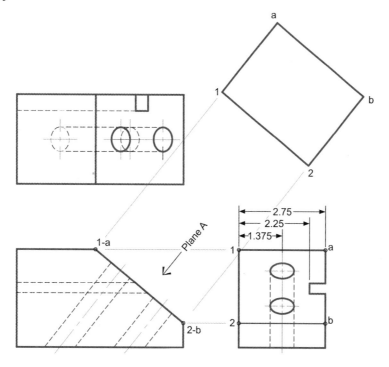

9.19 Connecting Point *1* to *a*, and Point *2* to *b*

STEP by STEP

4 Select the **OFFSET** command and pick line *1-2* in the auxiliary view as the line to offset. Enter **1.375** as the offset distance (the distance shown in the right-side view from the part's left edge to the center of the holes). Pick to the right of line *1-2* when prompted to *specify point on side to offset*: (see Figure 9.20).

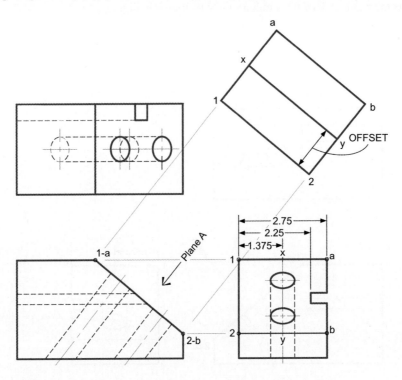

9.20 Offsetting Line *1, 2* to Create Line *x, y*

5 Set the **Projections** layer current and draw a line from point *3-g* on *Plane A* perpendicular to line *x-y* in the auxiliary view as shown in Figure 9.21. Repeat this step, drawing a line from point *4-h* perpendicular to line *x-y*.

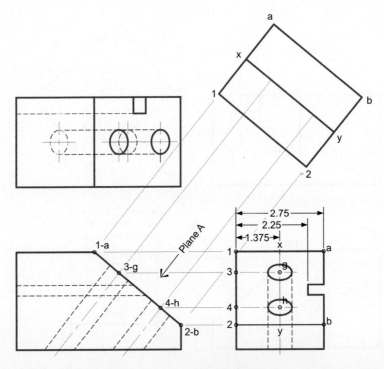

9.21 Projecting Points *3-g* and *4-h* to Line *x, y*

6 The points where line *x-y* and the projection lines from points *3-g* and *4-h* intersect are the centers for the two drilled holes. Set the **Visible** layer current and draw a **.75"** diameter circle at each intersection as shown in Figure 9.22.

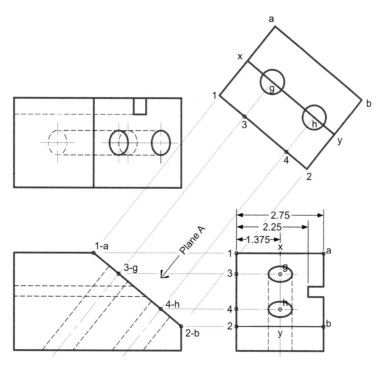

9.22   Adding Circles at Points *g* and *h*

7 Select the **OFFSET** command and type **2.25** for the distance to offset (the distance shown in the dimension on the right-side view from the part's left edge to the inside edge of the slot). Select line *1-2* and offset it to the right of the line as shown in Figure 9.23.

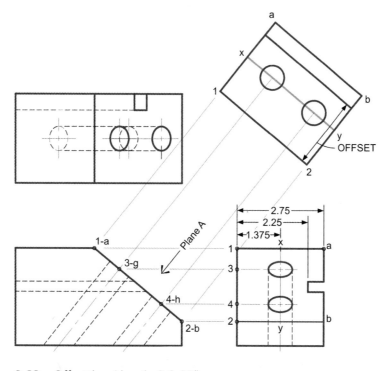

9.23   Offsetting Line 1, 2 2.25"

8 Set the **Projections** layer current and project two construction lines from the intersections of points *5-e, c* and *6-f, d* perpendicular to line *a-b* in the auxiliary view as shown in Figure 9.24.

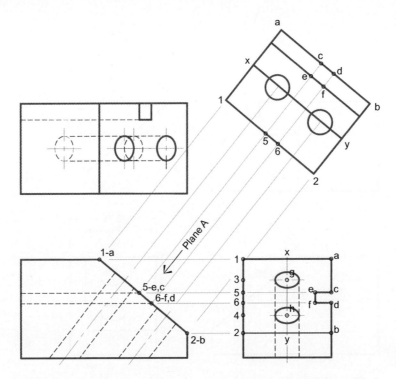

9.24 Projecting Points *5-e, c* and *6-f, d* to Locate Points *e* and *f*

9 Use the **TRIM** command to trim the lines representing the slot in the auxiliary view as shown in Figure 9.25. Set the **Visible** layer current and draw lines *c-e* and *d-f*. Erase line *x-y*.

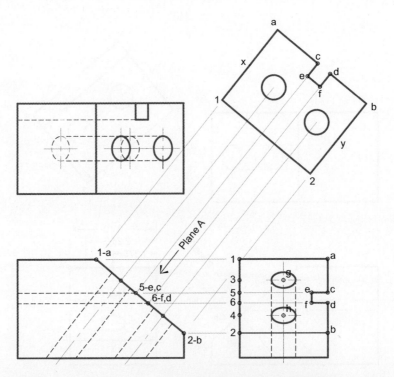

9.25 Connecting Lines *c, e, f,* and *d* and Trimming Line between Points *c* and *d*

10 Turn off the **Projections** layer and complete the drawing by adding centerlines to the holes and between the front view and the holes in the auxiliary view as shown in Figure 9.26.

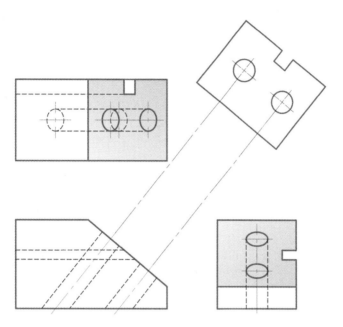

9.26   The Completed Auxiliary View of *Plane A*

This step completes the construction of the auxiliary view.

KEY WORDS

auxiliary views

partial auxiliary view

primary auxiliary view

secondary auxiliary view

CHAPTER SUMMARY

The techniques presented in this chapter have their origins in Gaspard Monge's *Géométrie Descriptive*, written in the eighteenth century. As mentioned in Chapter 1, many of Monge's ideas later became the foundation of modern technical drawing. However, with the advent of CAD software capable of 3D modeling, auxiliary views are more likely to be created by rotating a 3D model of the object until the inclined plane is perpendicular to the projection plane.

REVIEW QUESTIONS

Multiple Choice

1. In an auxiliary view, the plane of projection is _____ relative to the inclined plane.

    a. Oblique
    b. Parallel
    c. Skewed
    d. Perpendicular

2. A primary auxiliary view is drawn adjacent to, and aligned with, a(n) _____ view.

    a. Principal
    b. End
    c. Secondary auxiliary
    d. Perpendicular

3. An auxiliary view may be needed if the features of an object do not appear true shape in:

    a. An oblique view
    b. An isometric view
    c. Any of the regular views
    d. All the above

4. A partial auxiliary view omits:

    a. Phantom lines
    b. Cutting plane lines

    c. Foreshortened features of the object
    d. None of the above

5. What linetype is assigned to the lines that are drawn between the principal view and an auxiliary view?

    a. Center
    b. Phantom
    c. Hidden
    d. Visible

CHAPTER PROJECT

Project 9.1: Auxiliary View

Use the quick CAD method (refer to pages 326–331) to create a partial, primary auxiliary view for the object in the prototype drawing specified in the directions below. Project the auxiliary view from the inclined plane in the front view of the object.

Directions

1. Open the **Auxiliary View Prototype 2** drawing located in the student data files at **www.pearsondesigncentral.com.** To access this drawing, open the Pearson Design Central website and click on the *CAD Community* link, then select the *Click here to download student data files for our CAD titles* link. Next, click on the *Technical Drawing 101* link and select the *Prototype Drawings* zip file, then select the *Download* button and open (or save) the prototype drawing specified above.
2. Use **SAVE AS** to save the drawing to your **Home** directory, and rename the drawing **AUXILIARY VIEW PROJECT 1**.

CHAPTER TEN

BLOCKS

──── OBJECTIVES ────

After studying the material in this chapter, you should be able to:

1.   Describe what blocks are and how they are used in technical drawings created with AutoCAD.

2.   Create, insert, and edit blocks with AutoCAD software.

3.   Create a block library of architectural symbols and use them to produce a floor plan.

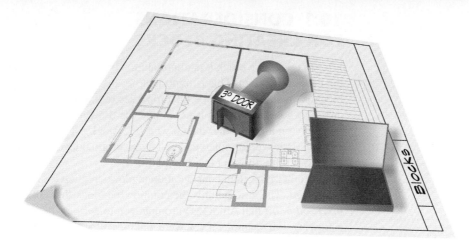

OVERVIEW

A **block** is an AutoCAD term that refers to a predrawn object stored in an AutoCAD drawing file that can be placed or inserted into the drawing whenever it is needed. For example, an architectural firm may create a block of door and window symbols. Later, when a door or window symbol is needed in a floor plan, the firm's drafters can select the symbol from the **block library** and insert it into the drawing rather than drawing each door and window from scratch. Thus, drafters save a huge amount of time and lower the cost of producing a drawing. Another advantage of using blocks is that when inserting a block, the drafter can change its scale, proportion, and rotation without redrawing the object.

Sometimes, architectural and engineering firms purchase premade block libraries from vendors, or in some cases, download them directly from vendors' websites.

10.1 CONSIDERATIONS FOR CREATING BLOCKS

Prior to creating a block it is important to consider the layer on which the entities of the block are drawn. This is important because objects that are on layer **0** when the block is created will assume the properties (color, linetype, etc.) of the layer that is current when the block is inserted into the drawing. Conversely, if the entities of a block are on a layer other than **0** when the block is created, the block will retain the characteristics (color, linetype, etc.) of the original layer, even if the block is inserted on a layer with different layer properties.

Another important consideration in block creation is the definition of the block's ***base point***. The base point is the point on the block that aligns to the location of the ***insertion point*** that AutoCAD prompts you to define when you insert the block into a drawing. For example, if you were making a block of the door shown in Figure 10.1, the corner of the door where the hinge would meet the door's opening is a logical base point. With this corner defined as the door's base point, the hinged corner of the door can be placed precisely into a floor plan by snapping to the corner of the door opening when you are prompted to define the block's insertion point.

Figure 10.2 shows the drawing for a ceiling fan. In a block of the fan, a logical base point is its center. Thus, when prompted to define the base point of the fan, you would select the center of the circle around which the blades are arrayed. Later, when the fan is inserted into a drawing, the fan's center point will align to the pick point, or coordinates, that you define when prompted by AutoCAD to define the block's insertion point.

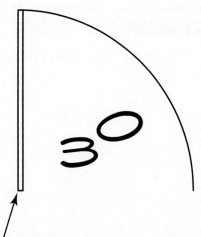

Select this corner to be the base point for the block of the door.

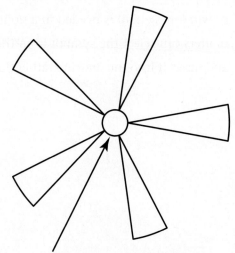

Select the center of this circle as the base point for the ceiling fan block.

10.1 Defining the Base Point of a Block of a Door

10.2 Defining the Base Point of a Block of a Ceiling Fan

CREATING BLOCKS

1 Draw the object to be blocked.

2 Select the **Make Block** icon from the **Draw** toolbar or the **Block** panel of the **Home** tab of the ribbon (see Figure 10.3). The **Block Definition** dialog box shown in Figure 10.4 will open.

3 Enter the block name in the **Name:** text box.

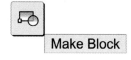

10.3 **Block** Icon

TIP
The layer on which the entities of a block are drawn is very important. For example, objects that are on layer **0** when the block is created will assume the color, linetype, and lineweight of the layer that is current when the block is inserted. Blocks created on a layer other than layer 0 will retain the characteristics of that layer, even when inserted on a different layer.

Step 5. Pick the **Select Objects** button and then select all the objects that will comprise the block. Press **Enter** when finished selecting objects.

Step 3. Enter the block's name in the **Name** text box.

Step 6. Selecting this box will allow the finished block to be exploded later if necessary.

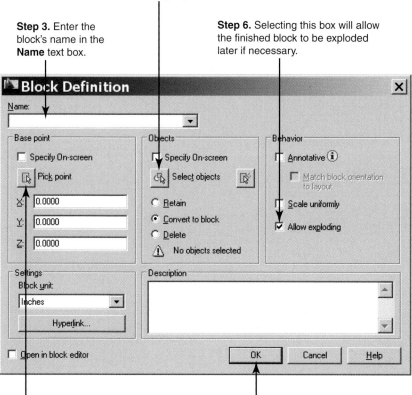

Step 4. Specify the **Base Point** of the block by picking on the **Pick Point** button and selecting the desired base point on the object. Remember to select a point that would make a "logical" Base Point.

Step 7. Pick the **OK** button to exit the Block Definition dialog box.

10.4 **Block Definition** Dialog Box

4 Specify the base point of the block by picking on the **Pick point** button and selecting the desired base point located on the object. Select a point that will make a "logical" base point for inserting the block into the drawing.

5 Pick the **Select objects** button and select all the objects that the block comprises. Press **<Enter>** when you have finished selecting objects.

6 Checking the **Allow exploding** box allows the finished block to be exploded later if necessary.

7 Click **OK** to exit the **Block Definition** dialog box.

INSERTING BLOCKS INTO A DRAWING

Blocks are placed into drawings by using the **Insert Block** command (see Figure 10.5). The steps involved in inserting a block into a drawing are as follows:

1. Select the **Insert Block** icon from the **Draw** toolbar or the from the **Block** panel of the **Home** tab of the ribbon (see Figure 10.5).

Insert Block

10.5   Insert Icon

2. When the **Insert** dialog box opens, click the down arrow on the right side of the **Name** window and select the block you wish to insert from the drop-down list (see Figure 10.6).

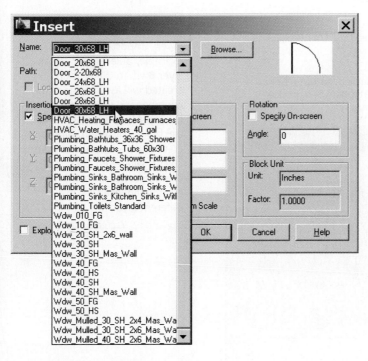

10.6   Insert Dialog Box

> ── TIP ──
>
> You can insert an entire existing AutoCAD drawing into your current drawing by selecting the **Browse . . .** button from the **Insert** dialog box, browsing to the AutoCAD drawing file you wish to insert, selecting its file name, and clicking **OK**. The **0,0** point on the inserted drawing will default as its base point. The inserted drawing will behave like a block (it will be inserted as one entity), and its layers, linetypes, and blocks will become part of the current drawing.

3. If the block needs to be rotated or scaled on placement, check the **Rotation Specify On-screen** box and/or the **Scale Specify On-screen** box in the **Insert** dialog box shown in Figure 10.7.

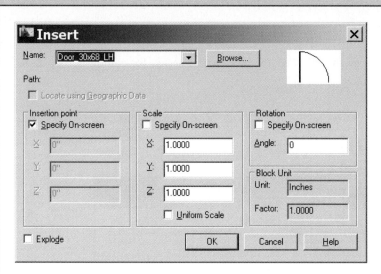

10.7   **Insert** Dialog Box

4 Click **OK** and select the insertion point on the drawing where you want to place the block's base point. You will also be prompted to define the block's scale and rotation if either of these boxes was checked in Step 3.

— TIP —

In most cases, exact placement of the block is important—at the endpoint of a line, for example. For this reason, use an appropriate **OSNAP** setting to facilitate accurate block placement whenever possible.

STEP by STEP

EDITING BLOCKS WITH THE BLOCK EDITOR COMMAND

The easiest way to make changes to a block is with the **Block Editor** command. The steps for using this command follow.

1 Open the **Block Editor** by selecting the **Block Editor** tool located on the **Blocks** panel of the **Home** tab of the ribbon or by double-clicking on a block that has already been inserted into the drawing or by typing **BEDIT** and pressing **<Enter>**.

2 When the **Edit Block Definition** dialog box opens [see Figure 10.8(a)], select the name of the block you wish to edit from the list on the left side of the box and click **OK**.

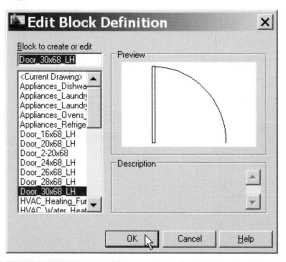

10.8(a)   **Edit Block Definition** Dialog Box

STEP by STEP

3 At this point two things will occur:

1. A window with a gray background will open that displays the block you selected for editing in Step 2. See Figure 10.8(b).

Save Block Tool   Block Editor Tab   Close Block Editor

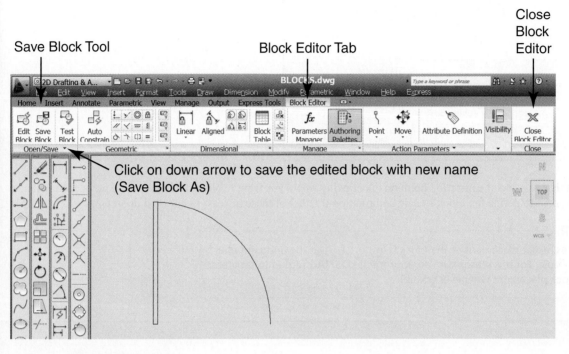

Click on down arrow to save the edited block with new name (Save Block As)

10.8(b)   **Block Editor** Screen

2. The **Home** tab of the ribbon will be replaced by the **Block Editor** tab.

4 Use the tools available on the **Draw** and **Modify** toolbars and on the **Block Editor** tab to make the desired changes to the block.

5 When you have finished editing the block, choose the **Save Block** tool from the **Open/Save** panel of the **Block Editor** tab of the ribbon. See Figure 10.8(b). To give the block a different name, pick on the down arrow next to the words **Open/Save** and select the **Save Block As** option. See Figure 10.8(b). To end the editing operation, choose the **Close Block Editor** tool from the **Close** panel.

> **TIP**
>
> Blocks with the same name as the redefined block that have been inserted into the drawing prior to editing will also be updated to reflect the redefined properties. This situation can be avoided by choosing the **Save Block As** tool from the **Open/Save** panel and giving the edited block a different name.

> **TIP**
>
> Another way to edit a block that has already been inserted into the drawing is to *explode* the block by selecting it and clicking the **Explode** tool located on the **Modify** toolbar. After a block has been exploded, its entities revert to individual objects that no longer constitute a block. It should be noted that block entities that were on layer 0 when the block was created will revert to layer 0 after the block is exploded. Block entities that were on layers other than layer 0 when the block was created will revert to their original layers after the block is exploded. After the entities have been edited, you can use the **Make Block** command to reblock the objects if desired.

KEY WORDS

Base Point

Block

Block Library

Insertion Point

CHAPTER SUMMARY

Creating and using blocks is another method employed by AutoCAD users to work more quickly and efficiently. This chapter presented the basics of creation, usage, and editing of blocks. Other, more powerful, methods of using blocks, including creating *attributed blocks* (an attribute is a label or tag that attaches data to a block) and *dynamic blocks* (blocks that can be edited in place rather than redefining them), are usually covered in more advanced AutoCAD texts.

Later in this text you will learn how to use an AutoCAD feature called *DesignCenter* to insert blocks from other drawings into the current drawing.

REVIEW QUESTIONS

Multiple Choice

1. What is a block?

   a. One set of a cube
   b. Predrawn object
   c. Group of drawing files
   d. None of the above

2. What AutoCAD command is used to place a block into a drawing?

   a. **INSERT**
   b. **ADD**
   c. **COPY & PASTE**
   d. All the above

3. What AutoCAD command is used to turn an object into a block?

   a. **GROUP**
   b. **BLOCK**
   c. Both a and b
   d. **Insert Block**

4. What is a block called that has a label (or tag) attached to it that contains data?

   a. Dynamic block
   b. Attributed block
   c. String block
   d. Wooden block

5. What command is used to edit a block?

   a. **BLOCKX**
   b. **BEDIT**
   c. **BEXPLODE**
   d. **BCLOSE**

CHAPTER PROJECT

Project 10.1: Adding Plumbing and Electrical Blocks to the Guest Cottage

In this project you will add plumbing and electrical symbols to the floor plan of the guest cottage you created in Chapter 4. This project will require you to create a block for each plumbing and electrical symbol. These blocks will be inserted into the floor plan in the locations shown in the designer's sketch in Figure 10.9.

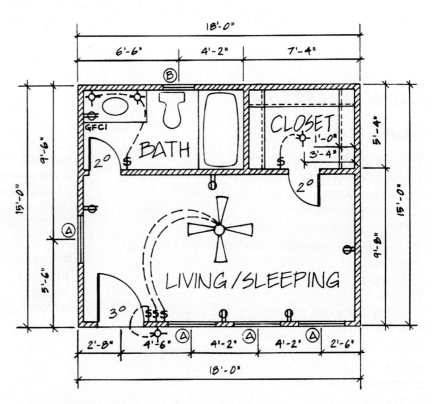

10.9   Designer's Sketch of the Guest Cottage Showing Plumbing, Electrical, and Wiring Symbols

Directions

1. Open the **Guest Cottage** drawing file you created in Chapter 4.
2. Create the following layers: **Plumbing, Electric,** and **Wiring.** Assign a color to each layer and set the Wiring layer's linetype to **Phantom.**
3. Use the following steps to create and place blocks for the plumbing and electrical symbols and to add switch lines between the switches, light fixtures, and ceiling fan.

Creating Blocks for the Guest Cottage

Follow the steps detailed on pages 343–345 to make blocks for the plumbing and electrical symbols. You will make five blocks in all. Insert the blocks into the **Guest Cottage** drawing in the locations shown in the designer's sketch in Figure 10.9.

TIP

Draw and create the blocks on layer **0.** Insert the plumbing symbols on the **Plumbing** layer and the electrical symbols on the **Electric** layer.

Drawing the Plumbing Symbols

Step 1. To draw the tub, draw a **2'6" × 5'0"** rectangle and offset it **4"** to the inside. Use the **FILLET** command to fillet the corners of the inside rectangle. Fillet the top corners **R6"** and the bottom corners **R2"** as shown in Figure 10.10.

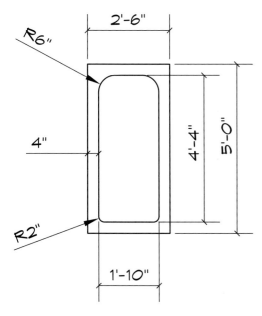

10.10 Size Dimensions for Tub

Step 2. Next, make a block for the tub, selecting the tub's upper right corner as the base point. Set the **Plumbing** layer current and insert the block of the tub into the corner of the bathroom as shown in Figure 10.9.

Step 3. To draw the lavatory, draw a **4'-6" × 1'-10"** rectangle for the sink top. Next, select the **ELLIPSE** command, and when prompted to *Specify axis endpoint:*, pick a point and draw a horizontal line **1'-8"** long. Then, at the prompt for the length of the other axis, type **7"** (1'-2" divided by 2) to create the bowl. Move the center of the bowl to the location on the rectangle shown in Figure 10.11.

Step 4. Next, make a block for the lavatory, selecting the lavatory's upper left corner as the base point. Insert the block of the lavatory into the corner of the bathroom as shown in Figure 10.9.

Step 5. To draw the flush toilet (also called a *commode* or *water closet*), draw a **1'8" × 6"** rectangle for the toilet tank. Next, draw a vertical line from the midpoint of the top edge of the rectangle to a point **1'-8"** below the first point. Select the **ELLIPSE** command and draw a horizontal line **1'-4"** long; then, at the prompt for the length of the other axis, type **10"** (1'-8" divided by 2) to create the toilet bowl. Move the ellipse by its center point to the endpoint of the **1'-8"** line drawn earlier and erase the line (see Figure 10.12).

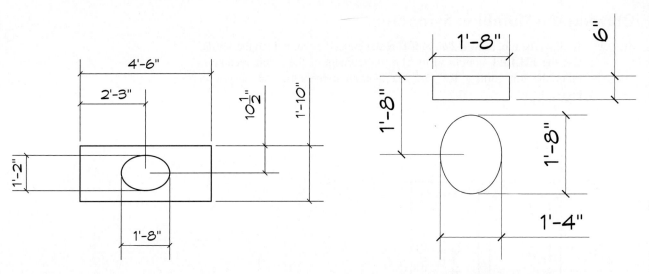

10.11   Size Dimensions for Lavatory

10.12   Size Dimensions for Toilet

Step 6.   Next, make a block representing the toilet. Select the midpoint of the toilet tank's top edge as the block's base point. Insert the block of the toilet into the **Guest Cottage** floor plan by centering it between the right edge of the lavatory and the left edge of the tub as shown in Figure 10.9. Move the toilet **2"** away from the inside edge of the wall.

Drawing the Electrical Symbols

Step 1.   To create the ceiling fan block, draw the fan blade and circle shown in Figure 10.13. Construct the fan inside a circle **3'** in diameter.

Step 2.   Use **Polar Array,** selecting the fan blade as the object to array and the center of the **4"** circle as the center point of the array. In the **Array** dialog box, enter **5** as the total number of items and **360** as the angle to fill. Check the box for **Rotate items as copied**. The finished fan should look like the one shown in Figure 10.14. Make a block of the fan, choosing the center of the array as the base point. Set the **Electric** layer current, and insert the fan in the location shown in Figure 10.9.

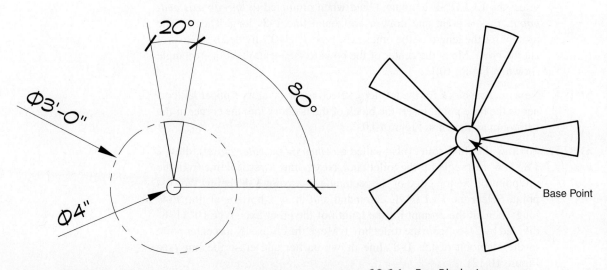

10.13   Fan Blade Construction

10.14   Fan Blade Array

Step 3.   To draw the light fixture (also called a *luminaire*), draw a **6"** diameter circle and then draw a **1-1/2"** line from each of the circle's quadrants as shown in Figure 10.15. Make a block of the light fixture, choosing the center of the circle as the base point. Insert two light fixture blocks above the lavatory as shown on the sketch of the floor plan in Figure 10.9.

Step 4. To add switches and outlets, you can use the blocks for the switches and outlets that are included in the prototype drawing for the **Guest Cottage** drawing. Use the **INSERT** command to place the electrical outlets (see Figure 10.16) and the switches (see Figure 10.17) from the list of blocks. Refer to the floor plan sketch in Figure 10.9 for placement of these symbols.

Set the **Labels** layer current, and label the outlet in the bathroom **GFCI** using **3"** text as shown in Figure 10.9. **GFCI** indicates that the type of outlet is a *ground fault circuit interrupt*. GFCI outlets are required near plumbing fixtures where an electric appliance, like a hair dryer, might come in contact with water and pose a risk of electric shock.

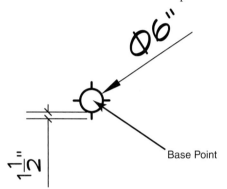

10.15 Size Dimensions for Light Fixture

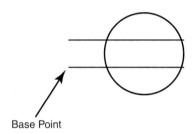

10.16 Electrical Outlet Symbol

10.17 Wall Switch Symbol

Adding the Switch Lines

Step 1. Set the **Wiring** layer current and use the **Spline** command to create the switch lines connecting the switches to the electrical fixtures as shown in Figure 10.18.

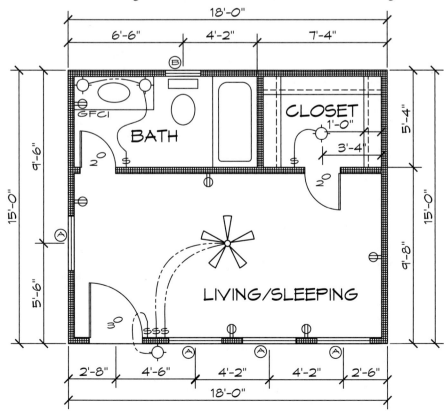

10.18 Switch Lines Added to Lights and Ceiling Fan

Step 2. You may need to set the **LTSCALE** (linetype scale) to a larger value for dashes to appear in the phantom lines. **LTSCALE** controls the size of dashes in noncontinuous lines such as hidden, center, and phantom lines. To change the **LTSCALE**, type **LTS** and press **<Enter>,** enter a new value (the default value is **1),** and press **<Enter>.** To change the **LTSCALE** of only one line, select the line, right-click, and select **Properties** from the menu; this will open the **Properties** palette. In the field next to **Linetype Scale,** set the value to a larger number.

This step completes the **Guest Cottage** project. Follow your instructor's directions to print the drawing. Be sure to save the drawing file when you close AutoCAD.

OPTIONAL CHAPTER PROJECT

Project 10.2: FM Tuner

Draw the schematic of the FM tuner shown in Figure 10.19. The schematic symbols needed in this drawing have already been drawn, but you will need to create a block for each symbol.

Directions

1. Open the **Electronic Schematic Template** drawing located in the student data files at **www.pearsondesigncentral.com.** To access this drawing, open the Pearson Design Central website and click on the *CAD Community* link, then select the *Click here to download student data files for our CAD titles* link. Next, click on the *Technical Drawing 101* link and select the *Prototype Drawings* zip file, then select the *Download* button and open (or save) the prototype drawing specified above.

2. Use **SAVE AS** to save the drawing to your **Home** directory, and rename the drawing **FM TUNER**.

3. Create two new layers named **Circuit** and **Symbols,** and follow the steps detailed on pages 347–348 to draw and label the schematic diagram shown in Figure 10.19.

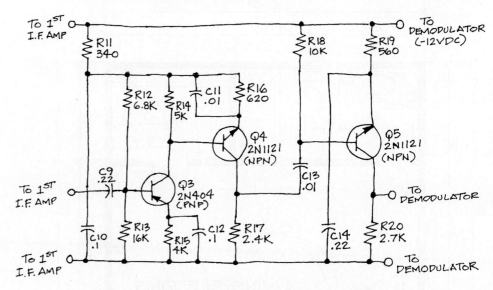

10.19 Designer's Sketch of the FM Tuner Schematic

4. Place Notes 1 and 2 (Figure 10.19) on the **Text** layer in the area to the left side of the title block using **.125"** text height.

Creating Blocks for the FM Tuner

Make a block for each of the symbols shown on the prototype drawing. There will be six blocks in all. Use the block names shown in Figure 10.20, and select the point displayed in red that accompanies each drawing as the block's base point.

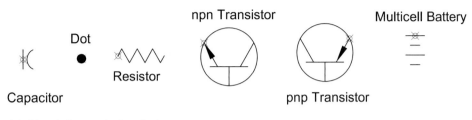

10.20   Schematic Symbols

TIP

You will need to have the **Node** object snap setting selected to snap to the red point included on each symbol, but **do not** include the *red point* when selecting the objects to be included in the block.

When you have finished making the blocks, turn the **Nodes** layer off and erase the symbols remaining on the screen.

Drawing the Schematic Diagram

Step 1.   Set the **Circuit** layer current and use **OFFSET** or **Rectangular Array** to draw a grid like the one shown in Figure 10.21 using **1.125"** spacing between lines. Begin the lower left corner of the grid at absolute coordinates **1.25, 2.5**.

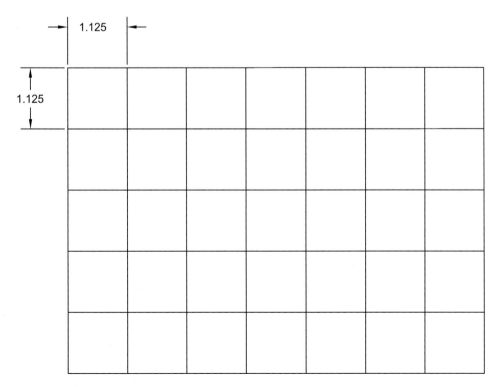

10.21   Construction of a Schematic Grid

Step 2.   Make the **Symbols** layer current and insert the blocks on the grid lines as shown in Figure 10.22. Visually center the symbols between the lines. You may need to move some lines at this point to reflect the sketch of the circuit accurately.

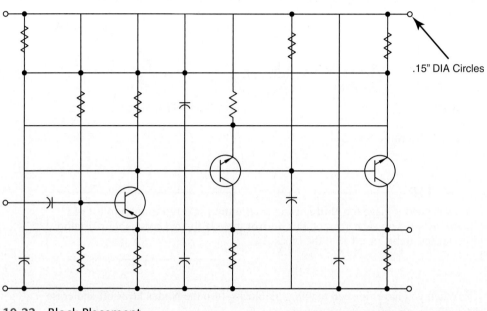

.15" DIA Circles

10.22   Block Placement

Step 3.   Trim the lines that run through the blocks of the electronic symbols. Next, trim or delete other layout lines as needed to create the circuit configuration shown in Figure 10.23.

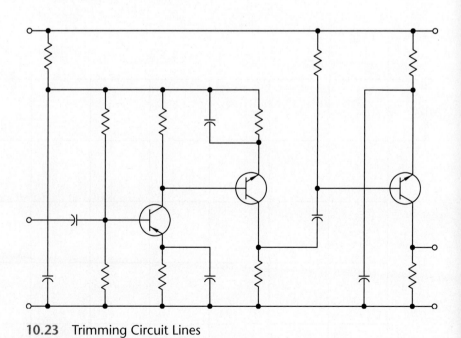

10.23   Trimming Circuit Lines

Step 4.   Refer to the sketch of the schematic shown in Figure 10.19, and add **.125"** labels on the **Text** layer as shown in Figure 10.24.

── TIP ──
Text height should be **.125**" for both labels and notes.

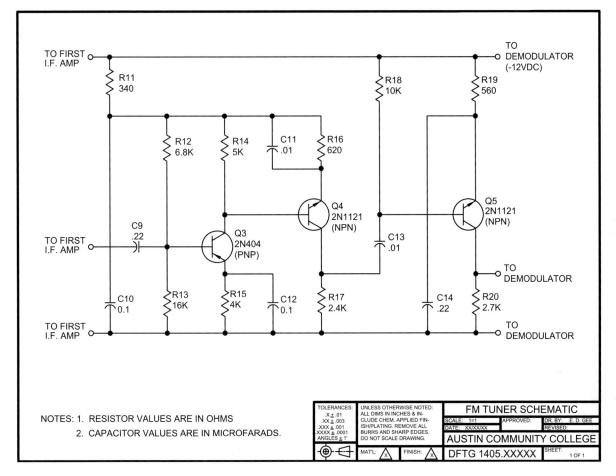

10.24 Finished FM Tuner Schematic Diagram

This completes the FM tuner project. Follow your instructor's directions to print the drawing. Be sure to save the drawing file before you close AutoCAD.

CHAPTER ELEVEN

MECHANICAL WORKING DRAWINGS

OBJECTIVES

After studying the material in this chapter, you should be able to:

1. Describe what mechanical working drawings are and how they are produced.

2. Use AutoCAD to create an exploded, isometric assembly view of a mechanism including balloons, part numbers, and a parts list.

3. Use AutoCAD to create detail drawings of mechanical parts, including all the necessary multiviews, dimensions, and notations required to manufacture each part.

4. Represent and specify fasteners and other hardware in a mechanical working drawing.

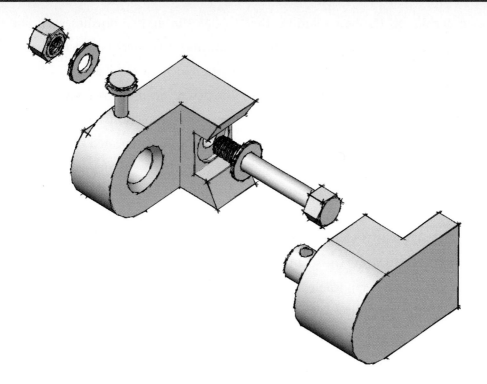

OVERVIEW

In the mechanical engineering field, drafters are often required to create complex sets of **mechanical working drawings** for entire mechanical assemblies. To better understand the creation of these drawings, it is helpful to step back and take a wider view of the mechanical design process itself.

For most mechanical designers, the first phase of a design project involves clearly defining the design problem and specifying the criteria that the finished design must meet to be considered a success. As stated earlier in Chapter 1, designers often refer to this phase in the design process as *problem identification*. For example, before beginning a design for a machine part, a mechanical designer must have a clear understanding of the following: the function the part serves; the ability of the part to work in conjunction with other parts; an idea of the shape, size, strength, and material of the finished part; any safety and reliability concerns the part may present; and an estimated budget for the project.

After the design problem is clearly defined, the *preliminary design* phase begins. This stage is also referred to by designers as the *ideation*, or *brainstorming*, phase of the process. During this phase, multiple solutions to the design problem are generated. The documentation for these preliminary designs may be in the form of freehand sketches or 2D and 3D CAD models.

In the next phase, the preliminary designs are analyzed and evaluated by the design team to decide which one best meets the design criteria defined in the first phase. During this process, the design may be further refined, and the best features of some of the rejected designs may be incorporated into the final design solution. The analysis of the designs may involve computer modeling or the preparation of actual prototypes of the part, which are subjected to performance testing. It is not unusual for a design to go through many revisions, or *iterations*, during this phase.

After the team decides on the best solution, the designer begins preparing design inputs that more clearly define the details of the project. Design inputs may include freehand sketches or CAD models that provide dimensional information and detailed notes about the project.

When the design inputs are finished, they are given to the drafter(s) responsible for preparing the working drawings for the project. In this phase, drafters usually work closely with designers, checkers, engineers, and other drafters to create the set of drawings. Drafters must follow any applicable drawing standards (such as ASME or ISO) during this phase.

As the drafter finishes each sheet in the set of drawings, the sheet is checked carefully for mistakes by designers or checkers. If mistakes are found, or if the design needs to be revised, the drafter makes the necessary corrections or revisions to the drawings. This process is repeated until the drawings are complete. Revisions are such an integral part of the design process that they are usually noted in a *revision history block* located on the upper right corner of the sheet.

The finished set of working drawings represents the master plan for the project. All the information required to manufacture and assemble the project should be included in these drawings.

11.1 PREPARING MECHANICAL WORKING DRAWINGS

Working drawings usually include assembly and detail drawings. ***Assembly drawings*** show how the separate parts of the assembly are related to each other, for example, how mating parts fit together. ***Detail drawings*** provide all the information required to manufacture or purchase each part in the assembly, including the necessary views, dimensions, notations, and specifications.

Assembly Drawings

The assembly drawing usually acts as the "cover" sheet in a set of working drawings and is numbered as the first sheet in the set of plans. For example, if a set of working drawings contains a total of 20 sheets, the drafter will put the label *SHEET 1 OF 20* in the assembly drawing's title block. The details for each part in the assembly are drawn on subsequent sheets, and these sheets are numbered sequentially, for example, *SHEET 2 OF 20, SHEET 3 OF 20,* and so on, through *SHEET 20 OF 20.*

Assembly drawings are often drawn pictorially with the parts pulled apart, or "exploded," to show how the device is assembled. Figure 11.1 shows an example of an exploded isometric drawing that is used to show how the parts in the assembly fit together.

> **NOTE**
> The layout of title blocks for the first sheet and continuing sheets, including the information that goes into the fields of the title block, is covered in the *ASME Y14.1-2005* standard.

> **NOTE**
> The ASME standards governing the size and format of drawing sheets, including borders, title blocks, and revision history blocks, are *ASME Y14.1-2005* and *ASME Y14.1M-2005* (metric).

The assembly drawing often includes a ***parts list*** (sometimes referred to as a *bill of materials or BOM*) itemizing all the parts in the assembly. In Figure 11.1 the parts list is located above the title block, and a revision history block is located in the upper right corner of this drawing.

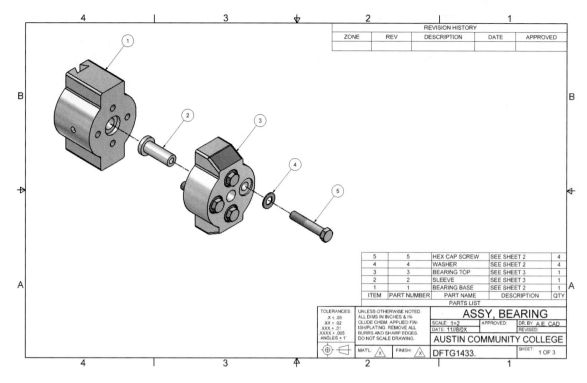

11.1 Exploded Assembly Drawing

CREATING AN EXPLODED ASSEMBLY DRAWING

1 Study the individual parts of the assembly and determine how they fit together. Make an isometric planning sketch of the assembly similar to the one in Figure 11.2. Sketch the parts of the assembly as if they were pulled apart along isometric axes.

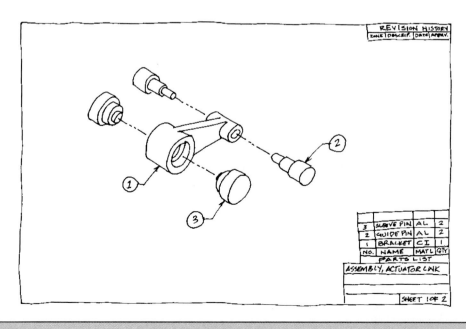

11.2 Planning Sketch of Exploded Assembly

STEP by STEP

Assign part numbers to the separate parts and enclose each number in a circle with a leader attached. Part numbers are also referred to as *find* numbers. In an assembly drawing, this combination of a part number, circle, and leader is called a *balloon*.

Refer to the part numbers assigned to the sketch, and plan a parts list. The categories the parts list must include are the part number, description, and the quantity required. The parts list may also include categories for material, Commercial and Governmental Entity Code (CAGE Code), and other information about the assembly.

② Begin a new AutoCAD drawing using an appropriate sheet size, border, and title block. Refer to the planning sketch made in Step 1, and construct an isometric view for each part in the assembly. Whenever possible, orient the isometric view to show as much detail about the assembly as possible. Align the parts as they would appear if they had been pulled apart from their normal assembled arrangement, as shown in Figure 11.3.

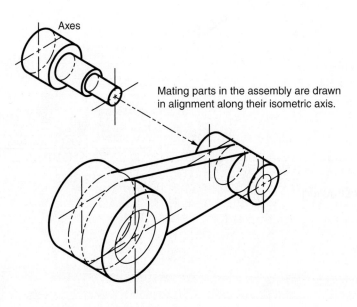

Axes

Mating parts in the assembly are drawn in alignment along their isometric axis.

11.3   Aligning Mating Parts along Their Isometric Axes

③ Add balloons and part numbers to each part.

┌─ **TIP** ───────────────────────────────────┐
Duplicate parts in an assembly receive the same part number.
└───┘

Add phantom lines along isometric axes to show the relationship between mating parts. See Figure 11.4.

④ Add a parts list to the drawing. An example of a parts list is shown in Figure 11.5. Parts lists are often placed above the title block in assembly drawings but may be placed in other areas of the drawing.

┌─ **NOTE** ──────────────────────────────────┐
The ASME standard governing location and format of a parts list is *ASME Y14.34-2008*. This standard also governs other types of lists used in engineering drawings.
└───┘

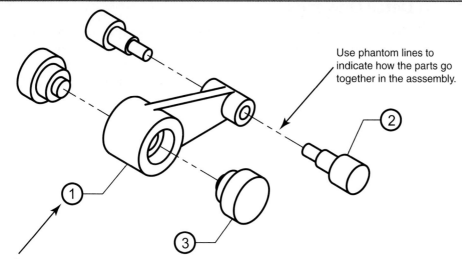

Use phantom lines to indicate how the parts go together in the asssembly.

Balloons are circles that enclose the part number. The balloons in this example were drawn .50″ in diameter, and .25″ text height was used for the part numbers.

11.4   Adding Balloons, Part Numbers, and Phantom Lines

STEP by **STEP**

5	HEX CAP SCREW	SEE SHEET 2	4
4	WASHER	SEE SHEET 2	4
3	BEARING TOP	SEE SHEET 3	1
2	SLEEVE	SEE SHEET 3	1
1	BEARING BASE	SEE SHEET 2	1
PART NUMBER	PART NAME	DESCRIPTION	QTY
PARTS LIST			

11.5   Example of a Parts List

5 Complete the information in the title block including the name, scale, and sheet number of the assembly. Compare the planning sketch shown in Figure 11.2 with the completed CAD drawing shown in Figure 11.6.

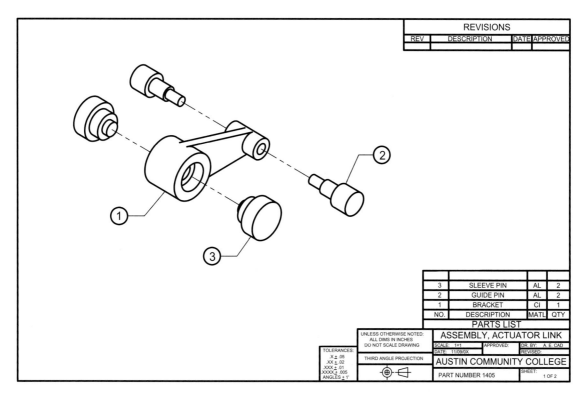

11.6   Completed Exploded Assembly

Detail Drawings

An example of a detail drawing is shown in Figure 11.7. To create this drawing, the drafter works from design inputs provided by an engineer or designer. Often, the design input is in the form of a rough sketch; however, in the modern practice of technical drawing, the drafter may receive this input in the form of a 3D CAD drawing file created by the designer.

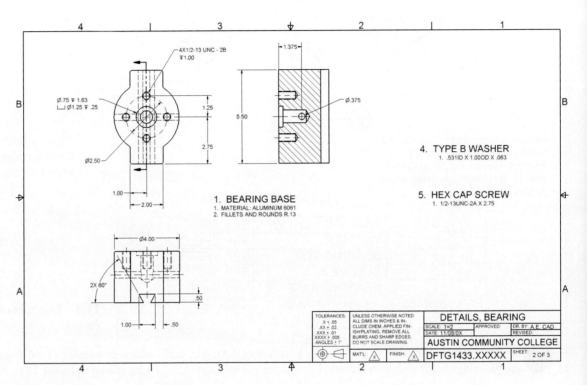

11.7 Example of a Detail Drawing

When the individual part is "detailed out," all the views, dimensions, and notes necessary to manufacture the part are included. Because the drafter's expertise is in creating technical drawings, decisions regarding the necessary views and correct dimensioning of the object are often left up to the drafter's judgment. The drafter may also be responsible for determining the sheet size and making sure that the drawing complies with any appropriate drafting or dimensioning standards (such as *ASME Y14.5-2009*).

JOB SKILLS

When creating a detail drawing of an object, the drafter must be careful not to change the design intent of the designer by incorrectly noting dimension values, changing the precision of dimensions, or referencing different datum features than the ones on the designer's sketch.

CREATING A DETAIL DRAWING

1 Make a planning sketch of the multiviews of the parts to be detailed similar to the one shown in Figure 11.8. This sketch may also include dimensions and notations.

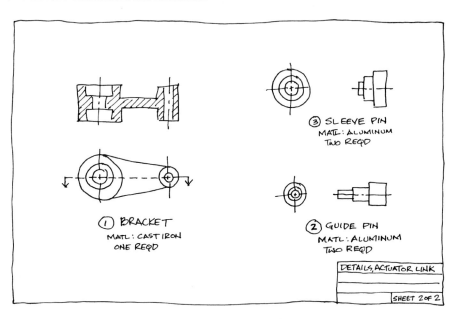

11.8 Planning Sketch for a Detail Sheet

If multiple parts are drawn on the same sheet, space the views of separate parts so there is no confusion concerning which view goes with which part.

Using the same part names and numbers defined in the assembly drawing, label each part. Include in the drawing the part's material, quantity (the number required for the assembly), and any other notes required for manufacture.

2 Begin a new AutoCAD drawing using the same sheet size, border, and title block used in the assembly drawing. Refer to the planning sketch and draw the necessary views for each part. Consider drawing section views of parts with complex interior details.

Include all the dimensions necessary to manufacture the part. When dimensioning, follow guidelines established by the *ASME Y14.5-2009* standard (refer to Chapter 5).

Add part numbers and part names. These are often placed using **.25"** text height for emphasis.

Include any notes required for manufacture and the total number of each part required for the assembly. These notes are often placed beneath the part name and number using the same text height as the dimension text.

3 Complete the information in the title block including the name, scale, and sheet number of the detail. Compare the planning sketch shown in Figure 11.8 with the completed CAD drawing shown in Figure 11.9.

STEP by STEP

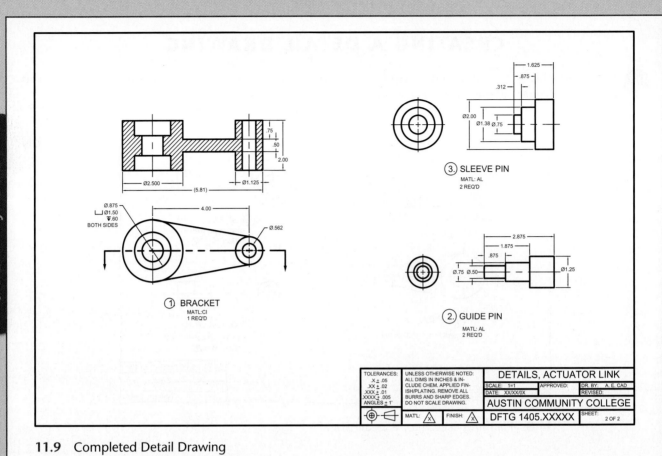

11.9 Completed Detail Drawing

KEY WORDS

Assembly Drawing

Mechanical Working Drawings

Detail Drawings

Parts List

CHAPTER SUMMARY

To be successful in the mechanical design field, drafters and CAD operators must be able to create working drawings consisting of both assembly and detail drawings. Assembly drawings illustrate how the parts in the assembly fit together and should include part numbers, balloons, and a parts list. Detail drawings should include all the views, dimensions, and notations required to manufacture each part of the assembly. Drafters and designers should also be familiar with specifying and representing threaded holes, shafts, and fasteners. It is important that the drafter represent every component of the assembly exactly as specified in the designer's inputs to ensure that the finished project is manufactured and assembled as intended.

Mechanical drafters must also be familiar with the numerous drafting and dimensioning standards that control the format, dimensioning, and tolerancing of engineering working drawings.

REVIEW QUESTIONS

Short Answer

1. Define what is meant by the term *assembly drawing*.
2. Define what is meant by the term *detail drawing*.
3. Explain the sheet numbering system used in mechanical working drawings.
4. Name four column headings that might be included on a parts list.
5. Explain how planning sketches are used in the creation of mechanical working drawings.

CHAPTER PROJECT

Project 11.1: Toe Stop Assembly

Create mechanical working drawings for the toe stop assembly detailed in Figures 11.10, 11.11, and 11.12. Draw the assembly as an exploded isometric view including balloons, part numbers, and a parts list. On the detail sheets, fully dimension each part and provide specifications for the standard hardware (hex screw, hex nut, and washer).

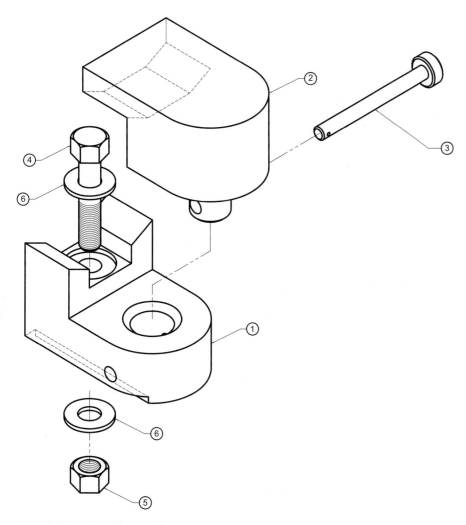

11.10   Toe Stop Assembly

PART NO	DESCRIPTION	MATERIAL	QTY
6	TYPE A PLAIN WASHER	SEE SHEET 3	2
5	HEX NUT	SEE SHEET 3	1
4	HEX CAP SCREW	SEE SHEET 3	1
3	CLEAT PIN	MILD STEEL	1
2	CLEAT	MILD STEEL	1
1	TOE STOP BASE	MILD STEEL	1

PARTS LIST

11.11   Toe Stop Assembly Parts List

$\tan 82 = \frac{.25}{x}$

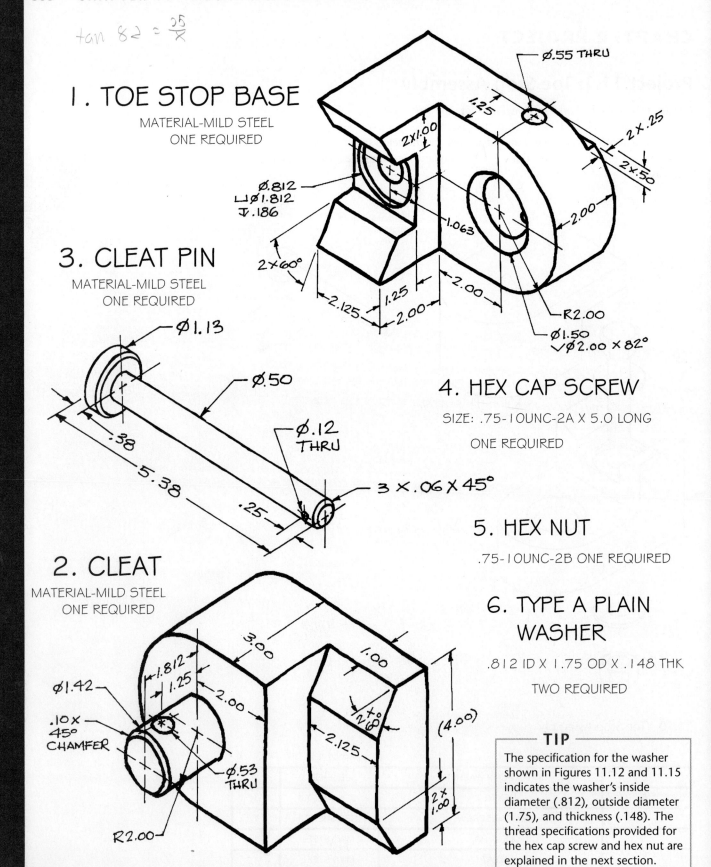

1. TOE STOP BASE

MATERIAL-MILD STEEL
ONE REQUIRED

Ø.55 THRU

1.25

2×1.00

2×.25

2×.50

2.00

Ø.812
⊔Ø1.812
⊽.186

2×60°

1.063

2.125

1.25

2.00

2.00

R2.00

Ø1.50
⊽Ø2.00 × 82°

3. CLEAT PIN

MATERIAL-MILD STEEL
ONE REQUIRED

Ø1.13

Ø.50

.38

5.38

Ø.12
THRU

.25

3 × .06 × 45°

4. HEX CAP SCREW

SIZE: .75-10UNC-2A X 5.0 LONG

ONE REQUIRED

5. HEX NUT

.75-10UNC-2B ONE REQUIRED

6. TYPE A PLAIN WASHER

.812 ID X 1.75 OD X .148 THK

TWO REQUIRED

2. CLEAT

MATERIAL-MILD STEEL
ONE REQUIRED

3.00

1.00

1.812

1.25

2.00

Ø1.42

.10 X
45°
CHAMFER

2 × 60°

2.125

Ø.53
THRU

(4.00)

R2.00

2 × 1.00

TIP

The specification for the washer shown in Figures 11.12 and 11.15 indicates the washer's inside diameter (.812), outside diameter (1.75), and thickness (.148). The thread specifications provided for the hex cap screw and hex nut are explained in the next section.

11.12 Designer's Sketch of Toe Stop Assembly Parts

Directions

1. Open the **Mechanical Working Drawing Prototype** drawing located in the student data files at **www.pearsondesigncentral.com.** To access this drawing, open the Pearson Design Central website and click on the *CAD Community* link, then select the *Click here to download student data files for our CAD titles* link. Next, click on the *Technical Drawing 101* link and select the *Prototype Drawings* zip file, then select the *Download* button and open (or save) the prototype drawing specified above.
2. Use **SAVE AS** to save the drawing to your **Home** directory, and rename the new drawing **TOE STOP ASSEMBLY**.
3. Draw and dimension the necessary views of the toe stop base, cleat, and cleat pin. In the **Dimension Style Manager** dialog box, create two new dimension styles named **ASME Small Radii** and **ASME Large Radii** that contain the following dimension style settings:

Text height:	.15
Arrow size:	.15
Center marks:	Line
Extend beyond dim lines:	.125
Precision:	Varies—match precision of dimensions on sketch
Zero suppression:	Leading
Offset from Dimension Line:	.062

For the **ASME Small Radii** style, set the **Fit** tab settings shown in Figure 5.57(a). For the **ASME Large Radii** style, set the **Fit** tab settings shown in Figure 5.57(c). When dimensioning small circles and arcs in the Toe Stop project, apply the **ASME Small Radii** dimension style. When dimensioning large circles and arcs in this project apply the **ASME Large Radii** style.
4. Create a full section view of the toe stop base on the details sheet for this part.
5. Draw an exploded isometric assembly showing all the parts, add balloons and part numbers, and complete the parts list. Insert the premade blocks representing the isometric views of the hex cap screw, hex nut, and washer contained in the prototype drawing.

Creating the Assembly and Detail Drawings for the Toe Stop Project

Planning the Sheets   This project will require three D-size (34″ × 22″) sheets. Sheet 1 will be an exploded assembly (including a parts list, balloons, and part numbers), and Sheets 2 and 3 will contain the details (multiviews, dimensions, and notations) for each part.

The exploded assembly will be the first sheet in the set and will be numbered Sheet 1 of 3. A planning sketch for this sheet might resemble the one shown in Figure 11.13. In this sketch the parts are sketched isometrically and positioned as they would look if the assembly had been pulled apart. Balloons, part numbers, and a parts list are also included on this sheet.

--- **TIP** ---
The CAD drawing of the exploded assembly should be drawn *after the detail sheets are drawn* because you will need to transfer measurements from the views of the detail drawings to construct isometric drawings of features such as the inclined planes and the countersunk hole.

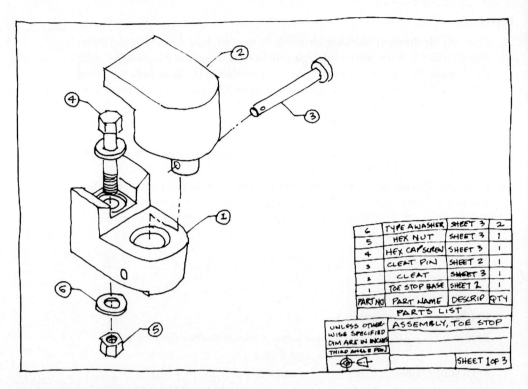

The parts list in the assembly drawing reads:

6	TYPE A WASHER	SHEET 3	2
5	HEX NUT	SHEET 3	1
4	HEX CAP SCREW	SHEET 3	1
3	CLEAT PIN	SHEET 2	1
2	CLEAT	SHEET 3	1
1	TOE STOP BASE	SHEET 2	1
PART NO	PART NAME	DESCRIP	QTY

PARTS LIST

UNLESS OTHERWISE SPECIFIED DIM ARE IN INCHES — THIRD ANGLE PROJ

ASSEMBLY, TOE STOP

SHEET 1 OF 3

11.13   Sheet 1 of the Planning Sketch

Begin the project by drawing the first sheet of details. Because the sheet containing the assembly drawing is numbered Sheet of 1 of 3, this sheet will be numbered Sheet 2 of 3.

This sheet will include the details of the toe stop base and the cleat pin. The toe stop base is considered the principal part in this assembly because all the other parts are aligned to or mate with it. Because it is the principal part, it will be labeled Part 1.

Figure 11.14 shows a planning sketch made for Sheet 2. Begin this sheet by determining which view of the toe stop base will be drawn as the front, or principal,

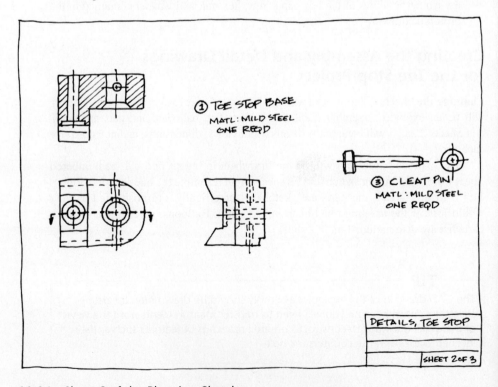

① TOE STOP BASE
MATL: MILD STEEL
ONE REQD

③ CLEAT PIN
MATL: MILD STEEL
ONE REQD

DETAILS, TOE STOP

SHEET 2 OF 3

11.14   Sheet 2 of the Planning Sketch

view and then determine the other multiviews necessary to describe the part. For the toe stop base, a full section should be included to show the interior detail of the object. Add the necessary dimensions and notations and follow the *ASME Y14.5-2009* dimensioning guidelines described in Chapter 5. Next, draw the necessary views of the cleat pin and add the required dimensions and notations to these views.

The next sheet drawn in this set will be the second sheet of details. which will be numbered Sheet 3 of 3. On this sheet you will draw the details of the cleat and include the specifications for the hex cap screw, hex nut, and washer. A planning sketch for this sheet is shown in Figure 11.15. Begin this sheet by determining which view of the cleat will be drawn as the front, or principal, view and then determine the other required views. Add the dimensions and notations required to manufacture the part.

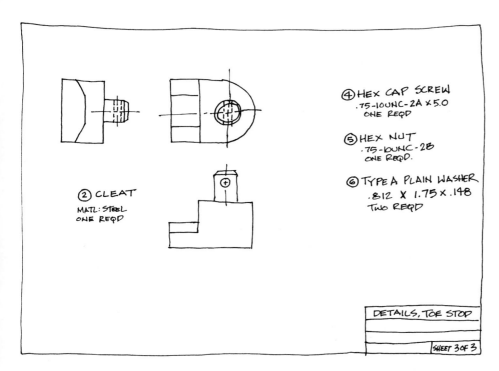

11.15   Sheet 3 of the Planning Sketch

Note in Figure 11.15 that instead of creating detail drawings for the hex cap screw, hex nut, and washer only their specifications for size and quantity are provided. This is because these parts are standard hardware that can be purchased from an outside vendor. However, it is necessary to note on the drawing the part name, part number, specification, and quantity for each part so that the correct hardware can be ordered.

Threads and Fasteners in Mechanical Working Drawings

Mechanical drawings often include threaded holes, shafts, and fasteners (hex nuts, bolts, screws, etc.). The threads on these features are specified with a thread note detailing the size and type of thread.

The Toe Stop Assembly project calls for a hex cap screw and a mating hex nut (see Figure 11.12). The thread specification for the screw is .75-10UNC-2A. This thread note is interpreted in the following way: the major diameter of the thread is **.75"**, the number of threads per inch is **10**, the thread series is **Unified National Coarse (UNC)**, the thread class is **2**, and the **A** indicates it is an external thread. The thread specification for the mating hex nut is exactly the same, except the **A** is replaced with a **B** to indicate an internal thread. Figure 11.16 shows how to interpret the thread specification for the hex cap screw.

> ── **NOTE** ──────────────────────
> The ASME standard governing the specification and dimensioning of screw threads is *ASME Y14.6-2001* (Reaffirmed 2007).

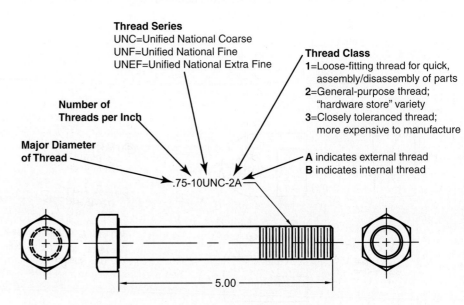

11.16 Interpreting a Thread Note for a Hex Cap Screw

Representing External Screw Threads on Mechanical Drawings There are three methods of representing external screw threads on a drawing: *schematic, detailed,* and *simplified.* The schematic method shown in Figure 11.17 is widely used because it can be drawn quickly using AutoCAD tools such as **OFFSET** and **ARRAY**. The detailed method shown in Figure 11.18 is used less frequently because it is more time consuming to construct. The simplified method shown in Figure 11.19 is also commonly used to represent screw threads on mechanical drawings.

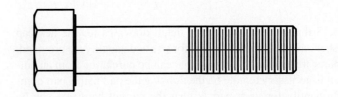

11.17 Schematic Method of Representing External Screw Threads

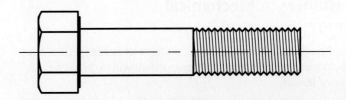

11.18 Detailed Method of Representing External Screw Threads

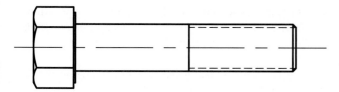

11.19   Simplified Method of Representing External
Screw Threads

Representing Internal Screw Threads on Mechanical Drawings   The end view
of a threaded hole is shown in Figure 11.20(a). In this view the major diameter of the
thread is represented by a circle drawn with a hidden line. The circle drawn with a
visible line represents the minor diameter of the thread. The threaded hole is represented in the side view by four hidden lines, as shown in Figure 11.20(b). These hidden lines are projected from the quadrants of the circles in the front view.

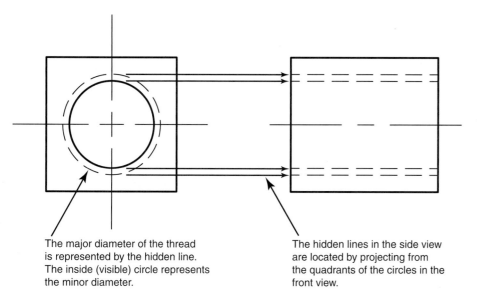

The major diameter of the thread
is represented by the hidden line.
The inside (visible) circle represents
the minor diameter.

The hidden lines in the side view
are located by projecting from
the quadrants of the circles in the
front view.

11.20(a)   Front View of a Threaded Hole; **(b)** Side View of a Threaded Hole

Drawing an Isometric Counterbored Hole

In creating the exploded assembly drawing for the toe stop base, you will need to construct an isometric view of a countersunk hole and a counterbored hole. Figures 11.21
through 11.25 illustrate the steps in constructing an isometric counterbored hole.

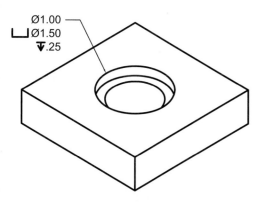

Ø1.00
⊔Ø1.50
▼.25

11.21   Isometric View of a
Counterbored Hole

The specifications for this counterbored hole are shown in Figure 11.21. In this example a **1.00″** diameter hole goes all the way through the object. Centered on this hole is a **1.50″** diameter counterbore that has a depth of **.25″**.

Step 1. Draw a **1.50″** diameter isometric ellipse, and copy it directly below the first ellipse at a distance of **.25″** as shown in Figure 11.22.

Step 2. Trim the bottom ellipse to the edge of the top ellipse as shown in Figure 11.23.

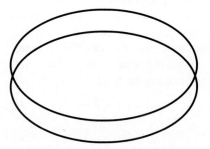

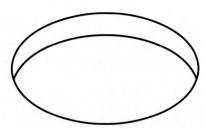

11.22 Isometric Ellipses

11.23 Ellipses after Trimming

Step 3. Draw a **1.00″** diameter ellipse at the center of the lower ellipse as shown in Figure 11.24.

Step 4. Trim the part of the ellipse drawn in Step 3 that extends below the first ellipse as shown in Figure 11.25. This completes the construction of the counterbored hole.

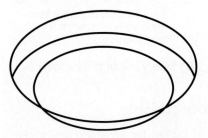

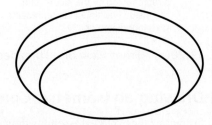

11.24 Adding the 1.00″ Ellipse

11.25 Finished Isometric Counterbored Hole

Drawing an Isometric Countersunk Hole

Figures 11.26 through 11.29 illustrate the steps in constructing an isometric countersunk hole.

TIP

When constructing the isometric countersunk hole for the toe stop base, substitute the dimensions noted on the designer's sketch in Figure 11.12 for those used in these examples.

The specifications for this countersunk hole are shown in Figure 11.26. In this example a **1.00″** diameter hole passes all the way through the object. Centered on this hole is a **1.50″** diameter countersunk hole. The angle between the sides of the countersunk hole is **82°**.

Step 1. Draw two concentric isometric ellipses, one with a diameter of **1.00″**, and the second with a diameter of **1.50″** as shown in Figure 11.27.

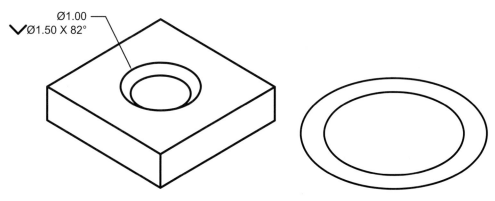

11.26 Isometric Countersunk Hole   **11.27** Isometric Ellipses

Step 2. Determine the value for **D** (the depth of the countersunk) by measuring from the multiview of the countersunk hole's side view as shown in Figure 11.28(a), and move the **1.00″** diameter ellipse straight down at distance **D** as shown in Figure 11.28(b).

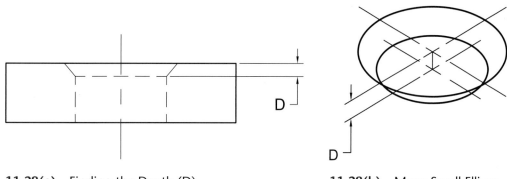

11.28(a) Finding the Depth (D) of the Countersunk Hole   **11.28(b)** Move Small Ellipse Down Depth (D)

> **TIP**
> For the toe stop assembly, you will transfer this distance from one of the multiview drawings of the toe stop base that shows the depth of the countersunk hole.

Step 3. Trim the smaller ellipse where it extends beyond the larger ellipse to complete the construction of the countersunk hole (see Figure 11.29).

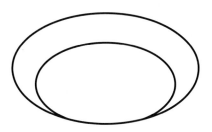

11.29 Completed Countersunk Hole

Constructing the Slots in the Isometric View of the Toe Stop Base

On each side of the bottom of the toe stop base is a slot that is **.50″** wide by **.25″** tall. The construction for the isometric drawing of these slots is shown in Figure 11.30(a). Figure 11.30(b) shows the toe stop base after the construction lines for the slots have been trimmed.

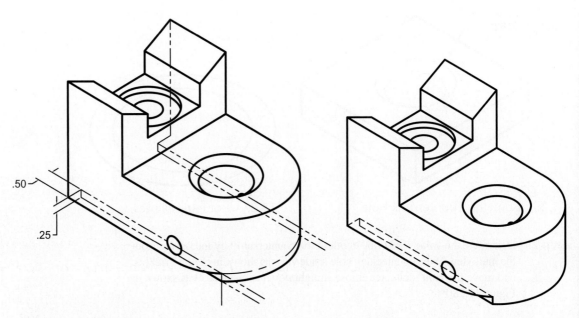

11.30(a)   Constructing Slots on the Toe Stop Base

11.30(b)   Completed Isometric Drawing of the Toe Stop Base

NOTE

Hidden lines showing the profile of the slot in the front side of the toe stop base have been shown for clarity in Figure 11.30(b).

Plotting the Sheets

Follow your instructor's directions to plot the sheets. If your plotter or printer allows, each sheet can be plotted on a 17″ × 11″ sheet using the monochrome setting at a scale of **1=2** (half size).

TIP

Follow the steps presented in Chapter 4 (pages 171–173) to create a page setup for plotting each sheet of this project.

OPTIONAL CHAPTER PROJECT

Project 11.2: Test Fixture Assembly

Create mechanical working drawings for the test fixture assembly detailed in Figures 11.31, 11.32, and 11.33(a)–(c). The assembly should be drawn as an exploded isometric view including balloons, part numbers, and a parts list (see Figure 11.32). On the detail sheets, fully dimension each part and provide specifications for the standard hardware (hex screw, hex nut, and washer).

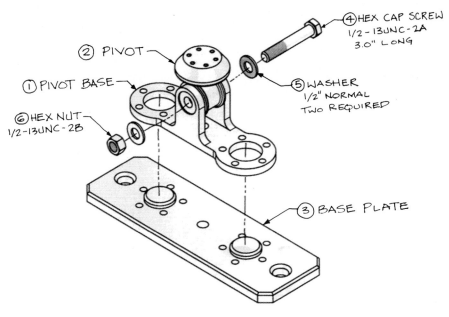

④ HEX CAP SCREW
1/2 - 13UNC - 2A
3.0" LONG

② PIVOT

① PIVOT BASE

⑤ WASHER
1/2" NORMAL
TWO REQUIRED

⑥ HEX NUT
1/2-13UNC-2B

③ BASE PLATE

11.31 Test Fixture Assembly

6	Hex Nut	SEE SHEET 3	1
5	Washer	SEE SHEET 3	2
4	Hex Cap Screw	SEE SHEET 3	1
3	Base Plate	SEE SHEET 3	1
2	Pivot	SEE SHEET 2	1
1	Pivot Base	SEE SHEET 2	1
PART NO	PART NAME	DESCRIPTION	QTY

PARTS LIST

11.32 Test Fixture Assembly Parts List

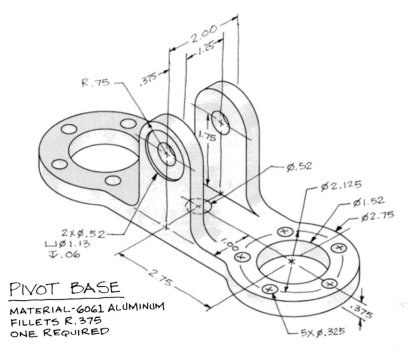

2.00
1.25
.375
R.75
Ø.52
1.75
Ø2.125
Ø1.52
Ø2.75
2X Ø.52
⊔ Ø1.13
⊥ .06
1.00
2.75
.375
5X Ø.325

PIVOT BASE

MATERIAL-6061 ALUMINUM
FILLETS R.375
ONE REQUIRED

11.33(a) Designer's Sketch of the Pivot Base

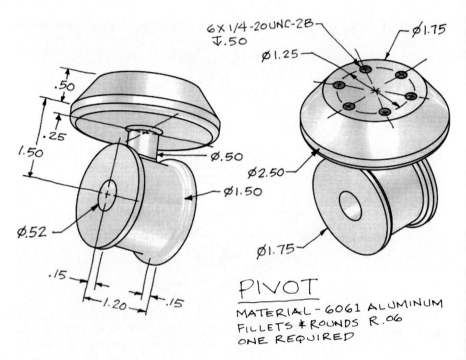

11.33(b) Designer's Sketch of the Pivot

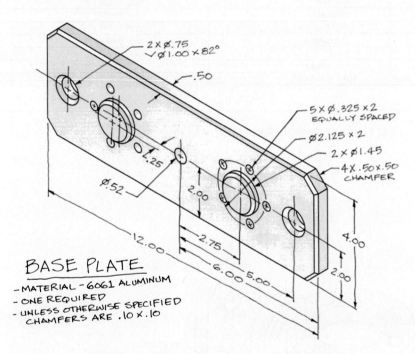

11.33(c) Designer's Sketch of the Base Plate and Hardware

Directions

1. Open the **Mechanical Working Drawing Prototype—Test Fixture** drawing located in the student data files at **www.pearsondesigncentral.com.** To access this drawing, open the Pearson Design Central website and click on the **CAD Community** link, then select the **Click here to download student data files for our CAD titles** link. Next, click on the **Technical Drawing 101** link and select the **Prototype Drawings** zip file, then select the **Download** button and open (or save) the prototype drawing specified above.

2. Use **SAVE AS** to save the drawing to your **Home** directory, and rename the new drawing **TEST FIXTURE ASSEMBLY**.

3. Draw and dimension the necessary views of the pivot, pivot base, and base plate. Create a full section view of the base plate.

4. Draw an exploded isometric assembly showing all the parts, add balloons and part numbers, and complete the parts list. Insert the premade blocks representing the isometric views of the hex cap screw, hex nut, and washer contained in the prototype drawing.

Plotting the Sheets

Follow your instructor's directions to plot the sheets. If your plotter or printer allows, each sheet can be plotted on a 17″ × 11″ sheet using the monochrome setting at a scale of **1=2.**

TIP

Follow the steps presented in Chapter 4 (pages 171–173) to create a page setup for plotting each sheet of this project.

CHAPTER TWELVE

ARCHITECTURAL WORKING DRAWINGS

---- OBJECTIVES ----

After studying the material in this chapter, you should be able to:

1. Describe architectural working drawings and their importance to the field of architecture.

2. Describe how floor plans and elevation drawings are planned and prepared.

3. Use AutoCAD to create a floor plan for a small house.

4. Use AutoCAD's **DesignCenter** to place blocks of electrical and plumbing symbols into the floor plan.

5. Use AutoCAD to create elevation drawings for a small house.

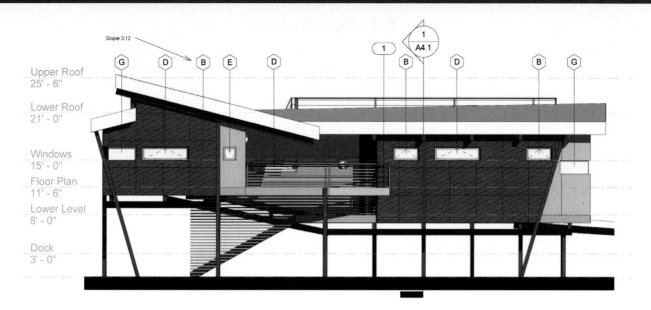

OVERVIEW

In many architectural offices, drafters work with architects and designers to prepare the drawings used in the construction of residential and commercial buildings. These drawings, which may include floor plans, elevations, foundations, wall sections, and roof framing plans, are called ***construction documents (CDs)***. Often, the separate sheets for a full set of plans are created on different CAD layers within the same CAD drawing file so that the drafter can selectively view and print the layers as needed.

12.1 FLOOR PLANS

Floor plans, like the one shown in Figure 12.1, provide home builders and contractors with the necessary information to lay out the building, including the locations of features such as walls, doors, electrical components (switches, lamps, etc.) and plumbing fixtures (tubs, commodes, sinks, etc.). Floor plans should include all the dimensions and notations required by the workers on the jobsite. Doors and windows are dimensioned to their centers, and continuous (also known as *chain*) dimensioning is typically employed on floor plans. Dimensions are labeled above the dimension line, and tick marks replace arrowheads.

Architectural firms create or purchase block libraries of doors, windows, electrical, plumbing, and other symbols frequently used on floor plans.

JOB SKILLS

The efficient use of blocks and layering techniques by drafters can increase productivity and lower the cost of creating a set of plans.

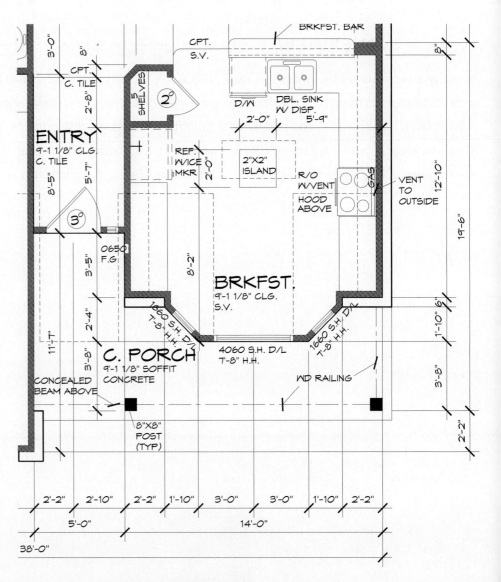

12.1   Example Detail from a Floor Plan

12.2 ELECTRICAL PLANS

An *electrical plan* provides electrical contractors information about the type, location, and installation of electrical components (switches, lamps, ceiling fans, electrical outlets, cable TV jacks, etc.) used in the project. All the information needed by the electrical contractor to wire the building should be provided by this plan.

Drafters can create a block library of electrical symbols to speed the process by which electrical plans are created. The electrical components and wiring are usually drawn on a separate layer that is superimposed on the floor plan layer(s). Figure 12.2 shows a detail from an electrical plan. A legend is included on the electrical plan to help workers identify all the components on the floor plan. Figure 12.3 shows an example of an electrical legend.

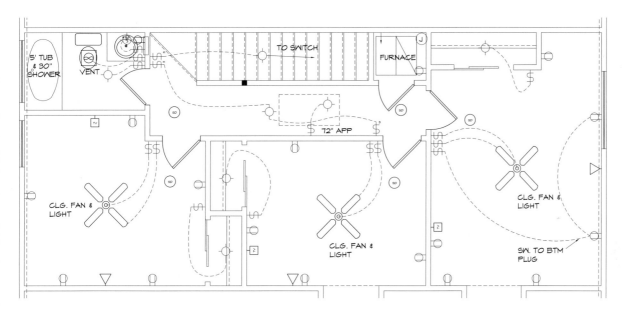

12.2 Electrical Plan Detail

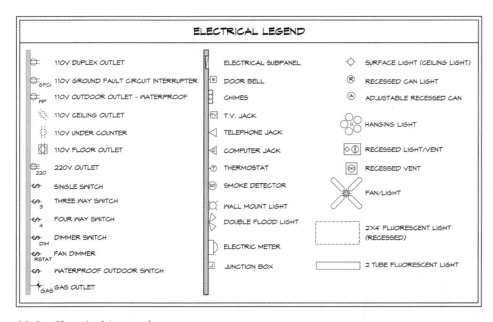

12.3 Electrical Legend

12.3 ELEVATIONS

Elevation drawings provide information about the exterior details of a building. This information may include roof pitch, exterior materials and finishes, overall heights of features, and window and door styles, as shown in Figure 12.4. All the dimensions and notations required by workers on the jobsite should be included on this sheet.

12.4   Front Elevation of a House

NOTE

Although Figure 12.5 shows the top view of the house, this view would not be included on the elevations sheet, because the top view reflects the roof plan of the building, which is typically drawn on a separate sheet.

Creating Elevations Using Multiview Drawing Techniques

In Figure 12.5 lines and arrows have been drawn between the views to show how the location and size of features on the house's exterior can be projected from one view to another using multiview drawing techniques. In fact, sometimes it is not possible to complete the construction of one elevation view without constructing an

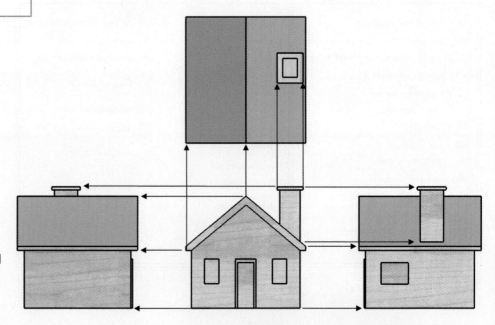

12.5   Projecting Points and Planes between Views of a House Using Multiview Drawing Techniques

adjacent elevation and projecting information from the new elevation back to the original view. For example, in Figure 12.5 it would not be possible to locate the top edge of the roof plane in either of the side elevations without first drawing the front elevation and projecting the roof peak to the side elevations.

Architectural Wall Sections

In architectural drawings, *wall sections* are often included to specify the composition of a wall as shown in Figure 12.6. Drafters often refer to an exterior wall section when determining roof angles, overhangs of rafters, and heights of walls and ceilings in the elevation view.

Sections are also included on *foundation* plans to show interior details of the composition of foundation beams, slabs, and footings.

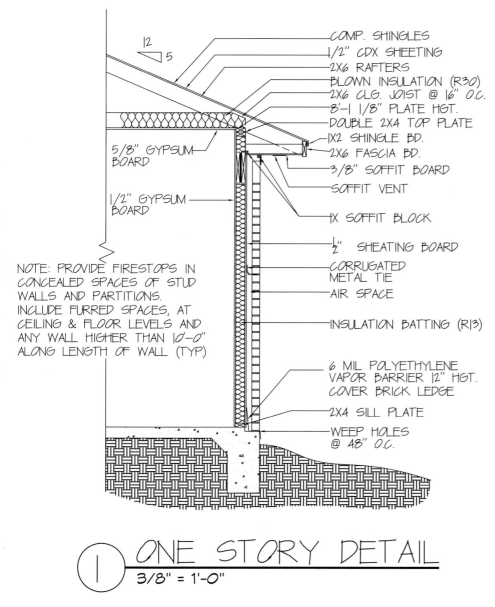

12.6   Architectural Wall Section

Roof Profiles on Architectural Elevations

The angle of a roof is called its ***roof pitch***. Pitch is specified as a ratio of the vertical *rise* of the roof (measured in inches) to the horizontal *run* of the roof (measured in inches). Using this notation, a roof with a "four-twelve" pitch (labeled as **4/12** on the drawing) would rise 4″ for every 12″ of horizontal run. A roof with a **12/12** pitch would rise 12″ for every 12″ of run. A **12/12** pitch would result in a roof angle of 45°.

A roof pitch symbol is created by drawing a horizontal line that is crossed near one end by a vertical line like the ones shown along the roof profiles in Figure 12.7. The rise is labeled next to the vertical line, and the run (usually 12″) is noted above the horizontal line.

In the roof profile shown in Figure 12.7, for every 12″ the roof runs along its horizontal axis, it rises 10″. A drafter would label this pitch specification as **10/12** on the drawing.

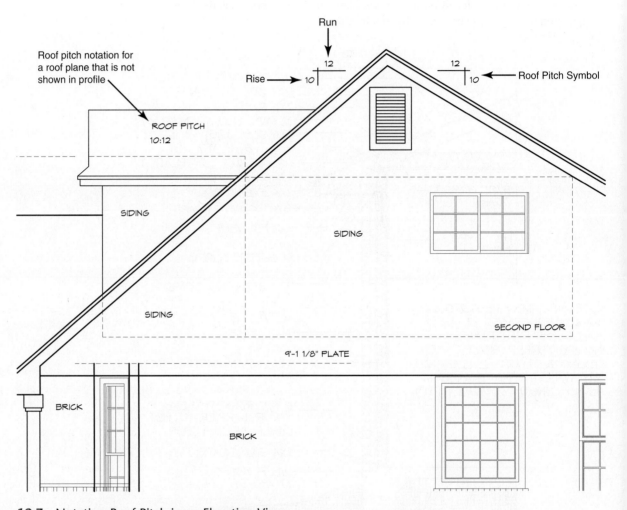

12.7　Notating Roof Pitch in an Elevation View

Using the Floor Plan to Locate Features on Elevations

When elevation drawings are created, the physical location of features on the floor plan, such as doors and windows, can be used to locate these same features in the elevation drawing.

Figure 12.8 shows the floor plan of the guest cottage you drew earlier in this course. Also shown in this figure are the front, back, and side elevations of the guest cottage. To speed the creation of the elevation views, information about the size and location of the windows, outside walls, and the front door was projected from the floor plan to the elevation views.

Locate the 45° miter lines in the corners of Figure 12.8 and note how information is projected among the front, back, and side views through these miter lines.

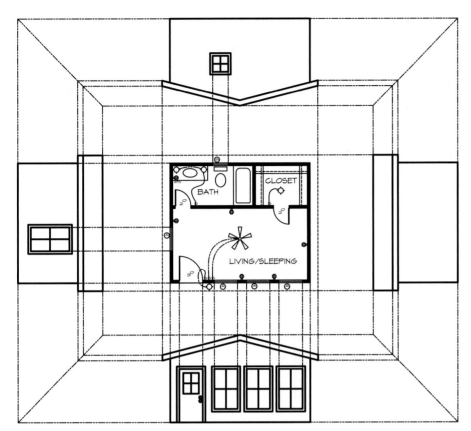

12.8 Projecting Elevation Features of the Guest Cottage from the Floor Plan

KEY WORDS

Construction Documents (CDs)

Electrical Plans

Elevation Drawings

Floor Plans

Roof Pitch

CHAPTER SUMMARY

In the early stages of an architectural project, designers and clients work together to produce a design that meets the client's needs *and* budget. During the design stage, the designer may communicate with the client through sketches, rendered CAD models, or scale models built of cardboard and foam-core.

When the client is satisfied with the initial design, drafters work under the supervision of the designer to create a set of construction documents (CDs) containing all the information necessary to build the project. CDs are the centerpiece of every construction project, and almost all who have a role in the construction of the project rely on architectural working drawings to accomplish their jobs, from lenders who review CDs to determine the levels of funding for the project, to contractors who use CDs during the bidding and construction phases of the project.

Drafters must understand how to apply CAD techniques, such as the use of block libraries, to produce CDs quickly without sacrificing detail and accuracy.

REVIEW QUESTIONS

Short Answer

1. What are construction documents?
2. Name four block libraries that might be used by architectural firms to produce drawings.
3. What is meant by the term *pitch* when used in the context of a roof?
4. Describe what is meant by a **3/12** notation on a roof plan.
5. Name three types of architectural drawings that may be drawn as section views.

CHAPTER PROJECT

Project 12.1: Cabin

In this project you will create the floor plan and elevations for a small cabin. The finished sheets will resemble the ones shown in Figures 12.9 and 12.10.

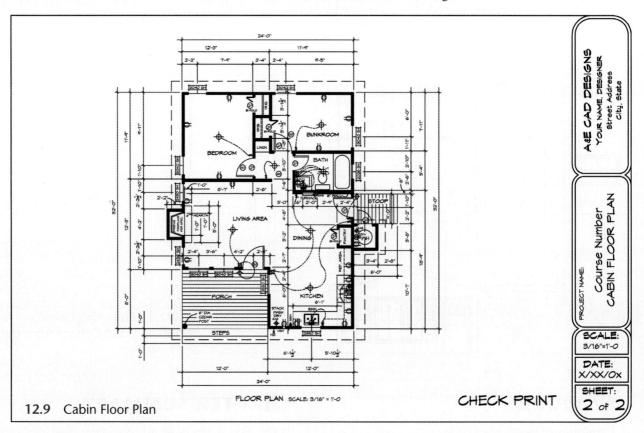

12.9 Cabin Floor Plan

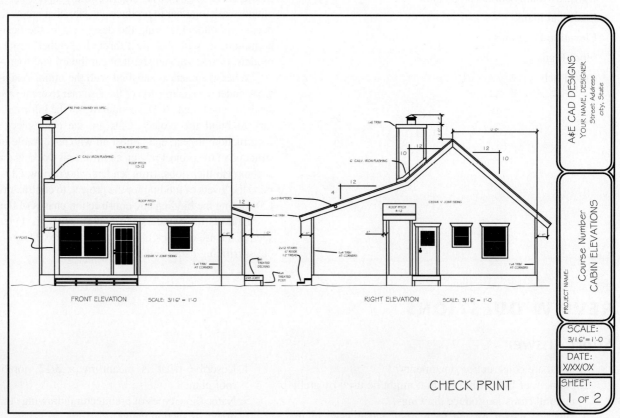

12.10 Cabin Elevations

Directions

1. Open the **Arch Cabin Prototype** drawing located in the student data files at **www.pearsondesigncentral.com/.** To access this drawing, open the Pearson Design Central website and click on the *CAD Community* link, then select the *Click here to download student data files for our CAD titles* link. Next, click on the *Technical Drawing 101* link and select the *Prototype Drawings* zip file, then select the *Download* button and open (or save) the prototype drawing specified above.

2. Use **SAVE AS** to save the drawing to your **Home** directory, and rename the drawing **CABIN PROJECT**.

3. Create the following layers: **Floor Plan, Doors, Electrical Plan, Switch Lines, Plumbing Plan, Kitchen, Labels, Dimensions, Wall Hatch, Elevations,** and **Notes.** Assign a color to each layer and set the linetype for the Switch Lines layer to **Phantom.**

4. Follow the directions on pages 381–404 to create the floor plan and the front and right elevations of the cabin.

Drawing the Floor Plan

Step 1. To draw the cabin's perimeter walls, set **Floor Plan** as the current layer, and draw the perimeter of the cabin using the dimensions shown in Figure 12.11. Use the **OFFSET** command to draw the walls **4″** thick.

TIP

Use the **Polyline** command to draw the perimeter as one entity. This will facilitate using the **OFFSET** command to create the wall thickness.

When architectural units are in effect, distances will default to inches unless you enter a foot mark (′). For example, for a line 24′ 6″ in length, enter **24′-6** (you do not need to type the inch mark after 6 because AutoCAD defaults to inches).

Enter dimensions with fractions by typing a dash between the inch value and the fractional value, for example, 15′9-1/2.

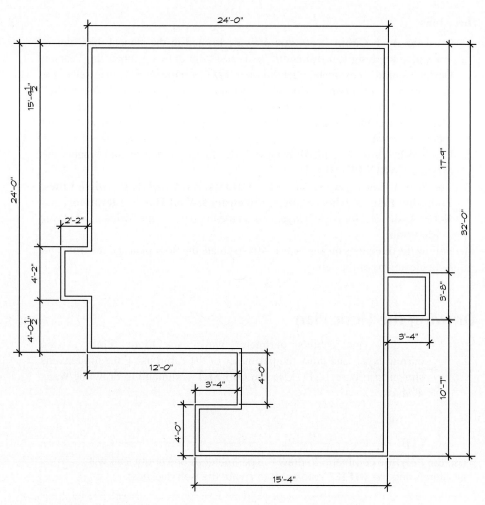

12.11 Perimeter Walls

┌─── **NOTE** ───┐
│ Do not add dimensions to the floor plan until you are instructed to do so in │
│ Step 12. │
└───┘

Step 2. To draw the interior walls, use the dimensions shown in Figure 12.12. You can locate these walls by offsetting their edges from the edges of known walls. Draw all interior walls **4″** wide except for the 6″ wide wall noted in the figure.

Step 3(a). In this step you will create a block library of architectural symbols that will be inserted into the floor plan. To create the block library, open the **Cabin Symbols** drawing located in the student data files at **www.pearsondesigncentral.com/.** To access this drawing, open the Pearson Design Central website and click on the *CAD Community* link, then select the *Click here to download student data files for our CAD titles* link. Next, click on the *Technical Drawing 101* link and select the *Prototype Drawings* zip file, then select the *Download* button and open (or save) the **Cabin Symbols** drawing using **Save As** to your **Home** folder. Make a separate block for each of the symbols

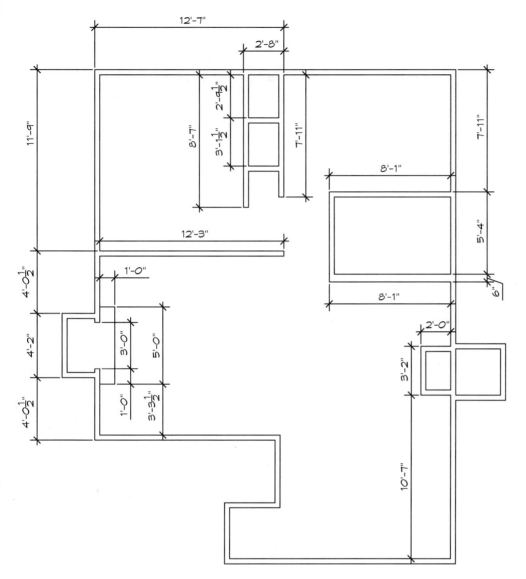

12.12   Interior Walls

shown in Figure 12.13 (refer to Chapter 10 on block creation and editing if necessary).

Make the blocks on layer **0** and assign base points that you think will facilitate the placement of the blocks into the drawing. When you have finished creating all the blocks, save and close the **Cabin Symbols** drawing to your **Home** folder. The next section explains how to insert the **Cabin Symbols** drawing's blocks into the **Cabin Project** drawing.

Using DesignCenter to Place the Blocks

DesignCenter is an AutoCAD feature that allows drafters to insert the blocks, layers, linetypes, dimension styles, and text styles created for one drawing file into a different drawing file. Steps 3(b) through 3(e) explain how to use **DesignCenter** to insert the blocks associated with the **Cabin Symbols** [that were created in Step 3(a)] into the **Cabin Project** drawing file.

Directions:

For each of the architectural symbols shown below, create a block.
Select insertion points that will facilitate placement of the block.

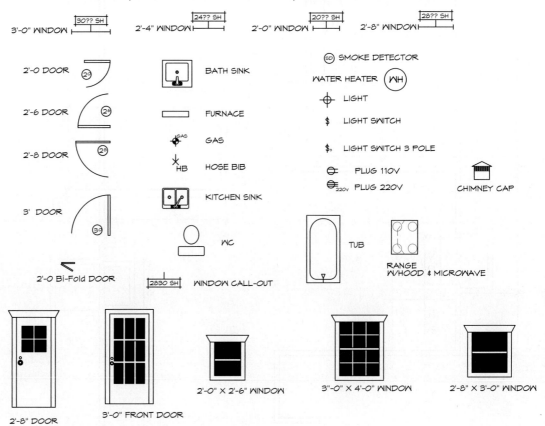

12.13 Block Library of Architectural Symbols

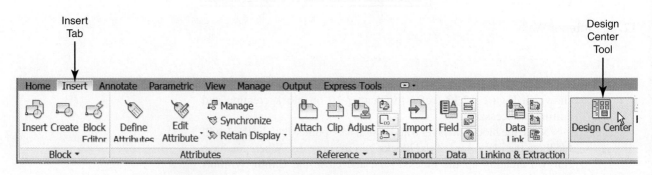

12.14 Locating the **DesignCenter** Icon on the **Standard** Toolbar

Step 3(b). Pick the **Design Center** tool located on the **Content** panel of the **Insert** tab of the ribbon (see Figure 12.14). Selecting this tool opens the **DesignCenter** window (see Figure 12.15). Note the location of the **Tree** pane and the **Contents Area** pane in the **DesignCenter** window shown in Figure 12.15.

Step 3(c). Move the cursor into the **Tree** pane and scroll through the file tree until you have located the **Cabin Symbols** drawing that you saved in your **Home** folder in Step 3(a). Double-click on the **Cabin Symbols.dwg** file name.

Tree Pane

Contents Area Pane

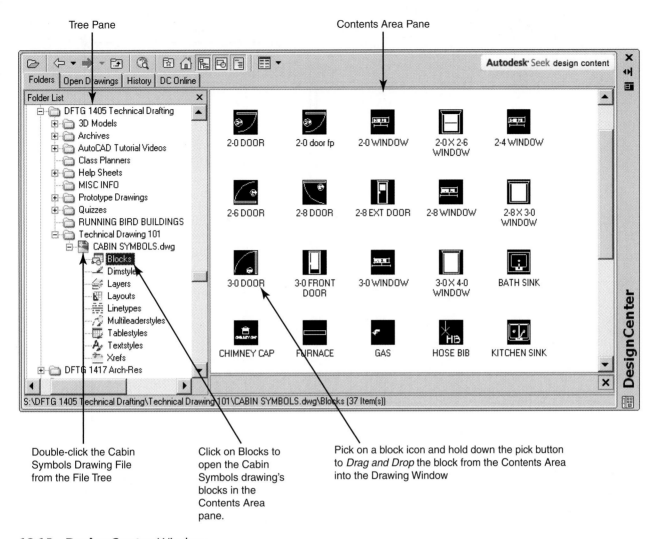

Double-click the Cabin
Symbols Drawing File
from the File Tree

Click on Blocks to
open the Cabin
Symbols drawing's
blocks in the
Contents Area
pane.

Pick on a block icon and hold down the pick button
to *Drag and Drop* the block from the Contents Area
into the Drawing Window

12.15   **DesignCenter** Window

Step 3(d).   Next, click on the word **Blocks** located in the tree below the **Cabin Symbols** file name (see Figure 12.15). The blocks associated with the **Cabin Symbols** drawing will appear in the **Contents Area** pane (see Figure 12.15).

Step 3(e).   You can insert the blocks shown in the **Contents Area** pane into the **Cabin Project** floor plan by "dragging and dropping" them into the drawing. You do this by clicking on a block icon and holding down the pick button of the mouse and dragging the block into the drawing window. You can also insert a block by selecting its icon in the **Contents Area** pane, right-clicking, choosing **Insert Block** from the menu, and inserting the block using the techniques presented in Chapter 10 (see Figure 10.7).

Step 4.   To locate the centers of the windows, offset the perimeter wall lines using the dimensions shown in Figure 12.16.

Use **DesignCenter** to access the block library created for the **Cabin Symbols** drawing and follow Steps 3(b) through 3(e) to insert the window blocks into the walls of the floor plan. Trim the walls to the edges of the windows as shown in Figure 12.16.

Step 5.   To place the doors, set the **Doors** layer current, and offset the wall lines to locate the centers and edges of doors—for example, the opening for a door

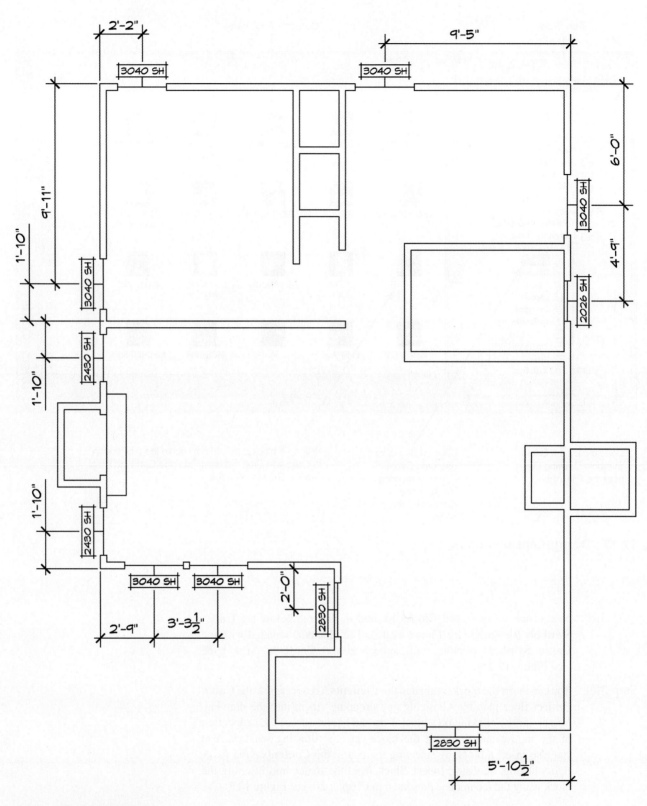

12.16   Window Placement

> **NOTE**
> The side of the door frame where the hinges are attached is referred to as the *hinge jamb*. The side of the door frame where the latching mechanism attaches is referred to as the *strike jamb*.

marked 2^6 will be 2'-6" wide. Allow a minimum length of **4"** for door jambs located on the hinged side of the bedroom, bunkroom, and bath doors. The pantry door and the bifold closet doors should be centered on their respective enclosures (see Figure 12.17). Insert the desired door block from the **DesignCenter** location and trim to the edges of the door block as shown in

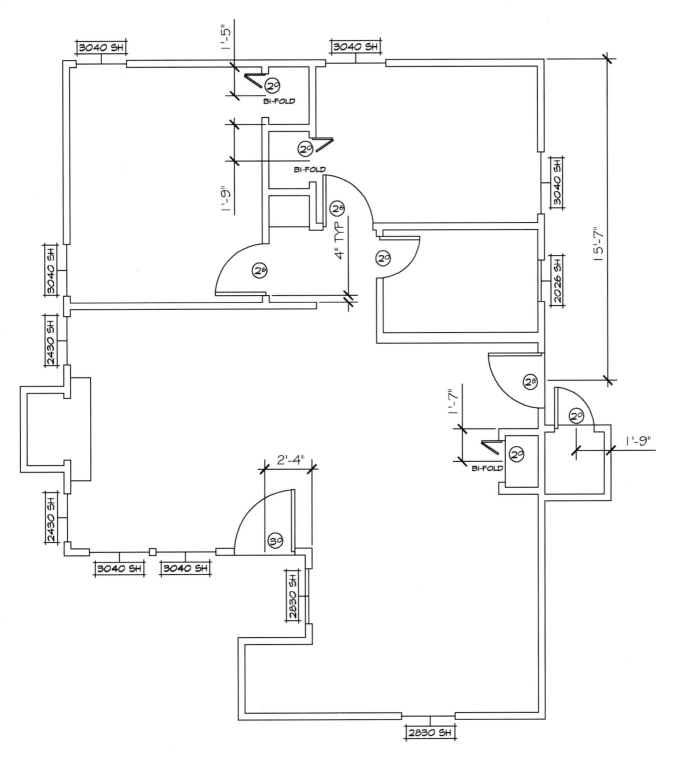

12.17 Door Placement

Figure 12.17. The construction details for the bifold door are shown in
Figure 12.18.

Step 6.   To draw the fireplace, refer to the details shown in Figure 12.19. Position
the fireplace in the floor plan as shown in Figure 12.20. The hearth is drawn
1' wide by **5'** long and should be centered on the fireplace.

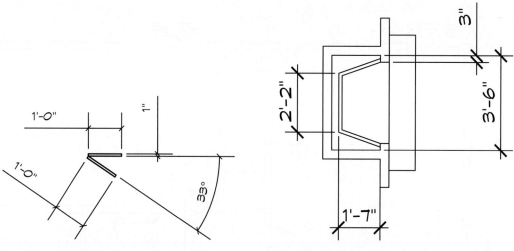

12.18   Bifold Door   **12.19**   Fireplace Details

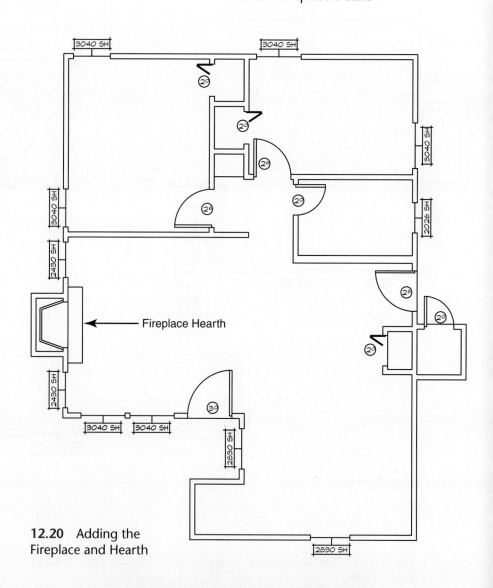

Fireplace Hearth

12.20   Adding the
Fireplace and Hearth

Step 7.   To draw the kitchen and bath, set the **Kitchen** layer current, and add the
kitchen cabinets and kitchen fixtures as shown in Figure 12.21. The lower
kitchen cabinets should be **24″** wide. The upper cabinets represented with
dashed lines should be **12″** wide. Open **DesignCenter** and insert the

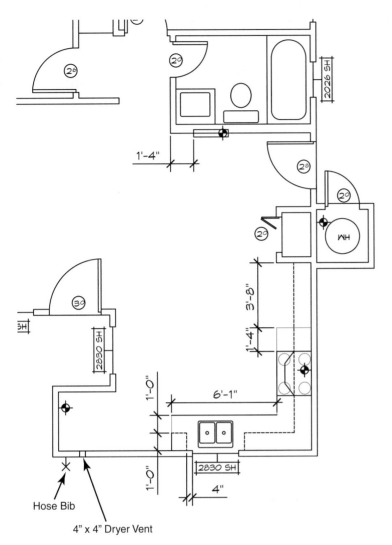

Hose Bib

4" x 4" Dryer Vent

12.21   Placement of Kitchen Cabinets and Plumbing Fixtures

blocks of the kitchen fixtures by selecting them from the **Cabin Symbols** drawing file.

Next, set the **Plumbing Plan** layer current, and insert the bathroom fixtures, furnace, and water heater as shown in Figure 12.21. Open **DesignCenter** and insert the blocks of the bathroom fixtures, furnace, and water heater from the **Cabin Symbols** drawing file. Add the dryer vent and hose bib as shown in Figure 12.21.

Step 8.   To draw the electrical plan, set the **Electrical Plan** layer current. Open **DesignCenter** and insert the blocks of the electric symbols from the **Cabin Symbols** drawing file into the floor plan as shown in Figure 12.22.

Then, set **Switch Lines** as the current layer, and using the **Spline** command, draw the *switch legs* from the switches to the lamps as shown in Figure 12.22. In an electrical plan, switch legs represent the electrical circuit that connects the switches to the lamps (or other electric fixtures) and are drawn as phantom lines.

TIP

You will probably need to set the **LTSCALE** of the drawing to a larger value for dashes to appear in the phantom lines.

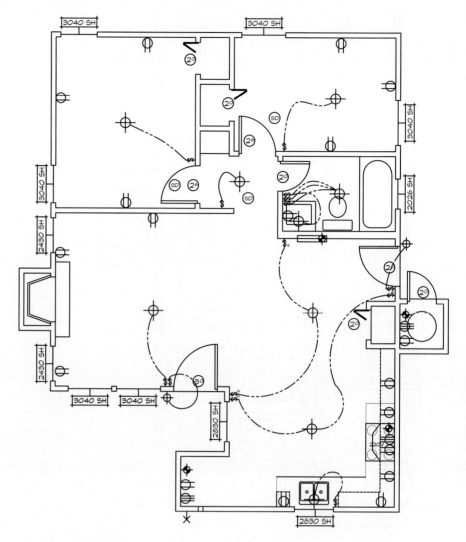

12.22 Electrical Plan

Step 9.   To add labels, set the **Labels** layer current and add the labels shown in Figure 12.23. Change the **Standard** text style's font to **Stylus BT**, and use the following text heights: for room names, use **6″** text height; for detail notes, or *callouts*, use **4″** text height; and for very small text use **3″** text height. In the title block, use **8″** text for the **Drawing Name** and **6″** text for the **Scale**.

Step 10. Set the **Floor Plan** layer current and draw the porch and stoop as shown in Figure 12.24. Draw the stoop **6′** long and **4′** wide. Use **6″** wide boards for the porch and stoop flooring. The treads of the porch steps should be drawn **12″** wide.

  Add an **8″** diameter cedar post to the front left corner of the porch roof. This post supports the roof above the front porch.

  Next, set **Wall Hatch** as the current layer, and hatch the walls and the cedar post with the **Net** pattern. Set the hatch pattern to a scale of **10**.

Step 11. During a meeting between the project architect and the Cabin Project's client, the client decided to change the design of the cabin's entry and kitchen area. The new layout is shown in Figure 12.25. Making these changes at this point in the design process may increase the fees the architectural firm will charge the client for this project. These changes also affect the final construction cost of the cabin.

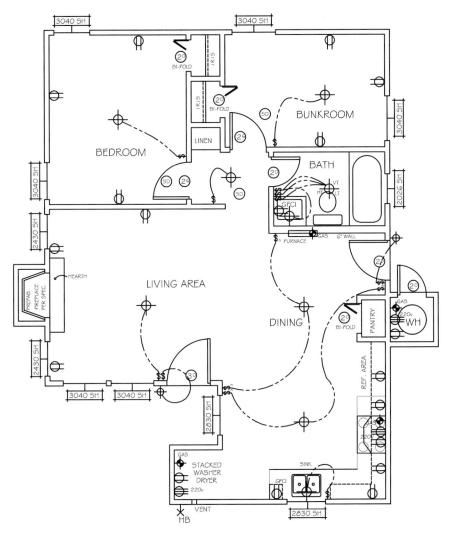

12.23   Adding to the Floor Plan

If the client instructs the firm to proceed with the design changes, the architect issues a formal *Architectural Change Order* to the drafting department to request the changes. The change order details the specific changes to be made to the floor plan. By following a formal process in making these changes, the architectural firm creates a record of what changes were made, when they were made, and by whom.

Edit your floor plan to reflect all the changes to the living area and kitchen shown in Figure 12.25 and reapply the hatch pattern to the walls when the changes are complete.

Step 12.   In this step you will add dashed lines around the outside of the floor plan's exterior walls, which represent the edges of the *roof overhang* as shown in Figures 12.26(a) and 12.26(b). You will also add the final dimensions to the floor plan. The directions for accomplishing these tasks follow.

Adding the Roof Overhang

Drafters can determine the placement of the dashed lines that represent the roof overhang by referring to the elevation sketches of the cabin and noting the rafter overhang distances. The roof overhang around the main living area of the cabin is **18″**, but the roof overhang around the water heater closet is **6″** on the top and bottom edges and **12″** along the right edge. Refer to Figures 12.26(a) and (b).

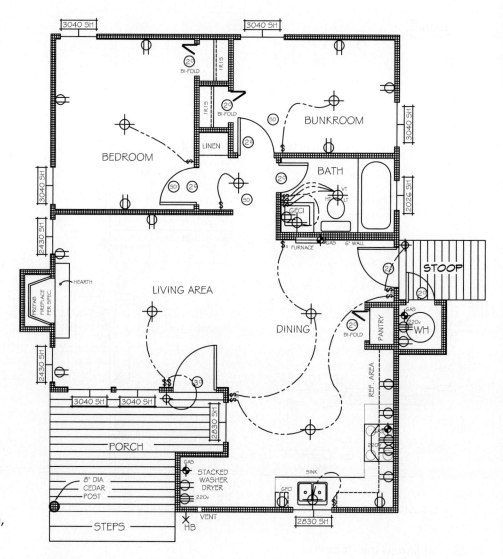

12.24   Floor Plan with Porch, Stoop, and Hatched Walls

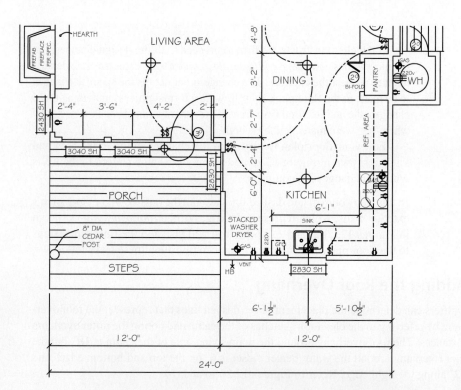

12.25   Changes to Floor Plan Resulting from the Architectural Change Order

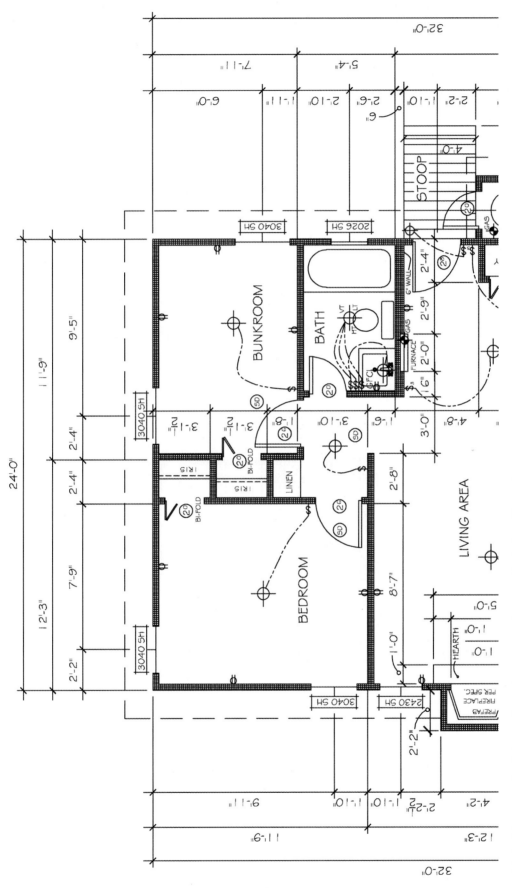

12.26(a)   Detail of Floor Plan Dimensions (Top Half of Plan Shown)

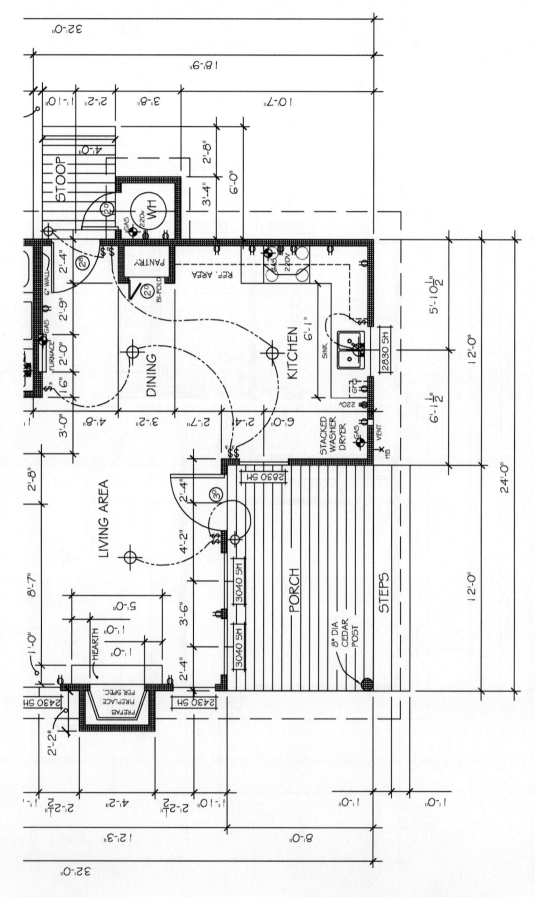

12.26(b) Dimensioning the Floor Plan (Bottom Half of Plan Shown)

Dimensioning the Cabin Project

Create a new dimension style named **ARCH48** that has the dimension style settings shown in Figures 12.27(a)–(e). Set the **Dimensions** layer current, and dimension the floor plan as shown in Figures 12.26(a) and (b).

The values shown in the **Dimension Style** tabs may seem large when compared with the settings for a mechanical drawing—for example, setting text height to 5″—but when the project is printed at a scale of 3/16″ = 1′-0″, the settings will be proportional to the size of the printed sheets.

After Step 12 is completed, the floor plan of the cabin is finished.

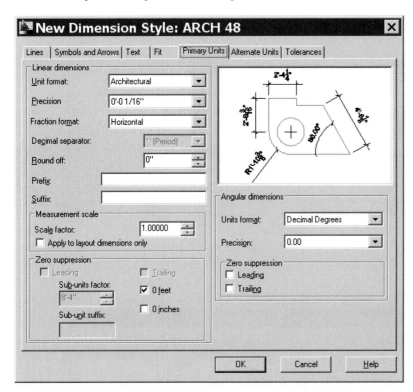

12.27(a) Cabin Project **Primary Units** Tab Dimension Style Settings

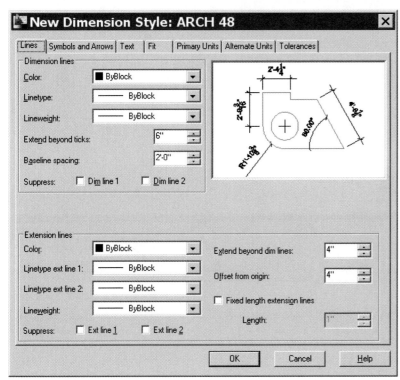

12.27(b) Cabin Project **Lines** Tab Dimension Style Settings

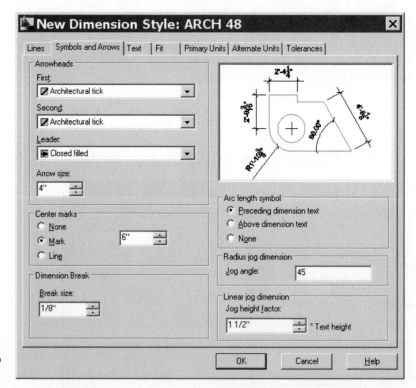

12.27(c) Cabin Project **Symbols and Arrows** Tab Dimension Style Settings

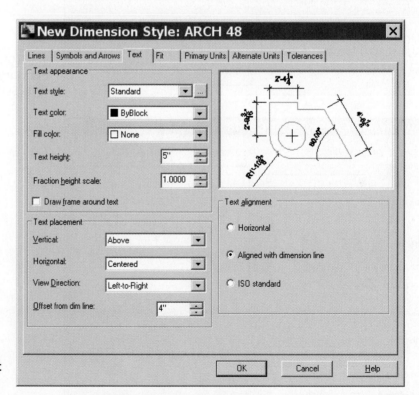

12.27(d) Cabin Project **Text** Tab Dimension Style Settings

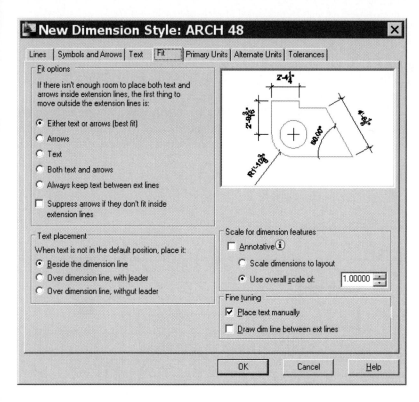

New Dimension Style: ARCH 48

Lines | Symbols and Arrows | Text | Fit | Primary Units | Alternate Units | Tolerances

Fit options
If there isn't enough room to place both text and arrows inside extension lines, the first thing to move outside the extension lines is:

- ◉ Either text or arrows (best fit)
- ○ Arrows
- ○ Text
- ○ Both text and arrows
- ○ Always keep text between ext lines

☐ Suppress arrows if they don't fit inside extension lines

Text placement
When text is not in the default position, place it:
- ◉ Beside the dimension line
- ○ Over dimension line, with leader
- ○ Over dimension line, without leader

Scale for dimension features
☐ Annotative ⓘ
- ○ Scale dimensions to layout
- ◉ Use overall scale of: 1.00000

Fine tuning
☑ Place text manually
☐ Draw dim line between ext lines

[OK] [Cancel] [Help]

12.27(e) Cabin Project **Fit** Tab Dimension Style Settings

Creating the Elevations of the Cabin Project

Using the same prototype drawing used to create the floor plan of the cabin, draw the front and right elevations as shown in Figure 12.28. Remember that architectural elevations are constructed using multiview drawing techniques and that information will be projected from one view to the next as the views are constructed.

The steps for creating the elevations are presented next.

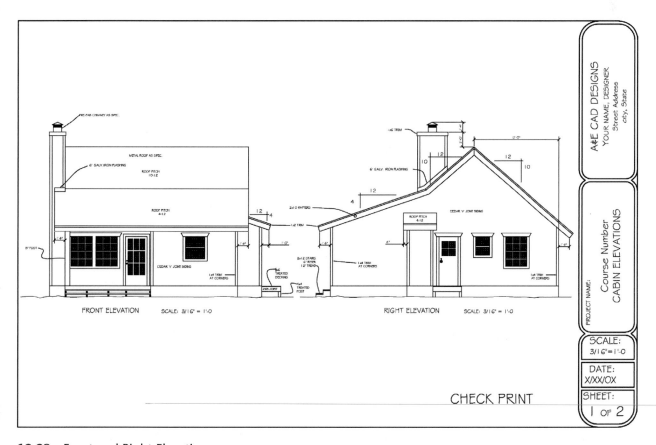

12.28 Front and Right Elevations

397

Relating the Cabin Elevations to Features on the Floor Plan When elevation drawings of the cabin are created, the dimensions shown on the floor plan are used to locate exterior features such as doors, windows, porches, and the chimney.

The dashed lines in Figure 12.29 illustrate how multiview drawing techniques can be applied to an architectural drawing to project the size and location of features in the floor plan to the front and side elevations. In Figure 12.29, locate the 45° miter line in the lower right corner and notice how information is projected between the front and side views through the miter line.

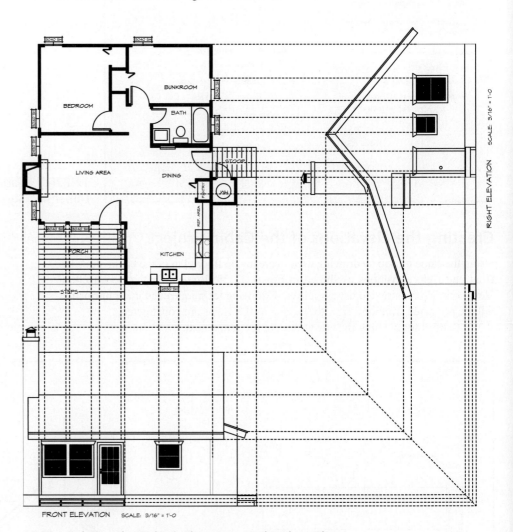

12.29 Relating the Cabin's Elevations to the Floor Plan

Wall Framing 101 An understanding of the basics of framing is very helpful to drafters in constructing elevation drawings. The method used to frame the wall will determine the heights of ceilings, windows, and other exterior features.

The example in Figure 12.30 shows the front and end views of a length of wall framing. In this example, the studs are placed 16″ on center. Figure 12.30 also shows the framing for the rough openings for a window and a door. The rough opening is sized by the framers to accommodate the size of the window or door specified on the plan. Generally, rough openings will be about 2 1/2″ wider and taller than the window or door specified on the floor plan.

Constructing the Right-Side Elevation Follow Steps 13 through 23 to draw the elevations of the cabin. The first view to be drawn is the right-side elevation shown in Figure 12.31. This view was chosen because it shows the profile of the roof's pitch. When this view is complete, construction lines will be projected from its features to assist in the construction of the front view of the cabin.

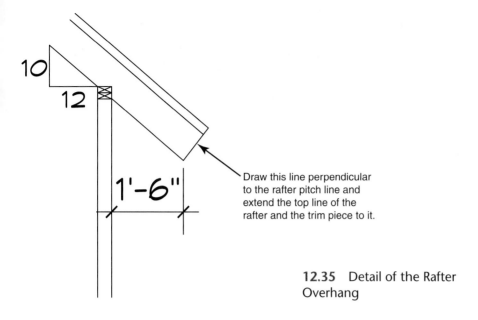

Draw this line perpendicular
to the rafter pitch line and
extend the top line of the
rafter and the trim piece to it.

12.35 Detail of the Rafter
Overhang

Extend the rafter and the finished floor and grade lines to the offset
line as shown in Figure 12.36.

Step 17. Mirror the rafter, foundation, and right outside wall as shown in
Figure 12.37. Select the offset line created in Step 15 as the mirror line.

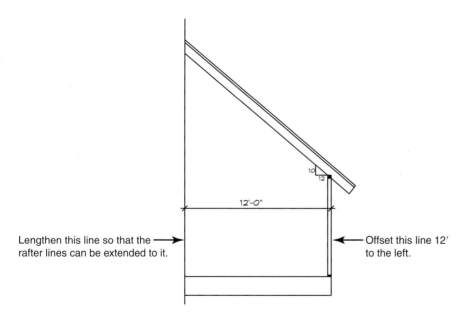

12'-0"

Lengthen this line so that the ⟶
rafter lines can be extended to it.

⟵ Offset this line 12'
to the left.

12.36 Extending the Rafter

Step 18. To construct the left side wall and roof profile, copy the side wall created
with the **MIRROR** command in Step 17, **8′** toward the left (**Ortho** should
be on) as shown in Figure 12.28. Then, construct the rafter as you did in
Steps 14 and 15 but this time with a **4/12** pitch. Extend the rafter lines until they intersect the **10/12** pitch roof section as shown in Figure 12.38.

Step 19. Use **TRIM**, **EXTEND**, and **ERASE** to complete the profile of the right
elevation as shown in Figure 12.39.

Step 20. Window dimensions for the $3^0 4^0$ window are shown in Figure 12.40. The
dimensions for the wood trim around the windows will be the same for
other windows and exterior doors.

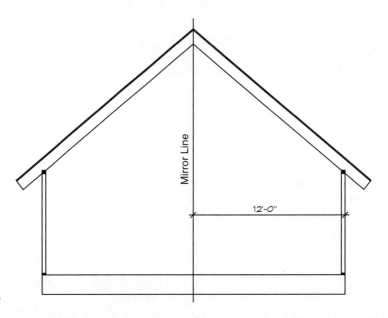

12.37 Mirroring the Roof Line

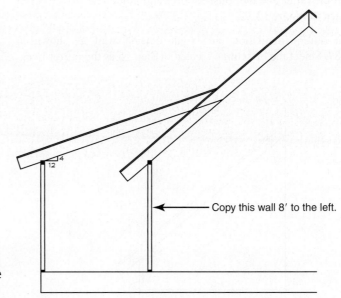

Copy this wall 8′ to the left.

12.38 Constructing the
Left Side Wall and Roof

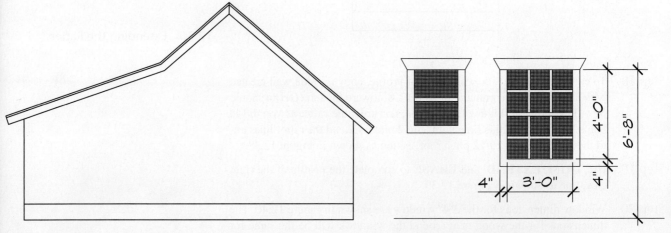

12.39 Right Elevation after Removal of Construction Lines   **12.40** Window Dimensions

To add windows, doors, and trim, open **DesignCenter** and insert blocks of the exterior door and windows from the **Cabin Symbols** drawing into the elevation view.

Use a **6″** wide trim piece along the top edges of doors and windows, and draw the angled cuts at **15°** from vertical.

Next, using dimensions from the floor plan, add the chimney and locate the edges of the water heater closet in the right elevation (refer to Figure 12.29).

> **─ NOTE ─**
> You will not be able to add the roof to the water heater closet at this time because you will need information projected from the front elevation.

Step 21. Information from features in the right elevation such as the roof height and location and height of the porch steps and chimney can be projected to the front elevation. The dashed lines in Figure 12.41 show where geometry is projected between the views.

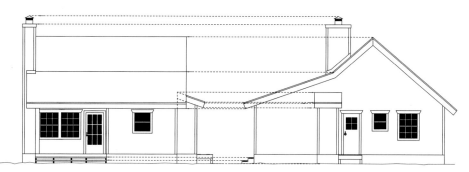

12.41 Projecting Information between the Right Elevation and the Front Elevation

Construct the side wall and the **4/12** roof pitch for the water heater closet in the front elevation using the same techniques used during the construction of the right elevation. Notice how the water closet's roof extends to the cabin's right side wall in the front elevation. It will be necessary to project the roof geometry of the water heater closet from the front elevation back to the right elevation to complete the construction of the water heater closet in the right elevation.

Step 22. Figure 12.42 shows the correct spacing for the front door and windows. The dimensions reflect the distances between centers. These dimensions are for reference only and should not be shown on the elevation view. To complete

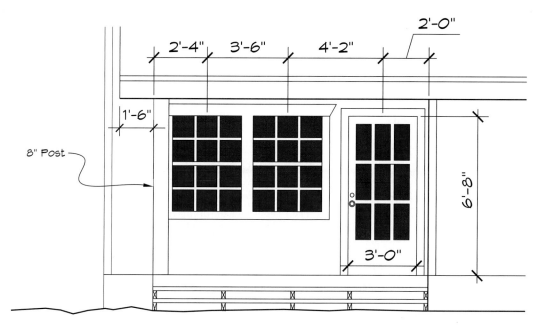

12.42 Front Door and Window Placement

the front elevation, open **DesignCenter** and insert blocks for the front door and windows from the **Cabin Symbols** drawing into the elevation view.

Step 23. Use splined multileaders to add leaders and notes to the elevation views as shown in Figures 12.31 and 12.43. To turn the **Spline** setting on, select the **Annotate** tab of the ribbon and select the arrow next to the word **Leaders** located on the **Leaders** panel. When the **Multileader Style Manager** dialog box launches, select the **Modify** button (or the **New** button to define a new style). Next, select the **Leader Format** tab and change the **Type** from **Straight** to **Spline,** and set the **Arrowhead Size** to **4″**. Then, select the **Leader Structure** tab and set the **Maximum Leader Points** to **3**. Next, select the **Content** tab and set the **Text Height** to **4″**. Then, click **OK** and **Close**. Select the **Multileader** tool from the **Leaders** panel (or type **MLD** and **<Enter>**) and follow the prompts to place the leaders as shown in the figures.

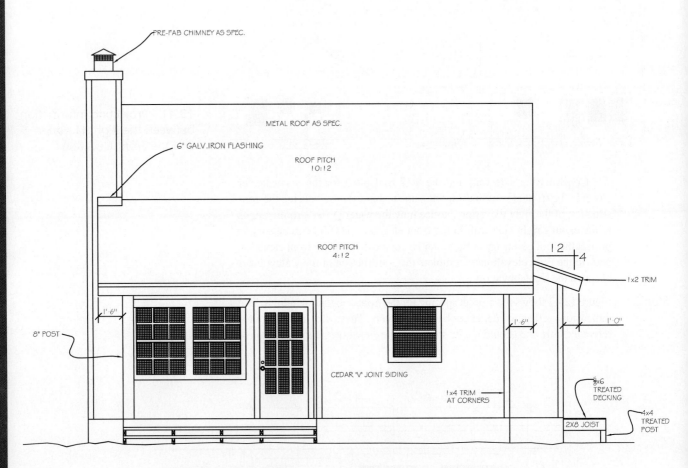

FRONT ELEVATION   SCALE: 3/16" = 1'-0

12.43 Front Elevation Notes

Step 24. Follow your instructor's directions to plot the sheets. If your plotter or printer allows, each sheet can be plotted on a 17 × 11 sheet using the monochrome setting at a scale of **3/16″ = 1′0″**.

TIP

Follow the steps presented in Chapter 4 (pages 171–173) to create a page setup for plotting each sheet of this project. The plotted sheets should resemble the examples shown in Figures 12.9 and 12.10.

CHAPTER THIRTEEN

3D MODELING BASICS

OBJECTIVES

After studying the material in this chapter, you should be able to:

1. Define coordinates along *X*-, *Y*-, and *Z*-axes.

2. Change the viewpoint to reveal the *Z*-axis of the user coordinate system in an AutoCAD drawing.

3. Use the **REGION** and **EXTRUDE** commands to convert 2D entities into 3D objects.

4. Use the **3DROTATE** command to rotate objects as needed in the creation of 3D models.

5. Employ the **SUBTRACT** and **UNION** commands to create complex 3D objects with AutoCAD.

6. Represent 3D models in wireframe or shaded form.

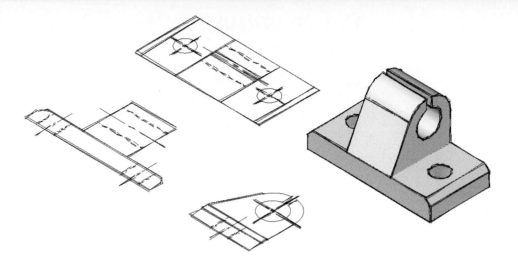

OVERVIEW

For years, drafters and designers in the mechanical engineering field have used CAD programs such as Inventor, SolidWorks, and ProE to produce 2D working drawings from 3D models. With the release of CAD software products such as Civil 3D and Revit, this technique is rapidly becoming the norm for civil and architectural drafters and designers as well. Working with 3D models gives designers a much more powerful way to conceptualize, edit, and analyze their designs.

Most 3D CAD software programs use a technique known as ***parametric modeling*** to create 3D geometry. In parametric models the geometry of the model is driven by the dimensions associated with the geometry. This allows designers to modify the features of the model by simply editing the dimensions. When a parametric dimension is changed, the 3D model updates to reflect the new dimension value.

JOB SKILLS

Finite element analysis (FEA) software is often used in conjunction with CAD modeling software to perform advanced design analysis on 3D models. FEA allows engineers and designers to calculate such properties as an object's mass, center of gravity, strength, distribution of stresses, and bending moments.

13.1 2D VERSUS 3D

Two-dimensional objects drawn with AutoCAD are described by specifying their *X*- and *Y*-coordinates. In a 2D drawing, the coordinate value of points located on the *Z*-axis is zero. Figure 13.1 shows a 2D drawing of an object created with AutoCAD. In the lower left corner of the screen, the user coordinate system (UCS) icon is visible. As you learned in Chapter 3, the UCS icon orients the drafter to the location of the 0,0 coordinates and the direction of the positive *X*- and *Y*-axes.

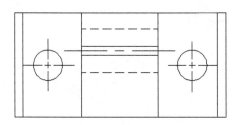

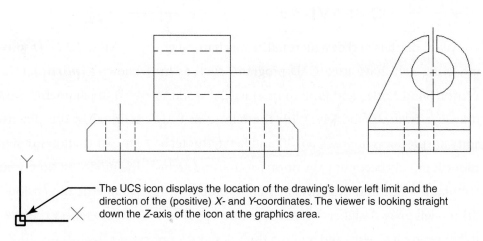

The UCS icon displays the location of the drawing's lower left limit and the direction of the (positive) *X*- and *Y*-coordinates. The viewer is looking straight down the *Z*-axis of the icon at the graphics area.

13.1   2D Views of an Object

In 3D drawing, objects are defined with coordinates that have *X*-, *Y*-, *and Z*- values. For example, the coordinates of the endpoint of a 3D line may be described as **6, 2, 4**, with **6** representing the *X*-value, **2** representing the *Y*-value, and **4** representing the *Z*-value. However, this line does not appear to be 3D if the graphics area is viewed from directly overhead, as in Figure 13.1. To view the *Z*-axis, it is necessary to change the point of view from which the 3D line is viewed.

13.2 CHANGING THE POINT OF VIEW OF AN AUTOCAD DRAWING

The point of view can be changed to show the Z-axis by opening AutoCAD's **View** toolbar and selecting the **SE Isometric** icon (see Figure 13.2). The AutoCAD drawing window will adjust to resemble the example shown in Figure 13.3. In this figure the

> **NOTE**
>
> Figure 13.1 shows the views of the tool slide as they would appear if the **Top** icon were selected from the **View** toolbar. With the view set to **Top**, the point of view is perpendicular to the *X-Y* plane. In other words, the viewer is looking straight down the *Z*-axis of the UCS icon to view objects on the *X-Y* plane.

Top View   Right View   SE Isometric View

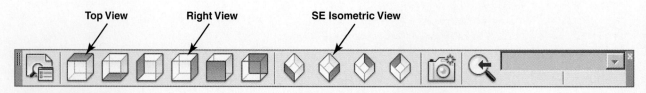

13.2   **View** Toolbar

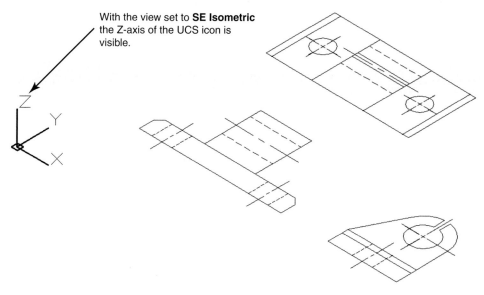

With the view set to **SE Isometric** the Z-axis of the UCS icon is visible.

13.3   SE Isometric View of 2D Objects

2D multiviews of the tool slide (drawn in Chapter 4) appear as they would if viewed from an elevated vantage point located on the southeast side of the drawing window. In fact, the *SE* in the **SE Isometric** icon on the toolbar refers to this *southeast* point of view. Likewise, *SW* refers to southwest, *NE* refers to northeast, and *NW* refers to a viewpoint located northwest of the viewed object.

More details about changing the point of view using the tools located on the ribbon will be presented later in this chapter.

13.3 AUTOCAD'S 3D MODELING ENVIRONMENT

AutoCAD's 3D environment has its own unique workspace named **3D Modeling**. When the **3D Modeling** workspace is selected, many of the tools found on the ribbon panels are replaced with specialized tools that are used in the creation, editing, and viewing of 3D models. In Figure 13.4 the workspace is set to **3D Modeling** and the view is set to **SE Isometric**. The **SE Isometric** tool is located on the **Views** panel of the **View** tab of the ribbon, as shown in Figure 13.4 (although the **View** tools can also be accessed by opening the **View** toolbar as discussed earlier in this chapter).

As you can see in Figure 13.4, the **3D Modeling** workspace looks different from AutoCAD's 2D workspace. For example, with the view set to **SE Isometric,** the Z-axis of the UCS icon is visible, the cursor displays the *X-, Y-,* and *Z-*axes, and the ViewCube (located in the upper right corner of the drawing window) resembles a 3D cube with the words **Top, Front,** and **Right** written on its surfaces. Clicking on a surface of the ViewCube will change the view displayed in the drawing window to match the selected surface; for example, clicking on the ViewCube surface labeled **Top,** will display objects as viewed from directly above. Clicking on a *corner* of the ViewCube (instead of a flat surface) will change the display to the corresponding isometric view. Right-clicking on the ViewCube and making a choice from the shortcut menu changes the display to show objects from either a perspective or a parallel (no perspective) point of view.

3D Modeling Workspace

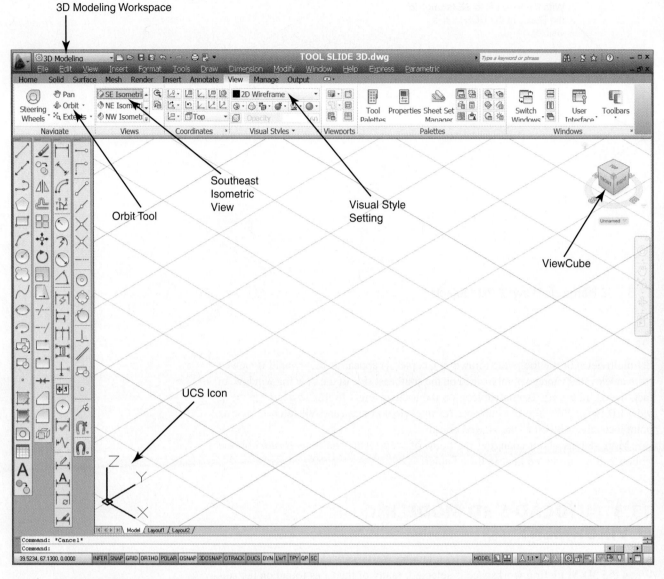

13.4   **3D Modeling** Workspace Environment

— NOTE —

In Figure 13.4, the menu bar is visible, and the **Draw**, **Modify**, **Dimension,** and **Osnap** toolbars have been docked along the left side of the drawing window. It should be noted however, that the choice of whether or not to display the menu bar and toolbars while in the **3D Modeling** workspace is left up to the user's discretion. It is the opinion of the authors that having these tools available is useful for new users of AutoCAD (refer to Chapter 4 (pages 82–83) for help opening the menu bar and the toolbars).

BEGINNING A NEW 3D DRAWING USING A 3D TEMPLATE FILE

To begin a new drawing using a template file that is preset to the 3D drawing environment, follow these steps:

1 Select **File**, pick **New**, select the **acad3D.dwt** template file from the **Select Template** dialog box, and click **Open**.

2 When the new drawing opens, select the **3D Modeling** workspace from the **Workspace Switching** drop-down menu located in the upper left corner of the interface (see Figure 13.4).

3 Next, select the **View** tab and pick the **SE Isometric** tool located on the **Views** panel.

4 Select the **Home** tab of the ribbon. The **Home** tab contains most of the tools necessary to create and edit 3D models.

CONVERTING THE 2D DRAWING ENVIRONMENT TO 3D

To convert the drawing environment of an existing 2D drawing to a 3D modeling environment, follow these steps:

1 Open the drawing and select **3D Modeling** in the **Workspace Switching** drop-down menu, as shown in Figure 13.4.

2 Select the **View** tab of the ribbon and select the **SE Isometric** tool from the **Views** panel, as shown in Figure 13.4.

3 Open the **Drafting Settings** dialog box. Under the **Grid Behavior** settings, check the box next to **Display Grid Beyond Limits** (refer to Figure 4.92) and turn the grid on.

4 Select the **Home** tab of the ribbon. The **Home** tab contains most of the tools necessary to create and edit 3D models.

When Steps 1 through 4 have been completed, the drawing's environment will resemble the screen layout shown in Figure 13.4.

13.4 3D MODELING TOOLS

Most of the tools necessary to create 3D solid models can be found on the **Modeling**, **Solid Editing**, and **Modify** panels of the **Home** tab (when the workspace is set to **3D Modeling**) or on the **Modeling** toolbar. In Figures 13.5(a) and 13.5(b) the icons for four essential 3D *modeling commands* are identified: **EXTRUDE**, **UNION**, **SUBTRACT**, and **3DROTATE**.

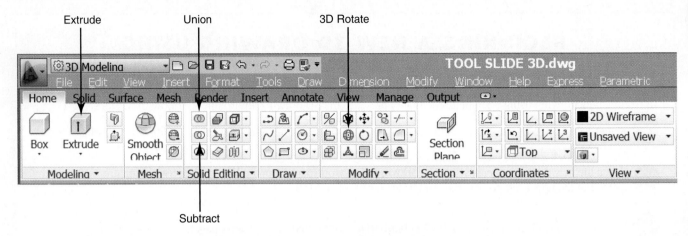

13.5(a)   Modeling Tools Located on the **Home** Tab of the **3D Modeling** Workspace

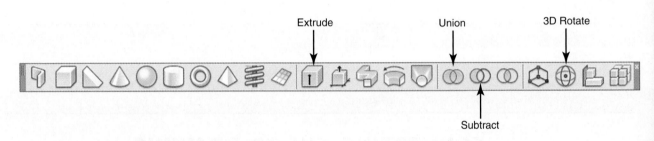

13.5(b)   The **Modeling** Toolbar

Extruding 2D Entities to Create 3D Solid Objects

In many cases, 2D objects can be converted to 3D objects by *extruding* them along their Z-axis using AutoCAD's **EXTRUDE** command. The **EXTRUDE** command can be selected from either the **Modeling** panel of the **Home** tab of the ribbon or the **Modeling** toolbar (see Figures 13.5a, 13.5b, and 13.6). (Objects that can be extruded include circles, rectangles, ellipses, polygons, closed polylines, and shapes that have been *regioned* with the **REGION** command. The **REGION** command is located on both the **Draw** panel of the **Home** tab and the **Draw** toolbar. Figure 13.7 shows the **Region** icon. The steps involved in using the **REGION** command are presented later in this chapter.

13.6   **Extrude** Icon   **13.7**   **Region** Icon

> **NOTE**
>
> At the *Specify height of the extrusion*: prompt, you can move the cursor in the desired direction of the extrusion along the Z-axis, then enter an extrusion height and press **<Enter>,** and the object will be extruded in the direction defined by the cursor.

Using the EXTRUDE Command

Select the **EXTRUDE** command and at the *Select objects prompt:*, pick the 2D object(s) to be extruded. Press **<Enter>** after the object(s) to be extruded has been selected. At the *Specify height of the extrusion (path):* prompt, type in the extrusion height as measured along the Z-axis (the height may be given as either a positive or a negative value depending on which direction is desired for the extrusion) and press **<Enter>**. The 2D shape will be extruded along its Z-axis, becoming a 3D object.

Unioning 3D Objects

Two or more 3D solid objects can be combined to form one object using the **UNION** command. The **UNION** command can be selected from either the **Solid Editing** panel of the **Home** tab of the ribbon or the **Modeling** toolbar. See Figures 13.5(a), 13.5(b), and 13.8.

Using the UNION Command

Select the **UNION** command and at the *Select objects:* prompt, select the 3D solid objects you would like to combine. When you have selected all the objects to be unioned, press **<Enter>**.

> ── NOTE ──────────────
> Unioning the solid objects combines their total volumes into one object, and they can no longer be edited as separate solids. An example of the union of the volumes of two solid cylinders with different diameters is shown in Figure 13.9.

Subtracting 3D Objects

When solid objects overlap, the **SUBTRACT** command can be use to remove the shared volume of one solid from the volume of the other solids. For example, subtracting a cylinder with a small diameter from a cylinder with a larger diameter forms a hole through the larger cylinder. The **SUBTRACT** command can be selected from either the **Solid Editing** panel of the **Home** tab of the ribbon or the **Modeling** toolbar. See Figures 13.5(a), 13.5(b), and 13.10.

Using the SUBTRACT Command

Select the **SUBTRACT** command. At the *Select solids or regions to subtract from:* prompt, pick the principal object and press **<Enter>**. At the *Select solids or regions to subtract:* prompt, pick the object whose mass you would like to subtract from the mass of the principal object and press **<Enter>**. An example of the subtraction of the volume of a solid cylinder (with a small diameter) from the volume of a solid cylinder with a larger diameter is shown in Figures 13.11 and 13.12.

13.8 Union Icon

13.9 Object Resulting from the Union of Two 3D Cylinders with Different Diameters

13.10 Subtract Icon

13.11 Two Intersecting Solid Cylinders (with Different Diameters) Prior to Use of the **SUBTRACT** Command

13.12 Object Resulting from the Subtraction of a Solid Cylinder with a Small Diameter from a Solid Cylinder of Greater Diameter

13.13 **Rotate 3D** Icon

13.5 ROTATING 3D OBJECTS

The **3DROTATE** command is used to rotate 3D objects around the *X-*, *Y-*, or *Z*-axis. The **3DROTATE** command can be selected from the **Modify** panel of the **Home** tab of the ribbon or the **Modeling** toolbar. See Figures 13.5(a), 13.5(b), and 13.13. When using the **3DROTATE** command, you are prompted to *Select objects:, Specify base point:, Pick a rotation axis:,* and *Specify angle start point or type an angle:.* The selected object(s) rotates around the base point, and the axis of rotation passes through the base point. The angle of the rotation is specified in degrees. Entering a positive value for the rotation angle will result in the counterclockwise rotation of the object, and entering a negative value for the angle will result in the clockwise rotation of the object.

NOTE

The step-by-step instructions for using the **3DROTATE** command are presented in Project 13.1 at the end of this chapter.

Free
Orbit

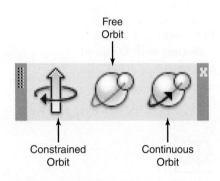

Constrained   Continuous
Orbit   Orbit

13.14 **Orbit** Toolbar

13.6 VIEWING 3D OBJECTS

In addition to the viewpoints available on the **View** toolbar, the **Orbit** tool is also helpful when viewing 3D objects. Using this tool allows you to "orbit" around a 3D object and view it from any angle. The **Orbit** tool can be selected from either the **Navigate** panel of the **View** tab of the ribbon(see Figure 13.4) or the **Orbit** toolbar shown in Figure 13.14. The **Orbit** tool is constrained to a horizontal and vertical orbit only. The **Free Orbit** tool shown in Figure 13.14 rotates the view in 3D space with no constraint on the roll.

Using the Free Orbit Tool

Select **Free Orbit** from the **Orbit** toolbar, and while holding down the left-click button of the mouse, move the mouse up and down or side to side. The viewpoint will change dynamically as the mouse is moved. To end the command, right-click and select **Exit**. To reset the object to a **SE Isometric** view, choose the **SE Isometric** tool from the **Views** panel of the **View** tab of the ribbon.

13.7 REPRESENTING 3D OBJECTS AS SHADED OR WIREFRAME MODELS

The **Visual Styles** tools control whether a solid is shown as a *shaded, unshaded,* or *wireframe* image in the drawing window. These tools can be accessed by picking on the down arrow located next to the word **2D Wireframe** located on the **View** panel of the **Home** tab of the ribbon [see Figure 13.15(a)] or by selecting them from the **Visual Styles** toolbar. See Figure 13.15(b).

Selecting either the **Conceptual Visual Style** or **Realistic Style** icons will result in shaded 3D representations.

TIP

Shading works best on objects that have been assigned a color other than black or white. Selecting the **2D Wireframe, 3D Wireframe,** or **3D Hidden Visual Style** icon will result in wireframe images of 3D objects. See Figures 13.15(a) and 13.15(b).

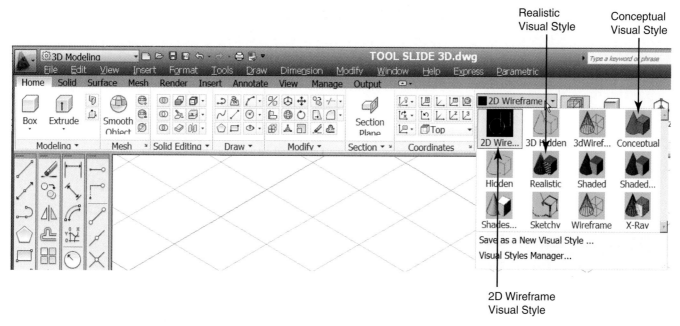

13.15(a) **Visual Styles** Tools Located on the **Views** Panel

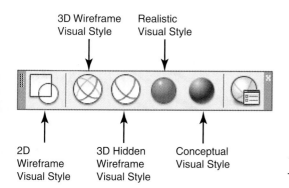

13.15(b) **Visual Styles** Toolbar Icons

KEY WORDS

Finite Element Analysis (FEA)

Modeling Commands

Parametric Modeling

CHAPTER SUMMARY

Compared with 2D CAD drafting, creating 3D models gives designers a more powerful and dynamic means to conceptualize, edit, and analyze their designs. The evolution of 3D CAD tools will allow many of the design functions currently performed by engineers to be performed by designers and designer/drafters. This will create career advancement opportunities for design drafters who adapt to these changes in CAD technology and master the design capabilities of these programs.

REVIEW QUESTIONS

Short Answer

1. Define the term *parametric modeling*.
2. What properties can be calculated using finite element analysis software?
3. What is the name of the AutoCAD command that combines the volumes of two or more 3D objects into one object?

4. Name the AutoCAD toolbar on which the **SUBTRACT** command is located.
5. When the **EXTRUDE** command is used, the height of the extrusion is defined along which axis (X, Y, or Z)?

CHAPTER PROJECTS

Project 13.1: 3D Tool Slide

Create a 3D model of the tool slide shown in the designer's sketch in Figure 13.16.

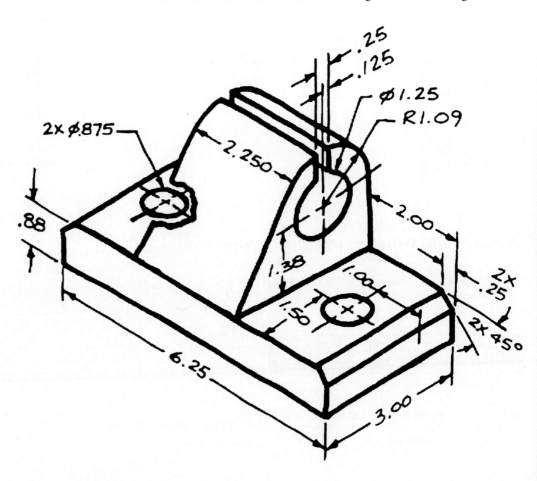

13.16 Designer's Sketch of the Tool Slide

Directions

1. Open the **Tool Slide 3D Exercise** drawing located in the student data files at **www.pearsondesigncentral.com.** To access this drawing, open the Pearson Design Central website and click on the *CAD Community* link, then select the *Click here to download student data files for our CAD titles* link. Next, click on the *Technical Drawing 101* link and select the *Prototype Drawings* zip file, then select the *Download* button and open (or save) the prototype drawing specified above.

2. Use **SAVE AS** to save the drawing to your **Home** directory, and rename the drawing **TOOL SLIDE 3D**.

3. The drawing should resemble the one shown in Figure 13.17. However, if it does not, follow the four steps outlined in the "Converting the 2D Drawing Environment to 3D" section presented on page 411.

Step 1.   Make a copy of the front and side views of the tool slide. Edit the views to create the profiles shown in Figure 13.18.

Step 2.   Select the **REGION** tool (see Figure 13.19), and create a separate region for each of the two profiles created in Step 1. When prompted by the command to *Select objects:*, select all the entities making up the profile to be regioned and press **<Enter>**.

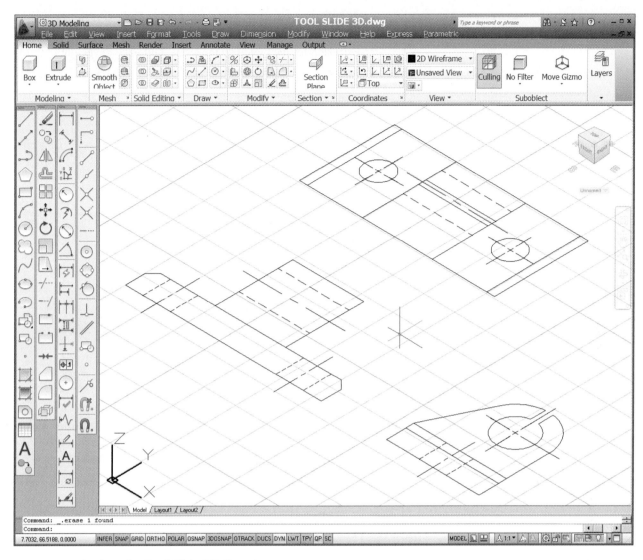

13.17   Beginning the Tool Slide 3D Drawing

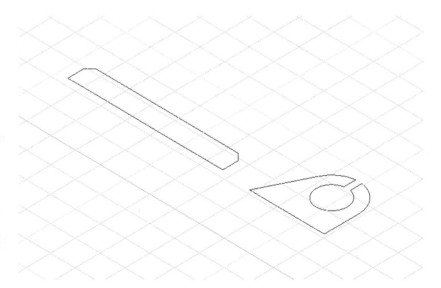

13.18   Profiles of the Front and Side Views of the Tool Slide

13.19   REGION Command Icon

Step 3.   Use the **EXTRUDE** command [refer to Figures 13.5(a) and 13.5(b)] to extrude the regions created in Step 2 as shown in Figure 13.20. The height of the extrusion for the region on the left is **3.00″**, and the height of the extrusion of the region on the right is **2.250″**.

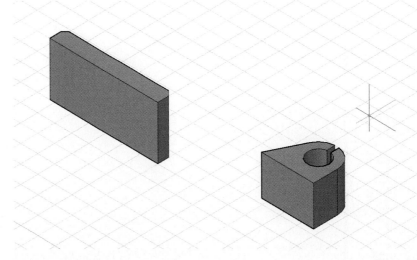

13.20   3D Models Created by Extruding

Step 4.   To rotate the 3D objects created in Step 3, select the **3D Rotate** icon [refer to Figures 13.5(a) and 13.5(b)]. When prompted to *Select objects:*, select both of the 3D objects created in Step 3 and press **<Enter>**.

Step 5.   When prompted to *Specify base point:*, select the endpoint shown in Figure 13.21.

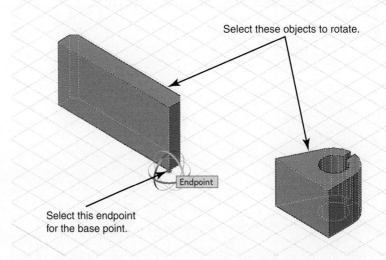

Select these objects to rotate.

Endpoint

Select this endpoint
for the base point.

13.21   Specifying the Base Point for the **3DROTATE** Command

Step 6.   When prompted to *Pick a rotation angle:*, pick the axis (ellipse) shown in Figure 13.22.

Step 7.   At the *Specify angle start point:* prompt, type **90** and press **<Enter>**. The object will rotate 90° around the base point in the positive direction of the rotation axis.

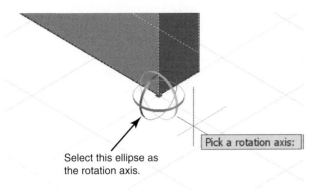

Select this ellipse as
the rotation axis.

Pick a rotation axis:

13.22   Selecting the Rotation Axis
of the **3DROTATE** Command

Step 8.   Use the **3DROTATE** command to rotate the object shown in Figure 13.23
again. This time, the rotation will be **90°** around the Z-axis.

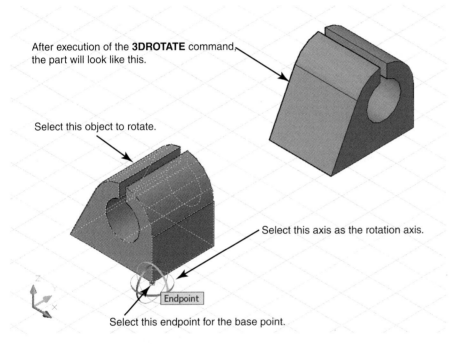

After execution of the **3DROTATE** command,
the part will look like this.

Select this object to rotate.

Select this axis as the rotation axis.

Endpoint

Select this endpoint for the base point.

13.23   Rotating the Object 90°
around the Z-Axis

Step 9.   Use the **MOVE** command to position the second object on top of the first
object as shown in Figure 13.24.

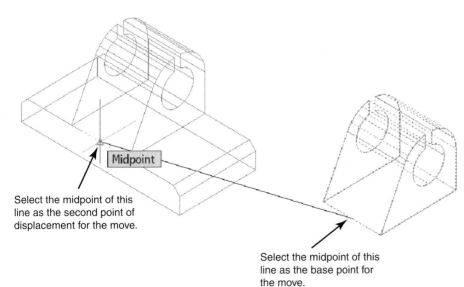

Midpoint

Select the midpoint of this
line as the second point of
displacement for the move.

Select the midpoint of this
line as the base point for
the move.

13.24   Positioning the Objects
with the **MOVE** Command

Step 10. Use the **UNION** command [refer to Figures 13.5(a) and 13.5(b)] to combine the two solids into one solid.

Step 11. Copy the two circles from the top view of the **Tool Slide** drawing to the 3D model. Use the bottom left corner of the top view as the base point and the front left corner of the 3D model as the second point of displacement as shown in Figure 13.25.

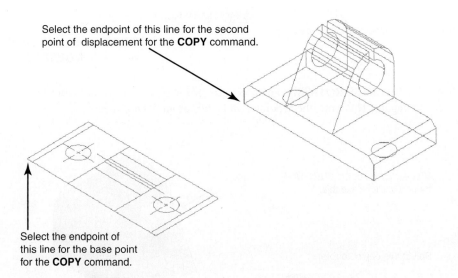

Select the endpoint of this line for the second point of displacement for the **COPY** command.

Select the endpoint of this line for the base point for the **COPY** command.

13.25   Copying the Circles from the Top View to the 3D Model

Step 12. Extrude the two circles copied in Step 11 to a height of **1.00″** to form two cylinders as shown in Figure 13.26.

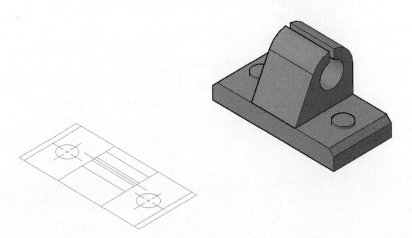

13.26   Model with Extruded Circles

Step 13. Use the **SUBTRACT** command [refer to Figures 13.5(a) and 13.5(b)] to subtract the cylinders (created in Step 12) from the larger solid object (created in Step 10) to create the holes in the solid. This step completes the construction of the 3D model of the tool slide.

Step 14. Select the **Conceptual Visual Style** icon [refer to Figures 13.15(a) and 13.15(b)] to add shading to the tool slide. The finished model should look like the one in Figure 13.27 after shading. Print the model per your instructor's directions.

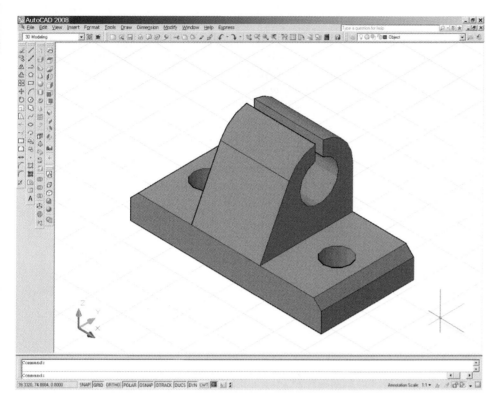

13.27   Completed 3D Model of the Tool Slide

Project 13.2: 3D Bracket

Create a 3D model of the bracket shown in Figure 13.28.

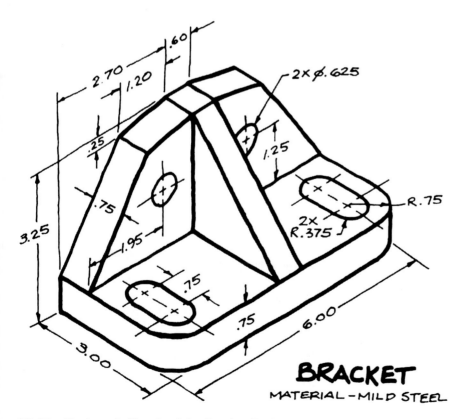

13.28   Designer's Sketch of the Bracket Project

Directions

1. Open the **Bracket 3D Exercise** drawing located in the student data files at **www .pearsondesigncentral.com.** To access this drawing, open the Pearson Design Central website and click on the *CAD Community* link, then select the *Click here to download student data files for our CAD titles* link. Next, click on the *Technical Drawing 101* link and select the *Prototype Drawings* zip file, then select the *Download* button and open (or save) the prototype drawing specified above.

2. Use **SAVE AS** to save the drawing to your **Home** directory, and rename the drawing **BRACKET 3D**.

3. Use the 2D geometry in the prototype drawing to create 2D profiles (set the **View** to **SE Isometric** if needed) and then use the **REGION** command to create a region for each profile (see Figure 13.29).

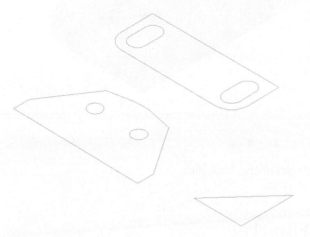

13.29   Creating Profiles and Regions

4. Use the **EXTRUDE** command to extrude the regions to the desired height (see Figure 13.30).

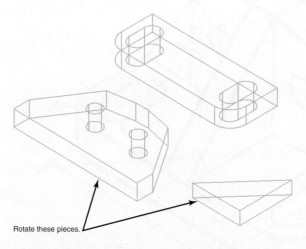

Rotate these pieces.

13.30   Extruded Profiles

5. Use the **3DROTATE**, **UNION**, **SUBTRACT**, and **MOVE** commands as needed to construct the 3D model (see Figure 13.31).
6. Print the model per your instructor's directions.

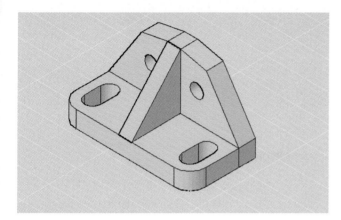

13.31   Completed 3D Model of the Bracket

Project 13.3: 3D Tool Holder

Create a 3D model of the tool holder shown in Figure 13.32.

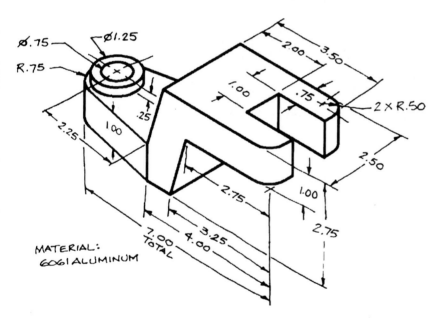

13.32   Designer's Sketch of the Tool Holder Project

Directions

1. Open the **Tool Holder 3D Exercise** drawing located in the student data files at **www.pearsondesigncentral.com.** To access this drawing, open the Pearson Design Central website and click on the **CAD Community** link, then select the **Click here to download student data files for our CAD titles** link. Next, click on the **Technical Drawing 101** link and select the **Prototype Drawings** zip file, then select the **Download** button and open (or save) the prototype drawing specified above.
2. Use **SAVE AS** to save the drawing to your **Home** directory, and rename the drawing **TOOL HOLDER 3D**.
3. Use the 2D geometry in the prototype drawing to create 2D profiles (set the **View** to **SE Isometric** if needed) and then use the **REGION** command to create a region for each profile (see Figure 13.33).

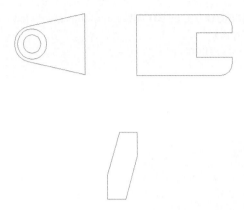

13.33   Creating Profiles and Regions

4. Use the **EXTRUDE** command to extrude the regions to the desired height (see Figure 13.34).

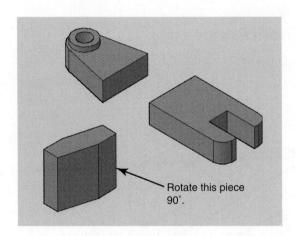

Rotate this piece 90°.

13.34   Extruded Profiles

5. Use the **3DROTATE**, **UNION**, **SUBTRACT**, and **MOVE** commands as needed to construct the 3D model (see Figure 13.35).

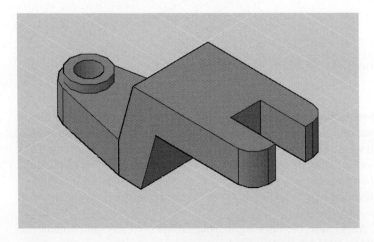

13.35   Completed 3D Model of the Tool Holder

6. Print the model per your instructor's directions.

APPENDIX A

ANSI/ASME STANDARDS

The American National Standards Institute (ANSI) oversees the creation of thousands of norms and guidelines that directly affect the manufacture and development of products and services in the United States. ANSI is also the U.S. representative to ISO, the International Organization for Standardization (see Appendix B).

A listing of all ANSI standards can be found at the ANSI website (www.ansi.org), but many of the the ANSI/ASME standards that are relevant to the creation of engineering drawings are as follows:

Y14.1-2005	*Decimal Inch Drawing Sheet Size and Format*
Y14.1M-2005	*Metric Drawing Sheet Size and Format*
Y14.2-2008	*Line Conventions and Lettering*
Y14.3-2003	*Multiview and Sectional View Drawings*
Y14.31-2008	*Undimensioned Drawings*
Y14.34-2008	*Associated Lists*
Y14.4M-1989	*Pictorial Drawing*
Y14.5-2009	*Dimensioning and Tolerancing*
Y14.6-2001	*Screw Thread Representation*

APPENDIX B

ISO STANDARDS

The International Organization for Standardization (ISO) is a consortium of the national standards institutes from more than 150 member countries. These institutes collaborate to establish standards for the development and manufacturing of products and services. The goal of ISO is not only to improve the quality of these products and processes but also to make them safer and more efficient. Another goal of international standards is to make trade between countries easier and fairer and to provide governments with a technical base for health, safety, and environmental legislation. ISO standards also help safeguard consumers and end users of products and services. The United States is represented in the ISO network by the American National Standards Institute (ANSI).

The first attempts at international standardization began in the early twentieth century, but it was not until 1946 that delegates from 25 countries met and created an international organization. The purpose of this organization would be "to facilitate the international coordination and unification of industrial standards." The new organization, which was named ISO, officially began operations on February 23, 1947.

In English, the acronym ISO stands for the International Organization for Standardization; in French, ISO stands for *Organisation internationale de normalisation*. Because of the many countries and languages represented in the ISO network, it was decided to use a word derived from the Greek *isos*, meaning "equal" to describe the organization. For this reason, regardless of the language, the organization is referred to as ISO.

A listing of most ISO standards can be found at the ISO website (www.iso.org), but a partial list of the ISO standards that relate specifically to the creation of technical drawings follows:

01.100.01	*Technical Drawings in General*
01.100.20	*Mechanical Engineering Drawings*
01.100.25	*Electrical and Electronics Engineering Drawings*
01.100.27	*Technical Drawings for Telecommunications/ Information Technology*
01.100.30	*Construction Drawings Including Civil Engineering Drawings*
01.100.40	*Drawing Equipment*
01.100.99	*Other Standards Related to Technical Drawings*

APPENDIX C

UNITED STATES NATIONAL CAD STANDARD

The United States National CAD Standard (NCS) coordinates CAD-related publications for the building design and construction industry in an attempt to make communication between design/construction teams and clients more consistent and direct.

Although adoption of the NCS by the building design and construction industry is voluntary, several government agencies have adopted the standard, and many public and private organizations are in the process of adopting it.

At its website (www.nationalcadstandard.org), the NCS lists the following benefits as the advantages of adopting the NCS standard:

BENEFITS TO CLIENTS AND OWNERS

- Consistent organization of data for all projects, from all sources
- Greater clarity of communication of design intent to the client
- Streamlined electronic data management of facility management data
- Enhanced potential for automated document storage and retrieval
- Streamlined construction document checking process

BENEFITS TO DESIGN PROFESSIONALS

- Consistent data classification for all projects, regardless of the project type or client
- Seamless transfer of information among architects, engineers, and other design team members

- Predictable file translation results between formats; reduced preparation time for translation
- Reduced file formatting and setup time when adopted by software application vendors
- Reduced staff training time to teach "office standards"
- Streamlined checking process for errors and omissions
- New opportunities for expanded services and revenue beyond building design
- Added value to design services; firms can feature compliance with the NCS

BENEFITS TO CONTRACTORS AND SUBCONTRACTORS

- Consistent drawing sheet order and sheet organization; information appears in the same place in all drawing sets
- Consistent detail reference system
- Reduction of discrepancies, reducing the potential for errors, change orders, and construction delays
- Enhanced potential for automated payment process
- Consistent organization of data for all projects, from all sources

INDUSTRY-WIDE BENEFITS FOR NCS ADOPTION

- Reduced in-office training time with "collective professional memory" of a drawing standard
- Improved training at undergraduate and graduate levels
- Enhanced potential for automated training and distance learning
- Substantial reduction of barriers to seamless exchange of building construction data, leading to greater efficiency and decreased costs

APPENDIX D

GEOMETRIC DIMENSIONING AND TOLERANCING BASICS

Applying plus/minus dimensioning to a drawing allows a mechanical designer to define the location and size of a part's features within a certain allowance, but applying the concepts of geometric dimensioning and tolerancing (GDT) allows the designer also to define the *form* (flatness, straightness, circularity, and cylindricity), *orientation* (perpendicularity, angularity, and parallelism), or *position* of a part's features.

Applying GDT increases the odds that a part will pass a quality control inspection, and fewer rejected parts will result in lower production costs.

On a drawing, GDT symbols are shown inside a rectangular box called a *feature control frame*. If the feature being defined by the GDT symbol is located relative to a datum feature (usually a surface or axis), the datum feature is defined with a *datum feature symbol*.

Figure D.1 shows a view of an object with GDT symbols added. Study this figure and note how the objects identified as the feature control frame and the datum feature symbol are represented.

INTERPRETING THE FEATURE CONTROL FRAME

The feature control frame contains the GDT characteristic symbol (parallelism, perpendicularity, etc.), the tolerance, and if the tolerance is referenced from a datum(s), the datum reference letter(s). Figure D.2 shows a feature control frame with its components identified.

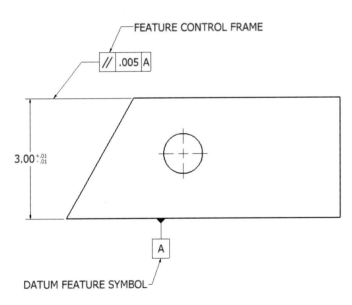

D.1   A Drawing with GDT Symbols

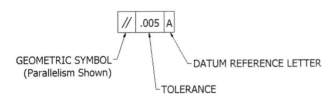

D.2   Interpreting a Feature Control Frame

431

GEOMETRIC CHARACTERISTIC SYMBOLS

The GDT characteristic symbols that may be included in a feature control frame are shown in Figure D.3. The symbols used to represent these characteristics are defined in the American Society of Mechanical Engineers standard for dimensioning and tolerancing, *ASME Y14.5-2009*. These symbols are included in the **Tolerance** command found on AutoCAD's **Dimension** toolbar. See Figures 5.42(a) and Figures 5.42(b).

Flatness-the amount that a surface can deviate from being perfectly flat.

Straightness-the amount a line on a surface can deviate from being perfectly straight.

Circularity-the amount a circle can deviate from being perfectly round.

Cylindricity-the amount a cylinder can deviate from being a perfect cylinder.

Profile of a Line-the amount a profile shape can deviate from the specified shape.

Profile of a Surface-the amount a surface can deviate from the specified shape.

Angularity-the amount an angled surface can deviate from a specified angle.

Perpendicularity-the amount that a surface can deviate from being perfectly perpendicular to a defined datum.

Parallelism-The amount a surface can deviate from parallel to a defined datum.

Position-The amount a feature can deviate from its true position as defined from a datum(s).

Concentricity-The amount the center axis of a revolved surface can deviate from being concentric with a defined datum.

Circular Runout-a measure of both the roundness and the location of circle.

Symmetry-the amount of deviation allowed from perfect symmetry.

Total Runout-the amount the surface of a cylinder can deviate as it is rotated around a center axis.

D.3 Geometric Characteristic Symbols

INTERPRETING GDT ON A DRAWING

Figure D.4 shows a drawing of an object with a feature control frame specifying the allowed deviation from perfect *flatness* for the bottom surface of the object. The distance between the two lines representing the .005 tolerance is exaggerated in this figure to better illustrate the concept.

INTERPRETING PARALLELISM

Figure D.5 shows a drawing of an object with a feature control frame specifying the allowed deviation that the top surface can have from being parallel to the bottom surface—identified with a datum feature symbol as *datum A*. The distance between the two lines representing the .005 tolerance is exaggerated in this figure to better illustrate the concept.

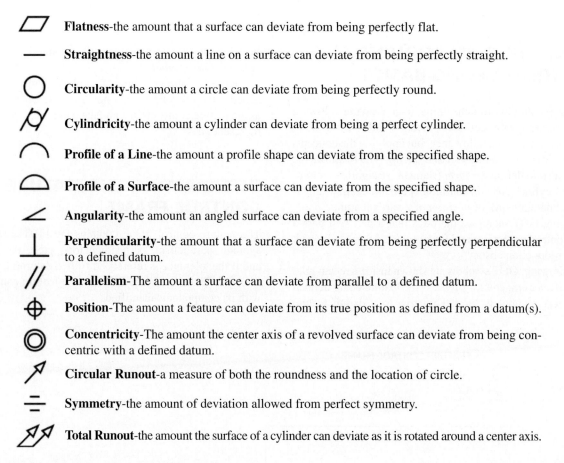

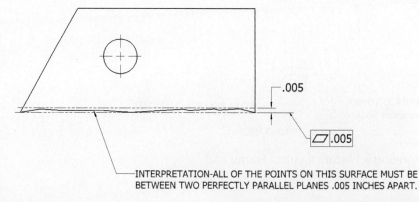

D.4 Interpreting Flatness on a Drawing

INTERPRETATION-ALL OF THE POINTS ON THIS SURFACE MUST BE BETWEEN TWO PERFECTLY PARALLEL PLANES .005 INCHES APART.

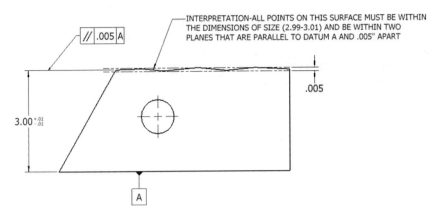

INTERPRETATION-ALL POINTS ON THIS SURFACE MUST BE WITHIN
THE DIMENSIONS OF SIZE (2.99-3.01) AND BE WITHIN TWO
PLANES THAT ARE PARALLEL TO DATUM A AND .005" APART

D.5   Interpreting Parallelism on a Drawing

ADDING GDT TO AN AUTOCAD DRAWING

Step 1.   Select the **Tolerance** icon from AutoCAD's **Dimension** toolbar (see Figure D.6). This will open the **Geometric Tolerance** dialog box shown in Figure D.7.

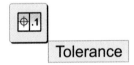

D.6   **Tolerance** Icon

Step 2.   Select the first black box below the word **Sym** located in the **Geometric Tolerance** dialog box shown in Figure D.7. This will open the **Symbol** box shown in Figure D.8.

Step 3.   Select the geometric characteristic symbol from the symbols available in the **Symbol** box (see Figure D.8). After you select a symbol, it will appear in the **Geometric Tolerance** dialog box in the window beneath **Sym,** as shown in Figure D.9.

Step 4.   Fill in the values for the desired tolerance and datum(s) as shown in Figure D.9 and click **OK**. Then, use the mouse to move the feature control frame to its desired location in the drawing.

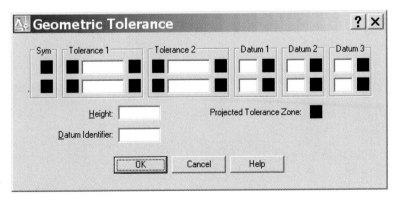

D.7   **Geometric Tolerance** Dialog Box

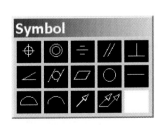

D.8   **Symbol** Box

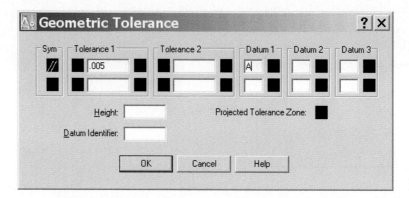

D.9   Adding Tolerance and Datum Information

ADDING A DATUM FEATURE SYMBOL

You can add a datum feature symbol by following Steps 1 and 2 in the preceding section, but instead of selecting the black box below the word **Sym**, type the desired datum identification character (an **A**, for example) in the **Datum Identifier** box and click **OK**. Then, use the mouse to move the datum feature symbol to its desired location in the drawing.

LEARNING TO APPLY GDT TO DRAWINGS

Learning to apply GDT to drawings is a process requiring instruction, study, and practice. GDT techniques are often included in the curriculum of advanced mechanical engineering drawing courses. Many organizations also offer continuing education GDT workshops for professionals.

A good resource for GDT materials and certification is the ASME website: www.asme.org.

APPENDIX E

AUTOCAD RIBBON TUTORIAL

When the AutoCAD CAD 2011 workspace is set to **2D Drafting & Annotation, 3D Modeling,** or **3D Basics,** the *ribbon* interface is displayed in the application window. The purpose of the ribbon is to maximize the AutoCAD drawing area by grouping commands and operations into compact *toolbar panels.* Toolbar panels are grouped together according to task to create seven *ribbon tabs.* These tabs are labeled **Home, Insert, Annotate, Parametric, View, Manage,** and **Output.** Selecting one of these tabs allows the user to select from the tools and operations contained on the toolbar panels of that tab. For example, when the **Home** tab

is selected, the **Draw, Modify, Layers, Annotation, Block, Properties, Utilities,** and **Clipboard** toolbar panels are displayed, along with their related tools and operations, as shown in Figure E.1(a).

NOTE

When the workspace is set to **3D Modeling** or **3D Basics,** the panels of the **Home** tab will be grouped into tools that facilitate the modeling, editing, and viewing of 3D objects. See Figure E.1(b).

E.1(a) The **Home** Tab of the Ribbon in the **2D Drafting & Annotation** Workspace

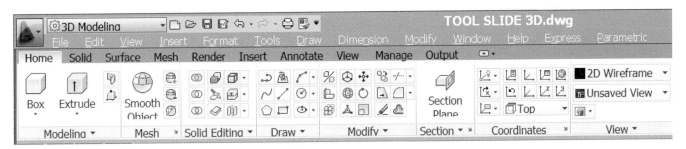

E.1(b) The **Home** Tab of the Ribbon in the **3D Modeling** Workspace

The Home Tab

The **Home** tab is the tab that new users of AutoCAD will utilize most frequently, because the draw, modify, and annotation tools (both text and dimensioning) are located on this tab. The tools used to control layer settings, including the **Layer Properties Manager,** can also be accessed from the **Home** tab. Most of the tools on this tab are discussed in Chapters 4 and 5 of this text.

Clicking on the down arrow next to the title at the bottom of a toolbar panel *expands* the panel to show additional command icons contained in the panel. Figure E.2 shows the **Draw** tool panel expanded in this manner. To "pin" the panel in its expanded view, click on the pushpin icon located on the bottom left corner of the expanded panel.

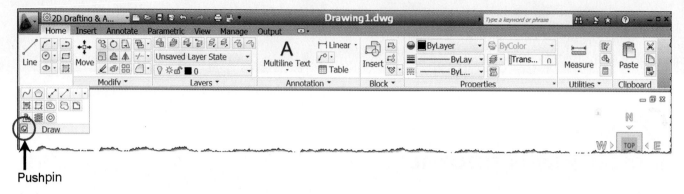

Pushpin

E.2 The **Home** Tab Showing the Expanded **Draw** Toolbar and Pushpin

The Insert Tab

Selecting the **Insert** tab displays toolbar panels related to blocks, attributes, references, importing, data, and linking and extraction, as shown in Figure E.3. Many of the tools and settings presented in Chapter 10 are found on this tab.

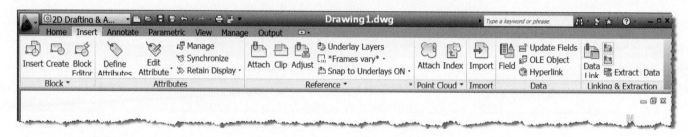

E.3 **Insert** Tab

The Annotate Tab

Selecting the **Annotate** tab displays toolbar panels related to placing annotations such as multiline text, dimensions, and leaders on drawings, as shown in Figure E.4.

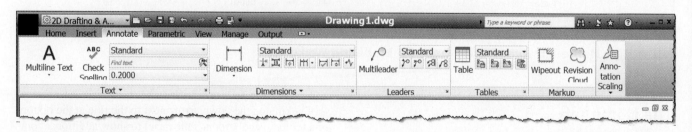

E.4 **Annotate** Tab

The Parametric Tab

Selecting the **Parametric** tab displays toolbar panels related to geometric constraints and parametric dimensioning tools (see Figure E.5). Adding geometric constraints to an object such as a line can constrain the line so that it will always remain perpendicular or parallel to another line, even if the other line is moved or rotated. Applying parametric dimensions to an object allows the size of the object to be driven by changing the value of the parametric dimensions. This can be done by double-clicking on a parametric dimension and entering a new dimension value in the text box. The use of the tools on this tab lend themselves to more advanced AutoCAD texts.

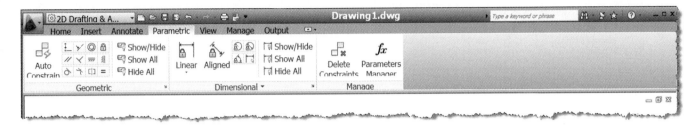

E.5   Parametric Tab

The View Tab

Selecting the **View** tab displays toolbar panels related to viewing and panning, the user coordinate system, viewports and views, tool palettes, changing an object's properties, arranging multiple drawings, and setting windows elements, as shown in Figure E.6.

> — NOTE —
> You can open AutoCAD toolbars by clicking on the **Toolbars** tool located on this tab, clicking on **AutoCAD** from the submenu, and selecting the desired toolbar from the toolbar menu.

E.6   View Tab

The Output Tab

Selecting the **Output** tab displays toolbar panels related to plotting and exporting drawings, as shown in Figure E.7.

E.7   Output Tab

The Express Tools Tab

Selecting the **Express Tools** tab displays a group of toolbar panels related to blocks, text, modify commands, layouts, draw tools, dimensioning tools, and tools used to accelerate the drawing process, as shown in Figure E.8.

E.8   Express Tools Tab

ACCESSING HELP TOOLS FROM THE RIBBON

AutoCAD has made it easier for users to access help with commands and settings. For example, holding the cursor over an icon located on a toolbar panel (but not picking the icon) for approximately one second causes a *tooltip* related to the icon to appear. Figure E.9 shows the tooltip that appears if the cursor is held over the **Circle** icon located on the **Draw** toolbar panel. If the cursor is held over the icon for two or more seconds, an extended tooltip will appear, as shown in Figure E.10. This tooltip offers additional information about the **CIRCLE** command.

Holding the cursor over the **Circle** icon and pressing the <**F1**> function key on the keyboard opens the **Quick Reference** help screen, which offers even more information about the **CIRCLE** command, as shown in Figure E.11.

Clicking on the down arrow located to the right of the **Circle** icon displays an expanded palette of circle creation options, as shown in Figure E.12.

> **— NOTE —**
> Holding the cursor over an icon (but not selecting the icon) can be used to access tooltip information about the tools located on any toolbar panel or toolbar.

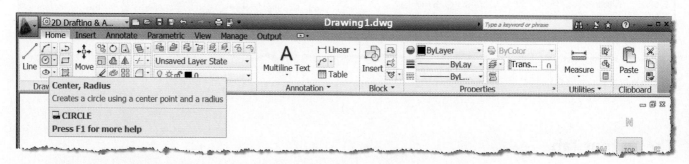

E.9   CIRCLE Command Tooltip

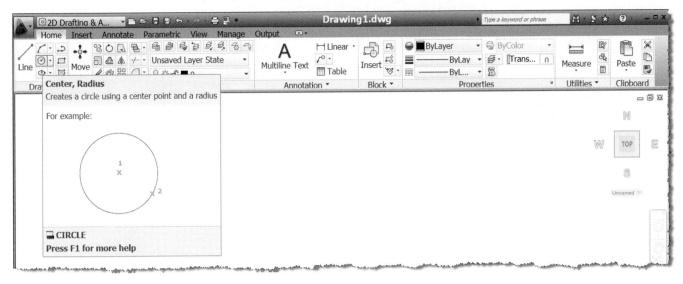

E.10   Expanded Tooltip for the **CIRCLE** Command

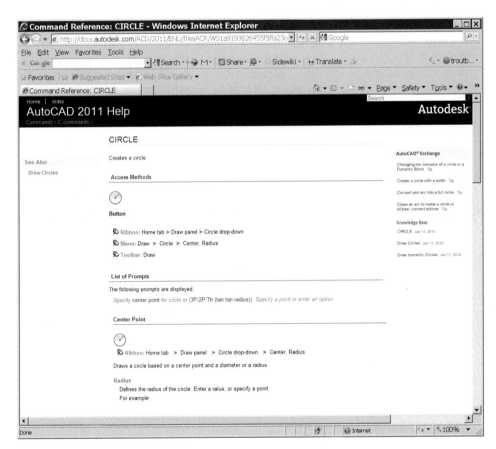

E.11   **Quick Reference** Help Screen for the **CIRCLE** Command

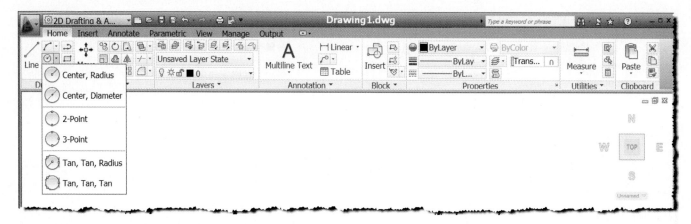

E.12   Circle Creation Options

MAXIMIZING THE DRAWING WINDOW BY MINIMIZING THE RIBBON INTERFACE

AutoCAD provides several ways to minimize the amount of screen space required to display the entire ribbon and its toolbar panels on the AutoCAD interface, thus maximizing the drawing window. The **Ribbon Minimize** button shown in Figure E.13 offers several ways to alter the size of the ribbon footprint on the screen.

Clicking the **Ribbon Minimize** button once minimizes the ribbon to display only the tab and toolbar panel buttons as shown in Figure E.13 Moving the cursor onto a panel button expands the panel and displays the tools associated with the panel. The expanded panel disappears when the cursor is moved away from the panel title.

> ─ **NOTE** ─
>
> By selecting the **Ribbon Minimize** button shown in Figure E.13, users can cycle this display between the following ribbon display options: **Minimize to Panel Buttons, Minimize to Panel Titles, Minimize to Tabs,** and **Show Full Ribbon.**

Ribbon Minimize Button

E.13   The **Ribbon Minimize** Button with the Ribbon Minimized to Tabs and Panel Buttons

Clicking the **Ribbon Minimize** button again minimizes both the ribbon and toolbar buttons to display only the tab and panel titles, as shown in Figure E.14 Moving the cursor onto a panel title causes an expanded tool panel to appear that displays the tools associated with the panel. If a tool is selected from the panel, the expanded panel disappears.

E.14   The Ribbon Minimized to Tabs and Panel Titles

Clicking the **Ribbon Minimize** button again, hides the toolbar panels leaving only the tabs displayed as shown in Figure E.15 Clicking on a tab will cause it to expand and display its tool panels, but the panels will disappear once a tool has been selected from a panel.

Double-clicking the **Ribbon Minimize** button will reset the ribbon to its full size.

E.15   The Ribbon Minimized to Tabs

GLOSSARY

absolute coordinates Points that are located along the *X-, Y-,* and *Z*-axes that are relative to a point defined as 0,0,0. In an AutoCAD drawing, 0,0,0 is usually located in the lower left corner of the graphics window.

actual size The measured size of a finished part. This size determines whether the part passes a quality control inspection.

aeronautical or aerospace drafters Drafters who prepare engineering drawings detailing plans and specifications used in the manufacture of aircraft and related equipment.

aligned text Text placed on a technical drawing that faces the bottom and the right side of the sheet. This technique is common on architectural drawings but is not allowed on drawings employing the ASME dimensioning standard.

allowance The minimum clearance or maximum interference between parts.

American Institute of Architects (AIA) The accrediting body for architects.

American National Standards Institute (ANSI) The national organization for the development of standards in the United States. ANSI represents the United States as a member of the International Organization for Standardization.

American Society of Mechanical Engineers (ASME) Publisher of standards for the creation of technical drawing in the United States. *ASME Y14.5-2009 Dimensioning and Tolerancing* and *ASME Y14.2 Line Conventions and Lettering* are two standards important to drafters.

architectural drafters Drafters who prepare the drawings used in construction industries.

assembly drawing A drawing that illustrates how the separate parts of an assembly are related to each other, for example, how mating parts fit together.

base point The point on a block that aligns to the insertion point in the field of the drawing defined when placing the block.

baseline dimensions A group of linear dimensions that are referenced from the same datum or baseline.

block AutoCAD term that refers to a predefined object or symbol stored in an AutoCAD drawing file that can be inserted into the drawing whenever it is needed.

block library A group of block definitions stored in a drawing file. For example, an architectural firm might create a block library of symbols like doors and windows that are frequently used on floor plans. See *block.*

broken-out section A view of an object that shows only a small area of the object as a section.

Building Information Model (BIM) A system of modeling and linking building system information into a digital, and increasingly 3D, database.

CAD (computer-aided design) A term often used to describe the creation of technical drawings. Also a term for the software used to create technical drawings. Some popular CAD programs include AutoCAD, SolidWorks, Revit, Pro/ENGINEER, and Inventor.

CAM (computer-aided manufacturing) Manufacturing processes in which manufacturing equipment and processes are controlled by computer commands.

Cartesian coordinate system A system of locating points along *X*- and *Y*-axes relative to a starting point representing "zero *X*" and "zero *Y*." Named for its originator, René Descartes.

checker An experienced designer/drafter with expertise in manufacturing, drafting techniques, and dimensioning conventions who is responsible for reviewing and approving the drawings prepared by other drafters.

civil drafters and design technicians Drafters who prepare construction drawings and topographical maps used in civil engineering projects.

construction documents (CDs) Drawings used in the construction of residential and commercial buildings. These drawings may include floor plans, elevations, foundations, wall sections, and roof framing plans.

continuous dimensions A dimensioning technique in which a linear dimension is placed using the second extension line origin of a selected dimension as its first extension line origin. This technique is also called *chain dimensioning.*

cutting plane An imaginary plane that slices through an object to reveal its interior features in a section view.

datum A theoretically perfect feature (plane, axis, or point) from which dimensions are referenced.

designer Individual who assists engineers or architects with the design process. Designers are often former drafters who have proven their ability to take on more responsibility and decision-making duties.

detail drawings Drawings that provide the information required to manufacture or purchase each part in an assembly including the necessary views, dimensions, notations, and specifications.

dimension commands The commands used to dimension an AutoCAD drawing. These commands are located on the **Dimension** toolbar and include **Linear**, **Baseline**, **Continue**, **Angular**, **Diameter**, and **Radius**.

dimensions Annotations that are added to a technical drawing specifying the size and location of the features of an object. There are two types of dimensions: *size* and *location.* For example, the diameter of a hole is a size dimension, whereas the dimensions that indicate the placement of the center of the hole are location dimensions. Dimensional information may include notes concerning the material from which the object is manufactured, special processes performed on the object (heat treating, polishing, etc.), and any other information needed during the manufacture of a part or the construction of a building.

dimension standards   Dimensioning rules that have been created to standardize dimensioning styles and techniques. Dimensioning standards for mechanical drawings have been defined by the American Society of Mechanical Engineers (ASME) and the International Organization for Standardization (ISO). Dimensioning standards for construction documents are defined by the United States National CAD Standard.

drafter   An individual with specialized training in the creation of technical drawings.

drafting   A term often used to describe the creation of technical drawings.

Draw commands   The commands used to place geometry in an AutoCAD drawing. These commands are located on the **Draw** toolbar and **Draw** panel and include **LINE**, **CIRCLE**, **ARC**, and **Multiline Text**.

drawing limits   The limits of an AutoCAD drawing define its drawing area; this is comparable to selecting the sheet size for the drawing. When setting limits, you are prompted to specify the lower left and upper right corners of the drawing area. In most cases, the lower left corner will default to **0,0**, and you will define the upper right corners by typing the coordinates of the corresponding sheet size. For example, in decimal units, an A-size sheet limits would be **0,0** and **12,9**; a B-size sheet limits would be **0,0** and **17,11**; a C-size sheet limits would be **0,0** and **22,17**; and a D- size sheet limits would be **0,0** and **34,22**.

drawing units   The units of measurement to be used in the creation of an AutoCAD drawing. For example, in an architectural drawing, one unit may equal one foot, whereas in a mechanical drawing, one unit may equal one inch or one millimeter. The drawing units should be set before beginning a drawing or defining the drawing limits.

electrical drafters   Drafters who prepare diagrams used in the installation and repair of electrical equipment and building wiring.

electrical plans   Drawings that provide electrical contractors information about the type, location, and installation of electrical components (switches, lamps, ceiling fans, electrical outlets, cable TV jacks, etc.) used in the project. All of the information needed by the electrical contractor to wire the building should be provided by this plan.

electro/mechanical drafters   Drafters who split their duties between mechanical drafting and electrical/electronics drafting.

electronics drafters   Drafters who prepare schematic diagrams, printed circuit board artwork, integrated circuit layouts, and other graphics used in the design and maintenance of electronic (semiconductor) devices.

elevation drawings   Drawings that provide information about the exterior details of a building. This information may include roof pitch, exterior materials and finishes, overall heights of features, and window and door styles. All the dimensions and notations required by workers on the jobsite should be included on this sheet.

engineering drawing   A term often used to describe the creation of technical drawings.

engineering graphics   A term often used to describe the creation of technical drawings.

engineer's, architect's, and metric scales   Precision measurement instruments used to make measurements during the creation or interpretation of technical drawings.

features   Geometric elements that are added to a base part. Features include holes, slots, arcs, fillets, rounds, angled planes, counterbored holes, and countersunk holes. Features are located on the object with location dimensions and are described with size dimensions.

fillet   A rounded inside corner of a part.

finite element analysis (FEA)   Software that is used in conjunction with CAD modeling software to perform advanced design analysis on 3D models. FEA allows engineers and designers to calculate such properties as an object's mass, center of gravity, strength, distribution of stresses, and moments of inertia.

first-angle projection   A technique for arranging multiview drawings in which the left-side view is drawn to the right of the front view, and the top view is placed below the front view, and so on. Commonly used on drawings prepared outside North America.

floor plans   Drawings that provide home builders and contractors with the necessary information to lay out the building, including the locations of features such as walls, doors, electrical components (switches, lamps, etc.) and plumbing fixtures (tubs, commodes, sinks, etc.). Floor plans usually include all of the dimensions and notations required by the workers on the jobsite. Doors and windows are dimensioned to their centers, and continuous (also known as *chain*) dimensioning is typically employed on floor plans.

foreshortening   A term used to describe the phenomenon that occurs when a feature on an inclined plane is not shown true size or true shape in a multiview drawing.

full section   A view of an object that shows its interior detail as if it has been cut in half.

geometric dimensioning and tolerancing (GD&T)   A dimensioning technique that is used to control the *form* (flatness, straightness, circularity, and cylindricity), *orientation* (perpendicularity, angularity, and parallelism), or *position* of a part's features.

graphic primitives   Geometric shapes such as boxes, cylinders, cones, spheres, wedges, and prisms that can be combined (unioned) or removed from one another (subtracted) to create more complicated shapes.

half section   A view of an object that shows its interior detail as if one fourth of it has been removed.

inclined plane   A plane located on an object in a multiview drawing that is sloping and is not perpendicular to the line of sight of the viewer.

Inquiry commands   Commands used to display information about AutoCAD entities such as distance between two points, area of a closed figure like a rectangle or circle, or the volume of a 3D object. These commands are located on the **Inquiry** toolbar and **Utilities** panel.

insertion point   The point defined in the field of the drawing that a block's base point will align to upon insertion.

International Organization for Standardization (ISO)   The international organization for the development of standards including technical drawing and dimensioning standards. ANSI represents the United States as a member of ISO. The ISO dimensioning standard is almost identical to the ASME dimensioning standard.

isometric drawing   A type of pictorial drawing in which receding lines are drawn at 30° relative to the horizon. Commonly used in the mechanical engineering field. See *pictorial drawing*.

layers   In AutoCAD drawings, lines and other entities are drawn on layers. Think of layers as sheets of clear glass layered one on top of the other. A layer can have its own properties such as color, linetype, or lineweight.

lead hardness grade   The scale that defines the hardness of graphite pencil leads. Soft leads range between 2B and 7B. Medium leads include 3H, 2H, H, F, HB, and B. Hard leads range between 4H and 9H.

least material condition (LMC)   The condition of a part when it contains the least amount of material. The LMC of an external feature, such as a shaft, is the lower limit of size defined by the tolerance. The LMC of an internal feature, such as a hole, is the upper limit of size defined by the tolerance.

limits   The maximum and minimum sizes of a feature as defined by its tolerances. For example, a feature with a nominal dimension of .50, with a tolerance of ±.02, has an upper limit of .52 and a lower limit of .48.

linetypes   Include *visible lines,* which show the visible edges and features of an object; *hidden lines,* which represent features that would not be visible; and *centerlines,* which locate the centers of features such as holes and arcs. Standard linetypes have been established by the American Society of Mechanical Engineers (ASME) in *ASME Y14.2.*

lineweight   Refers to the width of the lines in a technical drawing. Standard lineweights have been established by the American Society of Mechanical Engineers (ASME) in *ASME Y14.2.* In this standard, visible lines are drawn 0.6mm wide, and center and hidden lines are drawn .3mm wide.

maximum material condition (MMC)   The condition of a part when it contains the greatest amount of material. The MMC of an external feature, such as a shaft, is the upper limit. The MMC of an internal feature, such as a hole, is the lower limit.

mechanical drafters   Drafters who prepare detail and assembly drawings of machinery and mechanical devices.

mechanical working drawings   Drawings used in the fabrication and assembly of machine parts.

miter line   In drawings created with orthographic projection techniques, a construction line drawn at 45° that enables information to be projected from the top view to the side view, and from the side view to the top view. See *orthographic projection.*

modeling commands   Commands used to create 3D models in an AutoCAD drawing. These commands are located on the **Modeling** toolbar and include **UNION, SUBTRACT, 3DROTATE,** and **EXTRUDE.**

Modify commands   Commands used to modify the geometry of an AutoCAD drawing. These commands are located on the **Modify** toolbar and **Modify** panel and include **ERASE, MOVE, COPY, OFFSET, ROTATE,** and **SCALE.**

multiview drawing   A technique used by drafters and designers to depict a three-dimensional object (an object having height, width, and depth) as a group of related two-dimensional (having only width and height, or width and depth, or height and depth) views.

National Society of Professional Engineers   The accrediting agency for engineers.

nominal size   A dimension that describes the general size of a feature. Tolerances are applied to this dimension.

Object Snap settings   A technique used in the creation and editing of AutoCAD drawings that allows the user to snap to exact points on an object. Common object snap settings include snap to endpoint, snap to midpoint, snap to intersection, snap to center, and snap to quadrant.

offset section   A section that includes features that would not lie along the path of a straight cutting plane line. The cutting plane line is offset to take in these features.

orthographic projection   The technique employed in the creation of multiview drawings to project geometric information (points, lines, planes, or other features) from one view to another.

parametric modeling   A method of creating 3D CAD models in which the geometry of the model is driven by the dimensions associated with the geometry. This allows designers to modify the features of a model by simply editing its dimensions. When the parametric dimension is changed, the 3D model updates to reflect the new dimension value.

partial auxiliary view   An auxiliary view that is simplified by omitting planes and other features not shown true shape in the view.

parts list   A table placed on a technical drawing that itemizes all the parts in an assembly (sometimes referred to as a *bill of materials* or *BOM*). The parts list may include columns for part number, part name, description, quantity, and material.

perspective drawing   A type of pictorial drawing in which receding lines appear to converge at a vanishing point. Commonly used in the architectural field. See *pictorial drawing.*

pictorial drawing   A type of drawing in which an object appears to be three dimensional; that is, it appears to have width, height, and depth. But unlike an actual 3D model, a pictorial drawing is constructed using only X- and Y-coordinates. See *isometric drawing* and *perspective drawing.*

pipeline drafters and process piping drafters   Drafters who prepare drawings used in the construction and maintenance of oil refineries, oil production and exploration industries, chemical plants, and process piping systems such as those used in the manufacture of semiconductor devices.

polar coordinates   Coordinates defined by a length and an angle that are relative to the last point defined.

primary auxiliary view   A view that is adjacent to, and aligned with, a principal view of the object showing the true shape of features that are not parallel to any of the principal projection planes (front, top, side, etc.).

professional engineer (P.E.)   An engineer who is licensed by the National Society of Professional Engineers.

projection plane   An imaginary two-dimensional plane, like a sheet of clear glass, placed parallel to a principal face of the object to be visualized. The object's features (points, lines, planes) are projected perpendicular to the projection plane when visualizing a multiview drawing of the object.

properties   In an AutoCAD drawing, the properties of an object include its color, lineweight, layer, linetype, linetype scale, and so forth.

quality control inspection   A step in the manufacturing cycle performed by a quality control (QC) inspector using precise measuring equipment to determine the actual size of the part. The QC inspector compares the actual size of the part with the dimensions noted on the technical drawing. Parts that measure within the allowable size limits will pass the QC inspection, whereas parts that measure outside the limits will be rejected.

reference dimension   A dimension that is included on a technical drawing for information only and is not necessary to manufacture, or inspect, the part. No tolerances are applied to reference dimensions. Reference dimensions are enclosed in parentheses.

regular views   In a multiview drawing, this term refers to an object's front, top, bottom, right, left, and back (or rear) views.

relative coordinates   Points that are located along the X-, Y-, and Z-axes that are relative to the last point defined.

removed section   A section view that is not drawn in its normal projected position but somewhere else on the sheet. Requires labeling of both the cutting plane line and the view it references.

revolved section   A cross-sectional view of an object drawn on the object.

roof pitch   The angle of a roof. A roof's pitch is expressed as a ratio of the vertical *rise* of the roof (measured in inches) to the horizontal *run* of the roof (measured in inches). Using this notation, a roof with a "four-twelve" pitch (labeled as **4/12** on the drawing) would rise 4″ for every 12″ of horizontal run. Roof pitch is noted on elevation drawings in a set of construction documents.

round   A rounded outside corner of a part.

running object snaps   **Object Snap** modes that are activated whenever the user is prompted to select the location of a point.

sans serif   A typeface that does not include small marks, called *serifs*, at the ends of the main strokes of characters. Sometimes called gothic font.

secondary auxiliary view   A view that is adjacent to, and aligned with, a primary auxiliary view.

section   A drawing technique in which an object is drawn as if part of its exterior has been removed to reveal its interior features and details.

section lines   Diagonal lines drawn that are placed on a section view to indicate the areas of the object that came in contact with the cutting plane line. On AutoCAD drawings, section lines are placed with the **HATCH** command.

sheet sizes   Technical drawings are created on standardized sheet sizes. Sheet size varies with the type of drawing and/or the unit of measurement used to create the drawing.

technical drawing   Term used to describe the process of creating the drawings used in the field of engineering and architecture.

technical lettering   Freehand lettering that is added to a technical drawing or sketch. Technical lettering should be legible and consistent with regard to style.

text style   The characteristics of text used in a drawing such as font name, height, width factor, and oblique angle. These values are determined by the values set in the **Text Style** dialog box.

third-angle projection   A technique for arranging multiview drawings with the top view above the front view and the right-side view drawn to the right of the front view. Commonly used on drawings prepared in North America.

three-dimensional (3D) object   An object having height, width, and depth.

tick mark   A short diagonal line used to note the termination of dimensions in architectural drawings. Also referred to as a *slash*.

tolerance   The total permissible variation in the size and/or shape of the object's features as defined by applying tolerances to the nominal size dimension. The difference between the upper and lower size limits of the feature.

traditional drafting tools   The tools that were used to create technical drawings before CAD techniques became the standard. These tools include parallel straightedges, drafting machines, drafting boards, drafting triangles, protractors, circle and ellipse templates, and technical pens and pencils.

two-dimensional (2D) object   An object having height and width, width and depth, or height and depth.

unidirectional text   Text placed on a technical drawing that faces only the bottom of the sheet. This technique is required when the ASME text standard is applied to a drawing.

United States National CAD Standard (NCS)   A standard developed to unify the preparation, interpretation, and formatting of electronic drawing files across the fields of building design and construction.

user coordinate system (UCS)   The point in an AutoCAD drawing where the X-, Y-, and Z-axes intersect (0,0,0). This point is noted in the graphics window with the UCS icon.

INDEX